THE TRAFALGAR ROLL

VICE-ADMIRAL HORATIO, VISCOUNT NELSON, K.B.

THE TRAFALGAR ROLL

The Ships
and the Officers

COLONEL ROBERT HOLDEN MACKENZIE

F.S.A. SCOT.

NAVAL INSTITUTE PRESS

Published and distributed
in the United States of America by
the Naval Institute Press,
Annapolis, Maryland 21402.

This edition is authorized for sale only in the United States
and its territories and possessions.

Library of Congress Catalog Card No. 89-604447

ISBN 0-87021-990-1

Printed and bound in Great Britain
by Redwood Burn Limited,
Trowbridge, Wiltshire

"ENGLAND EXPECTS THAT EVERY MAN
WILL DO HIS DUTY"

Nelson's last Signal

PREFACE

IT is not proposed in this publication to add another to the many existing accounts of the battle of Trafalgar. The story has often been told. Nor are there wanting memorials of the great fight and of the principal actors in the historic scene. But the literature on the subject cannot be said to be complete until the names of all the officers of the Royal Navy and the Royal Marines who by their valour contributed to the day's success have been placed on permanent record. During the hundred and seven years which have elapsed since the supremacy of Great Britain's sea power was established on the memorable 21st of October 1805, no such record has been attempted, although the military victories of Blenheim and Waterloo have each their biographical roll. The present is an effort to repair this omission, by one for whom the life of the great Admiral has always possessed a peculiar fascination.

The preparation of these pages has demanded considerable application and research, not unaccompanied by many difficulties inseparable from the customs of the naval service a century ago. For instance, the fact of a young gentleman's name appearing in the ship's books of the period is no proof of that individual having been actually present : it frequently happened that he was in the nursery or at school. Great difficulty has also been experienced in tracing the services of others who, in accordance with the practice of the times, were borne in inferior ratings at Trafalgar, and subsequently attained commissioned rank.

I have given a short history of the British ships engaged in the battle, agreeing, as I do, with Admiral Mahan in his *Life of Nelson*, that "in Naval Biography and History, distinguished ships have a personality only less vivid than that of the men who fought them."

In times like the present, when medals and decorations are distributed with profuse liberality, it is melancholy to reflect that, with the exception of the admirals, and the captains of ships, who were rewarded with gold medals, comparatively few of those who contributed to the victory of Trafalgar received any official recognition of their services : the majority had gone to their last berths by the time Queen Victoria, on the 1st June 1847, nearly forty-two years after the fight, graciously repaired the omission of her predecessors by bestowing a silver medal with clasps on the survivors of the various actions, including Trafalgar, fought between 1793 and 1840.

It is probably not generally known that there were present at Trafalgar, as supernumeraries in His Majesty's ships, six Russian naval officers, of whom one died of wounds ; and that the Spanish statesman and soldier, Count de Alava, the friend and confidant of Wellington in his Peninsula and Waterloo campaigns, fought against us at Trafalgar as a naval officer in his uncle's flagship, the *Santa Ana.*

General Drouot, of the Artillery of the Imperial Guard, like the 2nd and 16th Regiments of the Line, served in the French fleet at Trafalgar. They were again our foes at Waterloo; while their 22nd, 34th, and 70th Regiments, which were with Grouchy not many miles away, had also as marines met the fire of our sailors at Trafalgar. It is somewhat remarkable that although every French line-of-battle ship, and the five regiments which served as marines, had with them at Trafalgar the Eagles which Napoleon had presented to them on the Field of Mars in 1804, not one of these trophies fell into our hands. They were somehow disposed of surreptitiously.

To Mr. G. E. Wheatly Cobb of Caldicot Castle, Monmouthshire, whose patriotism and public spirit has saved from the ship-breakers, and preserved to the nation, the *Foudroyant* and the *Implacable*, battleships intimately associated with the glorious life of Nelson, I am under a particular obligation for much valuable assistance and advice.   I have to thank the publishers of the *United Service Magazine*, in the pages of which this Roll first appeared, for permission to reproduce it in book form.   And I have derived considerable information from the interesting roll of the recipients of the Naval General Service Medal, compiled and kindly placed at my disposal by Lieut.-Colonel D. N. Hailes, Royal Marines.

R. H. MACKENZIE.

1913.

CONTENTS

ILLUSTRATIONS

CAPTAIN THOMAS MASTERMAN HARDY,
LATER VICE-ADMIRAL SIR THOMAS MASTERMAN HARDY,
Bart, G.C.B. *(1769-1839)*

VICE-ADMIRAL CUTHBERT COLLINGWOOD, K.B.
(1750-1810)

CAPTAIN CODRINGTON,
LATER ADMIRAL SIR EDWARD CODRINGTON, G.C.B.
(1770-1851)

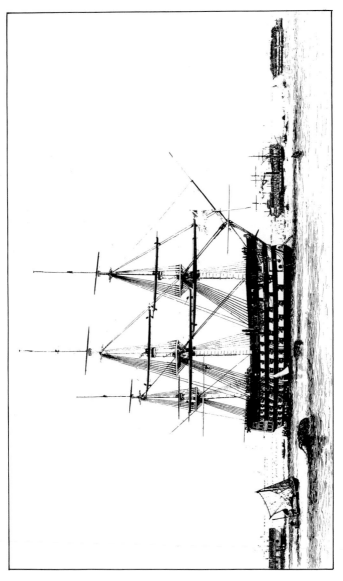

H.M.S. *VICTORY*

THE TRAFALGAR ROLL

H.M.S. *VICTORY*, 104 GUNS

Vice-Admiral, and Commander-in-Chief	Horatio, Viscount Nelson, K.B. (1). *Killed.*
Captain . . .	Thomas Masterman Hardy (2).
Lieutenants .	John Quilliam (3).
	Edward Williams (4).
	Andrew King (5).
	John Yule (6).
	George Miller Bligh (7). *Wounded.*
	John Pasco (8). *Wounded.*
	George Brown (9).
	William Alexander Ram (10). *Killed.*
	Alexander Hills (11).
Master . . .	Thomas Atkinson (12).
Master's Mates	William Chasman (13).
	Thomas Lowton Robins (14).
	Charles Chapell (15). *Wounded.*
	Samuel Spencer (16).
	William Henry Symons (17).
	Thomas Goble (18).
	James Green (19).
Midshipmen *	John Carslake (20).
	William Rivers (21). *Wounded.*

* Admiral W. W. P. Johnson, who died on Dec. 26, 1880, in his 91st year, is stated to have been present at Trafalgar as a guest in the *Victory*. He was a midshipman of the *Childers* at the time.

Midshipmen (*contd.*)	George Augustus Westphal (22). *Wounded.*
	Robert Cutts Barton (23).
	Richard Bulkeley (24). *Wounded.*
	Festing Horatio Grindall (25).
	Henry Cary (26).
	Thomas Thresher.
	John Felton (27).
	Richard Francis Roberts (28).
	James Sibbald (29).
	Oliver Pickin.
	Daniel Salter (30).
	Philip Thorez (31).
	David Ogilvie (32).
	John Lyons (33).
	James Pond (34).
	James Robertson Walker (35).
	John Pollard (36). *Wounded.*
	Daniel Harrington (37).
	Alexander Palmer (38). *Killed.*
	Robert Smith (39). *Killed.*
Volunteers 1st Class	William Randall (40).
	William Ferris.
	John Clay.
	John Scott.
	Henry Lancaster (41).
	Robert Twitchett.
	William Pope.
	William Doak.
	* *Francis Edward Collingwood* (42).
	Ralph Nevill (42 *a*), Supern.
Chaplain . .	Rev. Alexander John Scott (43).
Surgeon . . .	William Beatty (44).
Asst. Surgeon .	Neil Smith (45).
Surgeon's Mate	William Westerburgh.
Purser . . .	Walter Burke (46).
Admiral's Sec.	John Scott (47). *Killed.*

* Borne as A.B.

Captain's Clerk   Thomas Whipple (48).   *Killed.*

Secretary's
  Clerk . . . } George Andrews.

Agent Victualler   Richard Ford.

Agent
  Victualler's } John Geoghehan.   *Wounded.*
  Clerk . . .

Gunner . . .   William Rivers.

Boatswain . .   William Willmett (49).

Captain, Royal
  Marines . . } Charles William Adair (50).   *Killed.*

Lieuts., Royal { James Godwin Peake (51).   *Wounded.*
  Marines . . { Lewis Rotely (52).

2nd Lieut.,
  Royal Marines } Lewis Buckle Reeves (53).   *Wounded.*

The *Victory*, Lord Nelson's flagship at Trafalgar, and
the greatest and noblest of Britain's historical monuments,
was built in Chatham Dockyard from the design of Sir
Thomas Slade, Surveyor of the Navy, and was launched
on Sunday, the 7th May, 1765.   Her dimensions were as
follows : length from figure-head to taffrail, 226 ft. 6 in.;
length of keel, 151 ft. 3 in.; length of gun-deck, 186 ft.;
extreme beam, 52 ft.; depth of hold, 21 ft. 6 in.: and
tonnage, 2162 tons.

After laying quietly at her moorings for thirteen
years, she was commissioned in 1778 by Captain Sir J.
Lindsey, as the flagship of Admiral Hon. Sir Augustus
Keppel, commanding the Channel Fleet ; and took part
in his indecisive action with the French off Ushant in
the same year.   She was much cut up in the engagement
in her hull and rigging, and lost thirty-five killed and
wounded.   In 1779–80, she carried the flags of Admirals
Sir Charles Hardy, Geary, and Drake in the Channel.
She bore the flag of Vice-Admiral Hyde Parker, and the
broad pennant of Commodore Elliott, for a short time in

the North Sea in 1781 ; and was the flagship of Rear-Admiral Kempenfelt in his successful action with the French off Ushant, on the 12th December 1781. She carried Lord Howe's flag with the Channel Fleet at the relief of Gibraltar, and in the skirmish with the combined fleets in 1782, and was paid off at Portsmouth at the peace in the following year.

After bearing the flags of Lords Howe and Hood at the Nore in 1790–91, she became, on the recommencement of war in 1793, the flagship of Lord Hood, Commander-in-Chief in the Mediterranean ; was at the occupation of Toulon and in the action with the French fleet in 1793, and at the capture of Bastia and Calvi, in Corsica, in 1794, in which she lost several officers and men. After a thorough refit, she was selected to carry the flag of Rear-Admiral Man, with Hotham's fleet, and was engaged in the skirmish with the French in July 1795, when her rigging was much cut, all her lower masts badly wounded, and she lost twenty-one in killed and wounded. In October and November of the same year she bore the flag of Vice-Admiral Robert Linzee, cruising with the fleet off Toulon. During the two following years she was the flagship of Admiral Sir John Jervis, and played a prominent part in the great battle of St. Vincent, on the 14th February 1797, and in the blockade of Cadiz. Although much engaged at St. Vincent, she lost only nine killed and wounded, but the 112-gun ship *Salvador del Mundo* struck to her. It was on the quarter-deck of the *Victory* that Nelson, who had distinguished himself in the battle in the *Captain*, was embraced by Sir John Jervis on the very spot where, eight years later, he was destined to fall, covered with glory. Worn out and considered unfit for further active service, the *Victory* was degraded to the office of prison hospital ship at Chatham during the years 1798-1800 ;

but she was not done yet, and was afterwards thoroughly repaired and refitted.

On the recommencement of war with France in 1803, she became, with Captain Thomas Masterman Hardy as captain, the flagship of Lord Nelson, then Commander-in-Chief in the Mediterranean; and in that capacity took part in the blockade of Toulon, the recapture of the French frigate *Ambuscade*, formerly a British vessel, the pursuit of the combined fleets to the West Indies and back, and the glorious battle of Trafalgar on the 21st October 1805. The story of the great fight, which commenced at noon, needs no telling here. On the firing ceasing, the *Victory* was found to have lost 57 killed and 103 wounded, and was herself all but a wreck. The tremendous fire to which she had been exposed when leading her line into action had caused great damage at a very early period of the battle; and before she herself fired a gun, many of her spars were shot away, and great injury had been done to her hull, especially the fore part. At the conclusion of the action she had lost her mizen-mast, the fore-topmast had to be struck to save the fore-mast, the main-mast was not much better, while her figure-head had been struck by shot and part of it carried away. Her sails were badly wounded, and it took all the exertions of her crew to refit the rigging sufficiently to stand the bad weather that followed. Her trophy, the French 74 *Redoutable*, was one of those that sank after the action in deep water, and in her, as in many of the other vessels lost, went down her prize crew of gallant British seamen. On the 3rd November the *Victory* sailed from Gibraltar on the melancholy but proud duty of conveying the body of the dead hero to England. She reached Spithead on the 4th December, and Sheerness on the 22nd, where Nelson's body was removed to a yacht for conveyance to Greenwich and St. Paul's. During the ceremony of removing his remains, the hero's flag, which had flown half-mast ever since the action, was lowered for the last time. The *Victory* then went to Chatham, was paid off on the 16th January 1806, and underwent another thorough repair.

From 1808 to 1812 she carried the flag of Sir James Saumarez, as Commander-in-Chief of the Baltic Fleet, and was employed, amongst other duties, in the blockade of the Russian fleet. She had during that time for a short period borne the flag of Admiral Sir Joseph Yorke with a squadron which took reinforcements to Wellington. After Sir James Saumarez' flag had been rehoisted in her, her boats performed distinguished service in the capture of a number of Danish gunboats on the 20th September 1811. She arrived in England at the end of 1812, and was paid off at Portsmouth on the November, when the last active service of the glorious old ship ended. It was proposed to send her to sea again in 1815, and no fewer than six admirals, when applying for commands, named the *Victory* as the vessel they would wish to have as flagship. In 1824 she was made flagship in Portsmouth Harbour, and has ever since, with but few intervals, continued to bear the flags of admirals who, like her, have spent their lives in the service of their country, and terminate their active careers by holding the highest post in the British Navy—the command at Portsmouth. In 1903 she narrowly escaped sinking at her moorings. The condemned ship *Neptune*, breaking adrift when being towed out of harbour, collided with the old ship and made a large hole in her, and it was only by the promptest measures she was carried safely into dock. She still carries the flag of the Commander-in-Chief, but is used for no other active work, and has only a marine guard of ship-keepers aboard ; courts-martial, however, are still held in her. Dressed every year on the 21st October, and adorned with a wreath of laurel at each mast-head, the old ship remains a permanent memorial of the deeds of that memorable day when the naval supremacy of Great Britain was so firmly established.

NELSON

(1) The life and services of the greatest of Britain's naval heroes are too well known to need but a brief outline in these pages. The third surviving son of Rev. Edmund Nelson, Rector of Burnham Thorpe, in Norfolk, by Catherine, daughter of the Rev. Dr. Suckling, Prebendary of Westminster, Horatio Nelson was born at Burnham Thorpe in 1758. Under the auspices of his uncle, Captain Maurice Suckling, R.N., he entered the Royal Navy as Mid. of the *Raisonnable*, 1771, shortly afterwards transferring to the *Triumph*. While belonging to the latter he went a voyage to the West Indies in a merchant ship, but returned to the *Triumph* in 1772. In 1773 he served in the *Carcass* in an expedition towards the North Pole, on return from which in October of the same year he served as Mid. of the *Seahorse* frigate for two years. In 1776, as acting Lieut. of the *Worcester*, he was employed on convoy duty to Gibraltar. Was promoted Lieut., 1777, and served as Second Lieut. of the *Lowestoft*, a 32-gun frigate, in the West Indies until July 1778, when he was moved into the *Bristol*, flagship of Sir Peter Parker. Was promoted to Commander, 1778, and appointed to the *Badger*, brig, in the Bay of Honduras, for the protection of the trade against American privateers. Appointed Captain, 1779, and posted to the *Hinchingbroke*, frigate. In August 1779, when an attack on Jamaica by the French fleet was anticipated, he was appointed to the command of one of the

batteries for the defence of Kingston ; afterwards doing a three-months' cruise, during which he made some valuable prizes. In January 1780 he was sent as senior naval officer on a joint expedition against San Juan, but was soon invalided home. In 1781–83 he was in the *Albemarle*, a 28-gun frigate, part of the time escorting a large convoy to America, and afterwards in the West Indies. He was again in the West Indies in 1784–87 in the *Boreas* for the protection of commerce, and took several prizes. His next appointment was to the command of the *Agamemnon*, 74, in January 1793, in which he sailed for the Mediterranean under Lord Hood, and took part in the blockade of Toulon. In October his ship was in action with and roughly handled the French ship *Melpomene*, which escaped for the time. He performed valuable service on shore at the reduction of Corsica in 1794, including the capture of Bastia, and Calvi, where he lost his right eye ; and he bore a distinguished part with the fleet in Hotham's engagements in March and July 1795. He was afterwards sent with a small squadron to co-operate with the Austrians on the coast of Genoa. In 1796 he was appointed a Commodore 1st Class, and shifted his broad pennant to the *Captain ;* and on the 10th December to the *Minerve*, in which, in conjunction with the *Blanche*, he captured a Spanish frigate. Returning to the *Captain* in February 1797, he had a brilliant share in the battle of St. Vincent. For this service he was personally thanked by Lord St. Vincent on the quarter-deck of the flagship, was created a K.B., received the gold medal, and the freedom of the cities of London, Norwich, and Bath. His promotion to Rear-Admiral came to him in the ordinary course in 1797. In the *Captain* he commanded the attack on Santa Cruz, 1797, where he lost his right arm, and had to return home. In the *Vanguard*, of 74 guns, he rejoined the fleet under

Lord St. Vincent, in 1798, and in command of a squadron fought the decisive victory of the Nile, in which practically the whole French fleet was overpowered, captured, burnt, or blown up. For his brilliant services on this occasion, when he was again wounded, he was raised to the peerage, received the thanks of Parliament, a pension of £2000 per annum for three lives, and an honourable augmentation to his arms, a gold medal, a grant of £1000 from the East India Company, a sword from his captains, swords of honour from the City of London and the Sultan of Turkey, with the Order of the Crescent, besides handsome rewards from the Emperor of Russia and the King of Naples, and the Sardinian Order of San Joachim. For his services during the Neapolitan crisis he was created Duke of Bronte in Sicily, and was made a Knight Grand Cross of the Order of St. Ferdinand and Merit. He was also a Colonel of Marines. Promoted to Vice-Admiral, 1801, in February he went out in the *St. George* under orders of Sir Hyde Parker, Commander in-Chief of a Particular Squadron against the Northern Confederation, the armed neutrality of the Baltic. On the 1st April 1801, he fought and won the battle of Copenhagen ; was created a Viscount for his services during the campaign, but received no direct recognition for the battle. He succeeded Parker as Commander-in-Chief, but returned home in June 1801. He afterwards commanded the defence flotilla on the south-east coast until the peace in 1802. In 1803 he was appointed Commander-in-Chief in the Mediterranean, and sailed in the *Victory*, keeping watch on the French fleet for two years. In 1805 Napoleon resolved to make a gigantic effort to gain the command of the Channel by bringing into it the whole strength of France and Spain. On the 19th October, Nelson came up with the Franco-Spanish fleet of thirty-three sail of the line, and on the 21st won the glorious victory of Trafalgar. The battle commenced a little after noon ; about twenty minutes past one a musket shot from the *Redoutable's* mizen-top struck him on the left shoulder and penetrated his chest. The wound proved mortal, and after intense suffering he expired about half-past four in the afternoon, his last words being, " Thank God, I have done my duty." The actual number of prizes taken was nineteen, one short of the number bargained for by Nelson, but, from their disabled condition, they were nearly all wrested from us by the gales that succeeded the battle. His body, preserved in spirits, was brought home in the *Victory*, and he was buried in St. Paul's Cathedral on the 9th January 1806. His brother, the Rev. William Nelson, once a Chaplain, R.N., succeeded him as Baron Nelson of the Nile, but the viscountcy became extinct. He was, however, created Viscount Merton and Earl Nelson of Trafalgar and Merton, received a pension of £5000 a year, and a grant of £90,000 for the purchase of an estate. " Happy is he," says Admiral Mahan, in his *Life of Nelson*, " who lives to finish all his task. The words, ' I have done my duty,' sealed the closed book of Nelson's story with a truth broader and deeper than he himself could suspect. His duty was done, and its fruit perfected. Other men have died in the hour of victory ; but for no other has victory so singular and so signal graced the fulfilment and ending of a great life's work. *Finis coronat opus* has of no man been more true than of Nelson. There were, indeed, consequences momentous and stupendous yet to flow from the decisive supremacy of Great Britain's sea-power, the establishment of which, beyond all question or competition, was Nelson's great achievement ; but his part was done when Trafalgar was fought. The coincidence of his death with the moment of completed success has impressed upon that superb battle a stamp of finality, an immortality of fame, which even its own grandeur scarcely could have insured. He needed, and he left, no successor. 'There is but one Nelson,' said St. Vincent," and, as Lord Rosebery has said, " no figure like his among those who have ploughed the weary seas."

(2) Admiral Sir T. M. Hardy, Bart., G.C.B., was second son of Joseph Hardy, of Portisham, Co. Dorset, and Nanny, daughter of Thomas Masterman of Kingston Russel, in the same county. Born in 1769, and educated at Crewkerne school, he entered the service 1781, but returned to school in the following year at Milton Abbas, his name being retained on ship's books. After a period in the merchant service, he re-entered the Navy as Mid. in 1790. Was Mid. of *Amphitrite* in operations before Marseilles and Toulon, 1793. Promoted Lieut., 1793. Lieut. in *Minerve* under Nelson, and was taken prisoner in the encounter with the Spanish frigates *Sabina* and *Ceres* in 1796. Was present at the victory of St. Vincent, 1797. Nelson had a great affection for Hardy, and the story is well known how, when he was hastening in the *Minerve* to join Jervis, just before the battle of St. Vincent, and hotly chased in the Straits by several Spanish men-of-war, a man fell overboard, and Hardy, then a lieutenant, was lowered in a boat to pick him up. The man, however, could not be found, nor could the boat be recovered unless the way of the frigate was checked. The nearest Spaniard was almost within gunshot, and perhaps any other man than Nelson would have felt that the boat, even with Hardy in it, must be sacrificed to the safety of the frigate, and all that it meant to Jervis. But Nelson was not made in that mould. " By God, I'll not lose Hardy ! " he exclaimed. "Back the mizen-topsail." The boat was picked up, and Hardy was saved. Commanded the boats of the *Minerve* and *Lively*, and was wounded in the cutting out of the frigate *Mutine*, 1797, for which he was promoted Commander, and appointed by Nelson to the command of the *Mutine*. Commanded the *Mutine* in Nelson's victory of the Nile, 1798, and for his services was promoted Captain in 1798, and appointed

to the command of the *Vanguard*. Served in her and in the *Foudroyant* under Nelson in Naples and Sicily, 1798–99; and was present in his victory of Copenhagen in 1801. Flag-Captain of *Victory* during blockade of Toulon, and the pursuit of the combined fleets to the West Indies and back; and Captain of the Fleet at Trafalgar, 1805. Was a witness to Nelson's last will. Was with him when he received his mortal wound, and frequently in attendance during the hero's last hours, and at his funeral bore the "Banner of Emblems." For his services at Trafalgar he was created a baronet, received a gold medal, the thanks of Parliament, and swords of honour from the Patriotic Fund and City of London. Was Commander-in-Chief at Lisbon, 1809–12, and held the rank of Commodore in the Portuguese service; commanded a squadron on North American Station, 1812–13; K.C.B., 1815; commanded the yacht *Princess Augusta*, 1815–18; Commander-in-Chief, South American Station, 1819–24, during War of Independence. Colonel, Royal Marines, 1821; Rear-Admiral, 1825; commanded an Experimental Squadron, 1827; First Sea Lord of Admiralty, 1830–34; G.C.B., 1831; Governor of Greenwich Hospital, 1834; Vice-Admiral, 1837; Elder Brother, Trinity House, 1837; and died and was buried at Greenwich Hospital in 1839.

(3) Captain J. Quilliam, a native of the Isle of Man, was impressed into the service. Became Lieut., 1798. Third Lieut. of *Ethalion* at capture of *Thetis*, treasure ship, 1799, and received over £5000 as his share of the prize. Subsequently wrecked in the *Ethalion*. Was Lieut. of *Amazon* at Copenhagen, 1801. First Lieut. of *Victory* at Trafalgar, 1805—promoted Captain. In command of *Crescent* captured an American privateer, 1813. Died, 1839.

(4) Commander E. Williams became Lieut. 1796. Lieut. of *Victory* at Trafalgar, 1805 (promoted Commander, 1805). Carried a bannerol of lineage at Nelson's funeral, 1806. Commander of Greenwich Hospital, 1840. Died, 1843.

(5) Captain A. King, C.B., was son of William King of Southampton, and Harbest and Brockly, Suffolk, and brother of Admiral Sir Edward Durnford King. Mid. of *Bellerophon*

in Lord Howe's victory, 1794. Lieut., 1797. Second Lieut. of *Andromeda* at destruction of a French squadron in Dunkerque Harbour, 1799. Lieut. of *La Désirée* at Copenhagen, 1801 (wounded). Fourth Lieut. of *Victory* at Trafalgar, 1805 (promoted Commander, 1806). Was one of the supporters to the bearer of the Banner of Emblems at Nelson's funeral, 1806. Captain, 1807. Commanded *Hebe* in expedition to Copenhagen, 1807; commanded the *Venerable* in the attack upon Flushing, 1809; and the *Iphigenia* at reduction of Genoa, 1814. C.B., 1831. Died, when Superintendent of Packet Establishment, at Falmouth, 1835.

(6) Commander J. Yule was present in Cornwallis' retreat, 1795. Lieut., 1797. First Lieut. of *Alexander* at the Nile, 1798. Lieut. of *Victory* at Trafalgar, 1805 (promoted Commander, 1805). Carried a bannerol of lineage at Nelson's funeral, 1806. Greenwich Hospital pension, 1835. Died in Plymouth, 1840.

(7) Captain G. M. Bligh was son of Admiral Sir Richard Rodney Bligh, G.C.B., and entered service 1794. Mid. of *Alexander* when she was captured on the 4th November 1794; he, however, escaped. Lieut., 1801. Lieut. of *Victory* at Trafalgar, 1805 (severely wounded in the head by a musket ball—promoted Commander, 1806). Was one of the supporters to the bearer of the Banner of Emblems at Nelson's funeral, 1806. Commanded *Pylades*, sloop, at capture of privateer *Grand Napoleon*, 1808. Captain, 1808. Commanded the *Acorn*, protecting Lissa. Died in Southampton, 1834.

(8) Rear-Admiral J. Pasco was born in 1774. Entered service, 1784; Mid., 1790; Lieut., 1795. Lieut. of *Beaulieu* at reduction of St. Lucie, 1796. Lieut. of *Victory* at capture of French frigate *Ambuscade*, 1803. Senior Lieut. and Signal Lieut. of *Victory* at Trafalgar, 1805; but did not act as First. Arranged with Lord Nelson the memorable signal, " England expects that every man will do his duty." Was severely wounded in the right side and arm, for which he received a grant from the Patriotic Fund, and an Admiralty pension of £250 per annum. Was promoted Commander, 1805. Carried a bannerol of lineage at

Nelson's funeral, 1806. Captain, 1811. Good Service Pension, 1842. Captain of *Victory*, 1847. Retired Rear-Admiral, 1847. Medal and clasp. Died at Stonehouse, Devonport, November 1853, aged 78.

(9) Captain G. Brown, J.P., was born in Bridgewater, Somersetshire, 1784. Mid., 1797 ; Lieut., 1804. Lieut. of *Victory* in pursuit of combined fleets to West Indies and back, and one of Signal Lieuts. at Trafalgar, 1805. Carried a bannerol of lineage at Nelson's funeral, 1806. Flag-Lieut. to Vice-Admiral Lord Collingwood at the time of his death in the *Ville de Paris*, 1810, and accompanied his remains to England (promoted Commander, 1810). Called to Bar at Inner Temple, 1821. J.P. for Somerset and Bridgewater. Retired Captain, 1840. Medal and clasp. Died, 1856.

(10) Lieut. W. A. Ram was second son of Lieut.-Colonel Abel Ram, M.P., Wexford Militia, of Clonattin, Gorey, Co. Wexford. Born in 1784. Lieut., 1805. Killed at Trafalgar, 1805.

(11) Lieut. A. Hills was born at Bedhampton, 1780. Master's Mate, 1804. Lieut., 1805. Lieut. of *Victory*, at Trafalgar, 1805. Not traced after 1809.

(12) Mr. T. Atkinson was appointed Master, R.N., 1795. Master of *Theseus* at Teneriffe, 1797 ; at the battle of the Nile, 1798 ; and commanded one of the boats at the siege of Acre in 1799—wounded. Master of *Elephant*, under Nelson, at Copenhagen, 1801 ; and of the *Victory* at Trafalgar, 1805. Carried a bannerol of lineage at Nelson's funeral, 1806. Master-Attendant, Halifax Dockyard, 1806 ; 2nd Master-Attendant, Portsmouth Dockyard, 1810 ; and 1st Attendant from 1823 until his death, which occurred there in June 1836, in 69th year of his age. Held in great respect by Nelson, who stood godfather to his son, Horatio Nelson Atkinson, Lieut., R.N.

(13) Commander W. Chasman was born in Plymouth, and entered service 1794. Mid., 1799. As Mid. of *Amethyst* assisted at capture of three privateers and a French frigate and corvette in 1801. Master's Mate of *Victory* in pursuit of combined fleets to West Indies and back, and at Trafalgar, 1805 (promoted Lieut.,

1805). Second Lieut. of *Kent*, and did good service in bringing out a convoy at Noli, coast of Italy, 1808 (mentioned in despatches). Lieut. of *Rover* at capture, in the Channel, of French privateer, 1812. Lieut. of *Crescent* at capture, off Newfoundland, of an American privateer, 1814. Commander, 1821. Died, 1828.

(14) Captain T. L. Robins, son of Commander T. L. Robins, R.N., who died in 1836, was born at Portsmouth. Entered service as Volunteer 1st Class, 1798. Served in *Teazer* in expedition to Holland, 1799; attack on French frigates in Dunkerque Roads, 1800; and at Copenhagen, 1801. Mid. of *Arrow* when she was captured, after a gallant defence, 1805. Master's Mate, 1805. Master's Mate of *Victory* in pursuit of combined fleets to West Indies and back, and at Trafalgar, 1805 (promoted Lieut., 1805). Lieut. of *Pallas* in action with French squadron off Isle d'Aix, 1808; and in Walcheren expedition, 1809, and destruction of ships in Basque Roads, 12th April 1809. Wrecked in *Manilla* off the Haak Sand, near the Texel, 1812, and was a prisoner in France for two years. Commander, 1821. Captain, 1851. Medal and four clasps. Died, 1852.

(15) Commander C. Chapell was born in 1782, and entered service, 1798. Mid., 1799. Master's Mate of *Victory* at Trafalgar, 1805 (wounded). Served in boats of *Chiffone* at cutting out of a Spanish brig, 1807. Lieut., 1808. Retired Commander, 1845. Medal and clasp. Died, 1865.

(16) Lieut. S. Spencer was born at Halifax. Entered service, 1796; Mid., 1797; Mid. in the *Active* in the operations on the coast of Egypt, 1801. Master's Mate, 1803. Master's Mate of *Maidstone* in pursuit of a French privateer, 1803—wounded; and in boat attack on a convoy at La Vandour, 1804. Master's Mate of *Victory* at Trafalgar, 1805. Lieut., 1806. Afterwards Agent Transport Service and Admiralty Agent. Medal and two clasps. Died at Birkenhead, Cheshire, 1850.

(17) Commander W. H. Symons was born at Ashford, Kent, 1782; entered service, 1797. In *Canada* at defeat of French squadron, under Bompart, intended for the invasion of Ireland,

1798. Mid. of *Culloden* at recapture of the *Lord Nelson*, East Indiaman, 1803. Master's Mate of *Victory* at blockade of Toulon, pursuit of combined fleets to West Indies and back, and at Trafalgar, 1805 (promoted Lieut., 1805). Lieut. of *Conqueror* co-operating with the patriots on coast of Catalonia, 1809. Also on boat service in the Chesapeake, 1813–14. Retired Commander, 1842. Medal and clasps. Died at Plymouth November 1851.

(18) Mr. T. Goble, a son of James Holmes Goble, Major, Sussex Yeomanry Horse Artillery, was born in Arundel, in Sussex, about 1788. Rated as Master's Mate in the *Victory*, he served in the battle of Trafalgar as Secretary to Captain Hardy; and on the death of Mr. Scott, Lord Nelson's secretary, he acted as Secretary to the Fleet. He appears in Sir Benjamin West's celebrated picture of the battle. Appointed Purser, R.N., 1806. Retired, 1825. Medal and clasp. Died, 1869, and was buried in Porchester.

(19) Lieut. J. Green was born in Norfolk. Served as Master's Mate of *Victory* at Trafalgar, 1805. Lieut., 1806. Not in Navy List after 1812.

(20) Commander J. Carslake, J.P., was born in Colyton, Devonshire, 1785. Entered service 1799; Mid., 1800. Mid. of *Thames* in Saumarez' action near Cadiz, 1801. Mid. of *Victory* in pursuit of combined squadron to West Indies and back, and at Trafalgar (promoted Lieut., 1805). Saved an officer and bluejacket from drowning, when in the *Belleisle*, 1807. When Lieut. of *Proserpine* was captured, 1809, and was kept prisoner until 1814. Retired commander, 1852. Medal and two clasps. J.P. for Devon. Died in Clifton, 1865.

(21) Lieut. W. Rivers was born at Portsea, 1788. Volunteer, 1st Class, 1795. Served in *Victory* in Lord Hotham's second action, 1795. Mid., 1796. Mid. of *Victory* at St. Vincent, 1797; at pursuit of combined fleets to West Indies and back, and at Trafalgar, 1805 (severely wounded, lost a leg; promoted Lieut., 1806). For his wound he received a grant from the Patriotic Fund, and an Admiralty pension of £91, 5s. per annum. Lieut. of *Cossack* in expedition to Copenhagen, 1807. First Lieut.

Cretan, expedition to Walcheren, 1809. Warden at Woolwich Dockyard, 1824–26. Lieut. of Greenwich Hospital, 1826. Medal and clasps. Died at Greenwich Hospital, 1856.

(22) Admiral Sir G. A. Westphal, Kt., was the youngest son of George Westphal, of an old Hanoverian family. Born at Lambeth, 1785. Entered service, 1798. Mid. of *Victory* at Trafalgar, 1805 (severely wounded). While lying in the cockpit, Nelson's coat, hastily rolled up, was put under his head for a pillow. Lieut., 1806. When returning invalided in a merchant ship from the West Indies in 1807, the ship, after a gallant resistance, was captured by a privateer. He was severely wounded and taken prisoner, but escaped. Lieut. of *Belleisle* on shore at the reduction of Martinique, 1809. Afterwards commanded a division of gunboats on the Scheldt, 1809. Lieut. of *Indefatigable* in the expedition of Quiberon Bay, 1810, and the defence of Cadiz. Lieut. of *Marlborough* in the Chesapeake, and was repeatedly noticed for his gallant conduct in command of the boats of the squadron, 1813 (wounded, promoted Commander, 1813). Commanded *Anaconda*, sloop, in expedition against New Orleans, and was landed with the Naval Brigade. In command of *Jupiter* took Lord Amherst out to India, for which, in addition to his general gallant conduct, he was promoted Captain, 1819, and knighted in 1824. Flag-Captain to Admiral Sir George Cockburn on North American Station, 1832–34. Rear-Admiral, 1851. Vice-Admiral, 1857. Admiral, 1863. J.P. for Sussex and Hove. Medal and three clasps. Died at Hove, 1875. His eldest brother was Admiral Philip Westphal, who died in 1880.

(23) Commander R. C. Barton was born in Pembrokeshire. Mid. of *Victory* at Trafalgar, 1805. Lieut., 1806. Served in boats of *Apollo*, cutting out a convoy in Rosas Bay, 1809. Commander, 1819. Died at Bideford, 1827.

(24) Lieut. R. Bulkeley was son of Richard Bulkeley, of Pencombe, Bromyard. Mid., 1803. Mid. of *Victory* at Trafalgar, 1805—wounded; promoted Master's Mate. Lieut., 1806. Not in Navy List after 1810.

(25) Lieut. F. H. Grindal was son of Vice-Admiral Sir R.

Grindall, K.C.B., Captain of the *Prince* at Trafalgar. Born at Weymouth, 1787. Mid. of *Victory* at Trafalgar, 1805. Lieut., 1809. Died, 1812.

(26) Commander H. Cary was born at Portarlington, in Ireland, and entered service, 1799. Wrecked in *Resistance* off St. Vincent, 1803. Mid. of *Victory* in pursuit of combined fleets to West Indies and back, and at Trafalgar, 1805. Lieut., 1807. Lieut. of *Inflexible* in expedition to Copenhagen, 1807, and served on shore as Brigade Major. Served in boats of *Kent* at destruction of a convoy in mole of Palamos, 1810. Commanded a hired Packet under the Post Office, 1820–34. Retired, Commander, 1843. Died, 1847.

(27) Lieut. J. Felton was born in London. Served as Mid. in the *Bellona* in the battle of Copenhagen, 1801. Mid of *Victory* at Trafalgar, 1805. Lieut., 1806. Resigned 1810. Medal and two clasps.

(28) Mid. R. F. Roberts was eldest son of Richard Roberts of Burton Bradstock, Dorset. Born at Bridport. A.B. of *Victory* in pursuit of combined fleets to the West Indies and back, 1805. Mid., 1805. Mid. of *Victory* at Trafalgar, 1805. Left service, 1806.

(29) Commander J. Sibbald was born at Leith, near Edinburgh, 1788. Mid. of *Victory* at Trafalgar, 1805. Master's Mate, 1805. Commander, 1814. Died in Edinburgh, 1843.

(30) Lieut. D. Salter was born in Portsmouth. Mid. of *Victory* at Trafalgar, 1805. Lieut., 1809. Commanded a gunboat in operations in river Elbe, 1813. Died, 1842–43.

(31) Mr. P. Thorez was born in Naples. Mid., 1805. Mid. of *Victory* at Trafalgar, 1805. Purser, R.N., 1809. Died, 1839–40.

(32) Lieut. D. Ogilvie was born in London. Mid. of *Victory* at Trafalgar, 1805. Lieut., 1806. Not in Navy List after 1822.

(33) Admiral J. Lyons was son of John Lyons of Antigua, and Lymington, Hants, and brother of Admiral Sir E. Lyons, G.C.B. Born in London. Entered service, 1798. Served in *St. George* at Copenhagen, 1801. Wrecked in *Magnificent*, 1804. Mid. of *Victory* at Trafalgar, 1805 (promoted Lieut.,

1805). Lieut. of *Eagle* at reduction of Capri, 1806. Lieut. of *Montague*, and commanded a detachment of seamen and marines at reduction of St. Maura, 1810. Commander, 1814. Captain, 1830. Retired the 1st October 1850. Retired Rear-Admiral, 1855. Retired Vice-Admiral, 1862. Retired Admiral, 1866. Medal and two clasps. Died, 1872.

(34) Commander J. Poad was born at Devonport in 1789. Entered service, 1803. Mid., 1804. Mid. of *Victory* in pursuit of combined fleets to West Indies and back, and at Trafalgar, 1805. One of the supporters of Nelson's banner as a K.B. at his funeral. Lieut., 1812. In charge of a Semaphore Station, 1837–48. Greenwich Hospital Pension, 1853. Retired Commander, 1855. Medal and clasp. Died, 1858.

(35) Captain J. R. Walker was son of James Robertson D.L., J.P., of Stornoway, N.B., by Annabella, daughter of John Mackenzie, of Letterewe. Assumed the name of Walker. Born 1783. Entered service, 1801. Served in *Canopus* off Cadiz and in the Mediterranean, 1803–1804. Mid. of *Victory* in pursuit of combined fleets, and at Trafalgar, 1805. In *Thames* at attempted destruction of Boulogne flotilla by rockets, 1806. In *Belleisle* at reduction of islands of St. Thomas and St. Croix, 1807. Acting-Lieut. of *Fawn*, at capture of a privateer and three merchant vessels under the batteries of Puerto Rico, 1808; and in cutting out a merchant schooner. Acting-Lieut. of *Hazard* at capture of French 48-gun frigate *Topaze*, and the reduction of Martinique, 1809. Lieut., 1809. In boats of *Hazard* at destruction of a French privateer (mentioned in despatches); at capture of Guadaloupe, 1810; and at capture of several American vessels, 1812–13. In *Antelope* at capture of *Eleanor*, privateer 1813 (mentioned in despatches). Lieut. of *Confiance*, and succeeded to the command in her action with, and capture by U.S. Squadron, under Macdonough, 1814. Was tried by Court Martial, fully exonerated, and promoted Commander, 1815. Reserve Captain, 1851. Medal and three clasps. Died, 1858.

(36) Commander J. Pollard was born at Cawsand, Cornwall, in 1787, and entered service, 1797. Wrecked in 1800 off Jersey. Mid. of *Victory* in pursuit of combined fleets to West Indies and

back, and at Trafalgar, 1805 (wounded). Is said to have shot
the man who killed Lord Nelson. Lieut., 1806. Served in boats
of *Brunswick* at attack and capture of Danish brig *Fama*, and of
the cutter *Salorman*. Greenwich Hospital Pension, 1853,
Retired Commander, 1864. Medal and clasp. Died, 1868.

(37) Lieut. D. Harrington was born at Waterford, 1776.
Mid. of *Victory* at Trafalgar. Promoted Lieut., 1805. Lieut.
of *Standard* at forcing of Dardanelles, 1807—wounded. Died
at Dieppe, 1837.

(38) Mr. A. Palmer was born in London, 1783. Mid. from
A.B., 1805. Mid. of *Victory* in pursuit of combined fleets, and
at Trafalgar. Died of wounds on the 28th October 1805.

(39) Mr. R. Smith was born at Watford, Herts, in 1786.
Mid. of *Victory* in pursuit of combined fleets, and was killed at
Trafalgar, 1805.[1]

(40) Lieut. W. Randall was born in London. Volunteer 1st
Class of *Victory* in pursuit of combined fleets, and at Trafalgar,
1805. Lieut., 1810. Not traced after 1814.

(41) Commander H. Lancaster was youngest son of Rev.
Thomas Lancaster, Rector of Merton, Surrey. Born at Wimble-
don, 1791. Volunteer 1st Class, 1805. Served in *Victory* at Trafalgar; in *Apollo* at capture of French vessels in Bay of Rosas, 1809;
and capture of the *Merinos* and *Ulysse*, 1812. On shore at siege
of Trieste, 1813 (wounded—promoted Lieut., 1813.) Lieut. of
Prince of Wales in second partial action with Toulon fleet, 1814,
and fall of Genoa and Savona. Commander, 1851, Medal and
two clasps. Died in Connaught Square, Hyde Park, W., 1862.

(42) Commander F. E. Collingwood was only son of Francis
Collingwood, of Greenwich, and grandson of Edward Collingwood,
Master, R.N. Born at Milford, Pembrokeshire, 1785. Entered
service, 1799. Borne as A.B., but served as Mid. of the *Victory*
at Trafalgar, 1805, and with Mid. J. Pollard, is reputed to have
shot the Frenchman who killed Lord Nelson. Lieut., 1806.
Lieut. of *Pallas* at destruction of five French men-of-war in Aix
Roads, 1809. Was in Walcheren Expedition, 1809. Lieut. of *Iris*

---

[1] A Robert Smith, Midshipman, appears in the Medal Roll, 1848; but
only one of that name can be traced, and he was reported killed in the battle.

on north coast of Spain, and at capture of three American letters of marque, 1813. Twice wounded in command of *Kite*, revenue cutter, on coast of Ireland, 1820–23. Commander, 1828. Died at Tralee, Ireland, 1835, aged 50.

(42 *a*) Captain R. Viscount Nevill, son of the 2nd Earl of Abergavenny, K.T., and Mary, daughter of John Robinson, M.P., of Wyke House, Middlesex, was born in 1786. Served as Volunteer 1st Class in the *Victory* at Trafalgar, 1805. Lieut., 1806. Commander, 1808. Commanded the *Actæon*, brig, and assisted in capture of *Le Lezard*, French privateer, 1809; and was at the reduction of the Mauritius, 1810. Captain, 1811. Died in Boulogne, 1826.

(43) Rev. A. J. Scott, D.D., Chaplain, R.N., was son of Lieut. Robert Scott, R.N., and Jane Comyn. Born at Rotherhithe, 1768. Educated at Charter House. Obtained a scholarship at St. John's College, Cambridge, in 1786; graduated B.A., 1791; and was ordained, 1792. Chaplain, R.N., 1793. Private Secretary to Admiral Sir Hyde Parker, 1795–1801. Chaplain of H.M.S. *London* at Copenhagen, 1801. Chaplain of *Victory* and Private Secretary to Lord Nelson, 1803–5, including pursuit of the combined fleet to the West Indies and back, and the battle of Trafalgar, 1805. In that capacity it fell to his lot to soothe the last moments of his dying chief. He attended Nelson's funeral in 1806. M.A. of St. John's College, Cambridge, and D.D. by Royal Mandate, 1806. Vicar of Southminster, 1802–16, when he was appointed Chaplain to the Prince Regent, and presented to the Government living of Catterick, Yorkshire. Died at Ecclesfield Vicarage, Yorks, 1840.

(44) Sir W. Beatty, Kt., M.D., F.R.S., became Sugeon, R.N., 1793; and had seen considerable service before being appointed Surgeon of the *Victory*. Present in her at Trafalgar, 1805, and attended Lord Nelson at his death, of which he published an account in 1807. Physican, R.N., 1806. M.D. of St. Andrews, 1817. Licentiate, College of Physicians, 1817. F.R.S., 1818. Physician of Greenwich Hospital, 1822. Knighted, 1831. Died in York Street, Portman Square, London, 1842. He was brother to Colonel George Beatty, R.M.

(45) Surgeon N. Smith served as Assistant Surgeon of *Victory* at Trafalgar, 1805. Surgeon, 1806. Died, 1819.

(46) Mr. W. Burke was father of Commander Henry Burke, who, after being three times wounded in different actions, was lost in the *Seagull*, 1805; and of Lieut. Walter Burke, who was killed in the cutting out of the *Chevrette*, 1801. Mr. Burke was Purser of the *Victory* at Trafalgar, 1805; supported Nelson when he received his mortal wound, and remained with him to the last. Died at Wouldham, near Rochester, 1815, aged 75.

(47) Mr. J. Scott was appointed Purser of *Victory* and Secretary to Lord Nelson, 1803. One of the witnesses to the codicil of his last will, on the 6th September, 1803. Killed at Trafalgar by a round shot.

(48) Mr. T. Whipple was born at Plymouth. Killed at Trafalgar, 1805, by the wind of a round shot which never touched him; he had no wound or scratch on any part of his body.

(49) Boatswain W. Wilmett performed distinguished service during the battle. Was severely wounded in the thigh, but demanded to remain on duty till the end of the fight.

(50) Captain C. W. Adair, R.M., was the second son of Lieut.-Colonel Benjamin Adair, R.M., of Loughanmore, Dunadry, Co. Antrim, and Susannah, sister of Captain W. Prowse, R.N., who commanded H.M.S. *Sirius* at Trafalgar. He was born in 1776. His elder brother, General Thomas Benjamin Adair, C.B., R.M., was father of the late General Sir Charles William Adair, K.C.B., R.M., and grandfather of the present General Sir William Thompson Adair, K.C.B., R.M.L.I., of Loughanmore. Captain C. W. Adair joined R.M. as 2nd Lieut., 1782; Lieut., 1793; and served on shore as Adjutant of Royal Marine Battalion at the capture of the Cape, 1795. Captain, 1800. Senior Marine officer in the *Victory*, 1804-5, and Inspecting Officer for recruiting in the Mediterranean. Present at pursuit of combined fleets to West Indies and back, and at Trafalgar, 1805. Behaved with great gallantry in the fight. With a small party drove back the *Redoutable's* crew on their attempting to board the *Victory*. Met his death by a musket ball at the back of the neck while encouraging his men on the poop of the gangway.

(51) Captain J. G. Peake became 2nd Lieut., R.M., 1796. Lieut., 1799. Wounded in *Victory* at Trafalgar, 1805. Captain, 1808. Drowned by the upsetting of a ship's boat off Bermuda, 1809.

(52) Lieut. L. Rotely became 2nd Lieut., R.M., 1805. Served in *Victory* at Trafalgar, 1805. First Lieut., 1808. Served in the *Cleopatra* at the capture of Martinique in 1809 ; commanded a detachment at the capture of the French frigate *Topaze*, 48 guns, after an action of forty minutes near Guadaloupe, 1809. Saved four persons from drowning. The Rotely Scholarship at the Royal Naval School, Eltham, was founded in his memory. Retired on full pay, 1814. Medal and two clasps. Died at May Hill, Swansea, 1861.

(53) Lieut. L. B. Reeves was son of Thomas Reeves and Ellen, daughter of Lewis Buckle, of Borden, East Meon, Hants, and grandson of Robert Reeves of Besborough, Killimer, Co. Clare. Second Lieut., R.M., 1804. In *Victory* at Trafalgar, 1805 —severely wounded. Lieut., 1807. Present at defeat of French at Babagné, near St. Louis, 1809. Retired on half-pay, 1817. Medal and clasp. Died at Douglas, Isle of Man, 1861.

II

H.M.S. *ROYAL SOVEREIGN*, 100 GUNS

Vice-Admiral and Second-in-Command } Cuthbert Collingwood (1).

Captain . . . Edward Rotherham (2).

Lieutenants . John Clavell (3). *Wounded.*
Joseph Simmonds (4).
James Bashford (5). *Wounded.*
Francis Blower Gibbes (6).
Edward Barker (7).
Bryce Gilliland (8). *Killed.*

Master . . . William Chalmers (9). *Killed.*

Master's Mates Thomas Alltoff (10).
Charles Aubrey Antram (11).
Richard Davison Pritchard (12).
William Watson. *Wounded.*

Midshipmen . John Aikenhead. *Killed.*
William Stock.
John Doling Morey (13).
Samuel Weddel.
Thomas Pitt Robinson (14)
Charles Coucher.
Joseph Dell Carretto.
John Chaldicott.
Robert Edwards (15).
Henry Davis.
William Budd Boreham.
Gilbert Kennicott (16). *Wounded.*
John Dobson.

Midshipmen (*contd.*)	Thomas Currell.
	Granville Thompson (17). *Wounded.*
	George Castle (18).
	Thomas Dickinson (19). *Wounded.*
	John Campbell. *Wounded.*
	John Farrant (20). *Wounded.*
	Thomas Braund (21). *Killed.*
	John Redwood.
Volunteers 1st Class	Robert Julian (22).
	Archibald Nagle (23).
	Robert Duke Hamilton.
	Claudius Charles (24).
	William Lloyd.
	Charles Lambert (25).
	Charles Criswick (26).
	Meredith Milnekoff (Russian).
Chaplain . .	Rev. John Rudall (27).
Surgeon . . .	Richard Lloyd (28).
Assistant Surgeons . .	Primrose Lyon (29). Henry Towsey (30).
Purser . . .	Brinley Sylvester Oliver (31).
Clerk . . .	Richard Williamson.
Boatswain . .	Isaac Williamson.
Carpenter . .	George Clines.
Captain, Royal Marines . .	Joseph Vallack (32).
2nd Lieuts., Royal Marines .	Robert Green (33). *Killed.* Armiger Watts Hubbard (34). James Le Vesconte (35). *Wounded.*

The *Royal Sovereign*, the flagship of the second-in-command, was built in Plymouth Dockyard in 1787, by Mr. J. Pollard, Sir John Williams being Surveyor of the Navy. She was noted for her dull sailing qualities, and was facetiously known as the "West Country Waggon." After bearing the flag of Vice-Admiral Sir Alexander Hood as one of the ships of the Spanish armament, she

carried the flag in the Channel Fleet in 1790–94 of Vice-
Admiral Thomas Graves, afterwards Lord Graves.
Under Captain Henry Nicholls she was in Lord Howe's
action of the 29th May 1794, losing thirty-eight killed
and wounded ; and in his glorious victory of the 1st June.
On the latter occasion her losses amounted to fifty-eight
killed and wounded, the vice-admiral being amongst the
latter.   Her topmasts were badly injured, her fore and
main top-gallant-masts shot away, and her lower masts
injured.   Bearing the flag of Vice-Admiral Hon. William
Cornwallis, with Captain J. Whitby as flag-captain, she
was present in his memorable action with a superior
French fleet on the 16–17th June 1795.   From 1796 to
1800 she bore the flag, with the Channel Fleet, of Vice-
Admiral Sir Alan Gardner, Bart.   Her crew, two of
whom were hanged at the yard-arm, were unfortunately
implicated in the mutiny of the fleet in 1797.   In 1800–2
she flew Vice-Admiral Sir Henry Harvey's flag as second-
in-command of the Channel Fleet, and was with the
same fleet again in 1803.   In 1804–5 she carried the flag
of Rear-Admiral Sir Richard Bickerton off Toulon.

She carried the flag of the second-in-command, Vice-
Admiral Cuthbert Collingwood, with Edward Rotherham
as Captain, and led the lee column at Trafalgar, on the
21st October 1805.   In the actual fighting there was no
ship which covered herself with greater distinction.
For a time she was engaged single-handed with several
of the enemy's ships, before tackling Alava's flagship, the
Santa-Ana.   Her losses on this occasion amounted to
144, including 14 officers killed and wounded.   Her
injuries were very severe.   Her main and mizen masts
and fore-topsail-yard were shot away, and her fore-mast,
having been shot in several places and stripped of nearly
the whole of its rigging, was left in a tottering state.   By
the time the Spanish three-decker Santa-Ana struck to

her, the *Royal Sovereign* was almost unmanageable ; and at 6 P.M. Admiral Collingwood, who had succeeded the dead hero as Commander-in-Chief, was compelled to shift his flag into the *Euryalus*, frigate, by which, and afterwards by the *Neptune*, she was taken in tow. In November 1806 she was flying the flag of Vice-Admiral Edward Thornborough, and, after serving in the Mediterranean and at the blockade of Toulon, bore the flag of Lord Keith in 1812, for a short time Commander-in-Chief of the Channel Fleet ; as also that of Vice-Admiral Sir William Sydney Smith in 1813–14, after which she returned to Plymouth. In April 1814 Louis XVIII embarked in her at Dover for Calais. Her last service was 1815–16 when she flew the flag of Rear-Admiral Sir Benjamin Hallowell. Her name was changed in 1825 to *Captain ;* and as a receiving ship at Plymouth her existence was prolonged until 1841 when she was broken up. During her service she had earned the naval war medal with three clasps.

(1) Vice-Admiral Lord Collingwood, a member of an old Northumberland family, was son of Cuthbert Collingwood, Merchant, of Newcastle-upon-Tyne, and Milcha, daughter of Reginald Dobson of Barwess, Westmoreland. Born, 1750, at Newcastle. Entered service, 1761, and became Midshipman shortly afterwards. Master's Mate, 1767. Mate of *Preston* on the North American Station, and was present on shore with a party of seamen at Bunker's Hill, 1775—promoted Lieutenant. Tried by Court Martial in 1777 for disobedience of orders, and acquitted. Commander, 1779. Captain, 1780. Captain of *Hinchingbroke* in expedition against San Juan, 1780. In command of the *Pelican*, was wrecked on the Morant Keys, 1781. Captain of the *Mermaid* during the Spanish armament of 1790. Captain of *Barfleur* in Lord Howe's victory of the 1st June 1794, (gold medal). Was distinguished in command of the *Excellent* at St. Vincent, 1797 (gold medal, and thanked by Lord Nelson)

Rear-Admiral, 1799. With Channel Fleet was employed in blockade of Brest, 1800-2. He was with the detached squadron under Sir Charles Cotton which reinforced Lord Keith in the Mediterranean, and accompanied him back off Brest when the French fleet returned after an uneventful cruise. He continued attached to the Channel Fleet, employed for the most partin the blockade of Brest, till released by the peace of Amiens. On the recommencement of war in 1803 he was appointed to a command in the fleet off Brest under Admiral Cornwallis, was promoted to Vice-Admiral in 1804, but continued with Cornwallis till May 1805, when he was detached in command of a squadron to reinforce Nelson, then in pursuit of the French fleet. In accordance with his discretionary power, he took up his station off Cadiz, where, on July 18, he was joined by Nelson on his return from the West Indies, and where he still remained when Nelson, having intelligence that the combined fleet had been seen to the northward, sailed on July 25 to reinforce Cornwallis off Brest. He was still off Cadiz, keeping watch on the combined fleet, which had put into that port, when he was again joined by Nelson on September 28; and, commanding in the second post, with his flag in the *Royal Sovereign*, he led the lee line in the memorable battle of Trafalgar, 1805. By Nelson's death in the hour of victory, Collingwood succeeded to the chief command, and thus, in popular estimation, reaped a certain portion of the glory which, had Nelson lived, would have fallen to him alone. He, however, ably carried out the plan of the battle, so far as the duty was entrusted to him, though he took no initiative in the matter. Even his leading, in the *Royal Sovereign*, through the allied fleet some few minutes before the *Victory*, at the head of the weather line, was pre-arranged by Nelson. What Collingwood did under Nelson's directions he did gallantly and splendidly; what he did after Nelson's death left him commander-in-chief is another matter. That many of the prizes foundered in the subsequent gale is attributed by some to his neglect to act on Nelson's order to anchor immediately after the battle, but it is quite possible that the prizes would have been equally lost if the alternative course had been followed. Collingwood's brillant service was at once acknowledged by his being raised to the peerage as Baron Collingwood of Caldburne and Hethpoole, in Northumberland; by a pension of £2000 a year for life, with, after his death, £1000 a year to his widow, and £500 to each of his daughters; by the thanks of Parliament; by a valuable testimonial from Lloyd's Patriotic Fund; by a sword from the Duke of Clarence, and a gold medal.

Collingwood was continued in the command which had fallen to him by the death of Nelson, but the work had been done too thoroughly to leave him much opportunity for distinction. For eighteen months he remained on the coast of Spain; he then went to the Dardanelles on the failure of the expedition under Sir John Duckworth. He was in Sicily in 1807-8, and seems to have been unfortunate, to say the least, in his failure to engage the French fleet which, under Vice-Admiral Ganteaume, went to the relief of Corfu, and two months later returned unmolested to Toulon. He was a little more fortunate when, in 1809, the second attempt of the French to convoy troops and provisions from Toulon to Barcelona was frustrated by the action of his detached squadron under Rear-Admiral Martin. But his life's race was now nearly run. His health had long been failing, though he does not appear to have realised the very serious nature of his illness until too late. A typical north countryman, never unduly elated at success or depressed by failure, caring little for popular applause, quiet and retiring in his ways, anxious only to serve his country to the best of his ability, he has the right to be considered one of the noblest Englishmen who ever trod a quarter-deck. He died on the 7th March 1810—it may be said at his post in obedience to the call of duty. The body was brought to England, and, after lying in state in the Painted Hall in Greenwich, was buried in the crypt of St. Paul's by the side of Nelson. The monument to his memory is in the south transept of the cathedral.

(2) Captain E. Rotherham, C.B., was son of John Rotherham, M.D., of Newcastle-on-Tyne. Born at Hexham, Northumberland, 1753. Entered service, 1777. Mid. and Master's Mate, 1778-79. Acting-Lieut. of *Monarch* in Lord Howe's action, 1780-82,

Lieut., 1783. Senior Lieut. of *Culloden* in Lord Howe's victory of the 1st June 1794—promoted Commander. Captain, 1800. Captain of *Royal Sovereign*, and Flag-Captain to Admiral Collingwood at Trafalgar, 1805—gold medal, and sword from Patriotic Fund. Captain of the *Bellerophon* escorting the *Victory*, with the body of Nelson on board, to England, and commanded her in the Channel and the Baltic in 1806-9. Carried the guidon at Nelson's funeral, 1806. C.B., 1815. Captain of Greenwich Hospital, 1828-30. Died, 1830, at Bildeston, Suffolk.

(3) Captain J. Clavell, a son of Rev. Roger Clavell, was born in the Isle of Wight in 1779, and was entered in the ship's books of the *Centurion* at the age of one, but did not actually serve till he joined the *Duke* in 1792. Mid. of *Victory* at Toulon, 1793 ; on shore at capture of Bastia and Calvi, Corsica, 1794 ; in Hotham's action, July 1795 ; and at St. Vincent, 1797. Lieut., 1797. Senior Lieut. of *Royal Sovereign* at Trafalgar, the 21st October 1805 (wounded)—promoted Commander. Commanded *Weazel*, brig, at destruction and capture of French transports near Corfu, 1807. Captain, 1808. Captain of Ordinary, Portsmouth, 1825-27. Superintendent Packet Establishment, Falmouth, 1835-37. Superintendent Chatham Dockyard, 1837-41. Captain of Greenwich Hospital, 1841, and died there, the 11th March 1846.

(4) Commander J. Simmonds became Lieut., 1799. Lieut. of *Royal Sovereign* at Trafalgar, 1805. Commander, 1810. Died, 1838.

(5) Commander J. Bashford became Lieut., 1800. Lieut. of *Royal Sovereign* at Trafalgar, 1805—wounded. Commander, 1809. Died, 1816.

(6) Some difficulty has been experienced in tracing this officer. A Lieut. Francis Blower Gibbes, seniority 15th January 1802, appears in the official List of Sea Officers for 1805, who was incorrectly reported to have been drowned off Jamaica on 1st March 1805, when in acting command of the schooner *Redbridge*. The same name appears in later Navy Lists, but with seniority of 16th October 1806. This officer became a retired Com-

mander in 1841, and died at Arklow, Ireland, the 23rd November 1842, aged 70.

(7) Commander E. Barker. Lieut., 1798. In *Royal Sovereign* at Trafalgar—promoted Commander, 1805 ; not traced after 1820.

(8) Lieut. B. Gilliland. Lieut., 1802. Killed in *Royal Sovereign* at Trafalgar, the 21st October 1805.

(9) Mr. W. Chalmers. Master, 1793. Killed in *Royal Sovereign* at Trafalgar, the 21st October 1805.

(10) Mr. T. Alltoff. Master's Mate *Royal Sovereign* at Trafalgar, 1805. Master, 1812. Not traced after 1816.

(11) Lieut. C. A. Antram, son of Simon Antram, Paym. and Purser, R.N. Born in London, 1785. Master's Mate *Royal Sovereign* at Trafalgar, 1805 ; one of the supporters of the standard-bearer at Lord Nelson's funeral. Lieut., 1810. First Lieut. *Prometheus*, bombardment of Algiers, 1816. Died at Brambridge House, Twyford, Hants, 1831.

(12) Commander R. D. Pritchard, son of Samuel Perkins Pritchard, Master, R.N., who died in 1813, and brother to J. W. Pritchard, Mid. of *Britannia* at Trafalgar. Born at Portsmouth, 1788. Volunteer 1st Class, 1797. Master's Mate of *Royal Sovereign* at Trafalgar, 1805. Sub.-Lieut. of *Dextrous*, gun-brig, and served in her boats at capture of two gunboats near Gibraltar, 1807 (wounded, mentioned in despatches, and promoted Lieut., 1807) ; pension for wounds of £91, 5s. In *Avenger* at taking of Anholt, 1809 ; and while detached in a gunboat captured seven Danish vessels. Was afterwards taken prisoner. Commander, 1841. Medal and clasp. Died at Fareham, 1849, aged 60.

(13) Lieut. J. D. Morey was born in Havant. Mid. in *Royal Sovereign* at Trafalgar, 1805. Lieut., 1808. Not traced after 1824–25.

(14) Captain T. P. Robinson was only son of Admiral Mark Robinson, who died in 1834, and grandson of Rear-Admiral Mark Robinson, who died in 1799. Born at Bishop's Waltham, 1792. Entered service, 1804. Mid. of *Royal Sovereign* at Trafalgar, the 21st October 1805. Served in *Success* on coast of Italy, including the reduction of the Islands of Ischia and Procida, 1811. Lieut., 1812. Lieut. of *Genoa* at Navarino, 1827.

Commander, 1828. Inspecting Commander Coastguard, 1837–1851. Captain, 1851. Medal and two clasps. Died at Widcombe, Bath, 1861, aged 69.

(15) Lieut. R. Edwards was promoted Mid. from A.B., 1805. Mid. *Royal Sovereign* at Trafalgar, 1805—promoted Lieut. Not traced after 1809.

(16) Captain G. Kennicott was born in Devonshire, 1789. Entered service, 1803. Mid. of *Royal Sovereign* at Trafalgar, 1805 (severely wounded—pension for wounds). Master's Mate, 1807. Wrecked in *Hind* off Cyprus, 1807 ; kept prisoner by the Turks till 1809. Lieut., 1810. Lieut. of *Minorca*, and taken prisoner in an American prize and detained till 1814. Served in Coastguard, 1836–46. Commander, 1846. Captain, half-pay, 1859. Naval pension, 1867. Medal and clasp. Died, 1874.

(17) Lieut. G. Thomson was born in Newcastle. Mid. *Royal Sovereign* at Trafalgar—wounded. Master's Mate of *Scout*, cutting out convoy and gunboats near Cape Croisette, 1809. Lieut., 1809. Not traced after 1817.

(18) Lieut. G. Castle was born in Durham. Mid. of *Royal Sovereign* at Trafalgar, 1805. In boats of *Amphion* in cutting out and capture of Franco-Italian gunboats in the port of Cortelazzo, 1809. Lieut., 1811. In the unsuccessful attack on Fort Bowyer, West Florida, 1815. Not in Navy List after 1825–26.

(19) Captain T. Dickinson was born at Portsea. Entered service, 1796. In *Invincible* at reduction of St. Lucia and Trinidad, 1796. In *Dreadnought* when attacked by a flotilla of gunboats, 1801. Mid., 1804. Mid. *Royal Sovereign* at Trafalgar, 1805 (wounded). Lieut., 1806. First Lieut. *Andromache* at reduction of St. Sebastian, and capture of French 40-gun ship *Trave*, 1813 (severely wounded, promoted Commander, 1814). Pension for wounds, 1815. Commanded *Lightning*, 1831–32, in operations for recovery of treasure from *Thetis*. Captain, 1832. Captain of Greenwich Hospital, 1847. Medal and two clasps. Medal from Society of Arts for the application of the percussion principle of ignition to naval ordnance. Died at Greenwich Hospital, 1854.

(20) Commander J. Farrant was born at Exmouth, 1789. Volunteer 1st Class, 1801. Mid. of *Russell* at Copenhagen, 1801. Wrecked in *La Determinée*, frigate, near Jersey, 1803. Mid. of *Royal Sovereign* at Trafalgar, 1805 (severely wounded). Lieut., 1808, Served in boats of *Scout* at the storming of a battery near Marseilles, 1809; and in the *Tigre* at capture of vessels and a convoy of merchantmen in Bay of Rosas, 1809. Lieut. of *Plantagenet* in expedition against New Orleans, 1814; and Lieut. in the *Boxer*, and in her boats at destruction of twenty-seven American vessels in Connecticut, 1814. Pension for wounds, 1818. Greenwich Hospital Pension, 1839. Retired Commander, 1846. Medal and five clasps. Died at Coutances, Normandy, 1849.

(21) Mr. T. Braund was born at Plymouth Dock, 1788. Died on the 25th October 1805, of wounds received at Trafalgar when Mid. of *Royal Sovereign*.

(22) Lieut. R. Julian was born at Deptford. Volunteer 1st Class in *Royal Sovereign* at Trafalgar, 1805. Lieut., 1815. Not traced after 1823.

(23) Lieut. A. Nagle was born in London. Entered service, 1805. In *Royal Sovereign* at Trafalgar, 1805. In *Renown* at destruction of French ships *Robuste* and *Lion*, 1809; and at reduction of Isles of France and Java, 1810. Lieut., 1815. Medal and clasp. Died, 1849.

(24) Lieut. C. Charles was born in London. Volunteer 1st Class, 1804. In *Royal Sovereign* at Trafalgar, 1805. Lieut., 1815. Not traced after 1824–25.

(25) Commander C. Lambert was born in Lancaster, 1790. Entered service, 1804. In *Dreadnought* at blockade of Cadiz, and in *Royal Sovereign* at Trafalgar, 1805. In *Néréide* at capture of the fort of Jacotel, Ile de Bourbon, Ile de la Passe, and the sloop *Hector*, 1810. Wounded in *Néréide* and taken prisoner by French squadron, 1810. In *Peacock* when sunk by U.S. sloop *Hornet*, 1813—promoted Lieut. In *Euryalus* in expedition up the Potomac, 1814, including capture of Fort Washington, capitulation of Alexandria, and destruction of American batteries and shipping in the Potomac, 1814

C

—wounded. Commander, 1856. Medal and three clasps. Died at Topsham, 1856.

(26) Lieut. C. Criswick was born in Andover, Hants. Entered service, 1805; Volunteer 1st Class, 1805. In *Royal Sovereign* at Trafalgar, 1805. In *Southampton* at capture of Haytian frigate *Amethyst* and U.S. brig *Vixen*, 1812. Served on Canadian lakes, 1813-14, and was in the *Confiance* when captured by American squadron under Commodore Macdonough. Lieut., 1815. Medal and clasp. Died, 1854.

(27) Rev. J. Rudall was born 1754. Vicar of Credition, Devon, 1793. Leaving a curate in charge, served as Chaplain, R.N., 1799-1806. Chaplain of *Edgar* at Copenhagen, 1801; and of *Royal Sovereign* at Trafalgar, 1805. Died at Credition Vicarage, 1835, aged 81. Father of Lieut. J. Rudall, Mid. of *Defiance* at Trafalgar.

(28) Surgeon R. Lloyd, became Surgeon, R.N., 1781. In *Royal Sovereign* at Trafalgar, 1805. Not traced after 1816.

(29) Surgeon P. Lyon served in *Royal Sovereign* at Trafalgar, 1805. In *Canopus* in expedition to Egypt, 1807. Surgeon, 1812. Surgeon of *Glasgow* at Navarino, 1827. Medal and two clasps.

(30) Surgeon H. Towsey served in *Royal Sovereign* at Trafalgar, 1805. Surgeon, 1810. Medal and clasp. Died, 1860.

(31) Mr. B. S. Oliver became Paymaster and Purser, R.N., 1781. In *Royal Sovereign* at Trafalgar, 1805. Died, 1827.

(32) Lieut.-Colonel J. Vallack, R.M., became 2nd Lieut., 1782; Lieut., 1793; Captain, 1800. In *Royal Sovereign* at Trafalgar, 1805. Brevet-Major, 1812; Brevet-Lieut.-Colonel, 1816. Retired, 1826. Died at Kingsand, 1847, aged 81.

(33) Second Lieut. R. Green, R.M., became 2nd Lieut. 1803. Killed in *Royal Sovereign* at Trafalgar, 1805.

(34) Lieut. A. W. Hubbard, R.M., became 2nd Lieut. 1804. In *Royal Sovereign* at Trafalgar, 1805. Lieut., 1807. Retired half-pay, 1821. Died, 1844.

(35) Lieut. J. Le Vesconte, R.M., became 2nd Lieut. 1805. In *Royal Sovereign* at Trafalgar, 1805—wounded. Lieut., 1808 Not traced after 1814.

III

H.M.S. *BRITANNIA*, 100 GUNS

Rear-Admiral and Third-in-Command . } William, *Earl of* Northesk (1).

Captain . . . Charles Bullen (2).

Lieutenants . . Arthur Atchison (3).
John Houlton Marshall (4).
Francis Roskruge (5). *Killed.*
Charles Anthony (6).
Richard Lasham (7).
William Blight (8).
John Barclay, acting (9).

Master . . . Stephen Trounce (10). *Wounded.*

Master's Mates John Adamson (11).
James Sudbury.
William Grint (12). *Wounded.*
James Rattray (13).
Sylvester Austen (14).

Midshipmen . William Snell (15).
John White Pritchard (16).
Henry Canham.
Francis Daniel Lauzun (17)
Emanuel Blight (18).
William Geikie.
Joshua Thorndike.
Andrew Parry.
John Bramfield.
Joshua Peyton.
George Morey (19).

Midshipmen	William Benjamin Johnson (20).
(*continued*)	Charles Pitt (21).
	James Robinson.
	Radford Gundry Meech (22).
	James Lindsay.
	Richard Molesworth.
	Benjamin Shepherd (23).
	Bowham Tomkyns.
	Joshua Bailey.
	James Levett.
	Christopher Wilson.
	William Pyne (24).
	John Bidgood.
	John Lawrence.
	John Lang.
Volunteers	James R. Salmon.
1st Class	William P. Pinet.
	Richard Bayly Bowden (25).
	*John Wells (26).
Chaplain . .	Rev. Lawrence Hynes Halloran (27).
Surgeon . . .	Allan Cornfoot (28).
Assistant Surgeon . .	}John Evans (29).
Surgeon's Mate	John Owen Martin (30).
Purser . . .	James Hiatt.
Clerk. . . .	Richard M. Whichelo (31).
Gunner . . .	Michael Aylward.
Carpenter . .	John Simpson.
Captain, Royal Marines . .	{ Alexander Watson (32). William Jackson (33).
1st Lieuts, Royal Marines	{ Lawrence Boulcher Joseph Halloran (34). John Cooke (35).

The *Britannia,* Lord Northesk's flagship at Trafalgar, is believed to have been the oldest ship engaged in the battle on either side : she was built at Portsmouth in

---

* Borne as Quartermaster.

1762. She bore the flag of Vice-Admiral George Darby, as Second-in-Command of the Channel Fleet, in 1779–80; and when he was Commander-in-Chief in 1780–82. When the combined fleets of France and Spain invaded the Channel again in August 1780, Admiral Darby with his fleet took up a position at Torbay, but the allied commanders did not consider it prudent to attack him. Bearing Darby's flag, she took part in the second relief of Gibraltar in April 1781, and, with James Bradby as her captain, we find her with Vice-Admiral Richard Kempenfelt in his action with the French fleet off Ushant on the 12th–13th December 1781. In April 1782 Vice-Admiral Hon. Samuel Barrington hoisted his flag in her as Second-in-Command of the Channel Fleet, in which capacity she assisted at the final relief of Gibraltar, in October 1782, and in the repulse of the allied fleets of France and Spain on the twentieth of the same month: at the peace in the following year she returned home.

At the commencement of the war of the French Revolution in 1793, with John Holloway as captain, she bore the flag of Vice-Admiral William Hotham as Second-in-Command of the Mediterranean Fleet, and was employed in the blockade of Toulon. She still bore his flag on his becoming Commander-in-Chief, and was engaged in the action with the French fleet on the 14th March 1795, off Genoa, when she lost nineteen killed and wounded; and in his action of Hyères in July. Commanded by Captain Thomas Foley, and bearing the flag of Admiral Charles Thompson, she was present in Admiral Sir John Jervis's great victory over the Spanish fleet at St. Vincent, 14th February 1797; but did nothing of further importance during the remainder of the war.

On the recommencement of hostilities in 1803, she was commissioned at Portsmouth by Captain the Earl of

Northesk ; soon afterwards receiving visits on board from their Royal Highnesses the Dukes of York and Cumberland. Towards the close of the year we find her stationed at St. Helen's guarding that end of the Isle of Wight, in anticipation of a French invasion. She was with the fleet under Cornwallis at the blockade off Brest in 1804–5 ; and on the promotion of Lord Northesk to flank rank he continued his flag in her. Captain Charles Bullen was appointed his flag-captain in 1805, in August of which year she was detached under Sir Robert Calder to reinforce the fleet off Cadiz. She was with Lord Nelson at Trafalgar, and bore the flag of Lord Northesk as Third-in-Command on that eventful day. She was the fourth ship in the weather line led by Lord Nelson, and was thus early in the action, continuing closely engaged till the end, and sustaining a loss of fifty-two killed and wounded. She herself escaped with but slight loss to her masts and hull. In 1806 she escorted three of the prizes home to Plymouth, which was her last active service. She was laid up on the Hamoaze ; and her name was changed to *St. George* in 1812 ; renamed the *Barfleur* in 1819, she was finally broken up at Plymouth in 1826, after an existence of sixty-four years. She earned the naval war medal with three clasps.

(1) Admiral William, seventh Earl of Northesk, G.C.B., LL.D., Rear-Admiral of the United Kingdom, was the son of George, sixth Earl of Northesk, by his marriage with the Lady Anne Leslie, daughter of Alexander, fifth Earl of Leven and Melville ; and was born in 1756. Entering the service in 1771, he was promoted Lieutenant in 1777. Lieutenant in *Royal George*, under Sir John Lockhart Ross, at the capture of Caraccan fleet off Cape Finisterre, and of a Spanish squadron under Don Juan de Langara, 1779. Lieutenant in *Apollo* at first relief of Gibraltar, 1780. Lieutenant in the *Sandwich*, Lord Rodney's

flagship, in the battle with De Guichen, 1780—promoted Commander. Commanded the *St. Eustathius*, hired ship, at the reduction of the island of that name in the West Indies, in 1781. Captain, 1782. Commanded the *Heroine* for a few months in the Spanish armament in 1790. In 1792 he succeeded to the earldom on the death of his father. In 1796 he was appointed to the *Monmouth*, 64, in the North Sea Fleet, one of the ships which were implicated in the following year in the Mutiny of the Nore. He was detained by the mutineers as a prisoner in the *Sandwich*, and afterwards deputed by them to endeavour to effect a reconciliation with the King and the Government. In 1800–2 he commanded the *Prince*, 98, in the Channel Fleet. On the recommencement of war in 1803 he was appointed to the *Britannia*, of 100 guns, with the fleet under Admiral Cornwallis off Brest, and continued in her, on the same station, after his promotion to flag rank on the 23rd April in the following year. He was in her at the blockade of Brest in 1804–5, and was detached under Sir Robert Calder to reinforce the fleet off Cadiz. He was with Lord Nelson at Trafalgar, in which he commanded in the third post with his flag in the *Britannia*. She was the fourth ship in the weather line led by Lord Nelson, and was thus early in the action, continuing closely engaged till the end. For his service he was created a K.B., received the thanks of both Houses of Parliament, the gold medal, the thanks of the City of London, with the freedom of the city and a sword of honour, and a vase of the value of £300 from Lloyd's Patriotic Fund. Promoted Vice-Admiral, 1808; Admiral, 1814; and Rear-Admiral of the United Kingdom, 1821. Commander-in-Chief, Plymouth, 1827–30. Died in Albemarle Street, Piccadilly, London, in 1831, aged 75; and was buried on the 8th June in the crypt of St. Paul's Cathedral, near Nelson and Collingwood. His eldest son, Lord Rosehill, who was a Volunteer in the *Britannia* until within a few days of Trafalgar, was lost in 1807 when a Midshipman in the *Blenheim*.

(2) Admiral Sir Charles Bullen, G.C.B., K.C.H., Kt., was son of John Bullen of Weymouth, by his marriage with the daughter of Charles Liddell. Born at Newcastle, 1768. Entered service,

1779. Mid. of *Loyalist* at reduction of Charlestown, 1780. Lieut., 1791. Lieut. of *Ramillies* in action of 28th May, and in Lord Howe's victory of the 1st June 1794. Lieut. of *Monmouth* under Lord Northesk during the Mutiny of the Nore, 1797; 1st Lieut. of her at battle of Camperdown, 1797. Took possession of the Dutch ship *Delft*, and displayed great exertion and gallantry in saving many of the crew, being himself nearly drowned—promoted Commander. Captain, 1802. Flag-Captain of *Britannia* under Lord Northesk at Trafalgar, 1805 (gold medal, thanks of Parliament, and testimonial from Lloyd's Patriotic Fund). During the years 1807–11 he commanded successively the frigates *Volontaire* and *Cambrian* in the Mediterranean, off Toulon, and on the coast of Spain. Captain of *Akbar*, 50, on North American station, 1814–17. C.B., 1815. Commodore, West Coast of Africa, 1824–27. Superintendent Pembroke Dockyard, 1830. Commissioner Chatham Dockyard, 1831–32. Superintendent Pembroke Dockyard, 1832–37; Captain of *Royal Sovereign*, yacht, 1830–37. Rear-Admiral, 1837. Good service pension, 1843. Vice-Admiral, 1846. Admiral, 1852. Knighted, 1835; K.C.H., 1835; K.C.B., 1839; G.C.B., 1852. War medal and three clasps. Died, 2nd July 1853, at Shirley, Hants, aged 86. His portrait is in Painted Hall, Greenwich.

(3) Captain A. Atchison became Lieut., 1793. First Lieut. of *Britannia* at Trafalgar, 1805—promoted Commander. Commanded the *Scylla* at boarding and capture of the French gunbrig *Canonnière*, 1811. Captain, 1812. Died at Falmouth, 1818.

(4) Commander J. H. Marshall became Lieut., 1794. Lieut. of *Britannia* at Trafalgar, 1805. Commander, 1810. Commanded the *Halcyon*, 18, when she was wrecked and lost on a reef in the West Indies, 1814. Died, 1837.

(5) Lieut. F. Roskruge, son of Mr. John Roskruge, Master, R.N., became Lieut., 1796. Signal-Lieut. of *Britannia* at Trafalgar, 21st October 1805 and was killed by a double-headed shot.

(6) Commander C. Anthony entered service as Volunteer 1st

Class, 1793. Served in *Russel* in Lord Howe's victory of the 1st June 1794; and in Lord Bridport's action, 1795. Lieut., 1800. 1st Lieut. of *Blonde* in Egyptian War, 1801, including the disembarkation at Aboukir Bay, and battle of Alexandria (Turkish medal). Lieut. of *Britannia* at Trafalgar, 1805, and was placed in charge of the French 74-gun ship *Swiftsure*. Acting Captain of *Harpy* in Walcheren Expedition, and reduction of Flushing, 1809. Served in *Wolfe*, and commanded a division of gunboats in action with Americans at Forty Mile Creek, and at the capture of two schooners, 1813 (mentioned in despatches); also in three actions with Commodore Chauncey's squadron, 1813. Commander, 1813. Commanded the *Star* at capture of Fort Oswego, 1814 (mentioned in despatches). Governor of Preston Jail, 1827. Died, 1846.

(7) Lieut. R. Lasham became Lieut., 1801. Lieut. of *Britannia* at Trafalgar, 1805. Not in Navy List after 1812.

(8) Rear-Admiral W. Blight, brother of Commander Emanuel Blight, Mid. of *Britannia* at Trafalgar, entered service, 1793. Lieut., 1803. Lieut. of *Britannia* at Trafalgar, 21st October 1805. Was sent to take possession of the French 74 *Aigle*, but she was destroyed : he afterwards conducted the Spanish 112 *Santa-Ana* to Gibraltar. Lieut. of *Néréide* at attack on Buenos Ayres, 1807 ; at destruction of pirate vessels in Persian Gulf; and at recapture of *Sylph*, 1808. Commander, 1821. Captain, 1830. Retired Rear-Admiral, 1855. War medal and one clasp. Died at Stonehouse, Devon, aged 77.

(9) Commander J. Barclay entered service, 1797. Mid. of *Repulse* when lost off Ushant, 1800. Mid. of *Hydra*, and served in a boat at cutting out and capture of French armed lugger *Favori* near the mouth of the Tongue, 1803. Master's Mate of *Victory* in pursuit of combined fleet to the West Indies and back, 1805; and Acting-Lieut. of *Britannia* at Trafalgar, 1805— promoted Lieut. Lieut. in *Latona* at reduction of Curaçoa, 1807. Lieut. of *Fisgard* in expedition to Walcheren, 1809 ; and of *President* at storming of St. Sebastian, 1813. Retired Commander, 1838. War medal and three clasps. Died at Aldbury, Surrey, 1859, aged 77.

(10) Mr. S. Trounce was appointed Master, R.N., 1794. Master of *Britannia*, 1805—wounded. Died, 1839.

(11) Commander J. Adamson was born in Fifeshire, 1786. Became Mid., 1803. Master's Mate of *Britannia* at Trafalgar, 1805. Served in *Lavinia* in the Channel and Mediterranean, 1806-9, including the cutting out of a number of merchantmen. Commanded a gunboat in the expedition to Walcheren, and bombardment of Flushing, 1809. Lieut., 1811. Agent for Transport, 1825-32. Commander, Reserve List, 1853. Naval pension, 1861. War medal and clasp. Died, 1874.

(12) Captain W. Grint was born in Norfolk. Entered service, 1800. Served as Mid. in *Amazon* at battle of Copenhagen, 1801. Mid. of *Courageux* at capture of St. Lucia, 1803. Master's Mate, 1804. Master's Mate of *Britannia* at Trafalgar, 1805—wounded. Acting Lieut. *Latona*, frigate, at capture of Curaçoa, 1807. Lieut., 1808. Served in gunboats in Walcheren Expedition, 1809. Commander, 1818. Captain, 1851. War medal and three clasps. Died in Walworth, S.E., 1851.

(13) Vice-Admiral J. Rattray, D.L., J.P., son of David Rattray, M.D., was born in Coventry in 1790. Entered service, 1800. Served in *Courageux* in expedition to Terrol, 1800; in *Venerable* in action of 12th July 1801 with French and Spanish, Gut of Gibraltar; and again in *Courageux* at destruction of St. Lucia, 1803. Master's Mate of *Britannia* at Trafalgar, 1805. Lieut., 1807. Commander, 1812. Served in boats of *Contest* in cutting out U.S. gun-vessel *Asp* in the Chesapeake, 1813. Captain, 1815. Retired, 1846. Retired Rear-Admiral, 1851. Retired Vice-Admiral, 1857. War medal and two clasps. Died, 1862.

(14) Lieut. S. Austen was born in Falmouth. Mid. of *Venerable* in action off Algeciras, 1801—wounded. Master's Mate of *Britannia* at Trafalgar, 1805—promoted Lieut. Not in Navy List after 1816.

(15) Commander W. Snell was born in Antigua, 1790. Entered service, 1799. Mid. of *Britannia* at Trafalgar, 1805. Master's Mate, 1808. Lieut., 1811. In *Centaur* at defence of Tarragona, 1811. Retired Commander, 1853. Medal and

clasp. Died at Woopark, Neston, Cheshire, 1860. Brother of Lieut. J. C. Snell, who served in *Thunderer* at Trafalgar.

(16) Commander J. W. Pritchard was son of Samuel Perkins Pritchard, Master, R.N., and brother to R. D. Pritchard, Master's Mate of *Royal Sovereign* at Trafalgar. Born at Newington Butts. Volunteer 1st Class, 1800. Mid., 1801. Mid. of *Britannia* at Trafalgar, 1805. Lieut., 1808. Commander, 1828. Inspecting-Commander, Coastguard, 1835–38. Medal and clasp. Died at Kilmacoe, Ireland, 1851.

(17) Commander F. D. Lauzun was born in Jersey. Entered service, 1800. Mid. of *Britannia* at Trafalgar, 1805. In *Lavinia* at Brest and Toulon, 1806–8. In *Norge*, assisting at embarkation of army after Corunna, 1809; and served on shore at Ferrol, 1810. Lieut., 1811. Retired Commander, 1851. Medal and clasp. Died at Plymouth, 1861.

(18) Commander E. Blight, brother of Rear-Admiral William Blight, Lieut. of *Britannia* at Trafalgar, was born at Plymouth, 1790. Entered service, 1803. Mid. of *Britannia* at Trafalgar, 1805. Commanded a gunboat in the Walcheren Expedition, 1809, including the bombardment of Flushing. Lieut., 1815. Retired Commander, 1861. Medal and clasp. Died, 1864.

(19) Lieut. G. Morey served as Mid. in *Britannia* at Trafalgar, 1805. Lieut., 1815. Died at Milton, Gravesend, August, 1842, aged 53.

(20) Lieut. W. B. Johnson was born in Cork. Served as Mid. in *Britannia* at Trafalgar, 1805. Lieut., 1811. Not in Navy List after 1822.

(21) Lieut. C. Pitt was born in Yarmouth. Served as Mid. in *Britannia* at Trafalgar, 1805. Lieut., 1809. Not in Navy List after 1821.

(22) Lieut. R. G. Meech was born at Westbury, Wilts, 1790. Volunteer 1st Class, 1803. Mid. of *Britannia* at Trafalgar, 1805; and of *Royal George* in expedition to the Dardanelles, 1807. Lieut., 1810. Medal and clasp. Died in Jersey, 1849.

(23) Lieut. B. Shepherd entered service, 1804. Served as Mid. in *Britannia* at Trafalgar, 1805. In *Latona* at capture of Curaçoa, 1807, and the reduction of the Danish Islands, 1806.

In *Neptune* at capture of Martinique, 1809; and in *Pompée* at capture of Guadeloupe, 1810. Lieut., 1811. Lieut. of *Griffon* at the capture of two brigs of war on 27th March 1812. Medal and five clasps. Died, 1849–50.

(24) Lieut. W. Pyne was born in Tiverton. Served as Mid. in *Britannia* at Trafalgar, 1805. Lieut., 1812. Died, 1836.

(25) Commander R. B. Bowden was born in Somersetshire, 1792. Entered service, 1803. Served in *Britannia* at Trafalgar, 1805. Served in *Illustrious* in expedition to Copenhagen, 1807; and in *Nautilus*, sloop, in several engagements on the Portugal and Mediterranean stations, 1808–14. Lieut., 1815. Served in Coastguard, 1842–53. Retired Commander, 1853. Medal and clasp. Died at Herne Bay, Kent, 1861, aged 68.

(26) Lieut. J. Wells, son of Thomas Wells of Hull, was born there, 1784. Entered service, 1803. Served in *Britannia* at blockade of Brest, 1804–5. Borne as Quartermaster, but served as Signal-Midshipman in *Britannia* at Trafalgar, 1805. Lieut., 1812. Lieut., in *Julia*, at St. Helena during captivity of Napoleon, 1815–16. Resigned, 1816. Died, 1841, aged 56.

(27) Rev. L. H. Halloran, D.D., was formerly master at Alpington School, near Exeter. Chaplain, R.N., 1804. Chaplain of the *Britannia* at Trafalgar, 1805. Rector of Public Grammar School, and Chaplain to the troops, Cape of Good Hope, 1806–10. Died at Sydney, New South Wales, where he kept a school, 1831, aged 65.

(28) Mr. A. Cornfoot became Surgeon, R.N., 1795. Surgeon in *Britannia* at Trafalgar, 1805. Retired, 1839. Died, 1844.

(29) Mr. J. Evans became Assistant-Surgeon, 1799. Served in that capacity in *Britannia* at Trafalgar, 1805. Not in Navy List after 1818.

(30) Mr. J. O. Martin served as Surgeon's Mate in *Britannia* at Trafalgar, 1805. Surgeon, R.N., 1807. Surgeon of the *Hussar* at the capture of Java, 1811. Medal and two clasps. Died at Lee, near London, 1851.

(31) Mr. R. M. Whichelo, Purser, R.N., was born in Sussex, 1783. Was serving as Mid. of *Britannia* in 1804. Appointed Clerk, 1804. Clerk in *Britannia* at Trafalgar, 1805. Paymaster

and Purser, R.N., 1807.   When Purser of *Egeria* served in her boats at capture of part of Danish convoy on the Sleeve, 1809. Purser of *Blenheim* in first China War, 1840–42.   Had medal and clasp for Trafalgar, and medal for first China War.   Died, 1858.

(32) Captain A. Watson was appointed 2nd Lieut., Royal Marines, 1793.   1st Lieut., 1795.   Captain, 1803.   Senior Marine Officer in *Britannia* at Trafalgar, 1805.   Died, 1826.

(33) Captain W. Jackson was appointed 2nd Lieut., Royal Marines, 1795.   1st Lieut., 1797.   Captain, 1805.   Served in *Britannia* at Trafalgar, 1805.   Not in Navy List after 1819.

(34) Captain L. B. J. Halloran was appointed 2nd Lieut., Royal Marines, 1803.   1st Lieut., 1805.   Served in *Britannia* at Trafalgar, 1805.   Captain, 1827.   Retired, half-pay, 1833 Died, 1835.

(35) Lieut. J. Cooke was appointed 2nd Lieut., Roya Marines, 1803.   1st Lieut., 1805.   Served in *Britannia* at Trafalgar, 1805.   Died, 1825.

IV

H.M.S. *TÉMÉRAIRE*, 98 GUNS

Captain . . . Eliab Harvey (1).

Lieutenants . . Thomas Fortescue Kennedy (2).
Henry Coyngham Coxen (3).
Benjamin Vallack (4).
James Mould (5). *Wounded.*
William Smith.
John Wallace (6).
Alexander Davidson (7).
Thomas Coakley (8) (acting).

Master . . . Thomas Price.

Master's Mates James Arscott (9).
Francis Swaine Price (10). *Wounded.*
Alexander Black (11)

Midshipmen . William Pitts (12). *Killed.*
James John Blenkins (13).
John Knapman (14).
William Beale.
Lewis Davies.
Robert Henry Storck (15).
James Eaton (16).
Robert Sutton Bayly (17).
William Edward Hughes Allen (18).
John Eastman (19). *Wounded.*
Benjamin Dacosta (20).
Richard Elliott (21).
Robert Holgate (22).
Alexander Brenan (23).
William Napper (24).

Midshipmen . (*continued*)	Joseph Dixie Churchill (25).
	William Clark Jervoise (26).
	Thomas L. Cardew.
Volunteers 1st Class	William Shepheard (27).
	Henry C. Gordon
	Henry Walker (28).
	Francis Harris (29).
	John Hearle (30).
	Henry Douglas (31).
	* *Benjamin Mainwaring* (32).
	* *James Elphinstone Rivers* (33).
Chaplain . .	Rev. Joseph Sherer.
Surgeon . . .	Thomas Caird (34).
Assistant Surgeon . .	} William Scott.
Purser . . .	William Ballingall (35).
Clerk	John Augustus Matheson (36).
Gunner . . .	Francis Harris (37).
Boatswain . .	John Brooks. *Wounded.*
Carpenter . .	Lewis Oades. *Killed.*
Captain, Royal Marines . .	} Simeon Busigny (38). *Killed.*
2nd Lieuts., Royal Marines	{ Samuel John Payne (39). *Wounded.*
	John Kingston (40). *Killed.*
	William Nicolas Roe (41).

The *Téméraire* was built at Chatham, and launched
there in September 1798. She was commissioned by
Captain Peter Puget in April 1799, and between then
and 1801 bore the flags in the Channel Fleet of Rear-
Admirals Sir John Borlase Warren, K.B., and James
Hawkins Whitshed. In the autumn of 1801, Thomas
Eyles was appointed her captain, and Rear-Admiral
George Campbell hoisted his flag in her on taking over
command of the Western Squadron. On the conclusion
of the Peace of Amiens in 1802, the sailors, some of

* Rated as A.B.

whom had been several years at sea, expected to go home ;
and when the fleet rendezvoused at Bantry prior to pro-
ceeding to the West Indies, a serious mutiny broke out
on board. The officers burst in upon the men in con-
ference, and by nightfall the latter were in irons, under a
strong guard of marines. In January 1802 twenty of
them were tried by court-martial at Spithead, eighteen of
whom were found guilty and hanged at the yard-arm.
It is said that when the ship paid off in the following
year, the crew wore crape bands round their straw hats
in memory of the mutineers.

On the outbreak of the war with France in 1803, she
was commissioned by Captain Eliab Harvey, M.P. for
Essex, and "The Saucy *Téméraire*," as the seamen always
called her, commenced her career of distinction. For
eighteenth months in 1804–5 she served in the blockade
of Brest and in the Bay of Biscay, prior to joining the
fleet off Cadiz. At Trafalgar she was the second ship in
the weather line, closely following the *Victory*, and her
share in the action was particularly brilliant. When the
Victory was engaged with the *Redoutable*, the *Téméraire*
came up to starboard of the French 74, and also engaged
her. This was after Nelson had fallen, and the first
broadside of the *Téméraire* checked an attempt at boarding the *Victory* which the French were about to make.
The fight of the little two-decker against the pair of
three-deckers was heroic. The top-men of the *Redoutable*
flung down hand-grenades and fire-balls till they set fire
to the deck, larboard forechains, starboard foreshrouds,
and foresail ; one fire-ball rolled into the magazine
among the powder barrels, and only the presence of
mind of a master-at-arms saved the *Téméraire* from the
fate of the *Orient* at the battle of the Nile. In the mean-
time a new antagonist, the French 80-gun ship *Fougueux*,
had come up on the starboard quarter of the *Téméraire*,

which had been suffering also from the fire of the *Neptune*.
She looked nothing but a cripple, and the *Fougueux*
came up determined to board her. When less than fifty
yards separated the vessels, the starboard broadside of
the *Téméraire* crashed into the French ship, sweeping
her rigging and upper works bare, leaving her whole side
a mass of splinters. She drove into the *Téméraire*, was
lashed fast, and twenty-eight men under Lieut. T. F.
Kennedy sprang on to her deck—where the gallant
French captain lay mortally wounded—and fought their
way to the stump of the mainmast. In ten minutes they
had the British colours hoisted, and the *Fougueux*—which
unfortunately foundered in the subsequent gale, with the
prize crew on board—was a prize of war to the *Téméraire*,
which had also the *Victory's* prize, the *Redoutable*, lashed
to her. "Nothing could be finer," wrote Lord Collingwood, than her conduct in the fight—"I have no words
in which I can sufficiently express my admiration of it."
As the smoke of the battle cleared away she was seen
lying dismantled and temporarily helpless, but with
an enemy's ship, equally helpless, a prize on each side of
her. Her losses amounted to 121 killed and wounded,
including 9 officers, while 43 of her crew perished in the
prizes after the battle. She had her main top-mast, the
head of her mizen-mast, her foreyard, and her fore and
main topsail yards shot away ; her fore and main-masts
were so badly wounded as to be unfit to carry sail ; while
her bowsprit was shot through in several places. Her
rigging of every sort was cut to pieces, and she was
otherwise seriously damaged.

She had no opportunity of distinguishing herself during the remainder of the war. After the peace she was
employed until 1820 as a Receiving ship at Devonport,
and from then to 1836 as a Receiving and Victualling
ship at Sheerness. Her last duty was in 1836–38, when

she was commissioned at Sheerness, and her last captain, curiously enough, was Captain Thomas Fortescue Kennedy, who had been her First Lieutenant at Trafalgar. In 1838, forty years after she was launched, she was sold to Castle, the ship-breaker, for £5530. On the melancholy occasion of being towed up the river to her last berth at Rotherhithe, to be broken up for firewood, Turner, the Royal Academician, who was boating with a party of friends, saw her, and the idea of his celebrated picture, "The Fighting *Téméraire*," now in the National Gallery, came to him.   Ruskin took leave of her in an impassioned essay in which he said : "Never more shall sunset lay golden robe on her, nor starlight tremble on the waves that part at her gliding.   Perhaps where the low gate opens to some cottage garden, the tired traveller may ask, idly, why the moss grows so green on its rugged wood, and even the sailor's child may not answer nor know that the night dew lies deep in the war rents of the wood of the old *Téméraire*."   The fate of her timbers was little better than he had foreseen, but there are relics of the *Téméraire* to-day on the mantel-piece in Castle's ship-breaker's office at Millbank, which is supported by the two figures of "Atlas" taken from the quarter gallery of the old ship when she was broken up ; and the church of St. Paul, Rotherhithe, has, or had till very recently, heart of oak from the timber of this Trafalgar fighter in the altar table, altar rails, and sanctuary chairs.

(1) Admiral Sir E. Harvey, G.C.B., F.R.S., was the second son of William Harvey, M.P., of Rolls Park, Chigwell, Essex ; and was born in 1758.   Entered the service in 1771.   Served as Mid. in the *Eagle* under Lord Howe on the North American Station, during the war of American Independence, 1775–78. Appointed Lieut., 1779.   M.P. for Maldon, Essex, 1780–81. Commander, 1782.   Captain, 1783.   Commanded the *Santa*

Margaritta at the reduction of Martinique and Guadeloupe in 1794; and assisted in the same year at the destruction of the French frigate *La Félicité* and two corvettes. Commanded the Sea Fencibles of Essex in 1798–99. M.P. for Essex, 1802–12. On the recommencement of the war with France in 1803 was appointed to the *Téméraire*, 98, and in command of her greatly distinguished himself at Trafalgar on the 21st October 1805. Received the thanks of Parliament and of Lord Collingwood, a gold medal, a sword of honour from the Patriotic Fund, and was promoted Rear-Admiral. Was one of the pall-bearers at Lord Nelson's funeral. Was dismissed the service in 1809 for insubordination to Lord Gambier, but was restored in the following year and promoted Vice-Admiral. K.C.B., 1815. Admiral, 1819. M.P. for Essex, 1820–30. G.C.B., 1825. Died in 1830. Was at one time a great gambler, and is reported to have lost a fortune in one evening at hazard.

(2) Captain T. F. Kennedy was son of Dr. Kennedy, Inspector-General of Army Hospitals, and Physician to the Prince of Wales, afterwards George IV. Born, 1774. Entered service as Volunteer 1st Class, 1789. As Mid. in the *Terrible* served on shore with the army during the occupation of Toulon, 1793. Lieut., 1796. Lieut. in *La Sybille* at capture of a gunboat, 1798. First Lieut. of the *Téméraire* at Trafalgar, 1805; headed the boarders and planted the British flag in the French *Fougueux*, 80 guns—promoted Commander. Commanded the sloop *Cordelia* in Walcheren Expedition, 1809; and at capture of three privateers and some merchantmen; commanded a squadron of eight brigs at the blockade of two 40-gun frigates at Dunkerque. Captain, 1813. Superintendent Sheerness Dockyard, 1834–38, and Captain of the *Téméraire*, 1836–38. Died in 1846, aged 72.

(3) Commander H. C. Coxen became Lieut., 1803. Lieut. in the *Téméraire* at Trafalgar, 1805. Commander, 1809. Died at Mallow, Ireland, 1836.

(4) Lieut. B. Vallack became Lieut., 1801. Lieut. in the *Téméraire* at Trafalgar, 1805. Not in Navy List after 1811.

(5) Captain J. Mould became Lieut., 1797. Lieut. in the *Téméraire* at Trafalgar, 1805—slightly wounded. Commander,

1810. Commanded the *Mutine* in battle of Algiers, 1816—promoted Captain. Died in 1819.

(6) Lieut. J. Wallace became Lieut., 1797. Lieut. in the *Téméraire* at Trafalgar, 1805; took possession of the 74-gun ship *Redoutable*. Not in Navy List after 1809.

(7) Lieut. A. Davidson became Lieut., 1800. Lieut. in the *Téméraire* at Trafalgar, 1805. Not in Navy List after 1821.

(8) Commander T. Coakley was born in America, 1780. Entered service, 1798. Served in the *Lynx* at capture of *Le Mentor*, privateer, off Coast of North America, 1798. Acting-Lieut. of the *Téméraire* at Trafalgar, 1805 (promoted Lieut., 1806). Lieut. of the *Procris* in operations against Copenhagen, 1807. Lieut. of the *Raisonnable* at reduction of St. Paul's, Isle of Bourbon, 1809. Retired Commander, 1840. Medal and clasp. Died in 1851.

(9) Lieut. J. Arscott was born in Teignmouth. Master's Mate in *Téméraire* at Trafalgar, 1805, and was one of the boarders of the French 80, *Fougueux*. Acting-Master of *Confiance*, at the capture of Cayenne, 1809. Lieut., 1810. Died at Teignmouth, 1816.

(10) Commander F. S. Price was born at Bideford, Devonshire, in 1783. Entered service as Volunteer 1st Class, 1793. Mid. of the *Boadicea* in attack on a Spanish squadron in Aix Roads, 1799 (wounded); and in the cutting out of a Spanish packet and gunboat in the neighbourhood of Corunna (wounded). Master's Mate in the *Téméraire* at Trafalgar, 1805—wounded. Promoted Lieut., 1806. Retired Commander, 1839. Medal and clasp. Died in 1853–54.

(11) Mr. A. Black was born in Aberdeen in 1780. Served as Master's Mate in the *Téméraire* at Trafalgar, 1805; and with a prize crew of thirty was lost in the *Fougueux*, which foundered in the subsequent gale.

(12) Midshipman W. Pitts was born in London in 1784. Mid. in the *Téméraire* at Trafalgar, 1805, and was killed in the French ship *Redoutable*, having assisted to take possession of her. His leg was shattered by a shot, and he died after undergoing amputation by the French surgeon.

(13) Lieut. J. J. Blenkins was born in Essex in 1786. Mid. in the *Téméraire* at Trafalgar, 1805. Lieut., 1809. Not in Navy List after 1825.

(14) Commander J. Knapman was born at Plymouth in 1786; and entered service as Volunteer 1st Class, 1801. Mid. in the *Téméraire* at Trafalgar, 1805. In *Achille* at capture of four French frigates off Rochefort, 1806. Lieut., 1809. Served in the *Albacore* in the action with the French *La Gloire*, 1812. Served in Coastguard, 1827–32. Retired Commander, 1853. Medal and clasp. Died in 1866. Brother to Commander E. Knapman, who served in *Spartiate* at Trafalgar.

(15) Lieut. R. H. Storck was born in London in 1785. Served as a Mid. at the battle of Copenhagen, 1801. Mid. in the *Téméraire* at Trafalgar, 1805. Lieut., 1812. Died in 1816.

(16) Commander J. Eaton was born in London in 1783. Entered service, 1799. Was in *Hannibal* when she had to surrender in the action off Algeciras in 1801. Mid. in the *Atalante* cutting out vessels near St. Gilda's in Quiberon Bay, 1803. Signal Mid. of the *Téméraire* at Trafalgar, 1805—promoted Lieut., 1806. Was wounded in *Lion* when taking out a convoy to China. Present in her at the reduction of Java, 1811. Distinguished, when in the *Beaver*, in rescuing the crew of a Swedish vessel, 1813. Retired Commander, 1842. Medal and two clasps. Died in 1856–57.

(17) Lieut. R. S. Bayly was born in Poole, Dorsetshire, in 1787. Mid. in *Téméraire* at Trafalgar, 1805. Lieut., 1811. Not in Navy List after 1832.

(18) Captain W. E. H. Allen was a son of Admiral William Allen, who died in 1804. He was born in London in 1787. Volunteer 1st Class, 1802. Served as Mid. in the *Téméraire* at Trafalgar, 1805. Lieut., 1807. Lieut. of *Hercule* in expedition to Copenhagen, 1807; in *Akbar*, at reduction of Mauritius and capture of Java, 1811; and in command of her boats at capture of a French schooner, 1812. Wrecked in *Cygnet*, 1815. Commander, 1828. Inspecting-Commander Coastguard, 1831–34. Retired Captain, 1851. Greenwich Hospital pension, 1854. Medal and two clasps. Died in 1855-56.

(19) Midshipman J. Eastman was born in Plymouth in 1777. Served as Mid. in the *Téméraire* at Trafalgar, 1805—wounded. Medal and clasp. Living in 1848.

(20) Midshipman B. Dacosta was born in London in 1782. Mid., 1805. Mid. in the *Téméraire* at Trafalgar, 1805. Medal and clasp. Living in 1848.

(21) Midshipman R. Elliott was born in Dublin, in 1793. Volunteer 1st Class, 1804. Mid., 1805. Mid. in the *Téméraire* at Trafalgar, 1805. Not traced further.

(22) Lieut. R. Holgate was born in Essex in 1784. Mid. in the *Téméraire* at Trafalgar, 1805; and was one of the party which boarded the French 80 *Fougueux*. Lieut., 1806. Not in Navy List after 1811.

(23) Commander A. Brenan was born in Dublin in 1790. Volunteer 1st Class, 1804. Mid., 1805. Mid. in the *Téméraire* at Trafalgar, 1805. Lieut., 1814. Served in the *Merope*, one of the ships escorting Napoleon to Elba, 1814. Served in Coastguard, 1821–27. Retired Commander, 1857. Medal and clasp. Died in 1862.

(24) Midshipman W. Nipper was born in Rochester, Kent, in 1783. Served as Mid. in the *Téméraire* at Trafalgar, 1805. Died at sea in 1805.

(25) Lieut. J. D. Churchill was son of Rev. Joseph Dixie Churchill, Rector of Henstead, Suffolk, and was born in Norwich in 1788. Served as Mid. in the *Téméraire* at Trafalgar, 1805. Lieut., 1810. Died at Jamaica of yellow fever, in 1810–1811.

(26) Captain W. C. Jervoise was born in London, and entered service in 1800. Mid. of *Lapwing* at capture of French vessel *Henrietta*. Mid. in the *Téméraire* at Trafalgar, 1805. Lieut., 1806. Lieut. of *Alceste* in action with Spanish flotilla off Cadiz, 1808. Taken prisoner, 1808; escaped, 1814. Commander, 1814. Commanded the *Pandora* in expedition to Burburra on the African coast, 1826 (mentioned in despatches). Captain, 1828. Died at Lausanne in 1837, aged 48.

(27) Vice-Admiral W. Shepheard was born in London in 1793. Volunteer 1st Class, 1804. Served in the *Téméraire* at Trafalgar,

1805. Mid., 1806. Served in *Amelia* at destruction of French frigates under batteries of Sable d'Olonne, 1809; destruction of *L'Amazone*, 1811; destruction of Fort Winnebah, coast of Africa, 1812; and the action with the French frigate *L'Aréthuse*, 1813. Lieut., 1815. Commander, 1831. Served in Coastguard, 1835–1838. Captain, 1840. Retired, 1853. Retired Rear-Admiral, 1858. Retired Vice-Admiral, 1865. Medal and clasp. Died in 1870.

(28) Lieut. H. Walker was born at New Malton, Yorks, in 1790. Volunteer 1st Class, 1805. Served in the *Téméraire* at Trafalgar, 1805; and in *Africa* in unsuccessful attack on Buenos Ayres, 1807. In boats of *Mohawk* at destruction of forts and cannon foundry at French Town and Havre de Grace, 1813. Lieut., 1813. Medal and two clasps. Died in 1854.

(29) Commander F. Harris became Volunteer 1st Class, 1805. Served in the *Téméraire* at Trafalgar, 1805. In *Unité* at capture of French store-ship *Dromedaire*; the destruction of the *Giraffe* and *Nourrice*; and in the action with and capture of two French frigates, 1811. Lieut., 1815. Medal and two clasps. Died, a Retired Commander, in 1883, aged 87.

(30) Mr. J. Hearle was born at Plymouth in 1792. Volunteer 1st Class, 1805. Served in the *Téméraire* at Trafalgar, 1805. Not further traced.

(31) Commander H. Douglas entered the service as Volunteer 1st Class, 1805. Served in the *Téméraire* at Trafalgar, 1805. Served in *Belleisle* at destruction of the French 74 *L'Impéteux* off Cape Henry, 1806. In the *Astræa* was present at the capture of French frigates *Renommée* and *Néréide* off Madagascar, 1811; and the settlement of Tamatave, 1811. Served on the Canadian lakes, 1814–16. Lieut., 1815. Retired Commander, 1860. Medal and clasp. Died in 1885.

(32) Lieut. B. Mainwaring was son of Edward Mainwaring, and second cousin of Vice-Admiral T. F. C. Mainwaring, who served in the *Naiad* at Trafalgar, and died in 1858. Born in 1794. Borne on ship's books of *Téméraire* as A.B. at Trafalgar, 1805. Served in boats of *Revenge* at cutting out of two privateers from under the enemy's battery on the coast of Catalonia, 1814.

Lieut., 1814. Served in Coastguard, 1831–36. Medal and clasp. Died in 1852.

(33) Mr. J. E. Rivers was born in Portsea, Hants. Served as A.B. in *Téméraire* at Trafalgar, 1805—promoted Mid. Master, R.N., 1812. Afterwards joined the H.E.I. Co.'s Service, and died of fever at Chowinghee, in 1814, when Lieut. in the *Minto*.

(34) Surgeon T. Caird became Surgeon, R.N., 1779. Surgeon of *Téméraire* at Trafalgar, 1805. Died in 1821–22.

(35) Mr. W. Ballingall was appointed Paymaster and Purser, R.N., 1785. Purser of *Polyphemus* at the battle of Copenhagen, 1801; and of *Téméraire* at Trafalgar, 1805. Retired, 1843. Medal and two clasps.

(36) Mr. J. A. Matheson was born in London in 1780. Appointed Clerk from Mid., 1805. Clerk in *Téméraire* at Trafalgar, 1805. Resigned, 1806.

(37) Mr. F. Harris served as Gunner in the *Téméraire* at Trafalgar, 1805. Volunteer 1st Class, 1805. Mid. in the *Unité* in action with and capture of two French frigates at Pelagosa, 1811. Received the medal and two clasps in 1848.

(38) Captain S. Busigny was appointed 2nd Lieut., Royal Marines, in 1779. 1st Lieut., 1793. Captain, 1797. Senior officer of Marines in the *Téméraire* at Trafalgar, 1805, and died on the 23rd October 1805, from the severe wounds he received.

(79) Captain S. J. Payne was appointed 2nd Lieut., Royal Marines, in 1803. 1st Lieut., 1805. Served in the *Téméraire* at Trafalgar, 1805 (wounded). Commanded the Marines in *Amethyst*, frigate, in her action with, and capture of, French 40-gun frigate *Thétis*, 1808 (dangerously wounded). He was disabled for active service after this, and became Quartermaster, R.M., in 1808. Captain, 1826. Died at Bury St. Edmunds, while on recruiting service, in 1837, age 51.

(40) 2nd Lieut. J. Kingston was appointed 2nd Lieut., Royal Marines, in 1804. Served in the *Téméraire*, and was killed in action at Trafalgar, 1805.

(41) Lieut. W. N. Roe was appointed 2nd Lieut., Royal Marines, in 1804. Served in the *Téméraire* at Trafalgar, 1805. 1st Lieut., 1808. Placed on half-pay, 1814.

V

H.M.S *NEPTUNE*, 98 GUNS

Captain . . .	Thomas Francis Fremantle (1).
Lieutenants .	George Acklom (2).
	Amos Freeman Westropp (3).
	George William Hooper (4).
	Isaac Shaw (5).
	William Mowat (6).
	Hon. Granville Leveson Proby (7).
	Andrew Pellet Green (8).
Midshipmen .	Edward Andrews.
	Andrew English.
	Atwel Allen.
	John Hanns.
	George Cunningham (9).
	Thomas Wybrow (10)
	Francis Molesworth (11).
	George Flower Herbert (12).
	William Smith.
	George Loftin (13).
	Henry B. Middleton (14).
	William Stanhope Badcock (15).
	Edward Goodlad (16).
	Edward Potts.
	Daniel Hunt Sulivan (17)
	Alexander Mackenzie (18).
Volunteers	John Knight.
1st Class	Edward Moore (19).
	Frank Hastings (20).
	William Lancaster.

Volunteers 1st Cl.	William Wynne Eyton (21).
(*continued*)	* *Robert Newton* (22).
Master . . .	James Keith (23).
Master's Mates	Henry Hiatt (24).
	John Dodd.
	Robert Marr.
	James Pearl (25).
	William Hutchinson.
Chaplain . .	Rev. Charles Burne (26).
Surgeon . . .	Luke Farrington Nagle (27).
Assistant {	Edmund Smith
Surgeons . {	John Scott.
Purser . . .	Samuel Hodgson (28).
Clerk . . .	Richard Hurrell (29). *Wounded.*
1st Lieut., }	George Kendall (30).
Royal Marines }	
2nd Lieuts., {	William Burton (31).
Royal Marines {	Lewis Rooke (32).
Boatswain . .	John Scott.
Carpenter . .	John Hiatt.

The *Neptune* was built in Deptford Dockyard in 1797 from the design of Sir John Henslow, Knight, Surveyor of the Navy, and was commissioned in May of the same year by Captain Hon. Henry Edwin Stanhope. On the outbreak of the Mutiny of the Nore she bore the broad pennant of Commodore Sir Erasmus Gower, and was held in readiness to attack the mutineers. She was afterwards employed with the Channel Fleet until April 1799, when Captain James Vashon was appointed to her, and she joined Lord Keith off Brest in July, taking part in his unsuccessful pursuit of the allied fleet. In May 1805, under command of Captain Thomas Francis Fremantle, she joined the British fleet off Cadiz; and in October shared in the glories of Trafalgar. She was the

* Borne and served as A.B.

third ship in the weather column. She got into action about 1.45 P.M., when she hauled up for the nearest of the enemy's ships, and passing immediately under the stern of the French *Bucentaure*, delivered her broadside into it with terrible effect. She then continued under the stern and along the starboard side of the Spanish *Santisima Trinidad*, and luffed up to leeward of the huge four-decker, which had already suffered badly, and which she fought until the Spaniard became wholly unmanageable. The *Neptune* was afterwards somewhat severely handled by several ships of the combined van, which raked her after they bore up. She lost forty-four killed and wounded in the battle. Her masts and her standing and running rigging were all more or less damaged, and she had nine shots between wind and water. On the following day she took the *Royal Sovereign* in tow, but afterwards towed the *Victory* to Gibraltar. She was in the West Indies in 1808–9 under command of Captain Charles Dilkes, bearing the flag of Rear-Admiral Hon. Alexander Cochrane, K.B., and took part in the bombardment and capture of Martinique in January and February, 1809. In the following March she was with the squadron blockading the Saintes islands, and participated in the running fight with the three French 74's, *d'Hautpoult* (flagship), *Couragœux*, and *Polonais*, which ended in the capture by the *Pompée* and *Recruit* of the *d'Hautpoult* on the 17th April 1809. Her career ended in 1818, when she was broken up at Plymouth. She earned the naval war medal with two clasps.

(1) Vice-Admiral Sir T. F. Fremantle, G.C.B., was the third son of John Fremantle, of Aston Abbots, Bucks, by his marriage with Frances, daughter and co-heiress of John Edwards of Bristol. Born in 1765, he entered the service in 1778. Was a Midshipman in the *Phœnix* when she was lost on the coast of Cuba, in 1780. Lieut, 1782. Captain, 1793. Captain of the *Tartar*, 28, at the

blockade of Toulon, in 1793, and under Nelson at the reduction of Bastia, in Corsica, 1794. Captain of the *Inconstant*, which behaved so gallantly in Hotham's action off Genoa, in March 1795. Also in her at the capture of enemy's gunboats, 1795, the capture of the *Unité*, 1796, and particularly distinguished himself at the evacuation of Leghorn when threatened by the French, 1796 (mentioned in despatches), and the capture of Prombono in the same year. Commanded the *Seahorse* off Cadiz in 1797, and again distinguished himself under Nelson at Santa Cruz, 1797—wounded. Captain of the *Ganges* in Lord Nelson's victory of Copenhagen, the 2nd April 1801. Captain of the *Neptune* at Trafalgar, the 21st October 1805: she was the third ship in the weather column, and lost forty-four killed and wounded—gold medal, sword of honour from the Patriotic Fund. Appointed a Lord Commissioner of the Admiralty, 1807. Captain of the Royal Yacht *William and Mary*, 1807–10. Rear-Admiral, 1810. Commanded a squadron in the Adriatic, with his flag in the *Milford*, during the operations in 1812–14, including the capture of Fiume and Trieste; for which services he was created a K.C.B., a Baron of the Austrian States, a Knight of Maria Theresa, and a Knight of St. Ferdinand and Merit. Advanced to G.C.B., 1818. Vice-Admiral, 1819. Died in 1819, at Naples, aged 54, when Commander-in-Chief in the Mediterranean. Of his sons, the eldest, Thomas Frances (father of the present Admiral Hon. Sir Edmund Robert Fremantle, G.C.B., C.M.G., Rear-Admiral of the United Kingdom) was created a baronet in 1821 in acknowledgment of his father's services, and was raised to the peerage in 1874 as Baron Cottesloe. Another of his sons, Admiral Sir Charles White Fremantle, G.C.B., died in 1869.

(2) Commander G. Acklom entered service, 1788. Served on shore at occupation of Toulon, 1793. Became Lieut., 1794. Lieut. of *Hydra* at capture and destruction of the *Confiante*, 1798. 1st Lieut. of *Neptune* at Trafalgar, 1805—promoted ∫Commander. In command of *Ranger*, sloop, effected several captures on the Baltic station, 1807–12. Co-operated with the Russians at reduction of Dantzig, 1814 (2nd Class of St. Anne, and 3rd Class of St. Wladimir). Died at Wassand, near Hull, in 1837.

(3) Captain A. F. Westropp was the 3rd son of Captain Michael Roberts Westropp, of Cork, late 18th and 63rd Regiments, and Jane, daughter of Amos Godsell of Sunville, Co. Limerick. Born in 1782. Served as Midshipman of the *Monarch* at the battle of Camperdown, 1797—promoted Lieut. Senior Lieut. of the *Hebe* at the landing in Egypt, 1801. Second Lieut. of *Neptune* at Trafalgar, 1805. Senior Lieut. of *Surveillante* in the expedition to Copenhagen, 1807, and capture of Guadeloupe, 1809. In the *Peruvian*, brig, captured the American schooner *Yankee*, off the Leeward Islands, 1812. Commander, 1812. Conveyed the Duke of Wellington to Lisbon during the Peninsular War, and escorted Napoleon I. to St. Helena, 1815. Captain, 1818. Died at Cork in 1844, aged 61.

(4) Captain G. W. Hooper was promoted to Lieut. in 1800. Lieut. in the *Neptune* at Trafalgar, 1805. Commander, 1808. Captain, 1817. Died in 1839.

(5) Commander I. Shaw entered service as Volunteer 1st Class, 1793. Mid. of *Courageux* at occupation of Toulon, 1793, and reduction of Corsica, 1794; of *Romulus* in Admiral Hotham's action with the French fleet, 1795; and of *Barfleur* at battle of St. Vincent, 1797. Lieut., 1801. Lieut. of *Neptune* off Ferrol and Brest, and at Trafalgar, 1805. Lieut. of *Volontaire* in the Mediterranean, including capture of island of Pomégue, near Marseilles, 1809; destruction of Fort Rioux, near Cape Croisette, 1809 (mentioned in despatches); many boat actions, including the cutting out of privateer *La Décidé* from harbour of Palamos, 1811; capture and destruction of convoy near mouth of the Rhone, 1812; the capture of six vessels and the destruction of a battery at Morgion, the 2nd May 1813; and on other occasions (wounded, mentioned in despatches, and promoted Commander, 1813). War medal and four clasps. Died in 1848.

(6) Lieut. W. Mowatt was promoted to Lieut., 1803. Lieut. in *Neptune* at Trafalgar, 1805. Died, 1832–33.

(7) Admiral G. L., 3rd Earl of Carysfort, was second son of John Joshua, 1st Earl of Carysfort, K.P., by his first wife, Elizabeth, daughter of Rt. Hon. Sir William Osborne, Bart., of Newtown, Suffolk. He was born in 1781, educated at Rugby,

and entered service in 1798. Mid. of the *Vanguard* at battle of the Nile, 1798. Mid. of *Foudroyant* at blockade of Malta, capture of *Le Genereux* (74), the *Ville de Marseilles*, and the *Guillaume Tell* (84), 1800; and in expedition to Egypt, 1801. Lieut., 1804. Lieut. of *Neptune* at Trafalgar, 1805. Commander, 1806. Captain, 1806. M.P., Co. Wicklow, 1812–18, and 1820. Rear-Admiral, 1841. Vice-Admiral, 1851. Succeeded as 3rd Earl, 1855. Medal and two clasps. Died, 1868.

(8) Vice-Admiral Sir A. P. Green, K.C.H., Kt., entered the service in 1793. Mid. of *Illustrious* at investment of Toulon, 1793; siege and capture of Bastia, in Corsica, 1794; and in Admiral Hotham's action with the French fleet, 1795. Wrecked in *Illustrious*, 1795. Taken prisoner in the *Censeur*, 1795. Mid. of *Thunderer* at reduction of St. Lucia, 1795, the destruction of the *Harmonie*, and at St. Domingo, 1796–97. Lieut., 1800. Lieut. of the *Ganges* at the battle of Copenhagen, 1801. Lieut. of *Eurydice*, and commanded her boats at attack on a Spanish convoy, 1805 (mentioned in despatches). Lieut. of *Neptune* at Trafalgar, 1805, and at siege of Dantzig. Commander, 1812. Commanded *Shamrock* at capture of Cuxhaven, 1813 (mentioned in despatches), and served as a volunteer at siege and surrender of Gluckstadt, 1814 (promoted Captain, 1814; K.H.; Commander of the Sword of Sweden; and Knight of Iron Cross of Austria). Knighted, and K.C.H., 1832. A.D.C. to Queen. Rear-Admiral, 1849. Vice-Admiral, 1856. War medal and four clasps. Died in 1858 in James Street, Buckingham Gate, S.W., aged 81.

(9) Mr. G. Cunningham was born at Kilmarnock, Ayrshire, 1788. Mid. of *Neptune* at Trafalgar, 1805. Master's Mate of *Procris* at attack on Dutch gunboats at mouth of Indramayo River, and the capture of Java, 1811. Not traced further.

(10) Mr. T. Wybrow was born in Stonehouse, Plymouth. Volunteer 1st Class, 1805. Mid., 1805. Mid. in *Neptune* at Trafalgar, 1805. Not traced further.

(11) Lieut. F. Molesworth was son of Richard Molesworth, nephew of the 5th Viscount, and brother of the 7th Viscount Molesworth, and was born in London. He served as Mid. in

Neptune at Trafalgar, 1805. Lieut., 1806. Lieut. in the *Thames* and commanded her boats in the action with Danish gunboats, and the capture and destruction of a number of transports off Amanthea, coast of Calabria, 1810. Died, 1812.

(12) Rear-Admiral G. F. Herbert, son of Joseph Herbert, President of the Island of Montserrat. Born in London, entered the service in 1803. Mid., 1804. Mid. in the *Neptune* at Trafalgar, 1805. Lieut., 1811. Lieut. in the *San Josef*, in Sir Edward Pellew's action off Toulon, 1813, and at the capture of Genoa, 1814. Lieut. in the *Ulysses* at the destruction of a slave factory on the coast of Africa, 1815. Commander, 1828. Captain, 1852. Retired Rear-Admiral, 1867. Medal and clasp. Died in 1868.

(13) Mr. G. Loftin served as Mid. in the *Ganges* at the battle of Copenhagen, 1801; and as Mid. in the *Neptune* at Trafalgar, 1805. Became 2nd Lieut., Royal Marines, 1807 Placed on half-pay, 1809. Received the medal and two clasps in 1848. Died, 1848.

(14) Mr. H. B. Middleton was born in Cheshire. Served as Mid. in *Neptune* at Trafalgar, 1805. When Master's Mate of *Dreadnought*, was killed in an unsuccessful attempt to cut out a French vessel off Ushant, the 7th September 1810.

(15) Vice-Admiral W. S. Lovell, K.H., was son of Captain Thomas Stanhope Badcock, D.L., J.P., Bucks Militia, of Little Missenden, Bucks, by Anne, daughter of William Buckle, of the Mythe, Tewkesbury; and brother of General Sir Benjamin Lovell Lovell. He assumed the name of Lovell in 1840. Born at Buckingham, 1785. Entered the service, 1799. Mid. of *Neptune* at Trafalgar, 1805. Lieut., 1806. Lieut. of *Melpomene*, and in her boats at siege of Gaeta, 1806 (wounded and taken prisoner). Lieut. of *Renown*, and was with the boats of the squadron at capture and destruction of *La Thérèse*, 1809. Commanded *Brune*, and did good service on shore at siege of Badajos, 1812, and was otherwise actively employed on coast of Catalonia, 1812. Commander, 1812. Served during American War, 1813-14, including the expedition to Washington, capture of Barney's flotilla in the Patuxent, attack on Baltimore, and

destruction of enemy's junks on coast of Georgia. Captain, 1815. K.H., 1836. Retired, 1846. Retired Rear-Admiral, 1850. Retired Vice-Admiral, 1857. Medal and clasp. Died in 1859.

(16) Lieut. E. Goodlad was born in Calcutta. Volunteer 1st Class, 1804. Mid., 1805. Mid. in *Neptune* at Trafalgar, 1805. Served in the *Neptune* and *Pompée* in 1808-10, including the capture of Martinique, 1809, and Gaudeloupe, 1810. Lieut., 1814. Lieut. in *Edinburgh* at unsuccessful attack on Leghorn the reduction of the fortress of Santa Maria, and the fall of Genoa, 1814. Transport Agent, 1836-38. Medal and three clasps. Died in 1849.

(17) Lieut. D. H. Sulivan was born in Plymouth. Volunteer 1st Class, 1805. Mid., 1805. Mid. in *Neptune* at Trafalgar, 1805. Lieut., 1815. Served in Coastguard, 1830-35. Died in Stonehouse, Plymouth, in 1836.

(18) Commander A. Mackenzie was born in 1790. Became Volunteer 1st Class, 1804. Mid., 1805. Mid. in *Neptune* at Trafalgar, 1805. In *Lavinia* in expedition to Walcheren, 1809. In *Cumberland's* boats at capture of a convoy in the Bay of St. Euphemia, 1810. Acting-Lieut. in *Warrior* at defence of Cadiz, 1811. Lieut., 1811. Lieut. in *Cyane* in her gallant action with, and capture by, the U.S. frigate *Constitution*, 1815—severely wounded. Retired Commander, 1852. Medal and clasp. Died, 1869-70.

(19) Lieut. E. Moore entered the service, 1804, as Volunteer 1st Class. Served in *Neptune* at Trafalgar, 1805. Mid., 1805. Master's Mate *Dreadnought*, 1809-12; and commanded a boat cutting out a Spanish ship from under the batteries of Ushant, and several vessels in Basque Roads. Lieut., 1815. Medal and clasp. Died, 1857.

(20) Lieut. F. Hastings was born in London. Volunteer 1st Class, 1805. Served in *Neptune* at Trafalgar, 1805. Lieut., 1814. Died at Jamaica in 1819, when Lieut.-Commander of the surveying vessel *Kangaroo*.

(21) Commander W. W. Eyton was fourth son of Rev. Hope Wynne Eyton, of Leeswood, Co. Flint, by Margaret, daughter of Robert Wynne, of the Tower, Co. Flint. Born at Wrexham,

Denbighshire. Entered service, 1805, as Volunteer 1st Class. Served in *Neptune* at Trafalgar, 1805 ; in *Seahorse* at capture of Turkish frigate *Badere Zaffer*, 1808 ; and in *Milford* at capture of Fiume and Trieste, 1813. Lieut., 1814. Commander, 1852. War medal and two clasps. Died at Leeswood, near Mold, in 1857, aged 63.

(22) Lieut. R. Newton was born in Newcastle, and entered the service as A.B. in 1803. Served in that capacity in the *Neptune* at the blockade of Cadiz and at Trafalgar, 1805. Mid. in the *Ocean* in the partial fight with the Toulon fleet, 1814. Lieut., 1815. Medal and clasp. Died at Monkwearmouth, Durham, in 1856, aged 72.

(23) Mr. J. Keith was appointed Master, R.N., 1793. Master of the *Neptune* at Trafalgar, 1805. Died in 1838.

(24) Lieut. H. Hiatt was born in Portsmouth. Became Master's Mate, 1805. Master's Mate on *Neptune* at Trafalgar, 1805. Lieut., 1810. Not in Navy List after 1815.

(25) Commander Sir J. Pearl, Kt., K.H., was born in America. Mid., 1805. Master's Mate, 1805. Master's Mate in *Neptune* at Trafalgar, 1805. Lieut., 1808. Lieut. of *Mediator* at the destruction of French ships in the Basque Roads, 1809, on which occasion he was severely burned, and blown out of the ship. Presented with a sword by the Patriotic Fund. Lieut. in *Harpy*, sloop, in expedition to Walcheren, 1809. Commander, 1827. K.H., 1836. Knighted, 1838. Died in 1839.

(26) Rev. Charles Burne,, B.A., Chaplain, R.N., graduated B.A. at Oriel College, Oxford, 1799. Became Chaplain, R.N., 1801. Chaplain of *Neptune* at Trafalgar, 1805. Rector of Tedburn St. Mary, Devonport, 1808-52. War medal and clasp. Died, 1852.

(27) Surgeon L. F. Nagle was appointed Surgeon, R.N., in 1793. Surgeon of *Neptune* at Trafalgar, 1805. Died in 1838.

(28) Mr. S. Hodgson was appointed Paymaster and Purser R.N., in 1778. Served in *Neptune* at Trafalgar, 1805. Died in 1816.

(29) Mr. R. Hurrell was born at Plymouth in 1783. Served as Clerk in the *Neptune* at Trafalgar, 1805—wounded. Purser, 1806. Not in Navy List after 1824.

E

(30) Captain G. Kendall was appointed 2nd Lieut., Royal Marines, 1798. Was at Copenhagen, 1801. 1st Lieut., 1804. Senior Marine Officer in *Neptune* at Trafalgar, 1805. Captain, 1821. Retired on half-pay. Died in London in 1840, aged 58.

(31) Captain W. Burton was appointed 2nd Lieut., Royal Marines, 1803. 1st Lieut., 1805. Served in the *Neptune* at Trafalgar, 1805. Captain, 1826. Retired, 1834.

(32) Lieut. L. Rooke was appointed 2nd Lieut., Royal Marines, 1804. Served in *Neptune* at Trafalgar 1805. 1st Lieut., 1808. Served with a battalion of Marines in North America, 1813–14. Placed on half-pay. War medal and clasp. Died in 1871.

Flag Officers' Gold Medal—Obverse.

VI

H.M.S. *DREADNOUGHT*, 98 GUNS

Captain . . .	John Conn (1).
Lieutenants. .	Robert Morris (2).
	George Hewson (3).
	William Landless (4).
	James Llewin Lloyd (5). *Wounded.*
	George Stone (6).
	Nisbet Palmer (7).
	Christopher William Betty (8). *Wounded.*
	John Neale (9).
Master . . .	Richard Burstal (10).
Master's Mates	George Mitchener (11).
	George White (12).
	John James Callanan (13).
	William Sharp.
Midshipmen .	Thomas Miller.
	Methuselah Wills (14).
	Thomas Hannam (15).
	Andrew McCulloch (16). *Wounded.*
	John Dawes Haswell (17).
	Edward Rotton (18).
	James Sabben (19). *Wounded.*
	David John Burr.
	Edward Thomas Burr (20).
	Thomas Haswell.
	George Musson.
	Edward Hutton.
	John Rockwell (21).
	Richard Bane.
	William Henry Higden (22).

Volunteer 1st Class . . .	Thomas Hall.
Chaplain . .	Rev. Thomas Hardwick (23).
Surgeon . . .	Matthias Felix (24).
Assistant Surgeon . .	Thomas Bulkeley.
Surgeon's Mates . . .	William Dwyer. John Clark (25).
Purser . . .	John Hopper (26).
Clerk	Josiah Higden (27).
Gunner . . .	John M. Watkins
Boatswain . .	Edward Burr.
Carpenter . .	William Haswell.
Captain, Royal Marines . .	Thomas Timins (28).
1st Lieuts., Royal Marines	John McCallum (29). Thomas Lemon (30).
2nd Lieut., Royal Marines	David Marlay (31).

The *Dreadnought*, 98 guns, a sister ship to the " Fighting *Téméraire*," was built in Portsmouth Dockyard from the design of Sir John Henslow, Knight, Surveyor of the Navy. She was thirteen years on the stocks, and was not launched until the 13th June 1801, when she was christened by Captain Sir Charles Saxton, Bart., Kt., R.N., Commissioner of the yard. She was the first man-of-war launched after the union of Great Britain and Ireland. For a figure-head she carried a lion couchant on a scroll containing the imperial arms as emblazoned on the standard. She bore the flag of Admiral Hon. William Cornwallis, with the Channel Fleet, during the blockade of Brest in 1803 ; and that of Vice-Admiral Cuthbert Collingwood, with the blockading force before Cadiz, in 1805, only to be superseded as his flagship by the *Royal Sovereign* ten days before Trafalgar. So that she missed by only a trifle being flagship of the second-in-command in that great battle. She served in that fight under the command of Captain John Conn, and was one of the rearmost ships in Collingwood's division; but met with and gave some hard knocks. At one time she was engaged with two Spanish ships and one French vessel. She tackled the Spanish 74, *San Juan Nepomuceno*, which had already been severely handled, and although that ship was to some extent supported by the Spanish 112, *Principe de Asturias*, and the French 80-gun *Indomptable*, she ran on board the *San Juan* in little more than a quarter of an hour. But the *Principe de Asturias*, to which she next devoted her attention, got away. The *Dreadnought's* losses in the battle amounted to thirty-three killed and wounded. She had her masts cut with shot and her maintop sail-yard shot away. With Valentine Collard as Captain, she bore the flag of Rear-Admiral Thomas Sotheby with the Channel Fleet in 1808–10 ; and her boats lost heavily in an unsuccessful attempt to cut out a French vessel off Ushant, on the 9th September 1810. She earned the naval war medal with one clasp for Trafalgar, but performed no other service of distinction. She was employed as a hospital ship at Milford for some years ; and finished her career by serving for over a quarter of a century, from 1831 to 1857, as a Seamen's Hospital at Greenwich, when she passed into the hands of the ship-breakers on the Thames.

(1) Captain J. Conn, a member of the Irish family of that name at Mount Ida, Waterford, was born in Ireland in 1764, and entered the service in 1778. Became Lieut. in 1793. He was Lieut. in the *Royal Sovereign* in Lord Howe's victory of the 1st June 1794. Commander, 1800. Commanded the *Discovery*, bomb, at the battle of Copenhagen, 1801. Com-

manded a division of mortar boats in the attack on the French flotilla at Boulogne, on the 15th August 1801. Captain, 1802. Captain of the 80-gun ship *Canopus*, flagship of Rear-Admiral George Campbell, with Lord Nelson's force blockading the French in Toulon, 1803–5; and was in the affair off Cape Cepet, on the 24th August 1804, and in the pursuit of the French fleet in January and February 1805. Commanded the *Dreadnought*, 98, in the battle of Trafalgar, 1805, when the Spanish 74, *San Juan*, struck to her. Received a gold medal, and a sword of honour from the Patriotic Fund. When in command of the *Swiftsure*, was drowned off the Bermudas, in 1810. He was a cousin, by marriage, to Lord Nelson, having married a daughter of Rev. Isaac Nelson, Rector of Meldon and Vicar of Mitford.

(2) Lieut. R. Morris became Lieut. in 1800. Lieut. in the *Dreadnought* at Trafalgar, 1805. Died in 1823.

(3) Vice-Admiral G. Hewson was son of Rev. Francis Hewson, M.A., of Woodford, Listowel, Co. Kerry, by Margaret, daughter of Lancelot Sandes of Kilcavin, Queen's County. Born, 1776. Entered the service, 1788. When Mid. of the *St. George*, served on shore at occupation of Toulon, 1793; and in the operations against Corsica, 1794. Served as Mid. in *Britannia* in Admiral Hotham's action with the French fleet, 1795 —promoted Lieut. Lieut. of *Inconstant* at capture of French 28-gun frigate *Unité*, 1796. Lieut. of *Boadicea*, and commanded a division of gunboats at the cutting out of Spanish *Neptune* from Corunna, 1801; and present at cutting out of a lugger of 6 guns under the batteries of St. Matthew, 1803. Lieut. of *Dreadnought*, and succeeded as 1st Lieut. at Trafalgar, 1805. Lieut. of *Superb* in expedition to Copenhagen, 1807. Commander, 1807. Commanded *La Flèche* in expedition to Walcheren, 1809; wrecked in her off the Elbe, 1810. Captain, 1817. Retired Rear-Admiral, 1851. Retired Vice-Admiral, 1857. War medal and two clasps. Died in 1860.

(4) Commander W. Landless became Lieut., 1796. Lieut. of *Dreadnought* at Trafalgar, 1805. Commander, 1806. Not in Navy List after 1826.

(5) Lieut. J. L. Lloyd became Lieut. in 1799. Lieut. in the *Dreadnought* at Trafalgar, 1805—wounded. Died in 1806.

(6) Lieut. G. Stone became Lieut. in 1799. Lieut. in the *Dreadnought* at Trafalgar, 1805. Not in Navy List after 1810.

(7) Commander N. Palmer was Mid. in the *Berwick*, 74, when she was captured by the French fleet in the Mediterranean, in 1795. Lieut., 1799. Lieut. in the *Dreadnought* at Trafalgar, 1805—promoted Commander. Commanded the 18-gun brig *Alacrity* in her unfortunate action with, and capture by, the French 20-gun corvette *Abeille*, off Cape St. André, Corsica, on the 26th May 1811. He was wounded in the hand, and died in the following month from lockjaw.

(8) Commander C. W. Betty entered the service in 1793. Mid., 1793. Mid. of *Majestic* in Lord Howe's victory of the 1st June 1794 ; and of *Mars* at capture of the French 74, *L'Hercule*, 1798. Lieut., 1801. Lieut. of *Dreadnought* at Trafalgar, 1805 —wounded. Medal and three clasps. Retired Commander, 1832. Died at Cawsand, Cornwall, 1850.

(9) Lieut. J. Neale became Lieut. in 1805. Lieut. in the *Dreadnought* at Trafalgar, 1805. Not in Navy List after 1820.

(10) Mr. R. Burstal was appointed Master, R.N., in 1797. Master of *Atalante* in pursuit of two French ketches and a brig, and afterwards commanded a boat in cutting out the brig off the mouth of the river Pennerf, 1803. Master of *Dreadnought* at Trafalgar, 1805. Afterwards Master Superintendent Sheerness Dockyard. Died in 1838.

(11) Lieut. G. Mitchener was born in Havant, Hants. Served as Master's Mate in the *Dreadnought* at Trafalgar, 1805. Lieut., 1806. Not in Navy List after 1825.

(12) Commander G. White was son of Mr. George White, Purser and Paymaster, R.N., of Duns, N.B., and was born in Havant, Hants. Entered the service in 1798. Mid., 1804. Master's Mate, 1805. Master's Mate in *Dreadnought* at Trafalgar, 1805 ; and of the *Captain* at the capture of the French 40-gun frigate *Président*, 1806. Master's Mate at the reduction of Copenhagen in 1807 ; and served on shore at the capture of Martinique, 1809. Lieut., 1809. Lieut. of the *Pompée* in the

partial action with the French fleet at Toulon in 1813.   Retired
Commander, 1849.   Medal and two clasps.   Died in Plymouth,
in 1852.

(13) Lieut. J. J. Callanan was born in Cork, 1784.   Master's
Mate of *Dreadnought* at Trafalgar, 1805.   Lieut., 1807.   When
Lieut. of *Minotaur* was killed in action in a boat attack on
Russian vessels in the harbour of Frederikshamn in the Baltic,
the 25th July 1809.

(14) Lieut. M. Wills was born in Plymouth in 1780.   Mid.
in the' *Dreadnought* at Trafalgar, 1805.   Lieut., 1811.   Died in
Portsea, Hants, in 1842.

(15) Lieut. T. Hannam was born in Portsea in 1786.   Mid.
in the *Dreadnought* at Trafalgar, 1805.   Lieut., 1808.   Died
when in command of the *Opossum*, brig, 1830.

(16) Midshipman A. McCulloch was born in Ireland in 1785.
Mid. in the *Dreadnought* at Trafalgar, 1805—wounded.   Left the
service, 1806.

(17) Lieut. J. D. Haswell was born in Portsmouth, and
entered the service in 1803.   Mid. in the *Dreadnought* at
Trafalgar, 1805.   Lieut., 1815.   Medal and clasp.   Died in
1848.

(18) Lieut. E. Rotton was born in Bengal.   Mid. in
Dreadnought at Trafalgar, 1805.   Lieut., 1814.   Died in London,
in 1839, aged 53.

(19) Lieut. J. Sabben was born in Portsea in 1787.   After
a short period in the Merchant Service he entered the Royal
Navy as Volunteer 1st Class in 1803.   Was Mid. in the
Dreadnought at Trafalgar, 1805—wounded; gratuity from
Patriotic Fund.   Was in the schooner *Netley* in her action
with, and capture by, two French cruisers in the West Indies,
1806—taken prisoner.   Served in the flagship *Neptune* at the
capture of Martinique, 1809.   Acting-Lieut. in *Julia* at the
blockade of Guadeloupe, 1809.   Acting-Lieut. in *Ringdove* at
the storming of the batteries at Ans-la-Barque, and the capture
of the 40-gun frigates *Loire* and *Seine*, 1809—wounded.   Also in
the *Ringdove* at the capture of Guadeloupe, 1810.   Lieut., 1810.
Medal with four clasps.   Died in 1849, aged 62.

(20) Mr. E. T. Burr served as Mid. in the *Dreadnought* at Trafalgar, 1805. Received the medal and clasp in 1847.

(21) Mr. J. Rockwell served as Mid. in the *Dreadnought* at Trafalgar, 1805. Received the medal and clasp in 1847.

(22) Mr. W. H. Higden served as Mid. in the *Dreadnought* at Trafalgar, 1805. Received the medal and clasp in 1847.

(23) The Rev. T. Hardwick served as Chaplain in the *Dreadnought* at Trafalgar, 1805. Received the medal and clasp in 1848.

(24) Mr. M. Felix became Surgeon, R.N., in 1779. Served in *Dreadnought* at Trafalgar, 1805. Died in 1831.

(25) Mr. J. Clark served as Surgeon's Mate in the *Dreadnought* at Trafalgar, 1805. Surgeon, 1808. Medal and clasp. Died in 1864.

(26) Mr. J. Hopper became Purser and Paymaster, R.N., in 1782. Served in the *Dreadnought* at Trafalgar, 1805. Died in 1837.

(27) Mr. J. Higden served as Mid. in the *Royal Sovereign* in 1805. Clerk, 1805. Clerk in the *Dreadnought* at Trafalgar, 1805. Purser, 1806. Died in 1835.

(28) Lieut.-Colonel, T. Timins became 2nd Lieut., R.M., 1778. Served in Admiral Keppel's battle off Ushant, 1778. Served in America during the War of Independence, 1779–83, including the siege of Charlestown. Present in Admiral Marriot Arbuthnot's action with the French fleet off the Chesapeake, 1781 ; and served in the *Chatham* at the capture of the French 32-gun frigate *Magicienne* near Boston, 1781. 1st Lieut., 1781. Captain, 1796. Served in the *Dreadnought* at Trafalgar, 1805, and was the senior officer of Marines present in the battle— promoted Brevet Major. Major, 1810. Brevet Lieut.-Colonel, 1812. Lieut.-Colonel, 1822. Died in 1828.

(29) Colonel J. McCallum became 2nd Lieut., R.M.., 1798. Served in ship's boats at capture of a French privateer in 1800. 1st Lieut., 1803. Served in the *Dreadnought* at Trafalgar, 1805 ; and in *Endymion* at forcing of the Dardanelles, and destruction of Turkish squadron, 1807. Captain, 1812. Brevet Major, 1830. Lieut.-Colonel, 1837. Commanded Reserve

Battalion of Royal Marines in operations on coast of Syria, 1840. Colonel 2nd Commandant, 1842. Good Service pension, 1846. Colonel Commandant Plymouth Division, 1847–49. Retired full pay, 1849. Medal and two clasps, and Turkish medal for Syria. Died at Stonehouse, near Devonport, 1851, aged 71.

(30) Lieut.-Colonel T. Lemon became 2nd Lieut., R.M., 1798. 1st Lieut., 1803. Served in the *Dreadnought* at Trafalgar, 1805. Captain, 1812. Brevet Major, 1830. Hon. Lieut.-Colonel, 1854. Medal and clasp. Died in 1856.

(31) Lieut.-Colonel D. Marlay became 2nd Lieut., R.M., 1801. 1st Lieut., 1805. Served in the *Dreadnought* at Trafalgar, 1805. Captain, 1826. Lieut.-Colonel, 1841. Retired on full pay, 1841. Medal and clasp. Died in Hoddesdon, 1851, aged 66.

VII

H.M.S. *PRINCE*, 98 GUNS

Captain . . .	Richard Grindall (1).
Lieutenants * .	William Godfray (2).
	William Kelly (3).
	John Edwards (4).
	Abel Ferris (5).
	Samuel Burgess (6).
	Abraham Baldwin (7).
	James Hall (8).
Master . . .	Richard Anderson (9).
Master's Mates	Archibald McKillop (10).
	Allen Cameron (11).
	Peter Simpson Hambly (12).
Midshipmen .	Joseph Kirk.
	Philip Tomlinson (13).
	Matthew Foster.
	Alexander Martin (14).
	† *Robert Atwell* (15).
	Peregrine Bowen (16).
	Nicholas Colthurst (17).
	Thomas William Hunt (18).
	Thomas Carney (19)
	Thomas James.
	Dey Richard Syer (20).
	William Cunningham (21).
	George Tardrew (22).

* The medal roll gives the name of John Butt as Lieutenant in the *Prince* at Trafalgar, but no such name can be traced.

† Rated as Yeoman of Signals.

Midshipmen (*continued*)	William Greatwood (23). John Benjamin (24). William Watson. Robert Watson. James Burnett Elliott (25). Richard Bridges. Benjamin Morton Festing (26). William Henry Smart. John Hudson. Thomas Binford (27). George Wade (28). John Hoskins Brown (29)
Volunteer 1st Class	Henry Browne Mason (30).
	* *Thomas Akers* (31).
Surgeon . . .	James Fullarton.
Surgeon's Mates	Joshua Horwood (32). William Kettle Salton.
Purser . . .	Thomas Tait (33).
Clerk	Robert Dooley.
Gunner . . .	Thomas Hawkins.
Boatswain . .	Samuel Simpson.
Carpenter . .	William Johnson.
Captain, Royal Marines . .	Francis Williams (34).
Lieut., Royal Marines	Edward Pengelly (35).

The *Prince* was built at Chatham in 1788. At the commencement of the war of the French Revolution in 1793 Rear-Admiral George Bowyer hoisted his flag in her for service in the Channel Fleet under Lord Howe, with Cuthbert Collingwood as Flag-Captain. Under Captain Charles Powel Hamilton she was present with Lord Bridport's fleet in his successful action with the French off L'Orient on the 23rd June 1795; and she

* Served as A.B.

took one of the prizes in tow. In 1797 she was flying the flag of Rear-Admiral Sir Roger Curtis, with Captain T. Larcom as Flag-Captain. She was in the Mediterranean with the fleet under Lord St. Vincent in 1798; and her armed launch attended the execution of one of the ringleaders of the mutiny in the *Marlborough*, whose shipmates were compelled to hang him in their own ship. In March 1799 Captain Samuel Sutton was posted to her, and Rear-Admiral Sir Charles Cotton hoisted his flag in her as third-in-command of the Channel Fleet: on the 7th July she joined Lord Keith at Brest, and took part in the unsuccessful pursuit of the allied fleet. She was afterwards commanded in the Channel by Captain James Walker and Captain the Earl of Northesk until the end of the war.

On the recommencement of war in 1803 Captain Richard Grindall was appointed to her; and after being employed in the blockade of Brest and off Cadiz she fought in the lee column at Trafalgar, the 21st October 1805. Being a heavy sailer, she was allowed to depart from the prescribed order of sailing in line ahead, that she might steer obliquely between the two columns, and so get more of her sails to draw. She engaged the Spanish 112-gun ship *Principe de Asturias*, and the French *Achille*. When the latter was on fire and her mast had been cut in two by one of the broadsides of the *Prince*, and her dangerous situation was apparent, the boats of the *Prince* at great risk saved many of the French crew. Her own damages consisted of a shot in her bowsprit, three shots in her foremast, and the same in her mizen-mast; but she experienced the singular good fortune of being the only British ship in which no officers or men were killed or wounded.

Her career after this was an uneventful one. After the peace she was employed as a Receiving Hulk at Portsmouth until she " crossed the bar," and was broken up there in 1837, after an existence of just on half a century and having earned the war medal with two clasps.

(1) Vice-Admiral Sir R. Grindall, K.C.B., was born in 1750, and entered the Navy at a very early age. He was promoted to Lieut., 1776, Commander, 1781, and Captain, 1783. In command of the *Thalia*, 36, he captured the French ship *Requin*, 12, off Dunkirk, 1795. He commanded the *Irresistible*, 74, in Lord Bridport's successful action with the French off Isle Groix, 1795 —wounded. He was captain of the *Ramillies*, 74, with the blockading force off Rochefort in June 1799 ; and, in command of her, was detached in the following year by Lord St. Vincent with the squadron from Brest directed to co-operate with the insurgent French Royalists in the Morbihan. He was captain of the *Prince* at Trafalgar, 1805—gold medal, the thanks of Parliament, and a sword of honour from the Patriotic Fund. He was promoted Rear-Admiral, 1805, Vice-Admiral, 1810, and created a K.C.B. in 1815. He died in 1820.

(2) Captain W. Godfray, C.B., served as Mid. in the *Culloden* in Lord Howe's victory of the 1st June 1794. Lieut., 1795. First Lieut. of the *Prince* at Trafalgar, 1805—promoted Commander. Commanded the *Aetna*, bomb, at the attack on Copenhagen, 1807, and in the operations under Lord Gambier in the Basque Road, 1809—promoted Captain. Created C.B., 1815. Died in 1835.

(3) Commander W. Kelly was son of Benedict Marwood Kelly, of Holsworthy, Devonshire, and Mary, daughter of Arscott Coham. Born in 1782. Entered service, 1792. Mid., 1794. Served in *Solebay* at the reduction of the West India Islands, in 1794, including the capture of Martinique and Guadeloupe, and served as A.D.C. on shore. Lieut., 1798. Lieut. in *Minerve* at the capture and destruction of *La Succès* and *Le Bravoure*, 1801 —mentioned in despatches. Lieut. in *Prince* at Trafalgar, 1805, and was placed in charge of the *Santissima Trinidad* as prizemaster until she sank. Lieut. in *Caledonia*, and commanded her boats at the storming of the batteries at Point de Ché, Basque

Road, 1810. Commander, 1811. Greenwich Hospital pension, 1845. Medal and two clasps. Died in 1859.

(4) Commander J. Edwards served as a Mid. in Lord Howe's victory of the 1st June 1794. Lieut., 1798. Lieut. in the *Prince* at Trafalgar, 1805. Commander, 1813. Died at Torpoint, Cornwall, in 1838.

(5) Vice-Admiral A. Ferris, son of Abel Ferris, was born in 1776, and entered service in 1793. In *Thalia* witnessed the *Astræa's* capture of French frigate *Gloire*, 1795. Master's Mate, 1795. Master's Mate in *Irresistible* in Lord Bridport's successful action with the French off L'Orient, 1795. Master's Mate in *Colossus* at the battle of St. Vincent, 1797; and served in her boats in several actions with the Cadiz flotilla, 1797. Lieut., 1799. Lieut in the *Prince* at Trafalgar, 1805. Commander, 1807. Commanded the *Wizard*, sloop, in her action with the French brig-corvette *Le Requin*, 1808; and at the capture and destruction of coasting vessels off the coast of Italy same year. Captain, 1811. Greenwich Hospital pension, 1825. Retired Rear-Admiral, 1846. Retired Vice-Admiral, 1854. Medal and three clasps. Died in 1859.

(6) Captain S. Burgess was son of Commander William Burgess, R.N., who died in 1840. He was born in 1781, and entered the service in 1790. Mid., 1793. Served as Mid. in the *Impregnable* in Lord Howe's victory of the 1st June 1794. Mid. in the *Unicorn* at the capture of *L'Enterprise*, privateer, 1796. In the *Dryad* at the capture of four privateers in 1797. Mid. in the *Isis* in the expedition to the Helder, 1799. Lieut., 1799. Lieut. in the *Sylph* in her night action with *L'Artemise*, 1801. Lieut. in the *Prince* at Trafalgar, 1805. Commanded the *Pincher*, brig, in the North Sea and Baltic, including the capture and destruction of the fort at Bremerlé, Cuxhaven, 1809—mentioned in despatches. Flag-Lieut. to Lord Exmouth in the *Queen Charlotte* at the battle of Algiers, 1816—promoted Commander. Was wrecked when in command of the frigate *Thetis* off Cape Frio, 1830. Captain, 1830. Greenwich Hospital pension, 1846. Medal and five clasps. Died at Stourscombe House, near Launceston, in 1851.

(7) Lieut. A. Baldwin was promoted to Lieut., 1800. Lieut. in the *Prince* at Trafalgar, 1805. Died in 1815.

(8) Commander J. Hall was promoted to Lieut., 1801. Lieut. in the *Prince* at Trafalgar, 1805. Lieut. in the *Cyane* in the action with the French frigate *Cérès*, 40, off Naples, and the capture of eighteen gunboats, and destruction of four, 1809—dangerously wounded, mentioned in despatches, promoted Commander. Died of wounds in 1810, at Scarrington, near Bingham, Notts.

(9) Mr. R. Anderson was appointed Master, R.N., in 1795. Master of *Prince* at Trafalgar, 1805. Died in 1835–36.

(10) Lieut. A. McKillop was born in Campbeltown, in Argyllshire. Master's Mate, 1805. Master's Mate in the *Prince* at Trafalgar, 1805. Lieut., 1809. Not traced after 1820.

(11) Lieut. A. Cameron was born in Scotland. Master's Mate in the *Prince* at Trafalgar, 1805. Lieut., 1807. Not traced after 1812.

(12) Captain P. S. Hambly entered the service in 1797. Mid. in the *Emerald* at the capture of the Spanish frigates *Carmen* and *Florentina*, 1800—wounded; and in the capture of several privateers—wounded. Served in *Florentina* in Egyptian Campaign, 1801, including battle of Alexandria—wounded. Master's Mate in the *Prince* at Trafalgar, 1805, and was one of the party placed in charge of the Spanish *Santissima Trinidad* until she was sunk—promoted Lieut. Lieut. in the *Defence* in the Baltic, including the destruction of Russian vessels in 1809, and the blockade of Flushing, 1810. Commanded a division of gunboats at siege of Cadiz, 1810. Served on the Canadian lakes, 1814–15. Commander, 1819. Captain, 1841. Medal and clasp. Died in 1848.

(13) Mr. P. Tomlinson, a son of Commander Philip Tomlinson, R.N., who died in 1839, was born in Exeter. Served as Mid. in the *Prince* at Trafalgar, 1805. When Master's Mate in the *Valiant* was mortally wounded at the siege of Copenhagen, the 31st August 1807.

(14) Commander A. Martin entered the service in 1795. Served in the *Triumph* at the battle of Camperdown, 1797. Mid., 1802. Mid. in the *Prince* at Trafalgar, 1805. Lieut., 1811. Retired Commander, 1850. Medal and two clasps. Died in 1868.

(15) Mr. R. Atwell served in the *Irresistible* in Lord Bridport's action, 1795. As A.B. in the *Russell* in the battle of Camperdown, 1797. Yeoman of Sheets in *Ramillies* in the battle of Copenhagen, 1801. Yeoman of Signals in the *Prince*, but served as Mid. at Trafalgar, 1805. He received the medal and four clasps in 1848.

(16) Lieut. P. Bowen entered the service in 1801. Mid. in the *Prince* at Trafalgar, 1805. Served in *Vanguard* at bombardment of Copenhagen, 1807. Lieut., 1808. Lieut. of *Venus* in Walcheren Expedition, 1809. Admiralty agent in a contract mail steamer, 1839–48. Medal and clasp. Died in 1848.

(17) Commander N. Colthurst, the third son of John Colthurst, of Dripsey Castle, County Cork, was born in Cork, and entered the service in 1796. Mid., 1804. Mid. in the *Prince* at Trafalgar, 1805. Lieut., 1806. Senior Lieut. in the gunboat service on the Canadian lakes, 1812–14. Retired Commander, 1841. Medal and clasp. Died in Kensington, London, in 1854.

(18) Mr. T. W. Hunt served as Mid. in the *Prince* at Trafalgar, 1805. Received the medal and clasp in 1848.

(19) Mr. T. Carney served as Mid. in the *Prince* at Trafalgar, 1805. Received the medal and clasp in 1848.

(20) Commander D. R. Syer was a son of Rev. Barrington Blomfield Syer, rector of Kiddington, Suffolk. He was born in 1788, and entered the service in 1803. Mid., 1804. Mid. in the *Prince* at Trafalgar, 1805. Served in *Tigre* in expedition to Egypt, 1807 ; in pursuit of the *Robuste* and *Lion,* 1809 ; and at the capture and destruction of vessels in the Bay of Rosas, 1809—severely wounded ; promoted Lieut. Lieut. in the *Volontaire*, cutting out merchant vessels and privateers near Marseilles—wounded ; and served in her boats at capture and destruction of vessels and a battery in the harbour of Morjean, 1813. Commander, 1849. Medal and three clasps. Died in 1867.

(21) Mr. W. Cunningham served as Mid. in the *Prince* at Trafalgar, 1805. Received the medal and clasp in 1849.

(22) Commander G. Tardrew was born in 1784, and entered the service in 1804. Mid. in the *Prince* at Trafalgar, 1805. Master's Mate, 1806. Lieut., 1811. Served in the Coastguard, 1826–30. Retired Commander, 1852. War medal and clasp. Died in 1871.

F

(23) Lieut. W. Greatwood was born in Gloucester. Served as Mid. in the *Prince* at Trafalgar, 1805. Lieut., 1810. Not in Navy List after 1828.

(24) Mr. J. Benjamin served as Purser's Steward in the *Fairy* in her action with the French frigate *Pallas*, 1800; and in the *Renommée* in operations on coast of Egypt, 1801. Mid. in the *Prince* at Trafalgar, 1805. Received the medal and three clasps in 1848.

(25) Commander J. B. Elliott, brother of Captain Sir William Elliott, R.N., K.C.B., K.C.H., who died in 1838, was born in 1791, and entered the service in 1803. Mid., 1804. Mid. in the *Prince* at Trafalgar, 1805. In a boat of the *Plantagenet* assisted to rescue an English vessel near Lisbon, 1808. Lieut., 1815. Commander, 1859. Medal and clasp. Died in 1872.

(26) Captain Sir B. M. Festing, K.H., was the fifth son of Commander Henry Festing, R.N., who died in 1807, and Mary, eldest daughter of Rev. T. M. Colson of Dorchester; he had three brothers in the Royal Navy. Born at Andover, Hants, in 1794, and entered the service in 1805. Mid. in the *Prince*, commanded by his uncle, Captain Richard Grindall, at Trafalgar, 1805. Lieut., 1812. Lieut. in the *Eagle*, and commanded her barges in the action with, and capture of, seventeen gunboats at Maestro, coast of Italy, 1812; the reduction of Fiume, siege of Trieste, and on shore in co-operation with the Austrians, 1813. Was awarded the medal of the National Lifeboat Institution in 1825 for assisting to save the crew and passengers of the transport *Admiral Berkeley*, wrecked on Haslar beach. Commander, 1826. K.H., 1837. Inspecting-Commander, Coastguard, 1837–40. Captain, 1851. Medal and two clasps. Died in Weymouth in 1865.

(27) Mr. T. Binford served as Mid. in the *Prince* at Trafalgar. Received the medal and clasp in 1848.

(28) Lieut. G. Wade was born at Topsham, Devonshire, and entered the service in 1805. Served as Mid. in the *Prince* at Trafalgar, 1805. Lieut., 1813. Died at Jamaica in 1825, when Lieut. of the *Ferret*, sloop.

(29) Captain J. H. Brown, C.B., was born in South Wales in 1792, and entered the service in 1805. Mid., 1805. Mid. in

the *Prince* at Trafalgar, 1805. In *Vanguard* in the expedition to Copenhagen, 1807. In boats of *Tartarus* at destruction of two French privateers off Pillau, 1810. In *Prince Regent* in operations on Canadian lakes, 1813–14, including attack on Sackett's Harbour, action with American flotilla on Lake Ontario, and storming of Fort Oswego. Taken prisoner in 1813. Lieut., 1814. Retired Commander, 1858. Retired Captain, 1863. Was for many years Registrar-General of Seamen, for which services he was created a civil C.B. in 1862. Medal and clasp. Died at Brixton in 1864.

(30) Captain H. B. Mason, J.P., was born in 1791, and entered the service in 1803. Served as Volunteer 1st Class in the *Prince* at Trafalgar, 1805. When serving in the *Amphion* on the Mediterranean station was taken prisoner in 1809, but escaped in 1810. Lieut., 1811. Commander, 1815. Retired Captain, 1854. J.P. for Hants. Medal and clasp. Died in 1870.

(31) Commander T. Akers, one of four brothers in the Royal Navy, was born at Harwich in 1784, and entered the service in 1803. Served as A.B. in *Prince* at Trafalgar, 1805 ; in the *Goliath* in the expedition to Copenhagen in 1807 ; and as Mid. in the *Rolla*, brig, in the Walcheren expedition, 1809—severely wounded. Lieut., 1813. Greenwich Hospital pension, 1826. Retired Commander, 1856. Medal and clasp. Died in 1862–63.

(32) Mr. J. Horwood served as Surgeon's Mate in the *Prince* at Trafalgar, 1805. Surgeon, 1807. Medal and clasp. Died in 1850.

(33) Mr. T. Tait was appointed Paymaster and Purser, 1797. Purser of the *Prince* at Trafalgar, 1805. Died in 1825.

(34) Lieut.-Colonel F. Williams was appointed 2nd Lieut., R.M., in 1781. 1st Lieut., 1793. Captain, 1799. Served in the *Prince* at Trafalgar, 1805. Brevet Major, 1811. Brevet Lieut.-Colonel, 1819. Major, 1824. Died in 1825.

(35) Lieut. E. Pengelly became 2nd Lieut., R.M., 1803. 1st Lieut., 1805. Served in the *Prince* at Trafalgar, 1805. Retired on half-pay, 1823.

VIII

H.M.S. *TONNANT*, 80 GUNS

Captain . . .	Charles Tyler (1).
Lieutenants .	John Bedford (2)
	Charles Bennett (3).
	Frederick Hoffman (4). *Wounded.*
	Benjamin Clement (5).
	Hugh Brice White (6).
	William Smith Millett (7).
Master . . .	Edward Soper (8).
Master's Mates	Edward Collins Polwhele (9).
	John Treeve (10).
	Henry Ready (11). *Wounded.*
	James Little.
Midshipmen .	James Primrose Blennerhasset (12)
	Robson Cruse (13). .
	Joseph Symes (14).
	James Oldrini.
	J. M. H. Allen.
	George Rose Sartorius (15).
	Richard Langdon.
	William Brown.
	William Smith Stokes (16).
	John Marshall.
	William Peregrine.
	Thomas Bourne.
Surgeon . . .	Forbes McBean Chevers (17).
Assistant Surgeon . .	} Robert Evans (18).
Purser , , .	George Booth (19).

Clerk . . . . William Allen. *Wounded*
Gunner . . . Richard Rose.
Boatswain . . Richard Little. *Wounded*.
Carpenter . . John Chapman.
Captain, Royal } Arthur Hitchins Ball (20).
  Marines . . }
2nd Lieuts.,) James Cottell (21).
  Royal Marines) William Magin (22).

The *Tonnant* was built at Toulon for the French
Government in 1791–92. With the fleet under Rear-
Admiral Martin and M. Deputy Letourneur, she was
engaged in the action off Genoa with Vice-Admiral
William Hotham's fleet on the 14th March 1795. Under
Commodore A. A. du Petit-Thouars she was again opposed
to us in Lord Nelson's great victory of the Nile, 1st
August 1798. After a very gallant resistance, her three
masts having been shot away close to the deck, and
being a mere wreck, but with her colours still flying on
the stump of her mainmast, she was taken possession
of. Her gallant captain had first both his arms, and
then one of his legs, carried away by round shot; but
instead of allowing himself to be taken below, caused
himself to be placed in a tub of bran, whence he
continued to give his orders until he became insensible
from loss of blood. His dying command to the crew
not to surrender the ship was loyally obeyed till it was
impossible to save her. She was taken into the British
Navy, and commissioned by Captain Loftus Otway
Bland.

On the recommencement of war with France in 1803,
Captain Sir Edward Pellew, Bart., M.P., was appointed
to her. She was detached with a squadron blockading
Ferrol, and was in action with the *Duguay-Trouin* and
the *Guerrière* in August. In September 1805 Captain
Charles Tyler was posted to her, and under him she

fought at Trafalgar, on the 21st October. She was the fourth ship in the lee column. She was closely engaged with the Spanish 74, *Monarca* and *Algésiras*, the former of which struck to her, but rehoisted her colours on the *Tonnant* turning her attention to the other 74, whose bowsprit and anchors got entangled with the main rigging of the *Tonnant*, and the two ships were held fast together. Though the *Algésiras* made a plucky attempt to board, she got the worst of the encounter, and after a very gallant defence struck to the *Tonnant*, and was taken possession of by a party of bluejackets and marines. A party was sent at the same time to take over the Spanish *San Juan Nepomuceno*, but the boat capsized, nearly drowning the lieutenant in charge. The *Tonnant's* injuries were severe. She had all her three topmasts and mainyard shot away, was damaged in the hull, had a bad wound in the rudder, a portion of which was shot away, while a great portion of her starboard quarter piece with the rails and gallery was carried away. Her losses amounted to 76 killed and wounded, amongst the latter being her captain, who was taken below, and had to hand over the ship to the first lieutenant.

She was with the Channel Fleet in 1806–9, the chief portion of the time carrying the flag of Rear-Admiral Eliab Harvey, until his supersession in the spring of 1809. When with the Cadiz fleet her boats were engaged under Captain Sir R. Hall in the attack on, and destruction of, shipping at Port St. Mary, on 23rd November 1810. In 1814, under Captain John Wainwright, she was with the squadron under Rear-Admiral George Cockburn in the Chesapeake. Her boats' crews were in the operations in the Patuxent, and at the capture of Bladensburg and Washington. Under Captain Edward Codrington she was with the squadron under Vice-Admiral Sir Alexander

Cochrane in the expedition against New Orleans, and in Captain Lockyer's boat attack on, and capture of, six American gunboats and a sloop in Lake Borgue on the 14th December 1814. In 1815 Captain Edward Pelham Brenton was appointed to her, and for a short time she bore the flag of Rear-Admiral Sir Benjamin Hallowell on the Irish station. She served at Cork until 1818, when she returned to Plymouth, and was broken up in 1821. She earned the medal with two clasps.

(1) Admiral Sir C. Tyler, G.C.B., was the third son of Captain Peter Tyler, 52nd Foot, and Hon. Anna Maria Roper, daughter of Henry, 8th Lord Teynham. He was born in 1760, and entered the service in 1771. Became Lieut., 1779. Commander, 1782. Captain, 1790. Captain of the *Meleager*, 32, with the fleet under Admiral Hood at Toulon in 1793; and at the reduction of Calvi, Corsica, 1794. Captain of the *Diadem*, 64, in Vice-Admiral Hotham's action with the French off Genoa in 1795. Captain of the *Aigle*, 38, at the capture of privateers in 1796-97; and on the 18th July in the following year he was wrecked in her off Cape Farina. Captain of the *Warrior*, 74, at the blockade of Cadiz, and at the battle of Copenhagen, 1801— received the thanks of Parliament. Commanded Sea Fencibles, 1803-5. Captain of the *Tonnant*, 80, in the battle of Trafalgar, 1805—severely wounded, gold medal, the thanks of Parliament, and a sword of honour from the Patriotic Fund. For his wound —a musket ball in the right thigh—he received a grant from the Patriotic Fund, and a Government pension of £250 per annum. He was present at the surrender of the Russian fleet at Lisbon in 1808. Rear-Admiral, 1808. Vice-Admiral, 1813. Commander-in-Chief, Cape of Good Hope, 1812-15. K.C.B., 1815. Admiral, 1825. G.C.B., 1833. Died at the Spa, Gloucester, in 1835. He was father of Captain Charles Tyler, R.N., who died in 1846, and of Vice-Admiral Sir George Tyler, K.C.H., who died in 1862.

(2) Captain J. Bedford was promoted Lieut., 1794. 1st Lieut. of the *Tonnant* at Trafalgar, 1805, and took command of

the ship and continued to fight her when Captain Tyler was severely wounded and taken below—promoted Commander. Captain, 1813. Died in 1815.

(3) Captain C. Bennett was promoted Lieut., 1797. Lieut. in the *Tonnant* at Trafalgar, 1805. He took possession of the French 74, *Algésiras*, but with his party was subsequently overpowered by the French crew, who took the ship to Cadiz, where he was liberated. Commander, 1810. Retired Captain, 1840. Died in 1842.

(4) Captain F. Hoffman became Mid. in 1793. Served as Mid. on the *Blonde* at the reduction of the French West India Islands in 1794. Mid. in the *Hannibal* at the capture of the French frigate *La Gentille*, 1795. Lieut., 1799. 3rd Lieut. of the *Tonnant* at Trafalgar, 1805—wounded. Commander, 1808. In the *Apelles*, sloop, was run ashore off Boulogne, and taken prisoner, in 1812. Retired Captain, 1840. Medal and clasp. Died in 1849.

(5) Captain B. Clement, a son of Thomas Clement, solicitor, of Alton, Hants, entered the service in 1794. Served as Mid. of *Prince* in Lord Bridport's action with the French off L'Orient, 1795. Mid. in the *Monarch* in the battle of Camperdown, 1797 —three times wounded; at the capture of Texel Squadron, 1799; and the passage of the Sound, 1800–1. As Mid. commanded a flat-bottomed boat at the battle of Copenhagen, 1801. Lieut., 1801. 4th Lieut. of the *Tonnant* at Trafalgar, 1805. In trying to take possession of the Spanish 74-gun ship *San Juan*, his boat, damaged by shot, swamped, and he narrowly escaped drowning. Commander, 1806. Captain, 1811. Died at Chewton, Hants, in 1836.

(6) Lieut. H. B. White entered the service in 1794. In the *Jason* he assisted at the capture of French 40-gun frigate *La Seine*, 1798. Wrecked in *Jason*, 1798, and kept prisoner till the following year. Served in the *Pompée* in Saumarez' action with the French and Spanish squadrons in the Gut of Gibraltar, the 12th July 1801. Lieut., 1802. Lieut. in the *Tonnant* at Trafalgar, 1805. Inspecting-Commander Coastguard, Galway, 1827–47. Medal and two clasps. Died in Galway, Ireland, 1847.

(7) Lieut. W. S. Millett was promoted Lieut., 1802. Lieut. in the *Tonnant* at Trafalgar, 1805. Not in Navy List after 1814.

(8) Mr. E. Soper was appointed Master, R.N., 1799. Master of the *Tonnant* at Trafalgar, 1805. Not in Navy List after 1806.

(9) Lieut. E. C. Polwhele was son of the Rev. Richard Polwhele, J.P., of Polewhele, Cornwall, and Vicar of Newlyn, and Loveday, daughter of Samuel Warren, of Truro. Born, 1786. Served as Master's Mate in the *Tonnant* at Trafalgar, 1805. Lieut., 1807. Died at Gosport, Hants, in 1810.

(10) Commander J. Treeve was born in Penryn, Cornwall, in 1785, and entered the service in 1801. He served as Volunteer 1st Class in *St. George* in the battle of Copenhagen, 1801. Mid., 1802. Master's Mate in the *Tonnant* at Trafalgar, 1805. Lieut., 1809. Served in the *York* at the capture of Martinique, February, 1809; and in the expedition to Walcheren. Lieut. in the *Magnificent*, and served on shore, co-operating with patriots on the north coast of Spain, 1812. Commanded the *Rover* in unsuccessful attack on Baltimore, 1814. Retired Commander, 1848. Greenwich Hospital pension, 1851. Medal and three clasps. Died in 1855.

(11) Lieut. H. Ready was born in Sussex in 1784. Served as Master's Mate in the *Tonnant* at Trafalgar, 1805—wounded. Lieut., 1807. When 2nd Lieut. of the *Guerrière*, 38, was killed in action on her capture, after a gallant fight, by the U.S. 44-gun frigate *Constitution*, off Nova Scotia, 19th August 1812.

(12) Commander J. P. Blennerhasset was born in Hampshire in 1785. Entered service, 1800. Served in the *Pomone* at capture of the *Carrière*, 10 guns, and the frigates *Succès* and *Bravoure*, 1801. Mid. in the *Tonnant* at Trafalgar, 1805. Lieut., 1807. 1st Lieut. of the *Bedford* at blockade of Flushing, 1809. Retired Commander, 1844. Greenwich Hospital pension, 1853. Medal and clasp. Died in 1867-68.

(13) Lieut. R. Cruse served as Mid. in the *Tonnant* at Trafalgar, 1805. Lieut., 1810. Died in Speenhamland, Berks, in 1831.

(14) Rear-Admiral J. Symes was born in Somersetshire, in 1785, and entered the service in 1801. Served as Mid. in the

Tonnant at Trafalgar, 1805. Lieut., wrecked in the *Meleager* near Port Royal, 1808. Lieut. in the *Bonne Citoyenne* at capture of the French frigate *Furieuse*, 1809—mentioned in despatches; promoted Commander, 1810. In the *Thracian*, sloop, at destruction of a French privateer, 1811. Captain, 1812. Retired Rear-Admiral, 1846. Medal and two clasps. Died at Crewkerne, Somersetshire, in 1856.

(15) Admiral of the Fleet Sir G. R. Sartorius, Kt., G.C.B., was the eldest son of Colonel John Conrad Sartorius, East India Company Service, by Annabella, daughter of George Rose. Born at Bath in 1790, he entered the service in 1801. Mid. of the *Tonnant* at Trafalgar, 1805. Mid. in the *Daphne* in operations in the Rio de la Plata, 1806. Lieut., 1808. Lieut. in the *Success* at the reduction of Ischia and Procida, defence of Sicily, the destruction of vessels at Castiglione, and capture of a ship and three barks, 1810, and defence of Cadiz. Commander, 1812. Captain, 1814. Captain of the *Slaney*, which was in company with the *Bellerophon* when Napoleon surrendered on board her, 1815. Commanded the Portuguese Regency Fleet against Don Miguel, 1831–33, and for his services received the Grand Cross of the Tower and Sword, Grand Cross of St. Bento D'Avis, and the title of Viscomte de Piédale. He was restored to the British Navy in 1836. Knighted, 1841. Captain of the *Malabar* in the Mediterranean, 1841–44, and received the thanks of the United States Government for his efforts to save the U.S. frigate *Missouri*, which was burnt in Gibraltar Bay in 1842. Was one of the first to suggest to the Government the ancient idea of ramming an enemy's ship. A.D.C. to Queen, 1846-49. Rear-Admiral, 1849. Vice-Admiral, 1856. Admiral, 1861. K.C.B., 1869. Admiral of the Fleet, 1869. G.C.B., 1880. Medal and clasp. Died at East Grove, Lymington, Hants, 1885. Had three sons in the army, two of whom, Major-General Reginald W. Sartorius, C.M.G., and Major-General Euston H. Sartorius, earned the Victoria Cross,

(16) Lieut. W. S. Stokes served as Mid. in the *Tonnant* at Trafalgar, 1805. Lieut., 1811. Served on shore in Spain, 1812. Died in St. Leonard's, Bridgenorth, in 1826.

(17) Mr. F. McB. Chevers, Surgeon, R.N., served as Assistant Surgeon of the *Phaeton* at capture of the French frigate *Prompte*, and in Lord Howe's victory of the 1st June 1794. Surgeon, 1795. Surgeon of *Hydra* in the action with the French frigate *Confiante*, 1798 ; of *Tamar* at capture of French frigate *Républicaine*, 1799 ; and of *Robust* at the cutting out of *Chevrette*, 1801. Served in the *Tonnant* at Trafalgar, 1805. In the *Implacable* at the capture of the Russian 74-gun ship *Servolod*, 1808. Died in Upper Stamford Street, London, in 1847.

(18) Surgeon R. Evans, M.D., served as Assistant Surgeon in the *Tonnant* at Trafalgar, 1805. Surgeon, 1807. Retired, 1838. Died in 1846.

(19) Mr. G. Booth was appointed Paymaster and Purser, R.N., 1795. Purser of the *Tonnant* at Trafalgar, 1805. Died in 1839.

(20) Lieut.-Colonel A. H. Ball, R.M., joined the corps as 2nd Lieut., 1793. 1st Lieut., 1795. Captain-Lieut., 1803. Captain, 1803. Senior marine officer in the *Tonnant* at Trafalgar, 1805 ; and assisted in taking possession of the French 74, *Algésiras*. Brevet Major, 1814. Major, 1826. Lieut.-Colonel, 1828. Died in 1829.

(21) Captain J. Cottell became 2nd Lieut., R.M. 1798. 1st Lieut., 1804. Served in the *Tonnant* at Trafalgar, 1805. Present at capture of St. Paul, Isle de Bourbon, 1809, and at the capture of Isle de la Passe, Isle of France, and Isle de Bourbon, 1810. Planted the colours on the latter island—wounded. Captain, 1814. Retired half-pay, 1835. Died at Bedminster, Somerset, in 1842.

(22) Lieut. W. Magin, R.M., entered the corps as 2nd Lieut., 1803. 1st Lieut., 1805. Served in the *Tonnant* at Trafalgar, 1805. Served in the *Sirius* in the action with a French flotilla off Civita Vecchia, and at the capture of *La Bergère*, 1806. Retired half-pay, 1810.

IX

H.M.S. *BELLEISLE*, 74 GUNS

Captain . . . William Hargood (1).
Lieutenants . Thomas Fife (2).
Thomas Coleman (3).
William Ferrie (4). *Wounded.*
Robert Bastin (5).
Ebenezer Geale (6). *Killed.*
John Woodin (7). *Killed.*
Master . . . William Hudson (8).
Master's Mates William Henry Pierson (9). *Wounded.*
Henry Prior (10).
William Cutfield (11). *Wounded.*
Midshipmen . Peter Truppo (12).
Henry Garrett (13).
George Haydon (14).
Henry Parker (15).
William Wilmott Henderson (16).
Thomas Warton.
William Murley (17).
William Moore (18).
Thomas Redwood.
George Nind (19). *Killed.*
William Rowe (20).
John Alexander Philips (21).
Samuel Jago (22). *Wounded.*
James Walker (23).
Nickolas Koravaeff (Russian).
Volunteers, 1st George King Tyler.
   Class   William King Tyler.

John Singleton (24).

William Baker.

Thomas Coleman (25).

John Hodge. *Wounded.*

Surgeon . . .	William Clapperton (26).
Assistant Surgeon . . }	Moses Cotterell Woods (27).
Purser . . .	James MacFarlane (28).
Clerk	Andrew Thomson (29).
Gunner . . .	Barny Kinsley.
Boatswain . .	Andrew Gibson. *Wounded.*
Carpenter . .	John Hicks.
1st Lieut., Royal Marines }	John Owen (30). *Wounded.*
2nd Lieuts., Royal Marines {	Paul Harris Nicolas (31). John Weaver (32).

The *Belleisle* was formerly the French ship *Formidable*, and was built in 1793. In 1795 she was serving in the Mediterranean under the command of the celebrated C. A. L. Durand, Comte de Linois, and was present in Lord Bridport's victory over the French off Groix, on the 23rd June. On this occasion she was engaged with the British 100, *Queen Charlotte*, Captain Sir Andrew Snape Douglas, and the *Sans Pareil*, 80, Rear-Admiral Lord Hugh Seymour and Captain William Browell. In a quarter of an hour she caught fire on the poop, and from that moment suffered very severely, and began to drop astern. And when, at length, she lost her mizenmast, she bore up and struck, after a loss amounting to 320 officers and men. As there was already a *Formidable* in the service, the prize was renamed the *Belleisle*, under the mistaken impression that the action had been fought off Belle Isle, instead of, as was actually the case, off Isle Groix. Under Captains John Whitby and William Hargood, she was employed in the blockade of Toulon, in 1803-4, and in the following year accompanied Lord Nelson to the West Indies in his pursuit of the combined fleets.

She was present in the lee column, and bore a very distinguished part in the battle of Trafalgar, the 21st October 1805, under Captain William Hargood. Early in the action she suffered heavily from the fire of the ships in the allied rear, but only replied with a few shots directed at the Spanish *Monarca*. She then exchanged shots with the Spanish *Santa Ana* and the French *Indomptable*, and became somewhat distantly engaged with the Spanish *San Juan Nepomuceno*, which, with other vessels, had pressed up from the rear. At about 1 P.M. the *Fougueux* intervened, and, with her port bow, ran on board the *Belleisle*, nearly midships on the starboard side. The two ships briskly engaged one another for about twenty minutes, when the Frenchman dropped astern. The *Belleisle*, though by this time a wreck, was still further attacked until she was completely dismasted and shattered. But she remained unconquered, and suspended a Union Jack at the end of a pike and held it up to view, while an ensign was made fast to the stump of the mainmast. She was, however, succoured in time, and though unable to take further active part in the fighting, she subsequently sent her last remaining boat to take possession of the Spanish *Argonauta*, which had hauled down her colours, and lay not far off. The losses of the *Belleisle* amounted to 127 killed and wounded. Her hull was knocked almost to pieces, both sides of it being about equally damaged, while her three masts, bowsprit, and figurehead were shot away, together with her boats and anchors.

Under Captain William Hargood she sailed from Plymouth, in May 1806, with Sir Richard Strahan's squadron in search of the French fleet under M. Willaumez. On the 10th September, in conjunction with the *Bellona* and *Melampus*, she chased and destroyed the French 74-gun ship *Impéteux*, near Cape Henry, United States of America. She was the flagship of Rear-Admiral Hon. Sir Alexander Cochrane in the West Indies in 1807, and was at the capture of the island of St. Thomas. Under Captain George Cockburn she served in the Walcheren Expedition in 1809, and was at the bombardment of Flushing. Her last active service was at the capture of Martinique, in 1809, when she was commanded by Captain William Charles Fabie. She was sold out of the Navy in 1814. She earned the medal with two clasps.

(1) Admiral Sir W. Hargood, G.C.B., G.C.H., was the youngest son of Hezekiah Hargood, Purser, R.N., and was born in 1762. He entered the service in 1773. Mid. in the *Bristol* at the attack on Sullivan's Island, North America, 1776. Lieut., 1780. Lieut. in the *Port Royal* when captured by the Spaniards in the unsuccessful defence of Pensacola, 1781. Lieut. in the *Magnificent* in Lord Rodney's two actions off Dominica, 1782. Lieut. in the *Hebe*, frigate, with H.R.H. Prince William Henry, afterwards William IV., 1785; accompanying him as one of his lieutenants in the *Pegasus*, 1786, and as his 1st Lieut. in the *Andromeda* in 1788-89. Commander, 1789. Captain, 1790. Commanded the *Hyæna*, frigate, when she was captured off Cape Tiberon by the French frigate *Concorde* in 1793; was made prisoner, but escaped. On his return he was tried by court-martial for the loss of his ship, and was acquitted. Captain of the *Leopard*, the crew of which mutinied at the Nore in 1797, and put him ashore at Yarmouth. Captain of the *Belleisle* off Toulon with Nelson in 1803-4; in pursuit of the combined fleets to the West Indies and back in 1805; and at Trafalgar, 1805—gold medal, the thanks of Parliament, and a sword of honour from the Patriotic Fund. Captain of the *Belleisle*, in conjunction with *Bellona* and *Melampus*, at the capture and destruction of the French ship *Impéteux*, 1806. Colonel, Royal Marines, 1808. Captain of the *Northumberland* at the blockade of Lisbon, 1808, and co-operating with the Austrians in the Adriatic, 1809.

Rear-Admiral, 1810. Second in command, Portsmouth, 1810–1811. Commanded a squadron in the Channel Islands, 1811. Vice-Admiral, 1814. K.C.B., 1815. G.C.H. and G.C.B., 1831, at the coronation of William IV., with whom he was in personal friendship as an old messmate and shipmate. Commander-in-Chief at Plymouth, 1833–36. Died at the Royal Crescent, Bath, in 1839, aged 77. His portrait is in the Painted Hall, Greenwich.

(2) Captain T. Fife was promoted Lieut., 1800. 1st Lieut. of the *Belleisle* at Trafalgar, 1805—promoted Commander. Captain, 1812. Died in London, 1829.

(3) Lieut. T. Coleman was promoted Lieut., 1800. Lieut. in the *Belleisle* at Trafalgar, 1805. Resigned, 1811. Received medal and clasp in 1849.

(4) Commander W. Ferrie was promoted Lieut., 1800. Lieut. in the *Belleisle* at Trafalgar, 1805—wounded. Commander, 1809. Commanded the *Supérieure*, 16, at the capture of Martinique, 1809, and at the capture of the French 40-gun ship *Junon*, 1809. Died in 1816.

(5) Commander R. Bastin was the son of John Bastin, of Tidwell, East Chudleigh, Devonshire, and was born in 1780. He entered the service as Volunteer 1st Class in 1796. Served as Mid. in the *Nymphe* at the capture of the French frigates *Résistance*, 48, and *Constance*, 24, 1797. Master's Mate, 1802. Lieut., 1803. Lieut. in the *Belleisle* in the pursuit of the combined fleets to the West Indies, and at Trafalgar, 1805. Lieut. in the *Blanche* at the capture of the French 50-gun ship *La Guerrière*, 1806—wounded; mentioned in despatches. Was wrecked in the *Blanche* in 1807, and kept prisoner in France until 1814. Retired Commander, 1836. Medal and three clasps. Died in 1854.

(6) Lieut. E. Geale was promoted Lieut., 1800. Killed in action when serving as Lieut. in the *Belleisle* at Trafalgar, 1805.

(7) Lieut. J. Woodin was promoted Lieut., 1804. Killed in action when serving as Lieut. in the *Belleisle* at Trafalgar, 1805.

(8) Mr. W. Hudson was appointed Master, R.N., 1793. Master of the *Belleisle* at Trafalgar, 1805, and took possession of

the Spanish 80-gun ship *Argonauta*. Master-Attendant Bermuda Dockyard, 1828. Died in 1835.

(9) Rear-Admiral Sir W. H. Pierson, Kt., was born in Plymouth in 1782. Entered the service, 1796. Mid., 1798. Master's Mate in the *Belleisle* at Trafalgar, 1805—wounded; promoted Lieut. 1st Lieut. of the *Fylla* at capture of French privateer *L'Inconnu*, 1814—wounded. Commander, 1826. Commanded the *Madagascar* when the Lord-Lieut. of Ireland visited her in 1836, for which he was knighted. Captain, 1838. Retired, 1852. Retired Rear-Admiral, 1857. Medal and clasp. Died in Langstone, near Havant, Hants, in 1858.

(10) Lieut. H. Prior was born in Sussex. Served as Master's Mate in the *Belleisle* at Trafalgar, 1865. Lieut., 1808. Died in 1825.

(11) Commander W. Cutfield, eldest son of Mr. John Cutfield, of Deal, Master, R.N., was born in London, and entered the service, 1796. Master's Mate, 1805. Master's Mate in the *Belleisle* at Trafalgar, 1805—wounded in breast. Lieut., 1806. Lieut. in the *Grasshopper* in Mediterranean, 1807–8, and was frequently engaged in cutting-out expeditions and destruction of vessels and convoy—mentioned in despatches, promoted Commander, 1808. Served in Walcheren Expedition, 1809, and brought home the despatches from Sir R. Strachan. Commanded the *Woodhouse*, sloop, 1814–16. Captain of *Barracouta* on survey and exploration, east coast of Africa, 1822–23, and died of fever at Delagoa Bay, the 30th November 1823.

(12) Lieut. P. Truppo served as Mid. in the *Belleisle* at Trafalgar, 1805—promoted Lieut. Died in 1822.

(13) Commander H. Garrett was born in Hambledon, Hants, in 1786, and entered the service in 1799. Was wrecked in the *Impregnable* off Sussex, 1799. Served as Mid. in the *Belleisle* in pursuit of combined fleets to the West Indies and back, and at Trafalgar, 1805. Lieut., 1809. Lieut. in the *Psyche* at the reduction of Mauritius, 1810, and the capture of Java, 1811. Lieut. in the *Rhin*, and served on shore with the patriots on the north coast of Spain, 1812 ; commanded a battery at Santander—wounded. Commanded a semaphore station in Sussex, 1832–37,

G

and afterwards in Hants, 1841–47. Reserved Commander, 1851. War medal and two clasps. Died in Bedhampton, Hants, in 1865.

(14) Commander G. Haydon was born in Somersetshire, and entered the service in 1800. Served as Mid. in the *Belleisle* at Trafalgar, 1805. Lieut., 1807. Lieut. in the *Medusa*, 1808–13, including the capture of several privateers, the pursuit of French frigates to the coast of Labrador, and co-operating with the patriots on the north coast of Spain. Retired Commander, 1856. Medal and clasp. Died in 1859.

(15) Captain H. Parker was the son of John Robert Parker, of Green Park, Youghal, Co. Cork, and Catherine Uniacke. He was born in 1788, and entered the service as Volunteer 1st Class in 1801. Mid., 1801. Mid. in the *Belleisle* in the pursuit of the combined fleets to the West Indies and back, and at Trafalgar, 1805. Witnessed the destruction of *L'Impéteux*, 1806. Lieut., 1808. Flag-Lieut. to Admiral Sir J. B. Warren in the *Swiftsure* on the North American station, 1813–14 (twice wounded). Commander, 1814. Served in Coastguard, 1832–35. Commander of Greenwich Hospital, 1853–64. Retired Captain, 1864. Medal and clasp. Died in Greenwich Hospital, the 7th April 1873. His son, Captain George Frederick Hastings Parker, R.N., was father of the present Commander Reginald Francis Parker, R.N.

(16) Rear-Admiral W. W. Henderson, C.B., K.H., one of four brothers in the Royal Navy, was born in Poole, Dorsetshire, in 1782, and entered the service in 1799. Served as Mid. in the *Belleisle* in the pursuit of the combined fleets to the West Indies and back, and at Trafalgar, 1805. Lieut., 1806. Lieut. in the *Niobe* at the capture of the French corvette *Néarque*, 1806. When serving on shore, in co-operation with Portuguese army in 1809, was taken prisoner at Oporto, but escaped. 1st Lieut. of the *Active*, and commanded her boats at capture of a convoy at Grao, 1810. Served in her in the action and capture of frigates off Lissa, 1811—mentioned in despatches, promoted Commander. Commanded her boats at capture of several gunboats and twenty-one sail of convoy at Ragosniza, 1811. Was wrecked in the *Pomone* near the Needles, 1811. Commanded *Dasher*, sloop, at reduction

of Guadeloupe, 1815. Captain, 1815. K.H., 1835. Captain of *Edinburgh* in the operations on coast of Syria, 1840, including the bombardment of Acre—created C.B. Captain of *Victory*, 1841-44. Good Service Pension, 1847. Rear-Admiral, March 1851. Commander-in-Chief, south-east coast of America, with his flag in the *Centaur*, 1851-54. Medal and four clasps, and Turkish medal for Syria. Died at sea, the 12th July 1854.

(17) Captain W. Murley was born in Somersetshire, and entered the service in 1801. Served as Signal-Mid. in the *Belleisle* in the pursuit of the combined fleets to West Indies and back, and at Trafalgar, 1805. Served as Signal-Mid. in the *Diadem* in unsuccessful attack on Buenos Ayres, 1807. Lieut., 1808. Lieut. in the *Crocus*, and commanded a flat-bottomed boat at the siege of Flushing, 1809; and in the *Caledonia* in partial action with Toulon fleet, 1813. Commander, 1813. Retired Captain, 1849. Medal and clasp. Died in 1870.

(18) Mr. W. Moore was born in Scarborough, Yorks, in 1772. Promoted Mid. from A.B., 1805. Mid. in the *Belleisle* at Trafalgar, 1805. Left the service 1805.

(19) Mr. G. Nind was born in Reading, Berks, in 1776. When serving as Mid. in the *Belleisle* was killed in action at Trafalgar, the 21st October 1805.

(20) Mr. W. Rowe served as Mid. in the *Belleisle* at Trafalgar, 1805. Received medal and clasp in 1849.

(21) Lieut.-General J. A. Philips, R.M., son of Mr. Alexander Philips, Master, R.N., was born in 1790. He served as Mid. in the *Belleisle* in the pursuit of the combined fleets to the West Indies and back, and at Trafalgar, 1805. Entered R.M. as 2nd Lieut., 1806. 1st Lieut., 1813. Served with a battalion of marines in Spain and North America, 1812, and on the Canadian lakes, 1813-15. Captain, 1834. Brevet Major, 1846. Lieut.-Colonel, R.M.A., 1851. Colonel, R.M., 1854. Commanded Chatham Division, 1855-57. Major-General, 1857. Lieut.-General, 1863. Colonel of the Woolwich Division, R.M., 1865. Was in receipt of a Good Service Pension. Medal and clasp. Died at Farnbro', Hants, the 27th November 1865.

(22) Lieut. S. Jago was born at Plymouth Dock. Served as

Mid. in the *Belleisle* at Trafalgar—wounded. Lieut., 1812.
Not in Navy List after 1819.

(23) Mr. J. Walker was born in Scotland. Mid., 1805.
Served as Mid. in the *Belleisle* at Trafalgar, 1805. Clerk, 1806.
Purser, 1807. Not in Navy List after 1816.

(24) Mr. J. Singleton was born in Dover, 1791. Entered
service as Boy 3rd Class, 1803. Volunteer 1st Class, 1805.
Served in the *Belleisle* at Trafalgar, 1805. Left the service
same year.

(25) Commander T. Coleman entered the service as Volunteer 1st Class, 1805. Served in that capacity in the *Belleisle*
at Trafalgar, 1805. Mid., 1806. Mid. in the *Defiance* at the
destruction of the three French frigates under the batteries of
Sable d'Olonne, 1809 ; and in co-operating with the patriots on
the north coast of Spain. Lieut., 1815. Commander, 1837.
Medal and clasp. Died in 1849.

(26) Surgeon W. Clapperton was appointed Surgeon, R.N.,
1804. Surgeon of the *Belleisle* in pursuit of the combined fleets
to the West Indies and back, and at Trafalgar, 1805. Died
before 1849.

(27) Assistant-Surgeon M. C. Woods was appointed to that
rank, 1801. Served as Assistant-Surgeon of the *Belleisle* in the
pursuit of the combined fleets to the West Indies and back, and
at Trafalgar, 1805. Died in 1829-30.

(28) Mr. J. MacFarlane was appointed Paymaster and Purser,
R.N., 1798. Purser in the *Belleisle* at Trafalgar, 1805. Served
under Lord Gambier at the destruction of ships in the Basque
Roads, 1809. Retired, 1843. Medal and two clasps. Died in
1849.

(29) Mr. A. Thomson served as Clerk in the *Belleisle* at Trafalgar, 1805. Purser, 1806. Purser of the *Galatea* in her
action with Commodore Roquebert's squadron off Madagascar,
and the capture of the *Renommée* and *Néréide*, 1811. Not traced
after 1815.

(30) Lieut.-General Sir J. Owen, K.C.B., K.H., R.M., entered
the corps as 2nd Lieut., 1796. Served in the *Adamant* at the
battle of Camperdown, the 11th October 1797. 1st Lieut.,

1798. Was in the action with, and destruction of, the French frigate *Preneuse* off Port Louis, 1799; and at the boarding and capture of the ship *Sea Nymphe* in the harbour of Port Louis. Senior officer of marines in the *Belleisle* at Trafalgar, 1805—wounded, and was the first person to board the Spanish 80–gun ship *Argonauta*. Captain, 1807. Served in the expedition to Copenhagen, 1807, and at the destruction of the *Robuste* and *Lion*, French ships of the line. Landed with a party of marines, and carried a battery of five guns at Laigueglia, and witnessed the capture of a convoy in May 1812. Brevet Major, 1821. K.H., 1833. Commanded a battalion in the Carlist War, 1836–37, including the actions of Alza and Hernani. Lieut.-Colonel, 1837. C.B., 1838. Deputy Adjutant-General, R.M., 1838–54. Colonel 2nd Commandant, 1839. Colonel-Commandant, 1844. A.D.C. to the Queen. Major-General, 1851. K.C.B., 1852. Lieut.-General, 1855. Medal and three clasps, medal for Carlist War, and 2nd Class of St. Ferdinand. Died in 1857.

(31) Lieut. P. H. Nicolas, R.M., was second son of Retired Commander John Harris Nicolas, R.N., of East Looe, Cornwall, by Margaret, daughter and co-heir of J. Blake. He was brother of Rear-Admiral J. T. Nicolas, C.B., who died 1851, and of Sir N. H. Nicolas, G.C.M.G., K.H. Became 2nd Lieut., R.M., 1805. Served in the *Belleisle* at Trafalgar, 1805. 1st Lieut., 1808. Served in ship's boats at attack on French gunboats in Basque Roads, 1810. Retired half-pay, 1814. Medal and two clasps. Died in 1860.

(32) Captain J. Weaver became 2nd Lieut., R.M., 1803. 1st Lieut., 1805. Served in the *Belleisle* at Trafalgar, 1805. Captain 1826. Died in Plymouth, 1834.

X

H.M.S. *REVENGE*, 74 GUNS

Captain . . .	Robert Moorsom (1). *Wounded.*
Lieutenants. .	Lewis Hole (2).
	Peter Giles Pickernell (3).
	Francis Wills (4).
	Essex John Holcombe (5).
	William Wright (6).
	John Berry (7). *Wounded.*
Master . . .	Luke Brokenshaw (8). *Wounded.*
Master's Mates {	James Campbell.
	James Thomas.
Midshipmen .	John Sawyer.
	John Geary (9). *Wounded.*
	Samuel Cross.
	William Jackson.
	Thomas Grier (10). *Killed.*
	Matthew Corney (11).
	William Goddard.
	Daniel B. Kirby.
	John Hartnall.
	Bartholomew George Smith Day (12)
	Henry Patterson.
	Edward F. Brooke. *Killed.*
	James Blandford (13).
	William Henry Brand (14).
	Edward Herrick (15).
	Robert Alcock.
Volunteers, {	John W. Forster.
1st Class . .	Thomas Caven (supy.).

Chaplain   .   .   Rev. John Greenly, B.A. (16).   *Wounded*.

Surgeon .   .   .   William Dykar (17).

Assistant-   { Charles Gregson.
  Surgeons .   . { Thomas Fisher (18).

Purser   .   .   .   John Buckingham.

Clerk .   .   .   .   James Scott.

Gunner   .   .   .   John Tucker.

Boatswain   .   .   George Forster.

Carpenter   .   .   William Russell.

Captain, Royal }
  Marines   . . } Peter Lely (19).   *Wounded*.

2nd Lieuts.,   } Henry Blacker Fairtlough (20).
  Royal Marines } Arthur Copperthwaite (21).

The *Revenge* was built in Chatham Dockyard in 1805 from the design of Sir John Henslow, Knight, Surveyor of the Navy, and was commissioned in April by Captain Robert Moorsom for service with the Channel Fleet. She joined the blockading squadron before Cadiz, and witnessed Lord Nelson's arrival to take command. She was one of the first ships to be painted, in accordance with his idea, with her hull black, a yellow strake along each tier of ports, and black port-beds. This method of painting, known as double-yellow or chequer-painting, distinguished nearly every British ship which fought at Trafalgar, and was soon afterwards adopted as the regular uniform for British men-of-war; white, however, being eventually substituted for yellow in the colour of the strakes. In accordance with Nelson's order, the waists of all the ships were painted white.

Under Captain Robert Moorsom the *Revenge* took part in the victory of Trafalgar on the 21st October 1805, and was in the lee column. In attempting to pass through the enemy's line and secure an advantageous position athwart the hawser of the French *Aigle*, she fouled the latter's jib-boom, and while the ships were

interlocked delivered a couple of broadsides into the
Frenchman's bows. Then, standing on, she was in the
act of hauling up on the port tack, when a tremendous
fire was poured into her lee quarter by the Spanish
Principe de Asturias. Three two-deckers also hemmed
her in, and greatly punished her until they were driven
off by the approach of other British vessels. Her injuries
in the battle were in consequence severe and her losses
heavy, the latter amounting to twenty-eight killed and
fifty-one wounded, including her captain. Her bowsprit,
three lower masts, maintop mast, and gaff, were badly
injured. She received nine shots below the copper; her
stern, transoms, and timbers, and several beams, knees,
riders, and iron standards, were very much damaged,
and so was her hull generally. She had several chain
plates shot away, several of her lower deck ports destroyed, and three of her guns dismounted. After the
battle she was refitted at Gibraltar and returned to
Portsmouth, when Captain Hon. Charles Elphinstone
Fleming was appointed to her. He appears to have
been very unpopular, and to have caused great dis-
satisfaction amongst the crew by immediately painting
out Nelson's chequers and substituting a single stripe or
strake for them. He was, however, not long in the
ship, for early in 1806 Captain Sir John Gore, a very
good officer, succeeded him; and the *Revenge*, to the
great joy of the ship's company, was again painted as
one of "Nelson's chequer-players." On the 16th July
1806, her boats, with others, were employed in cutting
out, in the Gironde, the French corvette *Cæsar* and a
convoy, in which service her lieutenant was killed, the
boat sunk, and the crew taken prisoners. In September
of the same year she was with Sir Samuel Hood's
squadron, and took part in the pursuit of the French
frigates and corvettes from Rochefort. Early in 1807

she joined Lord Collingwood off Cadiz, where she remained until 1808, when Captain Hon. Charles Paget, M.P., was appointed to her, and she joined the squadron under Admiral Lord Gambier in the Channel. Captain Alexander Robert Kerr commanded her in 1809, and under him she participated in the action in the Basque Roads and in the destruction of the enemy's ships on the 12th April : her losses on this occasion amounted to eighteen killed and wounded. On the 15th November 1810, while cruising off Cherbourg under Captain Hon. Charles Paget, and bearing the flag of Rear-Admiral Hon. A. K. Legge, she took part in the attack on two 40-gun French frigates. In November 1812, Captain Sir John Gore was reappointed to her and took her out to the Mediterranean. In the summer of 1813 she was employed with the inshore squadron off Toulon ; on the night of the 8th November, her boats went into the harbour of Palamos, on the coast of Catalonia, and cut out a French felucca without losing a man killed or wounded. On the 4th December 1813, Captain Sir John Gore was promoted to the rank of Rear-Admiral, and hoisted his flag on board ; and in her he commanded the detached squadron in the Adriatic until the peace, when she returned to Chatham.

Between 1823 and 1832 she was employed in the Mediterranean and on particular service under Captains Sir Charles Burrard, Norborne Thompson, Hon. C. O. Bridgeman, James Hillyar, and Donald Hugh Mackay. Under the latter she was employed with the squadron under Vice-Admiral Sir Pulteney Malcolm blockading the ports of Holland in 1832. She was again in the Mediterranean a few years later, under command of Captain Sir William Elliott, K.C.B. In 1840 she was again on active service, when, under the command of Captain Hon. William Waldegrave, she took part in the

operations on the coast of Syria, under Admiral Hon.
Sir Robert Stopford, including the bombardment of
Acre. After this she returned to Sheerness, where she
remained until broken up in 1851, after an existence of
forty-six years, and having earned the naval war medal
with four clasps, and the Turkish medal for Syria.

(1) Admiral Sir R. Moorsom, K.C.B., was the second son of
Richard Moorsom, of Airy Hill, near Whitby, Yorkshire, and
was born in 1760. Became Midshipman, 1774. Served as Mid.
in the *Courageux* in Keppel's indecisive action in the Channel
with the French in June 1778; was at the relief of Gibraltar by
Vice-Admiral George Darby in 1781; the final relief by Lord
Howe in 1782; the action off Cape Spartel; and the capture by
Admiral Kempenfelt of part of a convoy going to the West
Indies, with Admiral De Guichen, 1782. Captain, 1790.
During the French Revolutionary War he commanded the *Niger*
and *Astrea* frigates, and the *Hindustan*, 50 guns. In 1803-4
he commanded the *Majestic*, and in April 1805 was posted to
the *Revenge*, 74, in which he served with the blockading squadron
before Cadiz, and in the battle of Trafalgar, 1805, in which his
ship was seriously engaged, and he himself wounded—received
gold medal, the thanks of Parliament, and a sword of honour
from the Patriotic Fund. He carried the great banner at Lord
Nelson's funeral. He was Private Secretary to the First Lord of
the Admiralty, Lord Mulgrave, in 1807; Colonel, Royal Marines,
1808; sometime a Lord Commissioner of the Admiralty; Surveyor-General of the Ordnance, 1810. M.P. for Queenborough,
Sheerness. Rear-Admiral, 1810. Vice-Admiral, 1814. K.C.B.,
1815. Commander-in-Chief, Chatham, 1824-27. Admiral, 1830.
Died in 1835, at Cosgrove Priory, Northamptonshire.

(2) Admiral L. Hole was son of Rev. William Hole, of Kuscott
Hill, Surrogate of Barnstaple. Born in Strodeley, Devonshire,
1779. Entered service as A.B., 1793. Mid., 1794. Mid. in
the *Belligueux* at the capture of Port au Prince, 1794. Lieut.,
1798. Mid. in the *Ramillies*, but served as a volunteer in the
Polyphemus at the battle of Copenhagen, 1801. First Lieut. of

the *Revenge* at Trafalgar, 1805—promoted Commander. While in *Egeria*, between 1808–12, he captured the *Naesois*, privateer, *Aalborg*, Danish cutter, and *Alvor*, privateer. Captain, 1813. Retired Rear-Admiral, 1846. Retired Vice-Admiral, 1856. Retired Admiral, 1861. Medal and two clasps. Died in 1870.

(3) Commander P. G. Pickernell was born in 1772, and entered the service, 1790. During his service in the *Magicienne*, and in command of the *Alexandra* tender to the *Prince of Wales*, in the West Indies, in 1793–1800, took part in several captures, and in the capture of Trinidad, the unsuccessful attack on Puerto Rico, and the reduction of Surinam. Lieut., 1800. Second Lieut. of the *Revenge* at Trafalgar, 1805 ; and 1st Lieut. of her at the capture, by Sir Samuel Hood, of four French frigates off Rochefort, 1806. Commanded the *Gallant*, brig, in the Walchern Expedition, 1809. Commander, 1810. Greenwich Hospital pension, 1846. Medal and clasp. Died at Blackheath, London, in 1859.

(4) Lieut. F. Wills was appointed Lieut. in 1801. Lieut. in the *Revenge* at Trafalgar, 1805. Not in Navy List after 1811.

(5) Lieut. E. J. Holcombe was appointed Lieut. in 1802. Lieut. in the *Revenge* at Trafalgar, 1805. Died in 1821–22.

(6) Lieut. W. Wright was appointed Lieut. in 1802. Lieut. in the *Revenge* at Trafalgar, 1805. Not in Navy List after 1809.

(7) Lieut. J. Berry was appointed Lieut. in 1805. Lieut. in the *Revenge* at Trafalgar, 1805—wounded. Died in Edinburgh in 1809.

(8) Mr. L. Brokenshaw was appointed Master, R.N., in 1803. Served as Master of the *Revenge* at Trafalgar, 1805—wounded. Master of the *Emerald* at the destruction of batteries and vessels of war at Vivero, 1808. Died in Porlipean, Cornwall, in 1840.

(9) Captain J. Geary, one of four brothers in the Royal Navy, was born in St. Margaret's, Kent, in 1787, and entered the service in 1797, as Volunteer 1st Class. Served in the *Scorpion* at the capture of a Dutch brig-of-war, 1798. Mid. in the *Revenge* at Trafalgar, 1805—wounded. Master's Mate in the *Monarch*, and served in her boats at the cutting out of the *César* at the mouth

of the Gironde, 1806—wounded; and in the capture of four
French frigates off Rochefort in the same year—wounded.
Lieut., 1807. Received the thanks of the Governor of the
Ionian Islands for his exertions, when Acting-Captain of *Mada-
gascar*, on the occasion of the wreck of a wing of the 90th Light
Infantry off Sicily, in 1830. Commander, 1831. Greenwich
Hospital pension, 1849. Captain, 1863. Medal and two clasps.
Died in 1874.

(10) Mr. T. Grier was killed in action, when serving as Midshipman in the *Revenge* at Trafalgar, 1805.

(11) Mr. M. Corney served as Midshipman in the *Revenge* at
Trafalgar, 1805. Became Purser, R.N., 1807. Not in Navy List
after 1827.

(12) Commander B. G. S. Day entered service as Volunteer
1st Class, 1804. Mid., 1805. Mid. in the *Revenge* at Trafalgar,
1805. Acting-Master of *Supérieure* at the capture of the 40-gun
French frigate *La Junon*, 1809; the capture of Martinique, 1809,
and Guadeloupe, 1810. Lieut., 1815. Retired Commander,
1860. Medal and four clasps. Died in 1867–68.

(13) Commander J. Blandford entered the service as Volunteer 1st Class, 1805. Mid., 1805. Served as Mid. in the
Revenge, and as A.D.C. to Captain Moorsom at Trafalgar, 1805.
Also in her at the capture of the French corvette *César*, 1806;
the pursuit and capture of four French frigates off Rochefort,
1806; the destruction of the enemy's ships in the Basque Roads,
1809; and the defence of Cadiz, in 1810–11. Lieut., 1811.
Retired Commander, 1853. Medal and three clasps. Died in
1867.

(14) Captain W. H. Brand, one of four brothers in the Royal
Navy, was a son of Mr. Alex. Brand, R.N., and Anne, daughter
of George Rollens. He was born in London in 1790, and
entered the service as Volunteer 1st Class in 1805. Served as
Mid. in the *Revenge* at Trafalgar, 1805; and in Lord Hood's
capture of four French frigates off Rochefort in 1806. Was taken
prisoner in the *Redwing* by a Spanish flotilla, 1807; and was
afterwards present in her action with, and the destruction of,
seven armed vessels near Cape Trafalgar, 1808. In *Apollo* he

was employed, co-operating with the patriots, on the north coast of Spain, 1812 ; at blockade of Barcelona ; the capture of the French *Merinos* off Corsica, 1812 ; and taking of the islands of Augusta and Curzola, 1813. Acting-Lieut. in the *Weazel*, and served in her boats at the capture of two vessels, 1812. Lieut., 1813. Lieut. in the *Badger* at the reduction of Guadeloupe, 1815. Inspecting-Commander of Coastguard, 1828–44. Commander, 1846. Retired Captain, 1858. Medal and two clasps. Died at Leigh, in Essex, the 22nd April 1867. His son, Mr. Ferdinand Brand, I.S.O., recently retired from the office of Librarian at the Admiralty.

(15) Captain E. Herrick, a son of Thomas Bousfield Herrick of Shippool, near Innishannon, Co. Cork, entered the service, in 1805, as Volunteer 1st Class. Served as Mid. in the *Revenge* at Trafalgar, 1805 ; at the destruction of shipping in the Basque Roads, 1809 ; and in the batteries during the operations against Flushing, 1809. Lieut., 1815. Employed in Packet service at Falmouth, 1838–46. First Lieut. of the *Victory*, 1847–49. Commander, 1849. In the Packet service at Dover, 1852–55. Captain, 1855. Retired Captain, 1860. Medal and two clasps. Died in 1862.

(16) Rev. J. Greenly, B.A., was appointed Chaplain, R.N., 1804. Served as Chaplain in the *Revenge* at Trafalgar, 1805— wounded. Afterwards Minor Canon of Salisbury Cathedral ; perpetual curate of St. Thomas, and Rector of Sharncote, Wilts. Medal and clasp. Died in 1862, at Salisbury.

(17) Surgeon W. Dykar was appointed Surgeon, R.N., in 1780. He served as Surgeon of the *Revenge* at Trafalgar, 1805. Retired, 1814. Died, 1829.

(18) Surgeon T. Fisher was appointed Surgeon, R.N., in 1808. Served as Assistant-Surgeon in the *Revenge* at Trafalgar, 1805. Medal and clasp. Died in 1861.

(19) Captain P. Lely became 2nd Lieut., R.M., 1793. First Lieut., 1795. Served in the *Glatton* at the battle of Copenhagen, 1801. Captain, 1803. Senior marine officer in the *Revenge* at Trafalgar, 1805—wounded. Retired half-pay, 1813. Died in Bath in 1832.

(20) Lieut. H. B. Fairtlough became 2nd Lieut., R.M., 1804. Served in the *Revenge* at Trafalgar, 1805. First Lieut., 1808. Retired half-pay, 1814. Received medal and clasp, 1848.

(21) Lieut. A. Copperthwaite became 2nd Lieut., R.M., 1803. First Lieut., 1805. Served in the *Revenge* at Trafalgar, 1805. Not traced after 1809.

Captains' Gold Medal—Reverse.

XI

H.M.S. *SPARTIATE*, 74 GUNS

Captain . . . *Sir* Francis Laforey, *Bart.* (1).
Lieutenants. . John McKerlie (2).
James Clephan (3).
George Bignell (4).
John James Ridge (5).
Frederick Jennings Thomas (acting) (6).
Hon. Michael de Courcy (supern.) (7).
Master . . . Francis Whitney (acting) (8).
Master's Mates Flowers Beckett (9).
Stephen Dillon (10).
Charles Taylor.
Midshipmen . Thomas S. Richards.
George Byron Winlack (11).
Edward Scott (12).
James Storey.
William Corke (13).
Vernon Lanphier (14).
James Henry Johnston (15).
William Franklyn Peter (16).
John Mawbey (17).
Edward Knapman (18). *Wounded.*
Henry Sara Hodge.
William Crump.
Henry Bellairs (19). *Wounded.*
Augustus James De Crespigny (20).
Henry Cowd Teed.
Copleston Radcliffe (21).
Michael Collins (22).

Surgeon . . . John Pritchard O'Berne (23).

Surgeon's Mates { Jacob Spencer.
{ William Henry Trotman (24).

Purser . . . Digory Forrest (25).

Clerk . . . Richard Sholl (26).

Gunner . . . Lockwood Baxter.

Boatswain . . John Clark. *Wounded.*

Carpenter . . Thomas Murray.

1st Lieut.,
Royal Marines } Samuel Holditch Hawkins (27).

2nd Lieuts., { John Rawlins Coryton (28).
Royal Marines { George Drew Hawkins (29).

The *Spartiate* was built for the French at Toulon, and was launched in 1793. On the 1st August 1798, under Captain M. J. Emeriau, she fought against the British in the battle of the Nile. After being engaged first by the *Theseus* and *Vanguard,* and fired on by the *Minotaur* and *Audacious* and completely dismasted, she struck. Taken on the list of the British Navy, she was commissioned in 1799 by Captain Henry Charles Herbert Pierrepont, and afterwards by Captain Lord William Stuart. Under command of Captain Sir Francis Laforey, Bart., she was in the West Indies with Rear-Admiral Hon. Alexander Cochrane in 1805 until she joined Lord Nelson. In the weather column she fought under Sir Francis Laforey in the great victory of Trafalgar, the 21st October 1805 ; her losses amounting to five killed and twenty wounded. The *Minotaur* and *Spartiate* were the two rearmost ships in the weather column, but exchanged broadsides with several of the combined fleet. They managed to cut off the Spanish 84-gun ship *Neptune,* of which they contrived to get alongside, and which, after a fight of over an hour, surrendered. The *Spartiate* had her foretopsail yard shot away, and her masts, yards, and rigging in general were a good deal damaged.

Under Sir Francis Laforey she served with Rear-Admiral Sir Richard Strachan's squadron at Rochefort in 1807–8, blockading Vice-Admiral Allemand's five ships of the line ; and in June 1809 she assisted in the capture of the Neapolitan islands of Ischia and Procida. After the war she returned to Sheerness. When Great Britain and France blockaded the ports of Holland in 1832, she was present, commanded by Captain Robert Tait, with the fleet under Vice-Admiral Sir Pulteney Malcolm : she continued on the South American station until 1835. She was made a sheer hulk at Plymouth in 1842, and was broken up there in 1857. She earned the medal with one clasp.

(1) Admiral Sir F. Laforey, 2nd Bart., K.C.B., was the son of Admiral Sir John Laforey, 1st Bart., and Eleanor, daughter of Colonel Francis Farley. He was born in Virginia in 1767, and entered the service in 1780. Lieut., 1789. Commander, 1790. Commanded the *Fairy*, 16, in the West Indies in 1791–1793, including the capture of Tobago in the Windward Islands in 1793, and was sent home with despatches—promoted Captain. In command of the 28-gun frigate *Carysfoot* recaptured, on the 29th May 1794, off Land's End, the 32-gun frigate *Castor*, which had been taken nineteen days earlier and commissioned by the French. Commanded the *Scipio*, 64, with his father, in the Leeward Islands in 1795–96, and assisted in the capture of the Dutch settlements of Demerara, Essequibo, and Berbice in 1796. In command of the 38-gun frigate *Hydra*, took part in the pursuit and destruction of the French frigate *Confiante* near Le Havre in 1798. Commanded the *Spartiate*, 74, in the West Indies in 1805, and at the battle of Trafalgar, 1805—gold medal, the thanks of Parliament, and a sword of honour from the Patriotic Fund. He carried the standard in the first barge in Lord Nelson's funeral from Greenwich. Still in command of the *Spartiate*, was with Sir Richard Strachan at Rochefort in 1807–8, blockading Vice-Admiral Allemand's fleet; and in 1809 assisted in the capture of the Neapolitan islands of Ischia and Procida.

Rear-Admiral, 1810. Commander-in-Chief, Leeward Islands, 1811–14. K.C.B., 1815. Vice-Admiral, 1819. Admiral, 1830. Died in Brighton in 1835.

(2) Rear-Admiral J. McKerlie, J.P., was born in 1774 in Scotland, and entered the service in 1794, as A.B. Mid. of *Indefatigable* at the capture of the French frigate *Virginie*, 1796, and the destruction of *Les Droits de l'Homme*, 1797—severely wounded, lost right arm. Present at attack on enemy's shipping in the Morbihan River, and assisted to board and blow up the *Insolente*, 1800. Lieut., 1802. 1st Lieut. of the *Spartiate* at Trafalgar, 1805—promoted Commander. In the *Calliope* at capture of Flushing, and commanded a division of gunboats in expedition to Walcheren, 1809, also actively employed in her in the German rivers, 1812–13. Made several captures, and commanded the boats at capture of two corvettes building in the Weser, 1813. Captain, 1813. Pension for wounds of £300 per annum. Acting Rear-Admiral, 1846. Medal and three clasps. Died at Caroisal, Wigtonshire, N.B., 1848.

(3) Captain J. Clephan was born in Fifeshire, N.B., and was pressed into the service in 1794. Master's Mate, 1795. Master's Mate of *Doris*, and served in her boats at the cutting out of the *Chevrette* near Brest, 1801—wounded; promoted Lieut. Lieut. in the *Spartiate* at Trafalgar, 1805. Commander, 1811. In *Charybdis*, sloop, captured the American privateer *Blockade* near Isle of Saba, 1812. Served in expedition against New Orleans, 1814–15. Retired Captain, 1840. Medal and two clasps. Died in 1851.

(4) Captain G. Bignell was son of John Bignell, Purser, R.N. Born in 1786, he entered the service in 1795. Acting Lieut. in the *London* at the battle of Copenhagen, 1801. Lieut., 1801. Lieut. in the *Spartiate* at Trafalgar, 1805; guarding coast of Sicily; landing troops in Bay of Naples; and reduction of islands of Ischia and Procida in 1809. In the *Dover* retook a schooner on banks of Newfoundland, 1812. Commanded the *Hunter*, brig, in action with American flotilla on Lake Erie, 1813—severely wounded; taken prisoner; pension for wounds. Commander, 1815. Retired Captain 1851. Medal and two clasps. Died in 1863.

(5) Commander J. J. Ridge was promoted to Lieut. in 1802. Served as Lieut. in the *Spartiate* at Trafalgar, 1805. Lost in command of the *Harrier*, 18, which is supposed to have foundered in the Indian Ocean in 1809.

(6) Rear-Admiral F. J. Thomas was a son of Sir John Thomas, 5th Bart., of Wenvoe Castle, Glamorganshire, and Mary, daughter of John Parker of Harfield Court, Gloucestershire. Born in New Forest in 1787. Entered service as Volunteer 1st Class, 1799. Served as Mid. in the *Prince of Wales* in Sir Robert Calder's action, 1805; and as acting Lieut. in the *Spartiate* at Trafalgar, 1805. Lieut., 1806. Lieut. in the *Spartiate* 1806–9, off Rochefort, and in the blockade of Toulon. Performed distinguished service on the coast of Spain, 1810–12, and commanded a division of gunboats at siege of Cadiz—wounded; thanked by the Commander-in-Chief; promoted Commander. Captain, 1813. Retired Rear-Admiral, 1846. Medal and clasp. Inventor of a lifeboat to pull and sail. Author of *England's Defence*. Died at Hill, near Southampton, in 1855.

(7) Commander Hon. M. de Courcy was the third son of John, 26th Lord Kingsale, and Susan, daughter of Conway Blennerhasset, of Castle Conway, Co. Kerry; his son became the 28th Lord Kingsale. Promoted Lieut., 1797. Was in the *Spartiate*, as supernumerary for passage at Trafalgar, 1805. Lieut.-Commander of the *St. Lucia*, 14, which was captured by the French in the West Indies, in 1807. Commander, 1808. Died in 1813.

(8) Mr. F. Whitney was appointed Master, R.N., in 1798. Acting Master of the *Spartiate* at Trafalgar, 1805. Died in Dartmouth in 1846.

(9) Lieut. F. Beckett entered the service in 1795. Served as Mid. in the *London* at the battle of Copenhagen, 1801. Master's Mate in the *Spartiate* at Trafalgar, 1805—promoted Lieut. Commanded Semaphore Station, Putney, 1839–47. Greenwich Hospital pension, 1847. Medal and two clasps. Died in 1862.

(10) Lieut. S. Dillon was born in Cornwall. Served as Master's Mate of the *Spartiate* at Trafalgar, 1805. Lieut., 1813. Not in Navy List after 1821.

(11) Lieut. G. B. Winlack was born in County Wexford, Ireland. Served as Mid. in the *Spartiate* at Trafalgar, 1805. Lieut., 1806. Not in Navy List after 1810.

(12) Mr. E. Scott was born in Newton, Devonshire, 1787. Served as Mid. in the *Spartiate* at Trafalgar, 1805. Invalided from the service, 1805.

(13) Lieut. W. Corke was born in Portsmouth. Served as Mid. in the *Spartiate* at Trafalgar, 1805. Lieut., 1811. Died in the Mauritius when serving in the *Thais* in 1816.

(14) Commander V. Lanphier was born in Ireland, and entered the service in 1799. Served as Mid. in the *Spartiate* at Trafalgar, 1805. Lieut., 1808. Lieut. in the *Leonidas* at the reduction of Cephalonia, 1809, and Santa Maura, 1810—wounded. Retired Commander, 1846. Medal and clasp. Died in 1867.

(15) Commander J. H. Johnston was born in London, and entered the service as Volunteer 1st Class in 1803. Served as Mid. in the *Spartiate* at Trafalgar, 1805. Lieut., 1810. Comptroller of the East India Company's steamers. Retired Commander, 1849. Medal and clasp. Died at sea, on passage home from Calcutta, in 1851.

(16) Lieut. W. F. Peter was born in Falmouth. Served as Mid. in the *Spartiate* at Trafalgar, 1805. Lieut., 1809. Died in 1830.

(17) Lieut. J. Mawbey was born in Portsmouth in 1781, and entered the service as Mid. in 1798. Served in the *Romney* at the capture of a Swedish convoy, 1799, in the expedition to Holland, 1799, and the surrender of the Dutch squadron under Admiral Storey. Served in the *Polyphemus* at the battle of Copenhagen, 1801. Mid. in the *Spartiate* at Trafalgar, 1805; and at the reduction of Ischia and Procida, 1809. Served in the *Caledonia* at the fall of Genoa. Lieut., 1815. Medal and two clasps. Died in 1852.

(18) Commander E. Knapman was born in 1794, and entered service in 1803. Served in the *Magnanime* at the bombardment of Havre de Grace, 1804. Mid. in the *Spartiate* at Trafalgar, 1805—wounded in arm and leg. Served in the boats of the *Dictator* at the capture of Danish luggers, 1810-11.

Lieut., 1812. Greenwich Hospital pension, 1858. Retired Commander, 1858. Medal and clasp. Brother of Commander John Knapman, who served in *Téméraire* at Trafalgar. Died in 1867-68.

(19) Rev. H. Bellairs, M.A., J.P., was third son of Abel Walford Bellairs, D.L., J.P., of Uffington, Co. Lincoln, and was born in 1790. Served as Mid. in the *Spartiate* in the pursuit of the combined fleets to the West Indies and back, and at Trafalgar, 1805—wounded. Resigned, 1806. Appointed cornet 15th Hussars, 1808; Lieut., 1809; resigned, 1811. Entered Holy Orders and became Rural Dean and Hon. Canon of Worcester Cathedral, and Domestic Chaplain to the Earl of Strafford. J.P., Co. Lincoln. Naval medal and clasp. Died in 1872.

(20) Commander A. J. De Crespigny, was 3rd son of Sir William Champion De Crespigny, 2nd Bart., M.P., and Sarah, daughter of the 4th Earl of Plymouth. Born in Italy. Entered service as Volunteer 1st Class, 1805. Mid., 1805. Mid. in the *Spartiate* at Trafalgar, 1805. Lieut., 1811. Received Royal Humane Society's medal, 1815, for gallantry in saving life from drowning. Commander, 1825. In command of *Scylla*, and died off Port Royal, Jamaica, of yellow fever, 1825.

(21) Lieut. C. Radcliffe was a son of the Rev. Copleston Radcliffe, M.A., Rector of Stoke Climsland, Cornwall, and Vicar of Tamerton Foliott, Devonshire. Born in Plymouth in 1785. Served in the *Spartiate* at Trafalgar, 1805. Lieut., 1807. Lieut. in the *Netley* during the American War, and was killed in action when boarding an American schooner, in the Canadian lakes, the 12th August 1814.

(22) Mr. M. Collins served as A.B. in the *Cæsar* in the action with the French and Spanish squadrons in Gut of Gibraltar, 1801. Mid. in the *Spartiate* at Trafalgar, 1805. Medal and two clasps.

(23) Surgeon J. P. O'Berne was appointed Surgeon, R.N., in 1798. Served as Surgeon of the *Spartiate* at Trafalgar, 1805. Died in 1821.

(24) Surgeon W. H. Trotman was born in the West Indies.

Surgeon's Mate, 1805.   Surgeon's Mate in the *Spartiate* at Trafalgar, 1805.   Surgeon, 1810.   Medal and clasp.   Died in 1862.

(25) Sir D. Forrest, Kt., J.P., was the son of Austen Forrest,
Storekeeper to the Victualling Office, Plymouth.   He was
appointed Paymaster and Purser, R.N., in 1795, and had acted
as Secretary to several flag-officers.   Served as Purser of the
Ardent at Copenhagen, 1801, and of the *Spartiate* at Trafalgar,
1805.   Knighted by the Prince Regent.   Retired, 1843.   Died
in Exmouth in 1846.

(26) Mr. R. Sholl was born in Truro, Cornwall, in 1784.
Served as Clerk in the *Spartiate* at Trafalgar, 1805.   Paymaster
and Purser, 1806.   Died in 1836.

(27) Lieut. S. H. Hawkins was appointed 2nd Lieut., R.M.,
1797.   1st Lieut., 1803.   Senior marine officer in *Spartiate* at
Trafalgar, 1805.   Not in Navy List after 1808.

(28) General J. R. Coryton, R.M., served as Mid., R.N.,
1800–2.   Was Mid. in the *Hunter* in action with batteries at Isle
of Bas.   Became 2nd Lieut., R.M., in 1803.   1st Lieut., 1805.
Served in the *Spartiate* at Trafalgar, 1805—mentioned in despatches.   Served in the *Argo* on the coast of Africa, 1807 ; at
the storm and capture of Teneriffe, and the capture of an enemy's
vessel—severely wounded, mentioned in despatches.   Also
during the siege of St. Domingo, 1809, and on one occasion
was the first to board a French felucca under the batteries of the
town (sword from Patriotic Fund).   Pension for wounds of £70
a year.   Good Service Pension £300 a year in 1838.   Adjutant,
Royal Marines, 1811.   Captain, 1826.   Brevet Major, 1841.
Lieut.-Colonel, 1844.   Colonel, 1849.   Commanded Plymouth
Division, 1851–55.   Major-General, 1855.   Lieut.-General, 1857.
General, 1858.   Medal and one clasp.   Died in Woolwich, 1867.

(29) Lieut. G. D. Hawkins was appointed 2nd Lieut., R.M.,
in 1804.   Served in the *Spartiate* at Trafalgar, 1805.   1st Lieut.,
1808.   Served in the *Dragon* on North American station,
including the operations under Sir George Cockburn in the
Chesapeake Bay, April and May 1813.   Retired, half-pay, 1814.
Medal and two clasps.   Died in 1856.

XII

H.M.S. *MARS*, 74 GUNS

Captain . . .	George Duff (1). *Killed.*
Lieutenants . .	William Hennah (2).
	James Black (3). *Wounded.*
	Benjamin Patey (4).
	Edward William Garrett (5). *Wounded.*
	George Lacey Decœurdoux (6).
	William Henry T. Boyce (7).
Master . . .	Thomas Cooke (8). *Wounded.*
2nd Master . .	James Lindsay (acting) (9). *Wounded.*
Master's Mates	Alexander Duff (10). *Killed.*
	James Horrie (11).
	James Wilkie (12).
Midshipmen .	Edward Perry Foster (13).
	John Jenkins. *Wounded.*
	George Dallas Barclay (14).
	Thomas Coates.
	Edmund Corbyn (15). *Killed.*
	George Edward Patey (16).
	Richard Merrish Goodwin (17).
	Alexander Dundas Young Arbuthnott (18).
	James Robinson.
	Norris Walker (19).
	George Guiren (20). *Died of Wounds.*
	M—— R—— Warren.
	William Dalrymple.
	John Yonge. *Wounded.*
	William John Cook. *Wounded.*
	Alfred Luckraft (21). *Wounded.*
	Michael Hervey (supy.).

Volunteers 1st   John Francis Cook (22).
  Class   Robert Snell.
                        Thomas Rawlins (23).
                        David Clerk.
                        Thomas Duff (24).
                        Edward Manners.
                        Jeremiah Pearcey.
                        *_Norwich Duff_ (25).
                        *_Henry Morgan_ (26).
Surgeon .   .   .   James Torkington (27).
Assistant-   ⎰ Michael Brown.
  Surgeons .   .   ⎱ John Millar.
Purser   .   .   .   Edward Hatfull (28).
Clerk .   .   .   .   William Barnell.
Gunner   .   .   .   Anthony Collis.
Boatswain .   .   John Bunt.
Carpenter .   .   William Cook.
Captain, Royal   ⎱
  Marines   ⎰ Thomas Norman (29).
2nd Lieuts.,   ⎰ Charles Holmes (30).
  Royal Marines ⎱ Robert Guthrie (31).

The _Mars_ was built at Deptford Dockyard in 1794,
from the design of Sir John Henslow, Knight, Surveyor
of the Navy; she was first commissioned on the 2nd
December 1794. Under Captain Sir Charles Cotton she
took part in Vice-Admiral Hon. W. Cornwallis' pursuit of
a French squadron on the 2nd June 1795; and in the
action with and brilliant repulse of a French fleet under
MM. Villaret-Joyeuse and Venne, four times superior in
force, on the 17th June, on which occasion she received
the approbation of the Admiral. Her loss on the latter
occasion amounted to thirteen killed and wounded; her
lower masts were damaged by shot, and all her standing
and running rigging cut and destroyed. In 1796 she

* Rated as A.B.

was with the squadron under Rear-Admiral H. Harvey, and afterwards in the Channel Fleet. In 1797 her crew were unfortunately implicated in the Mutiny of the Nore, and her captain and officers were compelled to leave the ship. Under the command of Captain Alexander Hood she took part in the determined action with, and captured, the French 74-gun ship *Herculae* off Bec du Raz on the 21st April 1798. On this occasion the *Mars* lost heavily. She had over seventy killed or wounded, including among the former her gallant Captain, Alexander Hood. He was wounded twenty minutes after the commencement of the action by a ball in the femoral artery, and died just after the enemy had submitted. She only lost her jib-boom, and suffered slight damage to her masts and rigging. She bore the flag of Rear-Admiral Hon. George Cranfield Berkeley in June 1798, with the blockading force off Rochefort; and in 1801–2 that of Rear-Admiral Thornborough in charge of the in-shore squadron off Brest; and was at the blockade of Rochefort in 1804–5.

Under command of Captain George Duff she was distinguished and lost heavily at Trafalgar, on the 21st October 1805. She was in the lee column, and followed the *Belleisle* into action. When endeavouring to find an opening at which to pass through the hostile line, she was engaged from astern by the French 74, *Pluton*. To avoid running into the Spanish *Santa Ana*, she was obliged to turn her head to wind, and so exposed her stern to the fire of the Spanish *Monarca* and French *Algésiras*, which punished her severely, until the coming of our *Tonnant* took off their attention. Quite unmanageable as she had become, the *Mars* paid off, but was further wounded by the French *Fougueux*, and again by the *Pluton*, one of whose shots carried off the head of Captain Duff. Her losses amounted to ninety-eight killed and wounded. Her main topmast and spanker boom were shot away, and all her lower masts left in a tottering state. She had several guns disabled, her rudder head injured, and all her yards more or less shot. On the surrender of the French Commander-in-Chief and his retinue, they were received on board the *Mars*.

In 1806, under command of Captain Robert Dudley Oliver, she was employed with Commodore Sir Samuel Hood's squadron off Rochefort, and captured the French 40-gun frigate *Rhin* on the 22nd July ; while on the 25th September in the same year, when cruising with the same squadron off Rochefort, she assisted at the capture of four French frigates. Under Captain William Lukin she was in the expedition to Copenhagen under Lord Gambier in 1807, and at the capture of the Danish fleet on the 7th September. She served in the expedition to the Baltic, and in Channel, in 1808–13, and was paid off in the latter year at Portsmouth, where, after being employed for a short time as a receiving hulk, she was broken up in 1823–24. She earned the war medal with three clasps.

(1) Captain G. Duff was the son of George Duff of Banff, N.B., and grandson of Alexander Duff, of Hatton, Banff, and Anne, eldest daughter of the 1st Earl of Fife. He was born in 1764, and entered the service in 1777. He was promoted to Lieutenant in 1779, and in the following year, when in the *Panther*, was present at the capture of the Spanish Admiral Don Juan de Langara. As Lieutenant in the *Montagu* he was present in Lord Rodney's action off Martinique, the siege of St. Kitts, and the capture of the French Commander De Grasse, in 1782. Commander, 1790. Captain, 1793. Commanded the *Duke*, 98, in the unsuccessful operations against Martinique in 1793, the *Vengeance* during the mutiny in Bantry Bay in 1797, and the *Glenmore*, 36, when she recaptured the East Indiaman *Calcutta* in 1799, which the French had just taken near Madeira. He

commanded the *Mars*, 74, during the blockade of Rochefort and Brest in 1804–5 and in the battle of Trafalgar, where he lost his life, 1805. He was killed early in the action by a shot which carried off his head; his body fell on the gangway, where it remained, covered with a Union Jack, till the end of the battle. A monument was erected to his memory in St. Paul's Cathedral; his family received the gold medal for the battle, a piece of plate from the Patriotic Fund, and an honourable augmentation of arms. He was grand-nephew to Vice-Admiral Robert Duff, who died in 1787, and father of Vice-Admiral Norwich Duff, who served as Volunteer in the *Mars* at Trafalgar, and died in 1862.

(2) Captain W. Hennah, C.B., was son of the Rev. Richard Hennah, Vicar of St. Anstell, Cornwall, and Domestic Chaplain to Viscount Falmouth. Promoted Lieut., 1793. Lieut. of *Magicienne* at capture and destruction of French corvette *Réolaise*, 1800. First Lieut. of the *Mars* at Trafalgar, 1805, and succeeded to the command of the ship on the death of Captain Duff—promoted to Captain, vase from Patriotic Fund, and testimonial from the crew of the ship. C.B., 1815. Died, 1832.

(3) Captain J. Black, C.B., served in the *Leviathan* at the siege of Toulon, 1793, and in Lord Howe's victory, the 1st June 1794. In the *Sans Pareil* in Lord Bridport's action, the 23rd June 1795. Lieut., 1799. Second Lieut. in the *Mars* at Trafalgar, 1805—wounded, and became 1st Lieut. on death of Captain Duff. First Lieut. of the *Mars* at the capture of French 40-gun frigate *Le Rhin*, 1806; and in the attack on Copenhagen, 1807. Commander, 1810. Commanded the *Weazel* at the destruction of six French gunboats, 1813—wounded, promoted Captain; also at the capture of the island of Mezzo, near Ragusa, and the island of Zera, 1813—severely wounded; and capture of two French gun vessels, 1813. C.B., 1815. Austrian Order of Maria Theresa. Died at sea between Leith and London, 1835.

(4) Lieut. B. Patey was promoted to Lieut. in 1801. Served as Lieut. in the *Mars* at Trafalgar, 1805. Not in Navy List after 1809.

(5) Commander E. W. Garrett was born in 1781, and entered

the service in 1794. Lieut., 1801. Lieut. in the *Mars* at Trafalgar, 1805—wounded ; at the capture of *Le Rhin, La Gloire*, and *L'Infatigable*, 1806 ; and in the expedition to Copenhagen, 1807. First Lieut. of the *Onyx* at the capture of the Dutch corvette *Manly*, 1809—wounded, mentioned in despatches, and promoted Commander. In command of the *Hope* captured an American privateer, 1813. Commander of Greenwich Hospital, 1844. Medal and two clasps. Died in 1860.

(6) Commander G. L. Decœurdoux entered the service as officer's servant in 1789. Served in the *Lion* in the action with four Spanish frigates and the capture of the *Santa Dorotea*, 1798, and was acting Lieut. in her at the capture of the French 80-gun ship *Gillaume Tell*, 1800. Lieut., 1802. Lieut. in the *Mars* at Trafalgar, 1805 ; at the capture of the French frigate *Le Rhin* and four others off Rochefort, 1806. Transport Agent, 1813–1817. Greenwich Hospital pension, 1839. Retired Commander, 1844. Medal and three clasps. Died in Southsea in March 1850.

(7) Commander W. H. Boyce entered service as officer's servant in 1792. Promoted Lieut., 1805. Lieut. in the *Mars* at Trafalgar, 1805. Greenwich Hospital pension, 1814. Retired Commander, 1864. Medal and clasp. Died in 1866.

(8) Mr. T. Cook was appointed Master, R.N., in 1796. Master of the *Mars* at Trafalgar, 1805—wounded. Died in 1831.

(9) Lieut. J. Lindsay was born in Aberdeen in 1783. Entered the service in 1803. Mid., 1804. Master's Mate, 1805. Acting 2nd Master of *Mars* at Trafalgar, 1805—wounded ; at the capture of French frigate *Le Rhin*, 1806 ; the capture of the *Gloire* and the *Infatigable*, 1806 ; and in the expedition to Copenhagen, 1807. Lieut., 1815. Died in 1845.

(10) Mr. A. Duff, Master's Mate, was the second son of Lachlan Duff-Gordon of Park, Banffshire, N.B., by Rachel Hog, of Newliston, and was elder brother of Thomas Duff (afterwards Gordon) who served as Volunteer 1st Class in the *Mars* at Trafalgar. Born in Edinburgh, 1785. Master's Mate of *Mars*, and was killed in action at Trafalgar, 1805, aged 20.

(11) Lieut. J. Horrie was born in Scotland. He served as

Master's Mate in the *Mars* at Trafalgar, 1805. Lieut., 1807. Died in 1826.

(12) Lieut. J. Wilkie was born in Haddington, N.B. Became Mid., 1805. Master's Mate, 1805. Master's Mate in the *Mars* at Trafalgar, 1805. Lieut., 1807. Lieut. in the *Dictator* in the action with a Danish squadron off Mardoe, coast of Norway, when two frigates and two brigs were destroyed, 1812. Died in the East Indies when 1st Lieut. of the *Topaze*, in 1821.

(13) Lieut. E. P. Foster was born in Plymouth Dock. Served as Mid. in the *Mars* at Trafalgar, 1805. Lieut., 1806. Died in 1844.

(14) Lieut. G. D. Barclay was born in London. He served as Mid. in the *Mars* at Trafalgar, 1805—promoted Lieut. Died in Yarmouth in 1834, aged 51.

(15) W. E. Corbyn was born in Plymouth in 1790. When Mid. in the *Mars* was killed in action at Trafalgar, 1805, aged 15.

(16) Commander G. E. Patey was the only son of Lieut. William Patey, R.N., who died on service in Spain, 1810. He was born in 1789, and entered service as Volunteer 1st Class, 1803. Served as Mid. in the *Mars* and A.D.C. to Captain Duff at Trafalgar, 1805. Served in *Crescent* at blockade of the Texel, 1806–8. Lieut. 1813. Served in the *Albacore* during American War. Retired Commander, 1856. Medal and clasp. Died in 1865.

(17) Lieut. R. M. Goodwin was born in Guernsey. He served as Mid. in the *Mars* at Trafalgar, 1805. Lieut., 1810. Not in Navy List after 1813.

(18) Admiral Sir A. D. Y. Arbuthnott, Kt., was son of Lieut.-Colonel Robert Arbuthnott, 31st Foot, who died of wounds received at St. Lucia, 1796. Born in Forton, Hants, 1789, and entered service as 3rd Class Boy, 1803. Mid., 1804. Served as Mid. in the *Mars* at Trafalgar, 1805; the capture of *Le Rhin*, 1806; the capture of four French frigates off Rochefort by Sir Samuel Hood's squadron, 1806; the expedition to Copenhagen, 1807; and in much gunboat service in the Baltic in 1808–9. Lieut., 1809. Lieut. in the *Impregnable* at reduction of islands of North and South Beveland, 1811; the capture of Antwerp;

and in escorting the Emperor of Russia and the King of Prussia to England, 1814. Assisted at the great Naval Review at Spithead, and was promoted Commander, 1814. Commander of *Jasper* on a mission to St. Petersburg in 1823—Order of St. George of Russia. Commanded the *Terror*, bomb, in the second expedition against Algiers in 1824. Captain, 1824. Served with the British Auxiliary Legion in Spain in 1835–37, as Colonel and Brigadier-General, including the relief of San Sebastian, and the storming of Irun—Knight Commander of Charles III., and the Order of San Fernando. Served in Syria in 1840–42 with the commissioners employed with the Turkish Army in driving the Egyptian forces under Ibrahim Pacha out of Syria—Turkish gold medal, and Order of Medjidieh. Retired Captain, 1846. Retired Rear-Admiral, 1853. Retired Vice-Admiral, 1858. Knighted, 1859. Retired Admiral, 1863. Naval medal and clasp. Was Gentleman of the Privy Chamber to George IV. and Queen Victoria. Died at Shenton Hall, Leicestershire, in 1871.

(19) Lieut. N. Walker was born in Falmouth. Served as Mid. in the *Mars* at Trafalgar, 1805. Lieut., 1809. Not in Navy List after 1813.

(20) Mr. G. Guiren was born in Portsmouth in 1788. Served as Mid. in the *Mars* at Trafalgar, 1805, and died on the 31st October of wounds received in the action.

(21) Admiral A. Luckraft was born in 1792. Entered the service in 1801. Served in the *Monarch* at the battle of Copenhagen, 1801; and in the *Mars* at Trafalgar, 1805—wounded. Lieut., 1810. Lieut. in the *Blonde* when employed in conjunction with French at the reduction of Morea Castle, 1828, and performed distinguished service on shore—mentioned in despatches, promoted Commander, Knight of the Legion of Honour, and the Order of the Redeemer of Greece. Captain, 1838. Retired, 1853. Retired Rear-Admiral, 1857. Retired Vice-Admiral, 1864. Retired Admiral, 1869. Medal and two clasps. Died in 1871.

(22) Lieut. J. F. Cook was born in Plymouth Dock. Served as Volunteer 1st Class in the *Mars* at Trafalgar, 1805. Lieut., 1815. Died in 1832.

(23) Commander. T. Rawlins was born in Dublin, and entered the service as Volunteer 1st Class, 1804. Served in the *Mars* at Trafalgar, 1805. Was in the *Ajax*, 74, when she was destroyed by fire in 1807. Mid., 1807. Mid. in the *Active* at the forcing of the Dardanelles, 1807. Served in the *Warspite* in a skirmish with a portion of the French Toulon fleet, 1810. Lieut., 1811. Lieut. in the *Severn* in the attack on Washington and Baltimore, 1814, the reduction of St. Mary's, coast of Georgia, and in several captures, 1815. Retired Commander, 1853. Medal and clasp. Died in 1860.

(24) Lieut.-Colonel T. Gordon, formerly Duff, D.L., J.P., of Park, Banffshire, N.B., Mid., R.N., was third son of Lachlan Duff-Gordon, of Park, Banffshire, by Rachel Hog, of Newliston, and younger brother of Alexander Duff, Master's Mate, who was killed in the *Mars* at Trafalgar. Born in Edinburgh, 1790. Entered the service as Volunteer 1st Class, 1805. Served in the *Mars* at Trafalgar, 1805. Left service, 1808, and became Lieut.-Colonel Inverness, Banff, &c., Militia (now 3rd Battalion Cameron Highlanders), 1812. Medal and clasp. Died at Fort George, Inverness, in 1855, aged 65.

(25) Vice-Admiral N. Duff, D.L., J.P., was the son of Captain George Duff, R.N., who was killed in command of the *Mars* at Trafalgar, and Sophia, 2nd daughter of Alexander Dirom, of Muiresk, Aberdeenshire. He was born in Edinburgh, and entered the service in 1805. Rated as A.B., but served as Mid. of *Mars* at Trafalgar, 1805. Volunteer 1st Class, 1805. Was in the *Ajax* when she was destroyed by fire in the Adriatic, 1807. Mid., 1807. Mid. in the *Active* at the forcing of the Dardanelles, 1807; the capture of the *Friedland*, Venetian brig of war, 1808; in ship's boats at capture of twenty fire vessels at Grao, 1810; in the action with and capture of frigates off Lissa, 1811; in ship's boats at capture of merchantmen off Ragosniza, and the capture of the *Pomone* and *Persanne*, 1811. Lieut., 1811. Commander, 1814. Commanded the *Espoir*, sloop, in expedition to Washington, Baltimore, and New Orleans, 1814. Captain, 1822. Rear-Admiral, 1852. Vice-Admiral, 1857. Medal and four clasps. Died in Bath, 1862.

(26) Mr. H. Morgan was rated as A.B., but served as Mid. in the *Mars* at Trafalgar, 1805.   Received the medal and clasp in 1860.

(27) Mr. J. Torkington was appointed Surgeon, R.N., 1790. Served as Surgeon of the *Mars* at Trafalgar, 1805.   Not in Navy List after 1809.

(28) Mr. E. Hatfull was appointed Paymaster and Purser, R.N., in 1795.   Served in the *Mars* at Trafalgar, 1805.   Died, 1829.

(29) Captain T. Norman was a son of Alderman Norman, of Coventry, and became 2nd Lieut., R.M., 1794.   1st Lieut., 1795. Captain, 1803.   Served as senior marine officer in the *Mars* at Trafalgar, 1805, and was mortally wounded.   Died from the effects in Naval Hospital, Gibraltar, the 6th December 1805.

(30) Lieut. C. Holmes became 2nd Lieut., R.M., 1803. Served in the *Mars* at Trafalgar, 1805.   First Lieut., 1806. Retired on half-pay, 1814.   Died in 1837.

(31) Lieut. R. Guthrie became 2nd Lieut., R.M., 1804. Served in the *Mars* at Trafalgar, 1805.   First Lieut., 1808.   Not in Navy List after 1809.

XIII

H.M.S. *DEFIANCE*, 74 GUNS

Captain . . .	Philip Charles Durham (1). *Wounded.*
Lieutenants. .	Thomas Simons (2). *Killed.*
	William Hellard (3).
	James Uzuld Purches (4).
	Andrew Bowden Pidgley (5).
	Henry John Smith Hargrave (6).
Master . . .	John Osman (7).
Master's Mates	James Spratt (8). *Wounded.*
	William Snowey (9).
	Colin Campbell (10).
Midshipmen .	George Simmonds.
	John Hodge. *Wounded.*
	James Williamson. *Killed.*
	Lewis Grant (11).
	Edmund Andrew Chapman (12). *Wounded.*
	Thomas Robin Longa.
	Peter Hannay (13).
	Henry Rich (14).
	James Hay (15).
	John Rudall (16).
	John Drake (17).
	Robert Maltman (18).
	Thomas Chrystie (19).
	Percy Watson.
	Spencer Smyth (20).
	James Young.
	*James Dott (21).
	* Robert Brown (22). *Wounded.*

* Rated as A.B.

Volunteers 1st   *_John Parsons_ (23).
  Class   Augustus Thomas Hickes (24).
                  John Osman.
                  John Pringle.
Chaplain   . .   Rev. Robert Henry Barker.
Surgeon . . .   William Burnett (25).
Surgeon's Mate   John Clerk.
Purser   . . .   George Jackson.
Clerk.   . . .   George Beck.
Gunner   . . .   Alexander Jacks.
Boatswain . .   William Forster.   _Killed._
Carpenter . .   William Caught.
Captain, Royal ⎱ Basil Alves (26).
  Marines . . ⎰
1st Lieut.,   ⎱ George I. Bristow (27).
  Royal Marines ⎰

The _Defiance_ was launched from the building yard
of Messrs. Randall and Co. on the Thames in 1783,
having been built from the design of Sir Thomas Slade,
Knight, Surveyor of the Navy.   First commissioned in
1794, her career for the next four years was somewhat
unfortunate.   There was a serious mutiny on board in
1794, which resulted in five of her crew being hanged,
and ten others severely punished.   She was seriously
implicated in the mutiny of the Channel Fleet at Spithead
in 1797, and when, on the 15th April, the ship's crew
were ordered by Lord Bridport to prepare for sea, they
ran up the shrouds and gave three cheers, the signal for
mutiny.   All efforts to persuade them to return to duty
failed until an inquiry into their grievances was promised.
On the 7th May Lord Bridport signalled to weigh and
put to sea, but, like those of the other ships, the crew of
the _Defiance_ refused to obey.   And it was not until Lord
Howe arrived with a full redress of their grievances and

* Rated as A.B.

a free pardon that discipline was restored, the men returned to their duty, and the fleet put to sea. Again, however, in 1798, the year of the Irish rebellion, ten of her crew were hanged and ten transported for life for being concerned in the conspiracy of the "United Irishmen." After this she quieted down and entered upon a career of distinction. In 1799, under Captain Thomas Revell Shivers, she was with Rear-Admiral Sir J. H. Whitshed, and joined Lord St. Vincent in the Mediterranean in his pursuit of the French fleet. Commanded by Captain Richard Retallick, and bearing the flag of Rear-Admiral Thomas Graves, she was present in Nelson's victory of Copenhagen on the 2nd April 1801, in which her losses in killed and wounded amounted to seventy-five. During the action she was several times set on fire by the hot 42-pound shot fired from the Danish batteries on shore, from which she was subjected to a very heavy fire, and which she returned with interest. She was considerably damaged in her hull, while her lower shrouds, lower masts, main-mast, mizen-mast, and bowsprit were badly wounded.

Under Captain Philip Charles Durham she was present in Sir Robert Calder's action of the 22nd July 1805, and was the first ship to discover the enemy. She lost eight killed and wounded, and some yards, but was not seriously damaged. She joined Lord Nelson on the 4th October, and under Captain Durham fought at Trafalgar on the 21st October 1805, in the lee column. As she got into the confusion of the allied line, she exchanged shots with the Spanish 112, *Principe de Asturias*, and about 3 P.M. ran alongside the French 74, *Aigle*, to which she lashed herself. The enemy was boarded, and appeared to be subdued, but no sooner had the boarding party hoisted the British colours over her than the *Aigle's* people rallied and drove them off. Captain Durham

thereupon cut loose the lashings, and, sheering off ten
yards or so, opened so heavy a fire that in about twenty
minutes the French ship, which had very gallantly
defended herself, asked for quarter, and was taken possession of.   The *Defiance* subsequently made a prisoner
of the Spanish *San Juan Nepomuceno*, which struck
to the *Dreadnought*.   Her losses in the battle amounted
to seventy killed and wounded, amongst the latter
being her captain.   Her bowsprit, fore and main-masts
were shot through, and her mizen-masts, three topmasts,
jib and driver booms, and gaff wounded.   Her rigging
and sails were likewise much cut, and her hull in several
places struck with shot.   It is noteworthy that of the
officers present in the battle sixteen were of Scottish
nationality.

Between 1806 and 1809 she assisted at the blockade
of L'Orient, was on the north coast of Spain co-operating
with the patriots, and landed the Duke of Wellington at
Corũna.   In 1808, under Captain Hon. Henry Hotham,
she was with Rear-Admiral Stopford's squadron blockading Rochefort.   On the 24th February 1809 she took
part in the successful action with three French 40-gun
frigates at Sables d'Olonne and with the batteries on
shore.   The *Defiance*, which bore the brunt of the action,
lost thirty killed and wounded ; while all her masts were
badly wounded and her rigging cut to pieces.   While
cruising off the north coast of Spain in 1809–10, she was
with the squadron which took possession of, masted, and
rigged in an incredibly short time, five Spanish sail of
the line, including two three-deckers, together with five
frigates and five sloops lying in the harbour of Ferrol, all
of which were sent to Cadiz.   She continued in service
till the 30th September 1813, when she was paid off at
Chatham.   She was afterwards employed for a short time
as a prison ship, and was broken up at Chatham in 1816,

after an existence of thirty-three years, and having earned the war medal with two clasps. Amongst the claimants for the medal and clasp for Trafalgar was Jane Townsend, a woman who was present in the ship in the battle. As the regulations for the award of the medal contained no reservation as to sex, and as her services were reported as highly satisfactory and useful, her claim was at first admitted ; but on reconsideration refused, as it appeared to the Board that complication would arise on account of there being so many other women in the ships of the fleet whose services were reported as equally useful.

(1) Admiral Sir P. C. Henderson-Calderwood-Durham, G.C.B., was the third son of James Durham, of Largo, Fifeshire, by Ann, daughter and heiress of Thomas Calderwood, of Polton, Lasswade, Midlothian ; he was brother of General James Durham, of Largo, to which property he succeeded in 1840. Born in 1763, he entered the service in 1777. He was present in the *Edgar* at the relief of Gibraltar by Admiral Darby in 1781, and was Acting-Lieutenant and Officer of the Watch in the *Royal George* when she sank at Spithead, 1782, being one of the few saved, after being an hour in the water. Served in the *Union* at the relief of Gibraltar by Lord Howe in 1782, and in the action with the combined fleets off Cape Spartel. Lieut., 1782. Commander, 1790. Captain, 1793. Commanded the *Spitfire* at the capture of the *Afrique*, French privateer, 1793. Captain of the *Anson* in the action off Isle Groix and L'Orient, 1795, and in the expedition to Quiberon Bay, 1795. Commanded the *Anson* in Sir J. B. Warren's action with the French squadron, and the capture of the 74-gun ship *Hoche* and two frigates off Tory Island, the 12th October 1798—thanks of Parliament. Captain of the *Defiance* in Calder's action off Finisterre, 1805, and in the battle of Trafalgar, 1805—slightly wounded ; gold medal, thanks of Parliament, and sword of honour from the Patriotic Fund. Bore Nelson's banner as a K.B., at his funeral, 1806. Served as Commodore in the Mediterranean, and, under Rear-Admiral Martain, was engaged

at the destruction of two French ships near Cette.   Rear-Admiral, 1810.   Commander-in-Chief, Leeward Islands, 1813–16, with his flag in the *Venerable*, including the capture of the two French frigates *Alcmène* and *Iphigénie*, the 16th January 1814 ; and at the reduction of Martinique and Guadeloupe, 1815—created a K.C.B., Knight Grand Cross of the French order of Military Merit.   Vice-Admiral, 1819.   Admiral, 1830.   G.C.B., 1830.   M.P. for Queenborough, 1830, and Devizes, 1835–36.   Commander-in-Chief, Portsmouth, 1836–39.   Equerry to H.R.H. the Duke of Cambridge.   Assumed additional surnames of Henderson in 1817, and Calderwood in 1840.   Died in Naples in 1845.   His portrait is in the Painted Hall, Greenwich.

(2) Lieut. T. Simons was appointed Lieut. in 1800.   Served as 1st Lieut. of the *Defiance* in Calder's action, 1805.   Killed in action at Trafalgar, the 21st October 1805.

(3) Captain W. Hellard was promoted to Lieut., 1783. Became 1st Lieut. of the *Defiance* at Trafalgar, 1805, on the death of Lieut. Simons—promoted Commander.   Promoted Captain, 1812.   Had a pension for wounds.   Died at Hythe, near Southampton, in 1837.

(4) Commander J. U. Purches was born in 1783, and entered the service in 1795.   Was wrecked in the *Espoir* on the Goodwins, 1799.   Mid. of *Voltigeur* when she repelled the attack of a flotilla of gunboats near Tarifa, 1800.   Lieut., 1804.   Lieut. in the *Defiance* in Calder's action, and in the battle of Trafalgar, 1805—was appointed Prize Master of *L'Aigle*, one of the captured 74's, in which he remained till she was dismasted and wrecked near Cadiz in the gale which followed the great battle. Was officially present at Nelson's funeral, 1806.   Lieut. of *Challenger* with squadron under Rear-Admiral C. V. Penrose forcing the passage of the Gironde ; and commanded her boats at capture of enemy's gunboats, 1813–14.   Retired Commander, 1851.   Pension for wounds, 1825.   Greenwich Hospital pension, 1866.   Medal and two clasps.   Died in 1869.

(5) Lieut. A. B. Pidgley was promoted to Lieut. in 1804. Lieut. in the *Defiance* at Trafalgar, 1805.   Not in Navy List after 1821.

(6) Commander H. J. S. Hargrave was the son of F. Hargrave, K.C. Was promoted to Lieut., 1804. Lieut. in the *Defiance* in Calder's action, and at Trafalgar, 1805. Commander, 1812. Died at Cork, when in command of the *Teazer*, the 18th March 1814.

(7) Mr. J. Osman was appointed Master, R.N., 1795. Master of the *Defiance* at Trafalgar, 1805. Afterwards Master-Superintendent of Portsmouth Dockyard. Died in 1832.

(8) Commander J. Spratt was the son of James Spratt, of Ballybeg, Co. Cork. Born at Harrel's Cross, Co. Dublin, in 1771. Volunteer 1st Class, 1796. Mid., 1797. Mid. in the *Bellona* at battle of Copenhagen, 1801. Master's Mate in the *Defiance* in Calder's action, 1805, and at Trafalgar, 1805. Distinguished himself in boarding the French 74-gun ship *Aigle*, to which he had to swim—wounded; promoted Lieut. Awarded a pension for wounds of £91, 5s.; and received a gratuity from Patriotic Fund. Inventor of the Homograph, the predecessor of the Semaphore. Retired Commander, 1838. Medal with two clasps. Died, in Teignmouth, the 15th June 1852. Was father of Vice-Admiral T. A. B. Spratt, C.B., F.R.S., who died in 1887.

(9) Lieut. W. Snowey was born in Inveraray, N.B. Served as Master's Mate in the *Defiance* at Trafalgar, 1805. Lieut., 1814. Died in 1837.

(10) Rear-Admiral C. Campbell, of Ardpatrick, Argyllshire, was fifth son of Walter Campbell, of Shawfield and Woodhall, Lanarkshire, and Islay, Argyllshire, by Eleanor, daughter of Robert Kerr, of Newfield, grandson of first Marquis of Lothian. Born at Woodhall, 1787. Entered service, 1799. Master's Mate of *Defiance* in Calder's action, and at Trafalgar, 1805—promoted Lieut., 1806. Commanded the sloop *Port d'Espagne* at capture of Martinique, 1809—promoted to Commander. Captain, 1812. Retired Rear-Admiral, 1846. Medal and two clasps. Died at Park Cottage, near Uxbridge, the 3rd March 1850.

(11) Lieut. L. Grant was born in Edinburgh. Served as Mid. in the *Defiance* at Trafalgar, 1805. Lieut., 1811. Died in 1822–23.

(12) Lieut. E. A. Chapman was born in Margate. Served

as Mid. in the *Defiance* at Trafalgar, 1805—wounded. Lieut., 1810. Died, 1811.

(13) Lieut. P. Hannay was the eldest son of George Hannay, of Kingsmuir, Fife, N.B., by Mary, daughter of John Hambly. Born at Kingsmuir, 1788. Mid., 1805. Mid. in the *Defiance* at Trafalgar, 1805. Lieut., 1815. Died, 1819.

(14) Commander H. Rich was the son of Robert Rich, of Orchardley Park, Somersetshire, and was born in 1787. Entered service, 1801. Mid. in the *Diligence* in Nelson's attack on Boulogne flotilla; and in the *Defiance* in Calder's action, and at Trafalgar, 1805. Lieut., 1808. Served in the *St. Alban's* and *Druid* at defence of Cadiz, 1810–11; and in *Druid* at defence of Tarifa, 1812. Retired Commander, 1846. War medal and clasp. Died in 1864.

(15) Rear-Admiral J. Hay, D.L., J.P., of Belton, East Lothian, was the son of James Hay, of Belton, and great-grandson of John, first Marquis of Tweeddale. Entered the service, 1799. Mid. in the *Defiance* in Calder's action and at Trafalgar, 1805—promoted Master's Mate. Lieut., 1806. Lieut. in *Amaranthe*, and commanded the boats of a small squadron at the boarding and capture of the French brig *Le Cigne* off Martinique, 1808; also present at capture of Martinique, 1809. Wrecked in the *Glommen*, sloop, in Carlisle Bay, Barbados, 1809. Commander, 1810. Captain, 1819. Retired, 1846. Retired Rear-Admiral, 1851. War medal and two clasps. Died, 1857, at Belton.

(16) Lieut. J. Rudall was a son of the Rev. J. Rudall, chaplain of the *Royal Sovereign* at Trafalgar, and brother to Mid. William Rudall, and Purser James Rudall, both of whom were also at Trafalgar. He was born in Crediton, Devonshire, in 1783. Served as Mid. in the *Defiance* at Trafalgar, 1805. Lieut., 1806. When Lieut. in the *Armada* was drowned off Brest on the 26th November 1809, in a gallant effort to save the life of a marine when boarding the French privateer *Glaveuse*.

(17) Vice-Admiral J. Drake was the son of Rev. William Drake, Vicar of Oadby, Leicestershire, and was born at Stoke Godlington in 1788. He entered the service in 1804. Mid. in the *Defiance* in Calder's action; at Trafalgar, 1805; and at the

destruction of three French frigates off Sables d'Olonne, 1809. Commanded a boat at recapture of *Elison*, timber ship, by cutting her out from Palais Harbour, Belleisle, 1809. Lieut., 1811. Lieut. in the *Northumberland* at the destruction of two French frigates and a brig off L'Orient, 1812. Senior Lieut. of the *Albion* at the battle of Navarino, the 20th October 1827—promoted Commander. Captain, 1835. Good Service Pension, 1851. Retired, 1851. Retired Rear-Admiral, 1857. Retired Vice-Admiral, 1863. War medal and three clasps. Died in Bath, 1864.

(18) Lieut. R. Maltman was born in Scotland, and entered the service in 1805. Mid., 1805. Mid. in the *Defiance* at Trafalgar, 1805. Lieut., 1814. Died, 1823.

(19) Commander T. Chrystie was born in Fifeshire, N.B., in 1787. Entered the service, 1800. Served in the *Ajax* in 1800–2, including expedition to Belleisle, Ferrol, Cadiz, and in the operations on the coast of Egypt in 1801. Mid. in the *Defiance* in Calder's action and at Trafalgar, 1805. Served in the *Neptune* and on shore at reduction of Martinique, 1809—promoted Lieut. When in *Cæsar*, with a party of seamen assisted at defence of lines of Torres Vedras, 1810. Commanded the boats of the *Sceptre* at the capture of a fort in Quiberon Bay, 1812. Served during the American War in 1814–15, and accompanied expedition against New Orleans. Retired Commander, 1847. War medal and three clasps. Died in 1867–68.

(20) Admiral S. Smyth was born in Portsmouth, 1791. Entered service as Mid. in 1803. Mid. in the *Defiance* in Calder's action, and at Trafalgar, 1805; at destruction of three French frigates under the batteries of Sables d'Olonne, 1809; and in co-operation with patriots on north coast of Spain, 1810. Served in the *Northumberland* at capture of two French privateers in 1810; and at the destruction of the 40-gun frigates *L'Arenne*, and *L'Andromaque*, and the 16-gun brig *Mamelouk*, 1812—promoted Lieut. in *Venerable* at the capture of *Le Jason*, letter of marque, and the frigates *Iphigénie* and *Alcmène*, 1814; and commanded ship's boats in the operations against Martinique and Guadeloupe, 1815. Lieut. in the *Dartmouth* at battle of

Navarino, 1827—wounded; promoted Commander. Captain, 1851. Harbour Master, Great Yarmouth, 1855–70. Retired Rear-Admiral, 1870. Retired Vice-Admiral, 1873. Retired Admiral, 1878. War medal and four clasps. Died, 1879, at Southtown, Great Yarmouth.

(21) Mr. J. Dott was born in Fifeshire, N.B. He served in the *Defiance* at Trafalgar, 1805—promoted Mid. Not traced further.

(22) Mr. R. Brown was born in Fifeshire, N.B. He served in the *Defiance* at Trafalgar, 1805—promoted Mid. Not traced further.

(23) Commander J. Parsons was born in Portsmouth in 1791. Entered the service, 1803. Served in the *Defiance* in Sir R. Calder's action, and at Trafalgar, 1805—promoted Mid. As Mid. in the *Podargus* witnessed the surrender of the Russian squadron in the ,Tagus, 1808; and assisted in the embarkation of the French army after Vimiero. Taken prisoner, 1809; escaped, 1813. Master's Mate in the *Wolverine*, and served in her launch at the attack on Baltimore, 1814. Lieut., 1815. Commander, Reserved, half-pay, 1854. War medal and clasp. Died in 1864.

(24) Commander A. T. Hickes entered the service in 1804. Served in the *Defiance* in Calder's action, and at Trafalgar, 1805; at the destruction of three French frigates under the batteries of Sables d'Olonne, 1809; and in co-operation with patriots on north coast of Spain, 1810. Lieut., 1811. Retired Commander, 1851. War medal and clasp. Died in 1857, at Berkeley, Gloucestershire.

(25) Sir W. Burnett, Kt., K.C.B., K.C.H., F.R.S., M.D., Director-General of the Medical Department of the Navy, was the son of William Burnett, of Montrose, N.B., was born in Montrose in 1779, and entered the service in 1796. Served as Assistant-Surgeon in the *Goliath* in the battle of St. Vincent, 1797; at the bombardment of Cadiz, 1797; and in the battle of the Nile, 1798. Surgeon, 1799. Surgeon of the *Athenian* in the expedition to Egypt, 1801; and of the *Blanche* at the capture of Cape François, 1803, and in the operations at Curaçoa, 1804.

Surgeon of the *Defiance* in Sir Robert Calder's action, and at Trafalgar, 1805. Physician, R.N., 1810. Inspector of Hospitals in the Mediterranean, 1810–13, and to the prisoners of war at Chatham during a dangerous epidemic of fever in 1814. M.D., Aberdeen University; L.R.C.P., 1825. Knighted and created K.C.H., 1831. C.B., 1832. Director-General of the Medical Department of the Navy, 1833. Physician in Ordinary to George IV, 1835. F.R.C.P., 1836. In 1841 the Naval Medical Service presented him with his portrait in oils, and with a service of plate. Was the author of several scientific publications. Medal and four clasps. Died in Chichester, Sussex, 1861.

(26) Captain B. Alves became 2nd Lieut., R.M., 1795. First Lieut., 1796. Captain, 1805. Served in the *Defiance* at Trafalgar, 1805. Retired, half-pay, 1807.

(27) Lieut. G. J. Bristow became 2nd Lieut., R.M., 1803. First Lieut., 1805. Served in the *Defiance* at Trafalgar, 1805. Captain, 1826. Died in 1828.

XIV

H.M.S. *MINOTAUR*, 74 GUNS

Captain . . .	Charles John Moore Mansfield (1).
Lieutenants .	James Stuart (2).
	Alexander McVicar (3).
	Nicholas Bell (4).
	Jeremiah Morgan (5).
	Charles Giddy (6).
	Roderick McLeod (acting) (7).
Master . . .	Robert Duncan (8).
Master's Mates	James William Eagle (9).
	Stephen Hilton (10).
Midshipmen .	John Parry.
	John Robertson.
	George Hancock.
	William Rawlins (11).
	William Martin (12).
	Christopher West (13).
	Charles Wolrige (14).
	John Samuel Smith (15). *Wounded*.
	William Woolcock.
	Charles B. Douce (16).
	Edward Simmons (17).
	John Waterman (18).
	William Pye (19).
Volunteers 1st {	John Hewey.
Class . . . {	John Finemore (20).
Surgeon . . .	Robert Crichton (21).
Surgeon's Mate	Thomas B. Anderson.
Purser . . .	George Jackson.

Gunner . . . Francis Graham.

Boatswain . . James Robinson. *Wounded*.

Carpenter . . Christopher Peake.

Captain, Royal }
  Marines . . } Paul Hunt (22).

2nd Lieuts.,   { Nathaniel Batt Grigg (23).
  Royal Marines { Thomas Reeves (24).

The *Minotaur* was built at Woolwich in 1793. Her dimensions are given as: length on the lower deck, 172 feet; breadth, 48 feet; depth, 19 feet; and tons burthen, 1721. She was commissioned in 1794 by Captain Thomas Louis, one of Nelson's band of brothers, and under him she joined the fleet in the Mediterranean, bearing the flag of Vice-Admiral MacBride; later on serving with Rear-Admiral George Montagu's force. In 1797 her crew were unfortunately implicated in the mutiny of the fleet at Spithead. She bore a distinguished part in the battle of the Nile, the 1st August 1798, in which she was sixth in the line, and the biggest ship engaged. She went into the bay immediately astern of the *Vanguard*, and was enabled to be of great assistance to the Commander-in-Chief. The *Vanguard* suffered greatly, as she was exposed to a destructive raking fire from the *Aquilon*, while she was engaged with the *Spartiate*. The *Minotaur*, however, went ahead and brought all her broadside guns to bear on the *Aquilon*, and when later that ship was attacked on the inner side by the *Theseus*, she was speedily dismasted and forced to surrender. The fierceness of the fight waged by the *Minotaur* is shown by the figures of her killed and wounded, which were twenty-three and sixty-four respectively. The timely assistance lent by Captain Louis was not allowed to pass unnoticed by Nelson. Despite the agony of a wound that he believed mortal, the Admiral sent for the captain, and in thanking him said :

" Your support has prevented me from being obliged to haul out of the line." Another exploit of Captain Louis in the *Minotaur* was the trip up the Tiber. In September 1799, shortly after Civita Vecchia had surrendered to Troubridge, Rome fell to the Neapolitan troops under Bouchard, with whom a detachment of the *Minotaur's* seamen was serving. On receipt of the news Captain Louis ordered his barge out, and rowed by his own men, went up the Tiber to the capital, where he hoisted the British flag.

In 1800 she bore the flag of Lord Keith for a short time; was at the siege and capture of Genoa, her cutter's crew distinguishing themselves in the cutting out of the *Prima* galley. On the 3rd September 1800 her boats assisted in the cutting out from Barcelona of the Spanish corvettes *Esmeralda*, 22, and *Paz*, 22. In 1801, under Captain Louis, she participated in the combined operations in Egypt. On the 20th May 1803, while cruising in the Channel under Captain C. J. Moore Mansfield, in conjunction with the *Albion* and *Thunderer*, she chased and captured the French 40-gun frigate *Franchise*, which she took to England.

Of the work of the *Minotaur* in the battle of Trafalgar there is not very much to be said. In company with the *Spartiate* in the weather division, she forced the Spanish *Neptune* to surrender, losing in the encounter three men killed and twenty-two wounded. Her only damage consisted in her spars being wounded. In 1807 she took part in the expedition to Copenhagen, bearing the flag of Rear-Admiral William Essington, third in command. In 1809 she was cruising off Finland under Captain John Barrett : in the evening of the 25th July her boats took part in the hard fight with, and capture of, four Russian gunboats and a brig in the harbour of Frederickshamn, near Aspo roads.

Her last service was in 1810, when, in company with the *Plantagenet* and *Loire,* she was ordered to convoy sixty sail of ships from the Baltic to Yarmouth. In a very severe storm she got separated from the others, and on the night of the 22nd December was unfortunately wrecked and lost on the Haak Sands at the mouth of the Texel. Of her ship's company three hundred and seventy lives were lost, including Captain Barrett. A picture of the wreck was painted by Mr. J. M. W. Turner, R.A., and what is believed to have been her figure-head is preserved in Sheerness Dockyard. In connection with the disaster a curious legend has arisen. A tame wolf that had become a ship's pet was on board at the time, and when the vessel went to pieces the wolf and one of the lieutenants got on to the mast together. At times they were washed off, but by each other's assistance regained their hold : exhausted by exertion and benumbed with cold, however, they sank together when within a very little distance of the shore.

(1) Captain C. J. M. Mansfield was promoted to Lieut. in 1778, Commander in 1793, and Captain in 1794. In 1796-97 he commanded the *Andromache,* 32, in the Mediterranean. On 31st January 1797, an Algerine corsair of twenty-four guns mistook her for a Portuguese frigate, and found that she had caught a Tartar. The Algerine lost sixty-four killed and forty wounded, to the *Andromache's* two killed and four wounded, and struck her colours. In command of the *Minotaur,* 74, and in conjunction with the *Thunderer,* he captured the French 40-gun frigate *Franchise* in the Channel on the 28th May 1803. He commanded the *Minotaur* in the weather column at Trafalgar, 1805 (gold medal, thanks of Parliament, and sword of honour from the Patriotic Fund) ; and in the expedition to Copenhagen in 1807, bearing the flag of Rear-Admiral William Essington, third in command. He died in May 1813.

(2) Captain J. Stuart was promoted to Lieut. in 1797. Served

as 1st Lieut. of the *Minotaur* at Trafalgar, 1805—promoted Commander. Captain, 1813. Died in 1838.

(3) Captain A. McVicar was promoted to Lieut. in 1798. Served as Lieut. in the *Minotaur* at Trafalgar, 1805. Commander, 1807. Captain, 1817. Died in May 1840.

(4) Lieut. N. Bell was promoted to Lieut. in 1799. Served as Lieut. in the *Minotaur* at Trafalgar, 1805. Died in 1827.

(5) Lieut. J. Morgan was promoted to Lieut. in 1800. Served as Lieut. in the *Minotaur* at Trafalgar, 1805. Died in 1817.

(6) Commander C. Giddy was promoted to Lieut. in 1800. Served as Lieut. in the *Minotaur* at Trafalgar, 1805. Commander, 1814. Died in Cheltenham in September 1839.

(7) Lieut. R. Macleod was promoted from the Lower Deck. He served as Acting-Lieut. in the *Minotaur* at Trafalgar, 1805. Lieut., 1806. Served in her in expedition to Copenhagen, 1807. Died at Greenock, 1810.

(8) Mr. R. Duncan was appointed Master, R.N., 1795. Served as Master of the *Minotaur* at Trafalgar, 1805. Master of the *Téméraire* with Sir E. Pellew's fleet in the Mediterranean, including the action with the French battery at Pointe des Mèdes, 1811—severely wounded. Afterwards Master of the yacht *Royal Charlotte*. Died in 1830.

(9) Lieut. J. W. Eagle served as Master's Mate in the *Minotaur* at Trafalgar, 1805—promoted Lieutenant. Died in 1822.

(10) Commander S. Hilton was born in Kent in 1785. Entered the service in 1795 as Volunteer 3rd Class. Mid., 1799. Mid. in the *Pearl* in various cutting-out affairs near Toulon, and in the operations on the coast of Egypt, 1801. Master's Mate, 1805. Master's Mate in the *Minotaur* at Trafalgar, 1805—promoted Lieut., 1806. Lieut. in *Revenge* at the capture of four French frigates off Rochefort, 1806; at the destruction, under Lord Gambier, of shipping in the Basque Roads, 1809; and at the bombardment of Flushing, 1809—wounded. Retired Commander, 1839. Naval pension, 1846. Medal and two clasps. Died in 1872.

(11) Commander W. Rawlins was born at Stratford-on-Avon. Served as Mid. in the *Minotaur* at Trafalgar, 1805. Lieut., 1807. Lieut. in the *Topaze* and served in her boats at capture of eleven

armed vessels in the Bay of Rosas, 1809. Commander, 1814. Died in 1818.

(12) Commander W. Martin was the son of Thomas Martin, J.P., of Springmount, Co. Cork, and was born at Glanmire, Co. Cork, in 1783. Entered the service as Volunteer 1st Class, 1799. Present in the *Hercule* at capture of the privateer *Le Premier Consul*, 1802. Served in the *Minotaur* at the capture of the French 48-gun frigate *Franchise*, 1803, and at Trafalgar, 1805. Lieut., 1806. Lieut. in the *Lion*, and commanded her launch in action with five piratical boats—wounded. Lieut. in *Aboukir* at blockade of Flushing, 1810. Commander, 1821. Retired Commander, 1856. Medal and clasp. Died in 1866.

(13) Captain C. West was born in 1788, and entered the service in 1800 as Volunteer 1st Class. Mid. in the *Thetis* in operations on the coast of Egypt, 1801. Mid. in the *Minotaur* at the capture of the French 40-gun frigate *Franchise*, 1803; at Trafalgar, 1805; and the expedition to Copenhagen, 1807. Sub-Lieut., 1807. Lieut., 1808. Lieut. in the *Blake* at the blockade of Flushing, 1810, and the defence of Tarragona, 1811. Commander, 1814. Retired Commander, 1851. Medal and clasp. Died at Teddington, Middlesex, 12 August 1854, aged 66.

(14) Commander C. Wolrige, one of four brothers in the Royal Navy and Royal Marines, was born in Plymouth, and entered the service as Volunteer 1st Class in 1799. Mid., 1803. Mid. in the *Minotaur* at blockade of Cadiz; at the battle of Trafalgar, 1805; and in the expedition to Copenhagen, 1807. Lieut., 1808. Served in the boats of the *Quebec* at the capture of three Danish gun-brigs in the river Jahde, 1811. Retired Commander, 1857. Medal and two clasps. Died in 1874.

(15) Lieut. J. S. Smith was son of Captain John Samuel Smith, R.N. Served as Mid. in the *Minotaur* at Trafalgar, 1805 —wounded. Lieut., 1813. Died in 1840.

(16) Lieut. C. B. Douce was born in Maling, Kent. Mid., 1805. Mid. in the *Minotaur* at Trafalgar, 1805. Lieut., 1809. Not in Navy List after 1812.

(17) Lieut. E. Simmons was born at Gillingham, Kent, in 1790. Entered service as Volunteer 1st Class, 1803. Mid. in

K

the *Minotaur* at Trafalgar, 1805; and in the expedition to
Copenhagen, 1807. Was wrecked in *Neptunos*, 1807, and in the
Astræa, 1808. Served in the *Ethalion* at capture of Martinique,
1809; and commanded a gunboat during operations in the
Scheldt. Lieut., 1811. Lieut. in the *Galatea* in the action off
Tamatave with French frigates, and the capture of the *Renomenée*
and *Néréide*, 1811. Medal and three clasps. Died in 1849.

(18) Commander J. Waterman was born in Ashford, Kent,
and entered the service as Volunteer 1st Class, 1803. Mid.,
1805. Mid. in the *Minotaur* at Trafalgar, 1805, and in the
expedition to Copenhagen, 1807. Lieut., 1809. Retired
Commander, 1848. Medal and clasp. Died in Wellesborough
in 1859.

(19) Commander W. Pye served as Mid. in the *Minotaur* at
Trafalgar, 1805. Lieut., 1810. Commander, 1851. Medal and
clasp. Died in 1876.

(20) Mr. J. Finemore was born in Plymouth in 1792. Served
as Volunteer 1st Class in the *Minotaur* at Trafalgar, 1805.

(21) Surgeon R. Crichton was appointed Surgeon, R.N.,
1796. Surgeon of the *Minotaur* at Trafalgar, 1805. Retired,
1820. Died in 1827.

(22) Major P. Hunt was appointed 2nd Lieut., R.M., 1780.
1st Lieut., 1793. Captain, 1797. Served in the *Minotaur* at
Trafalgar, 1805. Brevet Major, 1810. Retired, half-pay, 1813.
Died in 1818.

(23) Lieut. N. B. Grigg was appointed 2nd Lieut., R.M.,
1803. Served in the *Minotaur* at Trafalgar, 1805. First Lieut.,
1805. First Lieut., R.M. Artillery, 1817. Died in 1823.

(24) Lieut. T. Reeves was appointed 2nd Lieut., R.M., 1804.
Served in the *Minotaur* at Trafalgar, 1805. First Lieut., 1808.
Retired, half-pay, 1817. Died in 1845.

XV

H.M.S. *CONQUEROR*, 74 GUNS

Captain . . . Israel Pellew (1).
Lieutenants. . James Couch (2).
Richard Spear (3).
Humphrey Fleming Senhouse (4).
Gamaliel FitzMaurice (5).
William Molyneux St. George (6). *Killed.*
Robert Lloyd (7). *Killed.*
Midshipmen . Hamilton Davies (8).
Henry Taylor.
Robert Webber.
Thomas Story.
Thomas Helpman (9).
Richard Daniel.
John Pomeroy Peter.
Joseph Williams.
Charles Jolley (10).
Charles Harvey Norrington (11).
Edward Harding.
Edward Riou Owen Farquharson (12).
William Hicks (13). *Wounded.*
John Potts (14).
John Ellery.
      * *Thomas Leigh* (15).
Volunteers 1st   *Philip Mendel* (supernumerary), Russian.
  Class   *Wounded.*
Richard Hay (16).

* Rated as Ordinary.

Volunteers 1st Cl. John William Smith (17).
(*continued*)   Nathaniel Phibbs.
             Harry Brown Richards (18).
             Thomas Burke.
             Edward Connor.
             John Nicholson.
         * *William John Hawes* (19).

Master . . .	Joseph Seymour (20).
Master's Mates	Samuel Marshall.
	William Harrison.
	William Pringle Green (21).
Surgeon . . .	William Standbridge (22).
Assistant - Surgeon . . . }	Gabriel Bielle (23).
Surgeon's Mate	William Turner (24).
Purser . . .	Francis Beaty (25).
Clerk	James Brisben (26).
Gunner . . .	John Pearson.
Boatswain . .	Joshua Capie.
Carpenter . .	James McFarlane.
Captain, Royal Marines . . }	James Atcherley (27).
2nd Lieuts., Royal Marines {	John Nicholas Fischer (28).
	Thomas Wearing (29). *Wounded*.

The *Conqueror* was built at Graham's Yard, Harwich, in 1800, and was first commissioned in 1803 by Captain Sir Thomas Louis, Bart. On the 23rd April 1804, Captain Israel Pellew was appointed to her, and she was employed on Channel service till she sailed to join Lord Nelson in the Mediterranean, in the following year, and shared in the animating pursuit of the French fleet under Villeneuve to the West Indies and back. At Trafalgar she was the fourth ship in the weather column, following immediately after the *Victory*, *Téméraire*, and *Neptune*, and completing in part the work which they had well

* Rated as Ordinary.

begun. She engaged the French flagship *Buccntaurc* and the Spanish four-decker *Santissima Trinidada*. She shot away the former's main and mizen-masts by the board, her fore-mast in a few minutes sharing the same fate; when, after a loss of over four hundred killed and wounded, a white handkerchief was waved from her in token of submission, and Captain Atcherley, Royal Marines, and a party from the *Conqueror* was sent on board. There they received the swords of the French Commander-in-Chief, Villeneuve, and the senior military officer, General Contamin. The *Conqueror*, with the *Neptune*, then turned her attention to the *Santissima Trinidad*, whose main, mizen, and fore-masts were soon shot away, and she also struck to the two Britishers, which were immediately borne down upon by five of the enemy's ships until other British ships came to the assistance. While the remainder of the combined fleet were making their escape to Cadiz, the *Conqueror* hauled across the course of one of them which had only her foresail set. Her brave captain stood upon the poop holding the lower corner of a small French jack while he pinned the upper corner with his sword to the stump of the mizen-mast. She fired two or three guns, probably to provoke a return and so perhaps spare the discredit of a tame surrender. The *Conqueror's* broadside was ready, but Captain Pellew, unwilling to injure the brave French officer, fired a single shot across her bow. The captain lowered the flag, took off his hat, and bowed his surrender. The *Conqueror's* losses in the battle amounted to twelve killed and wounded, including four officers. She had her mizen topmast and main top-gallant mast shot away. Her fore and main-masts were badly wounded, and her rigging of every sort much cut, while several shot had struck her on the larboard side between wind and water. One of the enemy's shot also cut away the head of the figure at the ship's bow, and the crew, through the first lieutenant, asked permission to have it replaced by one of Lord Nelson. The request was granted, and when the *Conqueror* arrived at Plymouth after towing the *Africa* to Gibraltar, a figure of the hero, remarkable for the correct likeness and superior workmanship, and which the crew ornamented at their own expense, was placed at her bow.

In 1806 the *Conqueror* was with Sir Samuel Hood's squadron cruising off Rochefort. On the 16th July her boats, with those of other ships, assisted in the cutting out of the 16-gun French brig *César*, in the Gironde. In November 1807, still commanded by Captain Pellew, she was sent to the Tagus with the squadron of Rear-Admiral Sir William Sidney Smith to protect British interests, and to save the Royal Family of Portugal from the power of Napoleon. She afterwards formed part of the squadron blockading the Russian fleet in the Tagus until August 1808, when she returned home and was paid off. In 1810, under Captain Edward Fellowes, she was in the Mediterranean. We hear of her again in 1812, when, in conjunction with the *Sultan*, she was engaged with two French frigates entering Toulon. She was commissioned at Sheerness under Captain John Davie, in 1816, for service at Saint Helena guarding Napoleon, and she continued there till 1820, the last two years under the command of Captain Francis Stanfell. She then returned home, was paid off at Chatham, and broken up there in 1821.

(1) Admiral Sir I. Pellew, K.C.B., was the third son of Samuel Humphry Pellew, commander of a Dover Packet, by his marriage with Constance, daughter of Edward Langford; he was younger brother of Admiral Sir Edward Pellew, first Viscount Exmouth. Born in 1758, he entered the service in 1771. Served during the war of American Independence, 1778–79, and was in

the *Flora* when she was sunk off Rhode Island to prevent her capture by the enemy, 1778. Promoted to Lieut., 1779. Commanded the armed cutter *Resolution* when she captured the dangerous Dutch privateer *Flushinger*, 1783. Promoted to Commander, 1790. Served in the *Nymphe*, commanded by his brother, at the capture of the French frigate *Cléopatre*, the 18th June 1793—promoted Captain. Was in command of the *Amphion* when she was accidentally blown up at Plymouth, 1796. Was Captain of the *Greyhound* during the Mutiny of the Nore in 1797, and the crew of the ship put him on shore. Appointed Captain of the *Conqueror*, 74, in 1804, and was present in the pursuit of the French fleet to the West Indies and back, and in the battle of Trafalgar, 1805, when the French flagship *Bucentaure* and another struck to the *Conqueror*, which, with the *Neptune*, also accounted for the Spanish *Santissima Trinidada*—received a gold medal, the thanks of Parliament, and a sword of honour from the Patriotic Fund. Commanded the *Conqueror* till 1808, with Sir Samuel Hood's squadron off Rochefort, and protecting British interests in the Tagus. Became Rear-Admiral in 1810. Captain of the Mediterranean Fleet under Lord Exmouth, in 1811–15. Created a K.C.B., 1815. Vice-Admiral, 1819. Admiral, 1830. Died in Plymouth in 1832.

(2) Captain J. Couch entered the service as Officer's Servant, 1789. Lieut., 1800. Served in the *Woolwich*, store ship, during the operations on the coast of Egypt, 1801. First Lieut. of the *Conqueror* in the pursuit of the French fleet to the West Indies and back, and at Trafalgar, 1805. Served in the *Acasta* at the capture of the *Herald*, letter-of-marque, 1812—wounded. Commander, 1817. Captain, 1824. Retired, 1846. Greenwich Hospital pension, 1846. Medal and clasp. Died in 1850. His son, Lieut. Edward Couch, R.N., Mate of the *Erebus*, was lost in the Arctic regions with Sir John Franklin.

(3) Captain R. Spear was promoted to Lieut., 1800. Served as Lieut. in the *Conqueror* at Trafalgar, 1805. With a party took possession of the French 80-gun ship *Bucentaure*, which being wrecked on the Puerques, he and his party fell into the hands of the enemy—promoted Commander. Commanded the *Chanticleer*,

brig, in action with a Danish squadron, 1811. Captain, 1813. Died in 1825.

(4) Captain Sir H. F. Senhouse, Kt., K.C.H., C.B., was son of Lieut. William Senhouse, R.N., Surveyor-General of Barbados and the Leeward Islands, who died in 1810, by Elizabeth, daughter of Samson Wood, Speaker of the House of Assembly, Barbados ; and grandson of Humphry Senhouse, of Netherhall, Cumberland, by Mary, daughter and ultimately co-heir of Sir George Fleming, 2nd Bart., of Rydal, Bishop of Carlisle.   He had three brothers in the Royal Navy.   Served as Mid. at capture of Surinam, 1799, and was sent home with despatches.   Lieut. of *Conqueror* at Trafalgar, 1805.   Performed distinguished service at the capture of Martinique, 1809—promoted Commander.   Commanded *Martin*, sloop, in 1813-14, including the action with American flotilla of gunboats and block vessels, 1813 ; the capture of the *Snap Dragon*, privateer ; and was sent home with despatches from Sir Alex. Cochrane, announcing the successful result of the expedition against Castine, in the province of Maine.   Captain, 1814. Created a K.C.H., 1832.   Knighted, 1834.   Captain of the *Blenheim* in the first China War, 1839-41—medal, and created a C.B.   Died in 1841, on board the *Blenheim* in Hong-Kong Bay.

(5) Commander G. FitzMaurice was promoted to Lieut., 1802.   Served as Lieut. in the *Conqueror* at Trafalgar, 1805. Commanded a boat of the *Conqueror* at capture of the French brig *César*, in the Gironde, 1806.   Commander, 1812.   Died in 1836.

(6) Lieut. W. M. St. George was the fifth son of Thomas St. George, M.P., of Wood Park, Co. Armagh, by the Hon. Lucinda Acheson, fourth daughter of the first Viscount Gosford.   Born in Dublin in 1784.   Mid., 1804.   Lieut., 1804.   Third Lieut. of *Conqueror* at battle of Trafalgar, 1805, where he was killed by a cannon shot, aged 20.

(7) Lieut. R. Lloyd was promoted to Lieut., 1797.   Served as 1st Lieut. of the *Conqueror* in the pursuit of the French fleet to the West Indies and back, and at Trafalgar, 1805, when he was killed in action, his head being taken off by a cannon shot.

(8) Commander H. Davies was born at Liverpool, 1784, and

entered the service in 1795. Served in the *Virago* in the action with the Algeciras flotilla, 1798. Mid. in the *Conqueror* at Trafalgar, 1805. When in charge of a prize was taken prisoner by the French in 1808, and detained until 1814. Lieut., 1812. Retired Commander, 1855. Medal and clasp. Died in London in 1859.

(9) Mr. T. Helpman was born in Plymouth in 1784. Served as Mid. in the *Conqueror* at Trafalgar, 1805. Still in the *Conqueror*, he was killed in action at the attack on a convoy in the Gironde, when the French brig *César* was captured, the 16th July 1806.

(10) Lieut. C. Jolley was born in Plymouth. Served as Mid. in the *Conqueror* at Trafalgar, 1805. Lieut., 1806. Died in 1838.

(11) Lieut. C. H. Norrington was born in Exeter. Served as Mid. in the *Conqueror* at Trafalgar, 1805. Lieut., 1812. Died, when in command of the brig *Alert*, 1839.

(12) Lieut. E. R. O. Farquharson was born in Deptford, and entered service in 1803. Volunteer 1st Class, 1804. Mid., 1805. Served as Mid. in the *Conqueror* in the pursuit of the combined fleets to West Indies and back, and at Trafalgar, 1805. Witnessed the surrender of the Russian squadron in the Tagus, 1808. Lieut., 1810. Died in Haslar Hospital, 1846, aged 58.

(13) Rev. W. Hicks was born in St. Columb, Cornwall, in 1788. Served as Mid. in the *Conqueror* in the pursuit of the combined fleets to the West Indies and back, and as A.D.C. to Captain Israel Pellew at Trafalgar, 1805—wounded; also at the blockade of Brest and Rochefort, and at the cutting out of the French brig *César*, the 16th July 1806. As Mid. in the *Hydra*, was actively employed in boat service off Barcelona, and conveyed despatches to the leaders of the armed peasantry by swimming through the sea. Commanded the *Hydra's* yawl at the capture of an armed felucca off Toulon, 1809. Mate of *Spartan*, and in charge of a boat engaged a convoy in Quiberon Bay, 1811. Lieut., 1813. Commanded the *Finch*, 11, in the action on Lake Champlain, 1814. Left the Navy at the peace, and entered Magdalen College, Cambridge. In 1823 was ordained, and in 1830 was presented by the Duke of Rutland to the living of Sturmer,

Halstead, Essex, of which he was rector till his death. War medal and clasps. Died at Sturmer, 1874, aged 85.

(14) Lieut. J. Potts was born at Stoke, Devonport, and entered the service in 1800. Was wrecked in the *Assistance*, 1802. Mid., 1804. Served as Mid. in the *Conqueror* in pursuit of combined fleets to West Indies and back, and at Trafalgar, the 21st October 1805. Lieut., 1808. Died in 1847.

(15) Commander T. Leigh entered the service in 1803. Rated as Ordinary, but served as Mid. in the *Conqueror* in the pursuit of the combined fleets to the West Indies and back, and at Trafalgar, 1805. Master's Mate in the *Pilot* in the action with gunboats, and the capture and destruction of a number of transports at Amanthea, 1810—mentioned in despatches. Lieut., 1814. Served in Coastguard, 1827–35. Commander, 1835. Died in 1846.

(16) Mr. R. Hay was born in Checkland, Wilts, in 1789. Served as Volunteer 1st Class in the *Conqueror* at Trafalgar, 1805. Resigned same year.

(17) Lieut. J. W. Smith was born in Halifax, Nova Scotia, and entered the service in 1799. Was wrecked in the *Assistance*, 1802. Served in *Conqueror* in pursuit of combined fleets to West Indies and back, and at Trafalgar, 1805. Served in *Sceptre* and *Albion* in operations in the Chesapeake in 1813–14. Lieut., 1815. Medal and clasp. Died in 1860.

(18) Commander H. B. Richards was born in London in 1790. Volunteer 1st Class, 1805. Served in the *Conqueror* at Trafalgar, 1805. Lieut., 1812. Commander, 1834. Died in 1839.

(19) Mr. W. J. Hawes served as Captain's servant in the *Audacious* in Lord Howe's victory of 1st June 1794; and as Volunteer 1st Class in the battle of the Nile, 1798. Rated as Ordinary, but served as Volunteer 1st Class in the *Conqueror* at Trafalgar, 1805. Medal with three clasps.

(20) Commander J. Seymour was appointed Master, R.N., in 1796. Served as Master of the *Amphitrite* at the capture of Devil's Island, off Cayenne; of Surinam; and St Martin's; and of the Danish and Swedish islands; also of seven large privateers, and in command of her cutter captured a French

armed schooner lying near a privateer, and in the face of a heavy fire. He subsequently carried by boarding a Spanish armed schooner off Barbados. Master of the *Conqueror* at Trafalgar, 1805; of the Commander-in Chief's flagship at Corunna; of the *Barfleur*, flagship in the Tagus, 1809–12, and was one of the officers selected to fit for sea the Spanish line-of-battle ships in Ferrol. Master of the *Ramillies* during American War, 1813–1814. Retired Commander, 1846. Medal and two clasps. Died in 1862 at Bristol.

(21) Lieut. W. P. Green was born in Halifax, Nova Scotia, in 1785. Entered service as Volunteer 1st Class, 1796. In the *Tapaze* saw much active boat service in the West Indies in 1797–1801. Mid., 1804. Master's Mate, 1805. Served as Master's Mate in the *Conqueror* in the pursuit of the combined fleets to West Indies and back, and at Trafalgar, 1805, and was one of the party who took possession of the French flagship *Bucentaure*. Lieut., 1806. Died in 1846.

(22) Surgeon W. Standbridge was appointed Surgeon, R.N., in 1799. Served as Surgeon of the *Conqueror* at Trafalgar, 1805. Died in 1842.

(23) Surgeon G. Bielle served as Assistant-Surgeon in the *Conqueror* at Trafalgar, 1805. Surgeon, 1808. Died in Jamaica, when Surgeon of the sloop *Bann*, in 1819.

(24) Surgeon W. Turner served as Surgeon's Mate in the *Conqueror* at Trafalgar, 1805. In boats of *Conqueror* at the capture of the French brig *César*, 1806. Surgeon, 1807. Medal and two clasps. Died in 1859.

(25) Mr. F. Beaty was appointed Paymaster and Purser, 1781. Served as Purser of the *Conqueror* at Trafalgar, 1805. Died in Dorset Street, Portman Square, London, 1822.

(26) Mr. J. Brisben was born in Cawsand, Cornwall, in 1775. Appointed Clerk, 1804. Served as Clerk in the *Conqueror* at Trafalgar, 1805. Purser, 1806. Medal and clasp. Died in 1854.

(27) Captain J. Atcherley was appointed 2nd Lieut., R.M., 1794. First Lieut., 1795. In the *Hussar* was present and distinguished himself in her action with four French ships, and the capture of *La Raison* and *Prévoyante*, 1795. Captain-Lieut.,

1803. Captain, 1804. Senior officer of marines in the *Conqueror* at Trafalgar, 1805. Took possession of the French flagship *Bucentaure*, and received the swords of Admiral Villeneuve and General Contamin. Retired, half-pay, 1816. Died in 1834.

(28) Captain J. N. Fischer was appointed 2nd Lieut., R.M., 1803. First Lieut., 1805. Served in the *Conqueror* at Trafalgar, 1805. Senior Lieut. and Quartermaster at the defence of Anhalt by the Danes, 1811—promoted Brevet Captain. Retired, half-pay, 1814. Medal and two clasps. Died in 1858–59.

(29) Lieut.-General T. Wearing was appointed 2nd Lieut., R.M., in 1804. Served in the *Conqueror* at Trafalgar, 1805—wounded. First Lieut., 1807. Captain, 1827. Brevet Major, 1841. Lieut.-Colonel, 1846. Brevet Colonel, 1851. Commandant, Chatham Division, 1854. Major-General, 1855. Lieut.-General, 1857. Medal and clasp. Died in 1863.

Boulton's Medal—Obverse.

XVI

H.M.S. *ACHILLES*, 74 GUNS

Captain . . .   Richard King (1).

Lieutenants .   William Westcott Daniell (2).
Parkins Prynn (3). *Wounded.*
George Canning (4).
Josias Bray (5). *Wounded.*
William Hill (6).
Edward Barnard (acting) (7).

Master. . . .   Thomas Watson (8).

Master's Mates { George Pegge. *Wounded.*
John Man (9).

2nd Master . . William Woollard (acting) (10)

Midshipmen .   Digby Dent (11).
Arthur Short.
William Henry Staines. *Wounded.*
Louis Fazan.
William John Snow (12). *Wounded.*
Richard Douglas (13).
Samuel Priest.
Nicholas Pearce.
Francis John Mugg. *Killed.*
Samuel Hood Sulivan (14).
John Pengelley Parkin (15).
Lardner Dennys (16).
Joseph Collings Gill (17).
William Vicary (18).

Volunteers 1st
Class   Mark Grigg.
William Smith Warren (19). *Wounded.*
William John Thomson Hood (20).

Chaplain . . Rev. John Cobb Whicher (21).

Surgeon . . .   William Gray.
Assistant - Sur- ⎧ Chichester Wrey Bruton.
  geons . . . ⎩ David Gray.
Purser . . .   James Lamport.
Gunner . . .   Richard Hills.
Boatswain . .   Peter Johnson
Carpenter . .   John Wallis (acting).
Captain, Royal ⎫
  Marines . . ⎭ Palmes Westropp (22).   *Wounded.*
2nd Lieuts.,   ⎧ William Liddon (23).   *Wounded.*
Royal Marines ⎩ Francis Whalley (24).

The *Achilles*, frequently but incorrectly called the *Achille*, for she was never a French prize, but a British-built ship, was launched at Cleverley's Yard, Gravesend, early in 1798. In July 1798 she was commissioned by Captain H. E. Stanhope, who was succeeded in the following April by Captain G. Murray, under whom we find her in Lord Bridport's squadron off Rochefort. In the spring of 1805 Captain Richard King was appointed to her. She was with Lord Collingwood's little squadron watching Cadiz, and took part, under Captain King, in the battle of Trafalgar, the 21st October 1805. She was in the lee column and closely followed the *Colossus* into action; and, passing astern of the Spanish *Montañez*, luffed up and engaged that ship from leeward. When, in about twelve minutes, the *Montañez* sheered off, the *Achilles* headed for the *Belleisle*, which lay dismantled to leeward, seeming to be sorely pressed; but on her way she fell in with the Spanish *Argonauta*. Captain King brought to on the Spaniard's port beam, and fought her at close quarters for an hour. The *Argonauta* then endeavoured to make sail, but not being able to escape, shut her lower-deck ports, ceased firing, and, as was supposed, surrendered. Ere the *Achilles* could attempt to take possession of her, the French *Achille* passed her namesake and distracted her attention by firing into her ; and the French *Berwick*, which had already been distantly engaged with our *Defence*, interposed herself between the *Achilles* and her beaten opponent, the latter dropping to leeward and eventually surrendering. A hot action then began between the *Achilles* and the *Berwick;* the French ship, after more than an hour's fighting, hauled down her flag and was taken possession of by Captain King. The loss in the *Achilles* amounted to seventy-two killed and wounded, including nine officers. Her masts, though standing, were badly injured, and also her bowsprit and hull.

With Commodore Sir Samuel Hood's squadron, her boats assisted in the cutting out of the French corvette *César*, 16, at the entrance of the river Gironde, on the night of the 15th July 1806; and witnessed the capture off Rochefort, on the 24th September following, of the French 40-gun frigates *Armide, Minerve,* and *Gloire.* She was also in the expedition to Walcheren. and the blockade of Flushing in the same year, and in the blockade of Cadiz in 1810–11. When commanded by Captain Askew P. Hollis, her boats, in conjunction with those of the *Cerberus,* captured twelve sail of Trabbacolles off Venice, on the 17th July 1812 ; while in the same month, in conjunction with the *Milford,* she captured four other vessels. She remained in the service until the year 1865, when she was sold at Sheerness to Messrs. Castle & Sons, shipbreakers, for £3600.

(1) Vice-Admiral Sir Richard King, 2nd Bart., K.C.B., was the only son of Admiral Sir Richard King, Kt., M.P., and 1st Bart., by Susannah Margaretta, daughter of William Coker, of Maypowder, Co. Dorset. He was born the 28th November 1774, and entered the service in 1788. He was promoted to Lieut. in 1791, and to Captain in 1794. He was a member of the court-martial which tried Richard Parker, the ringleader in the Mutiny

of the Nore, in 1797. When Captain of the 36-gun frigate *Sirius* in 1797–1802, he captured the Dutch ships *Furie* of 36 guns and 153 men, and the *Waakzamheid* of 26 guns and 100 men, on the 24th October 1798 ; and in the same month made a prize of *La Favorie*, of 6 guns, off the coast of France, and a Spanish brig. Under him the *Sirius* did gallant service, in company with *L'Oiseau*, in capturing *La Dédaigneuse*, French frigate of 36 guns and 300 men, bound from Cayenne to Rochefort with despatches, on the 27th January 1801.

In the spring of 1805 he was appointed to the *Achilles*, of 74 guns, which he commanded in the battle of Trafalgar, 1805. In the lee column she did excellent service and lost heavily ; he was rewarded with the gold medal, received the thanks of Parliament, and a sword of honour from the Patriotic Fund. In 1806 he succeeded to the baronetcy. In 1808 he was employed in the blockade of Ferrol, and in 1810–11 at the blockade of Cadiz. He was Captain of the Fleet in the Mediterranean in 1811–12, when he obtained his promotion to Rear-Admiral ; after which, until the end of the war, he had his flag in the *San Josef*, of 110 guns, off Toulon. In 1815 he was nominated a K.C.B., and in the spring of 1816 was appointed Commander-in-Chief in the East Indies, which appointment he retained until 1820. He became Vice-Admiral in 1821 ; was Commander-in-Chief at the Nore in 1833–34 ; and died of cholera at Admiralty House, Sheerness in 1834. He was father of Admiral Sir George St. Vincent King, K.C.B., who died in 1891.

(2) Captain W. W. Daniell was promoted to Lieut. in 1798. Served as 1st Lieut. of the *Achilles* at Trafalgar, 1805—promoted Commander. Captain, 1813. Died in 1833.

(3) Commander P. Prynn entered the service in 1793. As Mid. served at the capture of a Dutch squadron at the Cape of Good Hope by Lord Keith in 1795. Lieut., 1800. Lieut. in the *Braakel* in the expedition to Egypt in 1801, and served on shore in the actions of the 13th and 21st March. Lieut. in the *Achilles* at Trafalgar, 1805—wounded. Retired Commander, 1830. Died at West Looe, 1838.

(4) Commander G. Canning served as Mid. in the *Tamar* at

Surinam in 1799, and at the capture of the French frigate *Republicaine*. Lieut., 1802. Was wrecked in the *Creole*, frigate, in 1804. Lieut. in the *Achilles* at Trafalgar, 1805. Lieut. in the *Brunswick* in the expedition to Copenhagen, 1807. Commander, 1814. Died in Gravesend in 1842.

(5) Commander J. Bray was promoted to Lieut. in 1800. Served as Lieut. in the *Achilles* at Trafalgar, 1805—wounded. Commanded the *Plumper*, brig, at the capture of three small American privateers in the Bay of Fundy, 1812; and was wrecked in her in Dipper Harbour, New Brunswick, the same year. Commanded the *Sprightly*, Revenue cruiser, which was wrecked at Blacknor, Isle of Portland, in 1821. Commander, 1825. Died in 1846.

(6) Captain W. Hill, a son of the Rev. John Hill, was born in Hennock, near Chudleigh, in 1783. Entered the service in 1795. Served as Mid. in the *Colossus* in Lord Bridport's action with the French fleet and capture of three sail of the line, 1795. Was wrecked in Diligence Bay, near Cuba, in 1800. Acting Lieut. in the *Rattler* in the West Indies in 1802-3—wounded. Lieut., 1803. Lieut. in the *Achilles* at Trafalgar, 1805. Senior Lieut. in the *Amethyst* at the capture of *La Thétis*, French frigate, 1808, and of *Le Meinen*, 1809—mentioned in despatches, promoted Commander. Captain, 1816. Died at Wood House, near Chudleigh, in 1840.

(7) Admiral E. Barnard entered the service in 1797. Served as Mid. in the *Sirius* at the capture of Dutch frigates *Furie* and *Waakzamheid*, 1798; and the capture of the *Dédaigneuse*, 1801. Acting Lieut. in the *Achilles* at the blockade of Cadiz, and at Trafalgar, 1805; took possession of French 74-gun ship *Berwick*. Lieut., 1806. Lieut. in the *Achilles* at the capture of four French frigates from Rochefort, 1806; expedition to Walcheren, including blockade of Flushing, 1809; and blockade of Cadiz, 1810. Present at the attack and destruction of shipping at Port St. Mary, 1810. Lieut. in the *San Josef* in the attacks on French fleet, 1813-14. Commander, 1814. Captain, 1817. Captain of the *Cambridge* in the operations on coast of Syria, 1840. Retired, 1846. Retired Rear-Admiral, 1851. Retired

L

Vice-Admiral, 1857. Retired Admiral, 1862. War medal and three clasps, and Turkish medal for Syria. Died at Hipswell Lodge, Richmond, Yorks, in 1863, aged 82.

(8) Mr. T. Watson was appointed Master, R.N., in 1781. Served as Master of the *Achilles* at Trafalgar, 1805. Afterwards Master-Superintendent, Portsmouth. Died in 1819.

(9) Lieut. J. Man was born in Falmouth. Promoted Master's Mate in 1805. Master's Mate in the *Achilles* at Trafalgar, 1805—promoted Lieut. Not in Navy List after 1811.

(10) Lieut. W. Woollard served as Acting 2nd Master in the *Achilles* at Trafalgar, 1805. Lieut., 1809. Not in Navy List after 1810.

(11) Captain D. Dent was son of Commander Digby Dent, R.N., who died in 1798, and grandson of Admiral Sir Digby Dent. Born in Plymouth, and entered the service in 1805. Mid. in the *Achilles* at Trafalgar, 1805; at the capture of four French frigates off Rochefort, 1806; expedition to Walcheren, and reduction of Flushing, 1809. Lieut., 1812. Lieut. of the *Minden* at the battle of Algiers, 1816. Commander, 1820. Retired Captain, 1856. War medal and two clasps. Died in 1861.

(12) Lieut. W. J. Snow was the son of Commander William Snow, R.N., and Sarah, daughter of Mr. Ewebank, Banker, of Hull. He was born in London in 1788. Served as Mid. in the *Achilles* at Trafalgar, 1805—wounded. Wrecked in a Danish prize, 1810. Master's Mate in the *Guerrière* in the action with the U.S. ship *Constitution*, 1812—severely wounded, mentioned in despatches. Lieut., 1815. Died at the Semaphore, Putney Heath, in 1827.

(13) Captain R. Douglas was born in Plymouth, and entered the service in 1799. Served in the *Achilles* at Trafalgar; and in action with four French frigates off Rochefort, 1806. Served in the *Neptune* at the reduction of Martinique, 1809. Lieut., 1809. Commander, 1823. Captain, 1851. Greenwich Hospital pension, 1856. Medal and two clasps. Died in 1866-67.

(14) Lieut. S. H. Sulivan was born in Plymouth. Served as Mid. in the *Achilles* at Trafalgar, 1805. Lieut., 1808. Died in 1836, in Stonehouse, Devonport.

(15) Captain J. P. Parkin entered the service as Volunteer 1st Class in 1805, and became Mid. a few months later. Served as Mid. in the *Achilles* at Trafalgar, 1805, at the blockade of Ferrol, and defence of Cadiz. Lieut., 1814. Commander, 1816. Second in command of the *Cambridge* in operations on coast of Syria, 1840. Captain, 1841. Medal with two clasps, and Turkish medal for Syria. Died in 1854.

(16) Commander L. Dennys was youngest son of Nicholas Dennys, of Ashley Park, near Tiverton, Devonshire, where he was born in 1791. Entered the service in 1805. Served as Mid. in the *Achilles* at Trafalgar, 1805; in Hood's capture of four French frigates off Rochefort, 1806; on shore in operations at Walcheren, 1809; and at the siege of Cadiz, 1810. Lieut., 1812. Lieut. of the *Horatia* at capture of Dutch islands of Shonwen and Tholen, 1813. Greenwich Hospital pension, 1852. Medal and clasp. Retired Commander, 1853. Died in London in 1864.

(17) Commander J. C. Gill was born at Plymouth Dock, and entered the service as Volunteer 1st Class in 1805. Served as Mid. in the *Achilles* at Trafalgar, 1805; at capture of four French frigates at Rochefort, 1806; in the expedition to Walcheren, 1809; and the defence of Cadiz, 1810–11. Lieut., 1812. Medal and clasp. Commander, 1842. Died in Devonport in 1858.

(18) Commander W. Vicary was born in Crediton in 1792; and entered service as Volunteer 1st Class in 1805. Served in the *Achilles* at Trafalgar, 1805; at the capture of four French frigates off Rochefort in 1806; in the Walcheren expedition, 1809; defence of Cadiz, 1810; and in a pinnace at the cutting out, in conjunction with the boats of the *Eagle*, of two merchant vessels on the coast of Istria, 1812. Lieut., 1815. Served in the Coastguard in 1828–48. Received gold medal of National Shipwreck Institution, and silver medal from Lloyd's for services at a wreck at Atherfield in 1843. Commander, half-pay, 1852. Medal and clasp. Died in 1882.

(19) Lieut. W. S. Warren was born in Plymouth Dock. Served as Volunteer 1st Class in the *Achilles* at Trafalgar, 1805— wounded. Lieut., 1815. Died in 1838.

(20) Captain W. J. T. Hood was born in 1794, and entered the service in 1805. Served as Volunteer 1st Class in the *Achilles* at Trafalgar, 1805. Served in the *Daphne* at the capture of Monte Video in 1807. Master's Mate in the *Malta* at the reduction of Gaeta, 1815. Commanded a Spanish gunboat co-operating with patriots on north coast of Spain. Lieut., 1815. Commander, 1828. Captain, 1843. Medal and two clasps. Died in 1857.

(21) The Rev. J. C. Whicher was appointed Chaplain, R.N., in 1797. Served as Chaplain of the *Achilles* at Trafalgar, 1805. Many years Rector of Stopham, Pulborough, Sussex, where he died in 1841.

(22) Lieut.-Colonel P. Westropp was the son of Palmes Westropp, of Cork, and Susanna, daughter of John Ross Lewin, of Fort Fergus, Co. Clare. Became 2nd Lieut., R.M., in 1780. First Lieut., 1793. Served in the *Orion* in Lord Howe's victory of the 1st June 1794. Captain, 1797. Senior officer of marines in the *Achilles* at Trafalgar, 1805—severely wounded, lost an arm. Brevet Major, 1809. Lieut.-Colonel, 1814. Had a pension for wounds. Died in Plymouth in 1826.

(23) Lieut. W. Liddon became 2nd Lieut., R.M., in 1804. Served in the *Achilles* at Trafalgar, 1805—wounded. First Lieut., 1808. Retired, half-pay, 1822. Died in 1831.

(24) Second Lieut. F. Whalley became 2nd Lieut., R.M., 1804. Served in the *Achilles* at Trafalgar, 1805. Resigned, 1806.

XVII

H.M.S. *COLOSSUS*, 74 GUNS

Captain . . . James Nicoll Morris (1). *Wounded.*

Lieutenants Thomas Richard Toker (2).
George Huish (3).
George Bulley (4). *Wounded.*
William Graves Nash (5).
George Bague (6). *Wounded.*
William Forster (acting) (7). *Died of Wounds.*
Mark Halpen Sweny (acting) (8). *Wounded.*

Master . . . Thomas Scriven (9) *Killed.*

Master's Mates Luke Anderson.
Silvester Barrell.
Henry Milbanke (10). *Wounded.*

Midshipmen . George D. Wilson.
Thomas Doughty.
Thomas Gwynne Rees (11). *Wounded.*
Henry Snellgrove (12). *Wounded.*
George Downing.
Henry Cook.
William Walpole (13).
William Carter.
William Allan Herringham (14). *Wounded.*
George Denton. *Wounded.*
William Carleton (15).
Rawdon McLean (16). *Wounded.*
Timothy Renou (17).
Richard Morgan.

Volunteers, 1st Class . . .	Frederick Thistlethwayte. *Wounded.*
	* *William Venus* (18).
Surgeon . . .	William McDonald (19).
Assistant-Surgeon . . .	Hugh Love.
Surgeon's Mate	James Dundas (20).
Purser . . .	Joseph Ault (21).
Clerk. . . .	Henry Ashton (22).
Gunner . . .	William Storar.
Boatswain . .	William Adamson (23). *Wounded.*
Carpenters . .	George Alderson.
	† *Thomas Goodricke* (24).
Captain, Royal Marines	Elias Lawrence (25).
2nd Lieuts., Royal Marines	William Laurie (26).
	John Benson (27). *Wounded.*

The *Colossus* was built in Deptford Dockyard in 1803, from the design of Sir John Henslow, Knight, Surveyor of the Navy, and was launched on the 23rd April 1803. In 1804 Captain James Nicoll Morris was appointed to her, and she served at the blockade of Brest in that and the following year, under Admiral Hon. William Cornwallis. We find her with Vice-Admiral Collingwood's little squadron watching Cadiz until September 1805, when she joined Lord Nelson. Under Captain Morris she was in the lee column at Trafalgar, on the 21st October 1805, her losses being more than those of any other ship in the fleet. She engaged the French 74, *Swiftsure*, and the Spanish 74, *Bahama*, which had been captured from the British on a previous occasion, both of which she obliged to surrender. Her losses in the battle amounted to forty killed and a hundred and sixty wounded, while she herself was badly injured. Her mainmast was so damaged that, during the ensuing

* Rated as A.B.   † Served as Carpenter's Mate.

night, it had to be cut away. Her foremast was shot through in several places, two of her anchors and three of her boats were destroyed, and some of her guns disabled. Four of her starboard lower-deck ports were also knocked away by running on board the Spanish 80-gun ship *Argonauta,* and her hull in every part of it was much shattered. Her master was killed, and fourteen other officers, including her captain, wounded. She had a hen-coop on board, and during the battle the cock flew out and perched on the captain's shoulder and crowed loudly, much to the amusement of the crew, who cheered while they kept up the fighting.

Still under Captain Morris, she was with Rear-Admiral Sir Richard Strachan's squadron watching Rochefort in 1807-8. On the 27th December 1811, she had the misfortune to lose two of her boats in an attack on the enemy's convoy in the Basque Roads, when forty-five men and officers were captured. In 1812, under command of Captain Thomas Alexander, she was with Captain Sir John Gore's little squadron blockading Vice-Admiral Allemand's five ships of the line in Orient, and when they escaped she took part in the pursuit. She performed no other service of any consequence, and was broken up at Chatham in 1827, having earned the naval war medal with one clasp.

(1) Vice-Admiral Sir J. N. Morris, K.C.B., was the son of Captain John Morris, R.N., who fell in command of the *Bristol* in the unsuccessful attack on Sullivan's Island, Charlestown, during the War of American Independence in 1776. He was born in 1763, and entered the service in 1775. He was present in the *Prince of Wales* in the actions of St. Lucia and Grenada in 1779, and was promoted to the rank of lieutenant in 1780. Lieut. in the *Plato,* sloop, at the capture of the French ship *Lutine,* on the Newfoundland station in 1793. Promoted to Captain, 1793. Captain of the frigate *Lively* when lost on Rota Point, near Cadiz,

1798. In the *Phæton* conducted Lord Elgin to Constantinople in 1799, and served near Genoa, co-operating with the Austrians in 1800. Captain of the *Colossus*, 74, at the blockade of Brest, and watching Cadiz in 1804-5, and at the battle of Trafalgar, 1805. He was severely wounded in the thigh, but the bleeding being stopped by a tourniquet, he remained on deck till the close of the action, when he fainted from loss of blood and was carried below, and landed some days later at Gibraltar. He received the thanks of Parliament, the gold medal, and a sword of honour from Lloyd's Patriotic Fund. Appointed a Colonel of Marines, 1810. Became Rear-Admiral, 1811. Third in command in the Baltic, 1812. K.C.B., 1815. Vice-Admiral, 1819. Died in Marlow on the 15th April, 1830.

(2) Captain T. R. Toker, was son of John Toker, of the Oaks, Ospringe, Kent. He entered the service in 1794. Became Mid., 1795. Master's Mate of the *Defence* at the battle of the Nile, 1798. When in the *Vanguard* served on shore at the capture of castle of St. Elmo, Naples. Lieut., 1800. First Lieut. of the *Colossus* at Trafalgar, 1805—promoted Commander. Commanded the *Cruizer* at capture of French cutter *Tilsit ;* recaptured the *Experiment ;* and captured Danish vessel *Christianborg,* 1809. Captain, 1813. When in command of the *Tartarus* was selected to quell the riots among the seamen at Sunderland and Shields, 1815, for which he received the thanks of H.R.H. Prince Regent and the Admiralty. When commanding the *Tamar* in 1817, introduced the use of the "sliding deadlights." Died at 8 Kent Terrace, Regent's Park, N.W., in 1846, aged 65.

(3) Lieut. G. Huish served as a Mid. in the boats of the *Phæton* in the attack on some Spanish ships near Malaga, 1800. Lieut., 1801. Lieut. in the *Colossus* at Trafalgar, 1805. Not traced after 1809.

(4) Commander G. Bulley was promoted to Lieut. in 1801. Served as Lieut. in the *Colossus* at Trafalgar, 1805—wounded. Commander, 1814. Died in London in 1817, aged 36.

(5) Lieut. W. G. Nash was promoted to Lieut. in 1803. Served as Lieut. in the *Colossus* at Trafalgar, 1805. Not in Navy List after 1806.

(6) Commander G. Bague, J.P., entered service in 1798 as

Volunteer 1st Class. Mid. of *Haarlem* at cutting out of the galley *Prima* off Genoa, and in the operations on the coast of Egypt, 1801. Lieut., 1805. Lieut. in the *Colossus* at blockade of Cadiz, and at Trafalgar, 1805—wounded. Lieut. in the *Bittern* in the Mediterranean, 1806–8—wounded. Lieut. in the *Leonidas* at reduction of Santa Maura, and defence of Scylla, 1810; and in the *Boyne* in action with French 74-gun ship *Romulus*, and at the fall of Genoa, 1814. Retired Commander, 1837. Medal and two clasps. J.P. for Middlesex. Died in 1856.

(7) Lieut. W. Forster served as Acting Lieutenant in the *Colossus* at Trafalgar, the 21st October 1805—mortally wounded. Died in Gibraltar Hospital, 30th October 1805.

(8) Captain M. H. Sweny was born in 1785, and entered service as Volunteer 1st Class in 1798. Acting Lieut. of *Colossus* at Trafalgar, 1805—severely wounded. Lieut., 1806. Lieut. of *Africa* in action with Danish flotilla in the Malmo Channel, 1808 —wounded. Senior Lieut. of *Northumberland* when she conveyed Napoleon I. to St. Helena, 1815. Commander, 1821. Captain, 1838. Pension for wounds, £91, 5s. Captain of Greenwich Hospital, 1854. Medal and clasp. Died in Greenwich Hospital, 1865.

(9) Mr. T. Scriven was appointed Master, R.N., in 1798. Served as Master of the *Colossus* off Cadiz in 1805, and in the battle of Trafalgar, the 21st October 1805, where he was killed in action.

(10) Lieut. H. Milbanke was born in Essex. He was promoted to Master's Mate in 1804. Served in that capacity in the *Colossus* at Trafalgar, 1805—wounded. Lieut., 1808. Not traced after 1808.

(11) Lieut. T. G. Rees was born in Dorsetshire. Served as Mid. in the *Colossus* at Trafalgar, 1805—wounded. Lieut., 1806. Killed in action when 1st Lieut. of the *Alacrity*, gun-brig, in her unfortunate action with and capture by the French brig-corvette *Abeille*, off Corsica, the 26th May 1811. When the command devolved upon him, although severely wounded, he remained on deck, displaying great gallantry, until killed by a second shot.

(12) Lieut. H. Snellgrove was born in London in 1872. Prior to entering Navy he served in the *Earl Howe*, East India-

man, at the attack on Seringapatam, 1799. Entered Royal Navy, 1803. Mid., 1803. Mid. in the *Colossus* at blockade of Brest, and battle of Trafalgar, 1805—wounded. Lieut., 1811. Served in the American War, 1814, including the operations in the Patuxent, the capture of Washington, and the attack on Baltimore, 1814. Medal and clasp. Died at Wells, Norfolk, in March 1848.

(13) Admiral W. Walpole was born in Lisbon, and entered the service in 1803. Mid. in the *Colossus* at Trafalgar, 1805 ; of *Ajax* when she was destroyed by fire, 1807 ; and of *Endymion* in the passage of the Dardanelles, 1807. Lieut., 1808. Lieut. in the *Imperieuse* in action with Toulon fleet, 1810 ; at destruction of merchant vessels in the gulf of Genoa, 1812—wounded ; and in the operations against Leghorn and Genoa, 1813-14. Commander, 1814. Commanded the *Curlew* in expedition against pirates in the Persian Gulf, 1819-20—mentioned in despatches, promoted Captain, 1819. Rear-Admiral reserve list, 1852. Vice-Admiral, 1857. Admiral, 1863. Medal and clasp. Died in 1875.

(14) Vice-Admiral W. A. Herringham was the son of Rev. William Herringham, B.D., Rector of Borley and Chadwell, Essex, and Prebendary of St. Paul's, by Anne, daughter of Rev. John Woodrooffe, Rector of Cranwell, Essex. He was born in 1790. Entered the service as Volunteer 1st Class, 1803. Mid., 1805. Mid. in the *Colossus* at Trafalgar, 1805—wounded. Served in the boats of the *Caledonia* at the storming of batteries at Pointe de Ché, Basque Roads, 1810. Lieut., 1810. Captured in the *Java* after severe action with the American 44-gun ship *Constitution*, 1812—mentioned in despatches. Commander, 1818. Captain, 1837. Retired Rear-Admiral, 1857. Retired Vice-Admiral, 1863. Medal and two clasps. Died at 27 Porchester Square, Hyde Park, W., in 1865, aged 75.

(15) Captain W. Carleton, a son of General Carleton, was born in America. Appointed Volunteer 1st Class, 1804. Mid., 1805. Served as Mid. in the *Colossus* at Trafalgar, 1805. When Master's Mate in the *Amazon* served in her boats at the cutting out of a merchantman in the Canaries, and in the capture of the French ships *Marengo* and *Belle Poule*, 1806. Lieut., 1810. Commander, 1826. Retired Captain, 1856. Medal and two clasps. Died in 1874.

(16) Captain R. Maclean was born at Berwick, N.B., and entered the service in 1798. Mid., 1800. Mid. in the *Colossus* at Trafalgar, 1805—severely wounded, left arm amputated. Lieut., 1806. Lieut. in the *Colossus*, and served on shore at defence of Rosas, 1808; commanded a gunboat during siege of Cadiz, 1810; and assisted at capture of a French convoy near Rochelle, 1811. Commander, 1823. Commanded a Royal Mail Steam Packet Company in West Indies, 1841–43. Retired Captain, 1856. Medal and clasp. Died in Dublin in 1863, aged 75.

(17) Lieut. T. Renou was born at Berwick in 1789. Entered the service, 1803. Mid. in the *Colossus* at the blockade of Brest and Rochefort, 1804–5; at Trafalgar, 1805—wounded. Master's Mate of *Norge* at siege of Cadiz. Lieut., 1812. In an armed boat of the *Bustard* cut out two armed feluccas on the coast of Catalonia; and was in the *Merope* in the unsuccessful attempt upon Tarragona, 1813. Served in Coastguard, 1822–41. Medal and clasp. Died in 1849, aged 59.

(18) Lieut. W. Venus was born in North Shields in 1782, and entered the service as A.B. Served as A.B. in the *Colossus* at Trafalgar, 1805. Master's Mate, 1809. Master's Mate in the *Hussar*, frigate, in Walcheren expedition, 1809, and the reduction of Java, 1811. Lieut., 1814. Served in the American War, 1814–15. Died in 1846.

(19) Surgeon W. McDonald was appointed Surgeon, R.N., in 1793. Surgeon of the *Colossus* at Trafalgar, 1805. Died when Surgeon of the *Driver*, sloop, on coast of Africa, in 1823.

(20) Surgeon J. Dundas served as Surgeon's Mate in the *Colossus* at Trafalgar, 1805. Surgeon, 1813. Medal and clasp. Died in 1848–49.

(21) Mr. J. Ault was appointed Paymaster and Purser, R.N., in 1788. Served in the *Colossus* at Trafalgar, 1805. Died in 1817.

(22) Mr. H. Ashton was born in London in 1784. Served as Clerk in the *Colossus* at Trafalgar, 1805. Resigned, 1805.

(23) Mr. W. Adamson was dangerously wounded when serving as Boatswain of the *Colossus* at Trafalgar, and died of wounds in hospital at Gibraltar, the 15th November 1805.

(24) Mr. T. Goodricke served as Carpenter's Mate in the

Colossus at Trafalgar, 1805.   Afterwards promoted to Carpenter.
Served as Carpenter in the *Unité* in the action with and capture
of two French frigates at Pelagosa, 1811.   Naval medal and two
clasps.

(25) General E. Lawrence, C.B., was appointed 2nd Lieut.,
R.M., 1793.   First Lieut., 1795.   Captain, 1801.   Served in the
Colossus at Trafalgar, 1805.   Was at defence of Cadiz, 1810.
Major, 1813.   Lieut.-Colonel, 1826.   Created a C.B., 1831.
Colonel, 1837.   Commandant Chatham Division, 1837–41.
Major-General, 1846.   Lieut.-General, 1854.   General, 1855.
Medal and clasp.   Died in Stoke, Devonport, in 1857.

(26) Major W. Laurie was appointed 2nd Lieut., R.M., 1803.
Served in the *Colossus* at Trafalgar, 1805.   First Lieut., 1806.
Commanded the marines in the *Pompée* at the capture of the
island of Capri, 1806 ; the attack and capture of a martello tower
on Cape Licora ; and in the forcing of the passage of the Dardanelles, 1807.   Was also in the expedition to Copenhagen, 1807.
Served in the *Cambrian* on the coast of Catalonia, 1810–11, including the capture of Bagur and Palmos—received Spanish medal.
Served at the siege of Tarragona, 1811 ; and in the Peninsula,
1813–14, as a Captain in the Spanish army.   Captain, 1826.
Brevet Major, 1841.   Died in 1842.

(27) Lieut. J. Benson was appointed 2nd Lieut., R.M., 1804.
Served in the *Colossus* at Trafalgar, 1805—wounded.   First Lieut.,
1808.   Retired, half-pay, 1815.

XVIII

H.M.S. *DEFENCE*, 74 GUNS

Captain . . .	George Johnstone Hope (1).
Lieutenants. .	James Green (2).
	William Hosie (3).
	Thomas Janverin (4).
	George Kippen (5).
	John Cooke (6).
	James Hanway Plumridge (acting) (7).
Master . . .	Richard Turner (8).
Master's Mates	Richard Marks (9).
	* *William Buchannan* (10).
	Thomas Skead (11).
	Adam Grieve (12).
Midshipmen .	Thomas Huskisson (13).
	Charles Hope Watson (14).
	William Robertson (15).
	William Thomas Morgan (16).
	Charles Reid.
	Hon. William John Napier (17).
	Richard Smith Simonds (18).
	William Dumbreck (19).
	John William Dalling (20).
	Alexander McDougall.
	William Hotham Littlejohn (21).
	William Appleby.
	George Richard Andrew.
	Edward Rowley (22).
Volunteer 1st Class . . . }	Samuel Enderby (23).

* Rated as A.B.

Surgeon . . . James Gillies (24).
Surgeon's { George Mitchell.
Mates . . { Lionel Gregg.
Purser . . . John Farr Bushell (25).
Clerk . . . . John Payton Lamey (26).
Schoolmaster . James Christie (27).
Gunner . . . Andrew Goldie.
Boatswain . . John Phillips.
Carpenter . . Peter Crusoe.
Captain, Royal } Henry Cox (28).
  Marines .
1st Lieut., } John Wilson (29).
  Royal Marines
2nd Lieut., } Alfred Burton (30).
  Royal Marines

The *Defence*, one of the most distinguished of the
Trafalgar ships, was launched from Plymouth Dockyard
in 1763, her builder having been Mr. Israel Pownall, and
Sir Thomas Slade, Knight, the Surveyor of the Navy.
In the period of peace which followed the Seven Years'
War, she was employed upon ordinary cruising duties,
and it was not until the rupture with the American
Colonies and the subsequent war with France and
Spain that she entered upon her real fighting career.
Under Sir Charles Hardy we find her in the Channel
Fleet in August 1779; the next year, under Captain Lord
Cranstoun, she set forth with Rodney to the relief of
Gibraltar, and immediately was in the thick of the fight-
ing. On the 8th January, off Finisterre, a convoy was
discovered, and Rodney, letting his own convoy stand by,
went in chase with the *Sandwich*, the *Prince George*, on
board which Prince William Henry, afterwards William
IV., was serving as a midshipman, the *Defence*, and some
others. By midday seven Spanish ships of war and all
the merchantmen were captured, and, although looked
upon at first no doubt by the officers and men of

Rodney's squadron as only a profitable adventure, this capture of the Caraccas convoy was of much importance historically. The greater part of the cargoes of the merchantmen consisted of articles of which the besieged garrison of Gibraltar, and the Spanish fleet lying in Cadiz Harbour, stood in need. The loss of those cargoes delayed the departure of the Spanish fleet for the West Indies, and saved Jamaica.

A week later—on the 16th January 1780—Rodney and the *Defence* were once more in action, when De Langara's squadron of fourteen Spanish ships of the line was discovered and chased. Rodney's command was of the same strength, but the Spanish commander was anxious to keep his fleet intact for siege work at Gibraltar, and sought to avoid an action. But the wind blew strongly, and some of the British ships, being coppered, gained rapidly, the *Defence* being among those which got near enough to commence action. From four o'clock in the afternoon until two in the morning, Rodney forced De Langara to keep up a running fight, blowing up the *San Domingo*, and capturing the *San Juliano*, with the *San Eugenio*, so that by daybreak De Langara's fleet was scattered, and he himself, with his flagship, the *Phœnix*, surrendered. The *Defence* had ten men killed and twenty-one wounded, the greatest loss sustained by any British ship in the engagement ; and she conducted the Spanish flagship to Gibraltar. As a corollary to this victory came the relief of Gibraltar ; and then, while Rodney went to the West Indies, the *Defence* went east under Captain Thomas Newnham, and was in Vice-Admiral Sir Edward Hughes' fifth and last action with Suffren off Pondicherry, on the 20th June 1783, which was fought five months after the preliminaries of peace had been signed. Her losses amounted to forty-five killed and wounded. Her fore and main masts, bowsprit, all three topmasts, and foreyard arm were shot away, her sails and standing and running rigging much cut, and her hull shattered.

In 1783–85 the *Defence* bore the flag of Vice-Admiral Sir Edward Hughes, and the broad pennant of Commodore Andrew Mitchell.

On the commencement of the war of the French Revolution in 1793 began the most glorious chapter in the history of the *Defence*, the days when she fought under Howe on the Glorious First of June, and under Nelson at the Nile and Trafalgar. Under Captain James, afterwards Lord, Gambier, she was one of Lord Howe's fleet which, on the 18th November 1793, fell in with and chased a French squadron under Commodore Vanstable. Several British vessels lost spars, and the *Defence* carried away both fore and main topmasts. In the following year she was still with Lord Howe, and in the engagements of the 28th and 29th May had five killed and, wounded. Her captain on the Glorious First of June was Gambier, a man whose notions of religion and morality were much stricter than those in vogue at the time. The *Defence* was spoken of as "a praying ship," and it was freely questioned whether it was possible for her to be a fighting ship as well. The doubt was set at rest in Howe's great victory, when the *Defence* was the first ship to break through the enemy's line, and engaged, with both broadsides at once, the *Mucius* and the *Tourville*. She lost fifty-four killed and wounded. Her three masts were all shot away, the quarter-deck and forecastle guns rendered useless, and, indeed, was so badly treated that she signalled for help and was taken in tow by the *Phæton*. Captain Gambier received the gold medal for the battle. In 1795, under Captain Thomas Wells, she bore the flag of Rear-Admiral Robert Man, and was in Admiral Hotham's chase of, and indecisive action with, the French fleet off Hyères, near Toulon, on the 13th July, in which she had seven killed and wounded. She was also in Admiral Man's unsuccessful pursuit of the French fleet under Rear-Admiral Richery, which slipped out of Toulon on the 5th October 1795.

Under Captain John Peyton she seems to have been one of Earl St. Vincent's fleet before Cadiz in 1798, being among the number that in May were sent to join Nelson in the Mediterranean. She accompanied him during the run to Alexandria, and until he discovered the objects of his search at anchor in Aboukir Bay. There, on the evening of the 1st August 1798, they were assailed by the British, the *Defence* being the eighth ship going into action, anchoring outside the hostile line at about seven o'clock, and plying her guns vigorously until her opponent surrendered. She lost her topmast, and her lower masts and bowsprit were shot through and through and in a most tottering state ; but generally seems to have been fortunate, as, out of a complement of 584, her losses did not exceed fifteen killed and wounded.

Her crew, which had been implicated in the mutiny of the Channel Fleet at Spithead in 1797, were unfortunately again in a state of gross insubordination ; and, on the 17th September 1798, nineteen seamen were sentenced to death and six to flogging and imprisonment. Under Captain Lord Henry Paulet she was with the fleet with which Vice-Admiral Lord Keith was watching Cadiz in 1799. In June of the following year she was one of a small squadron cruising near Brest, whose boats captured three armed and light merchant vessels that had taken refuge in the harbour of St. Croix, and on another occasion destroyed several batteries on the French coast. On the night of July 1st a similar expedition was despatched against a convoy lying near

M

the island of Noirmontier, mouth of the Loire. Though
protected by batteries on the land, a ship of twenty
guns, three other armed vessels, and fifteen merchant
craft were taken and destroyed without loss to the
British, who were returning in high spirits at their
success when, unfortunately, the boats grounded on
sand-banks, and, in spite of all their exertions, about
half of the party (some ninety) of the bold sailors and
marines became prisoners to the French. The *Defence*,
with Lord Henry Paulet as captain, was present in the
battle of Copenhagen on the 2nd April 1801. She was
in the fleet sent to the Baltic under Admiral Sir Hyde
Parker, but when the Danish force at Copenhagen was
attacked she was one of the division which that Admiral
kept with him, and, although afterwards ordered to
support the gallant Nelson, wind and current prevented
her taking any particular share in the battle. Under
Captain George Hope she was with Vice-Admiral Sir
John Orde's squadron on the 9th April 1805, and later
with Sir Robert Calder's and Collingwood's fleets. Then,
on the 21st October 1805, the *Defence* was one of the lee
column led by Vice-Admiral Collingwood, but, being
very close to its rear, was not able to engage the enemy
until some two and a half hours after firing had been
commenced by the foe. Then, for nearly half an hour,
she plied her guns at the French 74, *Berwick;* afterwards
assailing the Spanish *San Ildefonso*, also a 74, which
fought for about an hour and then struck her flag. It is
fair to say that she had been previously engaged by others
of the British, which had contributed materially to her
roll of casualties, amounting to something like 200 men
killed or wounded. The *Defence* had thirty-six killed
and wounded. Her damages were confined to a shot
through the mainmast, which was otherwise cut in
several places. Much of her lower and topmast rigging

was shot away, besides which her gaff was cut in two,
and she received some injury to her hanging knees and
chain plates.   The *Defence* and her prize, anchoring that
evening (as the dying Nelson had desired the fleet
should do), weathered the gale that followed the battle,
and thus the *San Ildefonso* became one of the few trophies
of victory saved from the tempest on this occasion.
It is noticeable that a large proportion of the officers
and crew of the *Defence* at Trafalgar were Scotsmen.

A second time the schemes of Napoleon made the
British Government determine to take possession of [the
Danish navy, so the *Defence* (with Charles Elkins as
captain) went again to Copenhagen and was present
at its bombardment and capture on the 7th September
1807.   In 1809 she was in the Baltic, and was present
at the destruction of a Russian battery at Porcola Point,
and the occupation of Fort Saumarez.   In 1810–11 she
was at the blockade of Flushing, and with the Baltic
and Flying squadrons until, after surviving the risks
of strife and storm for nearly half a century, she was
wrecked on the southern coast of Jutland on Christmas
Eve, 1811.   Under Captain David Atkins she was returning to England from the Baltic with Rear-Admiral
Robert Carthew Reynolds, whose flag was in the *St.
George*, when on the 20th December a great gale broke.
Four days and nights the vessels were the sport of the
elements, until on Christmas Eve the *St. George* was
driven ashore.   The *Defence* might have got away, as
indeed the *Cressy*, which was in company, did, but
Captain Atkins, when urged to leave, said : " I will
never desert my Admiral in the hour of danger and
distress," and the *Defence* was also stranded on a lee
shore.   Of her crew of about 530 not half a dozen lived
to see Christmas Day.   The Rear-Admiral, Captain
Daniel Oliver Guion of the *St. George*, and Captain

David Atkins of the *Defence* perished. The *Defence* had earned the naval war medal with four clasps, besides Davison's Nile medal and Boulton's Trafalgar medal.

(1) Rear-Admiral Sir G. J. Hope, K.C.B., was a son of Hon. Charles Hope-Vere by his third wife, Helen, daughter of George Dunbar, and was grandson of Charles, 1st Earl of Hopetoun, K.T. He was born in 1767, and entered the service in 1782. He was promoted to Lieutenant in 1788, and Commander in 1790. On the commencement of war with France in 1793 he was in command of the *Bulldog*, 14, in the Mediterranean, and was for some time employed on convoy service at Toulon under Vice-Admiral Lord Hood. He was promoted Captain in 1793. He commanded the *Romulus*, 36, in Vice-Admiral Sir William Hotham's action with the French off Genoa, 1795. In 1798 he was commanding the *Alcmène* before Alexandria under Captain Samuel Hood, and on the 22nd August chased and captured the French gunboat *Légère*, carrying despatches for Napoleon. A French officer, at the moment of capture, threw the papers overboard, but they were recovered by two seamen of the *Alcmène* who jumped in after them. Commanded the *Leda*, 38, during the operations on the coast of Egypt in 1801. He commanded the *Defence*, 74, in the battle of Trafalgar, 1805, and was much distinguished—received the gold medal, the thanks of Parliament, and a sword of honour from the Patriotic Fund. He was captain of the *Victory*, 100, bearing the flag of Vice-Admiral Sir James Saumarez, in the expedition to the Baltic in 1808, when, though the army was not employed and returned to England, the navy rendered excellent service; he continued as captain of the Baltic Fleet until promoted to Rear-Admiral in 1811. He was a Lord of the Admiralty in 1812–13, when he was sent to bring over the Russian fleet to England during the French invasion of Russia. He then returned to the Admiralty, where he remained till his death. He was for some time M.P. for East Grinstead in Sussex, and was appointed a Major-General in the Royal Marines in 1818. He died at the Admiralty in 1818, and was buried in

Westminster Abbey. He was father of Admiral of the Fleet Sir James Hope, G.C.B.

(2) Captain J. Green was promoted to Lieut. in 1799. Served in the expedition to Egypt, 1801. First Lieut. of the *Defence* at Trafalgar, 1805—promoted to Commander. Captain, 1812. Had a pension for wounds. Died in Hanover Square, London, in 1836.

(3) Lieut. W. Hosie was promoted to Lieut. in 1800. Served as Lieut. in the *Defence* at Trafalgar, 1805. Not in Navy List after 1808.

(4) Lieut. P. Janverin was promoted to Lieut. in 1800. Served as Lieut. in the *Defence* at Trafalgar, 1805. Died in 1826.

(5) Captain G. Kippen was born in 1781, and entered the service in 1796. Served as Mid. in the *Captain*, under Nelson, in the battle of St. Vincent, 1797; and was also in the unsuccessful attempt at Teneriffe, 1797, and in the battle of the Nile, 1798. Promoted to Lieut., 1802. Lieut. in the *Defence* at Trafalgar, 1805. Commander, 1812. Commanded the *Peruvian*, brig, during the American War, 1812–14, including the capture of the American privateer, *John*, 16 guns, and in the expedition to Penobscot. Captain, 1814. Died in Scotland in 1826.

(6) Lieut. J. Cooke was promoted to Lieut. in 1802. Served as Lieut. in the *Defence* at Trafalgar, 1805. Accidently killed while out shooting at Wilford, near Nottingham, in 1813.

(7) Admiral Sir J. H. Plumridge, K.C.B., was the son of James Plumridge, of Littleworth, Berks., and was born in Hertford Street, London, W. Entered the service in 1799 as Volunteer 1st Class. Mid. in the *Leda* in the expedition to Egypt in 1801. Acting Lieut. in the *Defence* at Trafalgar, 1805. Lieut., 1806. Senior Lieut. in the *Melpomene*, and commanded her boats at the capture of a Danish cutter and some merchant vessels off Jutland in 1809. Senior Lieut. of *Menelaus* at reduction of the Isle of France, 1810. Commanded the boats of the *Resistance* at the capture of a convoy in Port d'Anzo, 1813; and served as A.D.C. to Sir Edward Pellew in 1814—promoted to Commander Captain, 1822. M.P. for Falmouth, 1841–47. Storekeeper of the Ordnance, 1842. Good Service Pension, 1847. Rear-

Admiral, 1852. Third in command in the expedition to the Baltic in 1854, including the bombardment of Bomarsund, and the command of two detached squadrons employed in the destruction of war material in the Gulf of Bothnia—mentioned in despatches, K.C.B., and Baltic medal. Admiral Superintendent Devonport Dockyard, 1855–57. Vice-Admiral, 1857. Admiral, 1863. Naval medal and clasps. Died at Hopton Hall, Suffolk, in 1863.

(8) Mr. R. Turner was appointed Master, R.N., in 1796. Served as Master of the *Defence* at Trafalgar, 1805. Queen's Harbour Master, Plymouth, 1823–38. Died in 1838.

(9) Lieut. R. Marks served as Master's Mate in the *Defence* at Trafalgar, 1805—promoted Lieut. Not in Navy List after 1814.

(10) Captain W. Buchannan was born in 1777, and entered the service as A.B. in 1795, but was invalided in 1796. Rejoined, 1799, and served in the *Alarm* at the capture of privateers on the Jamaica station in 1800. Rated as A.B., but served as Master's Mate in the *Defence* at Trafalgar, 1805—promoted Lieut. Served in the *Audacious*, landing troops under Sir John Moore in Portugal in 1808, and as Assistant Beach Master at the embarkation of the army after Corūna, 1809. First Lieut. of the *Dictator* at the destruction of a Danish squadron, 1812— mentioned in despatches—promoted Commander. Retired Captain, 1846. Medal and two clasps. Died in 1859.

(11) Lieut. T. Skead was born in Scotland. Served as Mid. in the *Defence* at Trafalgar, 1805. Lieut., 1808. Died at Chatham in 1841.

(12) Commander A. Grieve was born in Leith in 1770, and entered the service as Master's Mate in 1797. Served in the *Leda* on coast of Egypt in 1801. Master's Mate in the *Defence* at Trafalgar, 1805. Lieut., 1807. In command of a signal station in Alderney, 1812–14. Retired Commander, 1843. Died in Weymouth, 1845.

(13) Captain T. Huskisson, half-brother of the Rt. Hon. William Huskisson, was born in Oxley, near Wolverhampton, in 1784, and entered the service in 1800 as A.B. Mid., 1800. Mid.

in the *Defence* in 1803–5, including the battle of Trafalgar, 1805. Lieut., 1806. Lieut. in the *Prince of Wales*, and Flag-Lieut. to Admiral Gambier, in the expedition to Copenhagen in 1807. Served in the *Fleur de la Mer*, schooner, at blockade of St. Domingo, 1808. Commander, 1809. Commanded the *Pelorous* at the capture of Guadeloupe, 1810. Captain, 1811. In the *Barbados* captured the U.S. Revenue cruiser *James Maddison*, 1812. Wrecked in the *Barbados*, 1812. Captain of the *Euryalus*, 1815, and in 1818–19, and was twice temporarily Commodore of the squadron in the West Indies. Paymaster of the Navy 1827–30. Captain of Greenwich Hospital, 1830, until his death there in 1844.

(14) Captain C. H. Watson was the son of Charles Watson, of Saughton, Edinburgh, and Lady Margaret Carnegie, daughter of Admiral George, 6th Earl of Northesk. Served as Mid. in the *Defence* at Trafalgar, 1805. Lieut., 1807. Lieut. in the *Unité*, frigate, at the capture of three Italian brigs in the Adriatic, 1808. Commander, 1812. Captain, 1814. Died in 1836.

(15) Rear-Admiral W. Robertson was born in Leith, N.B., in 1786, and entered the service as Mid. in 1803. Served in the *Defence* in 1803–5, including the battle of Trafalgar, 1805. Mid. in the *Spencer* in the expedition to Copenhagen, 1807; taken prisoner, but escaped in 1809. Lieut., 1810. Lieut. in the *Isabella*, sloop, Captain John Ross, 1815–18, in her Arctic exploring expedition. Commander, 1827. Captain, 1837. Retired Rear-Admiral, 1857. Medal and clasp for Trafalgar, and Arctic medal. Died in Bath in 1861.

(16) Commander W. T. Morgan was born in London. Served as Mid. in the *Defence* at Trafalgar, 1805. Lieut., 1809. First Lieut. of the *Endymion* at the capture of the American frigate *President*, 1815—mentioned in despatches, promoted Commander. In command of the *Confidence*, 18, when she was lost, with all hands, off Mizen Head, the 21st April 1822.

(17) Captain W. J. Lord Napier, F.R.S., was the eldest son of Francis, 8th Lord Napier of Merchiston, and Maria, daughter of Lieut.-General Sir William Clavering, K.B. He was born in 1786, and entered the service in 1802. Served as Mid. in the

Defence at Trafalgar, 1805. Mid. in the *Imperieuse* in a boat attack on Fort Roguette, 1806—mentioned in despatches; at the capture of a privateer in 1807—wounded; at the cutting out of a French vessel in the Bay of Almeria, 1808; and in the destruction of shipping in the Basque Roads, 1809. Present in the attack on Polamos, 1810. Commander, 1812. Wrecked in the *Goshawk*, 1813. Captain, 1814. Succeeded as 9th Lord Napier, 1823. Captain of the *Diamond*, 1824-27. Principal Superintendent of British Trade and Interests in China, 1833-34. Died at Macao, China, 1834.

(18) Commander R. S. Simonds was born in Islington, London, in 1788, and entered the service as a Volunteer in 1803. Served in the *Defence* in 1803-5, including the pursuit of the combined fleets to the West Indies and back, and at Trafalgar, 1805. Mid., 1805. Lent to the *Spencer*, and was in her in the Walcheren expedition, 1809. Master's Mate in the *Caledonia*, and served in her boats at attack on batteries at Point de Ché, 1810. Acting Lieut. in the *Courageux* at defence of Cadiz, and other operations in 1810-11. Served with a flotilla at the defence of Riga, and in the ship's boats of the *Aboukir* in the attack on Mittau, 1812. Lieut., 1812. Medal and three clasps. Retired Commander, 1855. Died in 1865.

(19) Lieut. William Dumbreck was born in Edinburgh in 1789, and entered the service as Volunteer 1st Class in 1802. Mid., 1804. Served in the *Defence* at Trafalgar, 1805. Served in the boats of the *Victory* at the embarkation of Sir John Moore's army at Coruna, 1809. Lieut., 1810. Medal and clasp. Died in 1862.

(20) Captain J. W. Dalling was the youngest son of Colonel Sir John Dalling, Bart., of Burwood Park, Surrey, Governor of Jamaica, and Louise, daughter of Excelles Lawford. Entered service as Volunteer 1st Class in 1803. Mid., 1804. Mid. in the *Defence* at Trafalgar, 1805. Served in the *Amphion* at capture of Reggio, and the fortress of Cotrone, 1806; and in her boats at the destruction of a battery, and capture of six gunboats and a convoy at Cortellazzo, 1809. Master's Mate, 1809. Lieut., 1810. Commander, 1814. Captain, 1828. Retired, 1848.

Medal and two clasps. Died at Earsham House, Norfolk, in 1853.

(21) Lieut. W. H. Littlejohn served as Mid. in the *Defence* at Trafalgar, 1805. Lieut., 1811. Died in 1812.

(22) Commander E. Rowley was the son of Sir William Rowley, M.P. for Suffolk. Served as Mid. in the *Defence* at Trafalgar, 1805. Lieut., 1810. Commander, 1815. Died at Nassau, New Providence, when commanding H.M.S. *Shearwater*, 1817.

(23) Captain Samuel Enderby was born in London in 1789, and entered the service as Volunteer 1st Class. In that capacity he served in the *Defence* at Trafalgar, 1805—promoted Mid. Left the service in 1808, and later on joined the army. He became 2nd Lieut., 17th Light Dragoons, 1811. Lieut., 22nd Light Dragoons, 1812. Captain, 1819. Captain, 5th Dragoon Guards, 1820. Captain, 16th Lancers, 1822. Captain, 59th Regiment, 1831. Retired, half-pay, 1832. Served with the 22nd Light Dragoons at Belgaum and Sholapore, 1818, and with the 16th Lancers at the siege and capture of Bhurtpore, 1825–26. Received the naval war medal and clasp for Trafalgar, and the Indian war medal and clasp for Bhurtpore, both in 1849. Died in 1873.

(24) Surgeon J. Gillies, M.D., was born in Scotland. Was appointed Surgeon, R.N., 1798. Surgeon of the *Defence* at Trafalgar, 1805. Died at Castle Cary, Somersetshire, in 1827.

(25) Mr. J. F. Bushell was appointed Paymaster and Purser, R.N., in 1796. Served as Purser of the *Defence* at Trafalgar, 1805. Died in 1826.

(26) Mr. J. P. Lamey served as Clerk in the *Defence* at Trafalgar, 1805. Purser, 1826. Died at the Cape of Good Hope, when serving as Secretary to Rear-Admiral Fred. Warren, Commander-in-Chief, 1834.

(27) Mr. J. Christie served as Schoolmaster in the *Defence* at Trafalgar, 1805, and received the medal and clasp in 1848.

(28) Colonel H. Cox was appointed 2nd Lieut., R.M., 1793. First Lieut., 1795. Captain, 1803. Served in the *Defence* at Trafalgar, 1805. Brevet Major, 1814. Major, 1826. Lieut.-Colonel, 1829. Brevet Colonel, 1829. Retired, 1829. Died in 1830.

(29) Lieut.-Colonel J. Wilson was appointed 2nd Lieut., R.M.,

1803. First Lieut., 1805. Served in the *Defence* at Trafalgar, 1805; was sent with a guard to take possession of the Spanish *San Ilde-fonso*, and did good service in securing her preservation as a prize. Was one of the two officers saved from the *Boreas*, frigate, wrecked near Guernsey in 1807; served at the reduction of the islands of Les Saintes; the expedition to Walcheren in 1809; the siege of Cadiz, 1810; in the celebrated action between the 38-gun frigate *Macedonia* and the U.S. 44-gun frigate *United States*, in which the former, after a gallant fight of an hour, and a loss in killed and wounded of 104, was compelled to surrender, 1812; was with the Naval Brigade on shore in the battle of New Orleans, 1814. Adjutant Chatham Division, 1825–26. Captain, 1826. Assistant-Adjutant-General, 1834–46. Brevet Major, 1841. Lieut.-Colonel, 1846. Retired, 1846. Medal and clasp. Died in Tunbridge Wells in 1850. His medal is in the collection of the Royal Marines at Plymouth.

(30) Captain A. Burton was appointed 2nd Lieut., R.M., 1804. Served in the *Defence* at Trafalgar, 1805. First Lieut., 1806. Captain, 1827. Died in 1840.

XIX

H.M.S. *LEVIATHAN*, 74 GUNS

Captain . . .	Henry William Bayntun (1).
Lieutenants .	Eyles Mounsher (2).
	James Harding (3).
	John Baldwin (4).
	Alexander Burgoyne Howe (5).
	Francis Baker (6).
	John Carter (acting) (7).
Master . . .	John William Trotter (8).
Master's Mates	Jeremiah William Boham (9).
	James Cumming (10).
	John Lemon.
Midshipmen .	John Jolley.
	William Anderson.
	George Dunsford (11).
	Davis Thomas (12).
	James Stone.
	Erasmus Pepys.
	George Compston.
	J. W. Watson (13). *Wounded.*
	Alfred Smith (14).
	Peter A. Mouatt.
	George Crisp (15).
Volunteers 1st	Henry Francis Spence (16).
Class	* *Robert Mowbray* (17).
	William Stone.
	Arthur Shakespear (18).

* Rated as Boy.

Volunteers 1st Cl.   Thomas Ebenezer Jessop.
    (*continued*)   Wassily Skripzine (supernumerary).
Surgeon . . .   William Shoveller (19).
Assistant - Sur-⎫
    geon . . .⎬ Paul Johnstone.
Surgeon's 2nd⎫
    Mate . . .⎬ Matthew Capponi (20).
Purser . . .   Samuel Rickards (21).
Clerk. . . .   James Nuttall.
Gunners. . .   Joseph Wells.
                  Robert Chien (22).
Boatswain . .   Alexander Mowbray.
Carpenter . .   James Avory.
Captain, Royal⎫
    Marines . .⎬ George Prescott Wingrove (23).
1st Lieuts.,   ⎰ Nathaniel Cole (24).
    Royal Marines ⎱ Thomas James Waldegrave Tane (25).

The *Leviathan* was built at Chatham in 1789. She
was commissioned in 1793 by Captain Lord Hugh
Seymour, and was employed with the fleet under Vice-
Admiral Lord Hood at Toulon—Captain Benjamin
Hallowell temporarily commanded her when Lord Hugh
Seymour was sent home with despatches. On the
evacuation of Toulon she received some of the British
troops on board. In the Channel Fleet, under Lord
Howe, she participated, under Lord Hugh Seymour, in
the actions of the 28th and 29th May, and in the battle
of the 1st June 1794. On the 28th she was engaged
with the French 110 *Révolutionnaire;* on the 29th, following the *Queen Charlotte,* she broke through the French
line, was a good deal engaged, and somewhat damaged.
She was soon, however, made fit for action, and did
good service in the great battle of the 1st June, her
captain being awarded the gold medal for his distinguished service. She engaged the French 74, *America,*

* Served as Coxswain.

which she dismantled and left a mere log on the water, after an hour's hard fighting, and was of great assistance to the *Russell*, when she was being badly mauled by the *Trajan* and *Eole*. She suffered a loss in killed and wounded of forty-three; her foretopsail yard was shot away, and her masts, sails, and rigging injured. In April 1795, Captain John Thomas Duckworth was appointed to her, and she joined Rear-Admiral William Parker in the West Indies, taking part in the combined attack upon Leogane on the 21st March 1796, in which she was considerably damaged aloft by the guns on shore, and lost twenty-four killed and wounded. In August 1796, Duckworth hoisted his broad pennant in her. Returning home in the following year, she served on the coast of Ireland early in 1798, and then joined Lord St. Vincent in the Mediterranean, bearing Commodore Duckworth's pennant with the squadron which conveyed the troops to Minorca, and covered the operations in that island until its capture on the 15th November 1798.

On the 6th February 1799, under Captain John Buchanan, and in company with the *Argo*, 44, she chased and captured the Spanish frigate *Santa Teresa*, 34, near Majorca, in the Mediterranean. On the 20th May 1799, bearing the flag of Rear-Admiral J. T. Duckworth, and with Henry Digby as captain, she joined Lord St. Vincent off Minorca; and in the following month was sent to reinforce Lord Nelson at Palermo. On the 5th April 1800, under the command of Captain James Carpenter, and carrying Duckworth's flag, she attacked a Spanish convoy off Cadiz; her boats captured a Spanish brig on the following day; while on the 7th April, in company with the *Emerald*, she made prizes of the Spanish frigates *Carmen*, 32, and *Florentina*, 34, and took them to Gibraltar.

In 1804 Captain Henry William Bayntun was appointed to her, and under him she joined Lord Nelson at Toulon in May. She had thus a share in the pursuit of the combined fleets to the West Indies and back in the following year, and in the great victory of Trafalgar on the 21st October 1805. On the latter occasion, in the weather column, she was closely engaged with the French flagship *Bucentaure*, 80, and the Spanish 140 *Santisima Trinidad* and 74 *San Augustin*, the latter of which she easily outmanœuvred, boarded, and carried without opposition. Lashing the Spaniard to her port side, she brought on herself a nasty fire from the French 74 *Intrépide*, until the *Africa*, *Orion*, and other ships came to the rescue. Her losses in the battle amounted to twenty-six killed and wounded. The mainpiece of her head was shot through, all three masts, bowsprit, and most of her lower and topsail yards wounded, her mizen topsail yard shot away, and a great part of the rigging cut to pieces. She received eight shots between wind and water, and had three guns completely disabled.

In October 1809, commanded by Captain John Harvey, she joined the force under Rear-Admiral George Martin which pursued five men-of-war, transports, and a convoy under Rear-Admiral Baudin, inflicted a serious loss on him, and prevented his succouring Barcelona. In 1811 she was with the fleet in the Mediterranean under Vice-Admiral Sir Edward Pellew. On the 29th April 1812, under Captain Patrick Campbell, her boats, with those of the *Undaunted*, attacked a French privateer and several merchantmen in the port of Agay, near Fréjus; the privateer was boarded and captured, but had to be left; several of the merchant vessels were, however, brought off. On the 9th and 10th May 1812, she landed a party of marines, with some from the *America*, at Laigueglia, and attacked the batteries, while a party of seamen captured a convoy which had taken refuge under the batteries. On the 27th June following, she participated in the capture and destruction of a French convoy of eighteen vessels in Laigueglia and Alassio. Her last commission was under the command of Captain Thomas Briggs, on the Lisbon, Cork, and Mediterranean stations, in 1814-16. From the latter year until 1844 she was employed as a convict hulk at Portsmouth. She was then used as a target until broken up at that port in 1848. She had earned the naval medal with two clasps.

(1) Admiral Sir H. W. Bayntun, G.C.B., was the son of Mr. Bayntun, H.M. Consul-General at Algiers, and was born in 1766. Entering the service at an early age, he was promoted to the rank of lieutenant in 1783 at the age of sixteen. He saw considerable service during the war with France commencing in 1793. He served with the fleet under Sir John Jervis, in the West Indies; was engaged on shore at the capture of Martinique in 1794. Commanded the *Avenger*, 16, after the death of her commander, James Milne, the boats of which assisted in boarding and capturing the French frigate *Bienvenue*, 32, and other vessels in Fort Royal Bay on the 17th March 1794; and was present at the capture of Guadeloupe in April of the same year. For his distinguished services on these occasions he was promoted to Commander and Captain within four months. He commanded the *Réunion*, 36, which was wrecked in the Swin on the 7th December 1796; and was present at the capture of Trinidad in February 1797. When Captain of the *Cumberland*, 74, commanded a squadron off San Domingo in 1803, and on the 30th June captured the French frigate *Créole*, 40, with troops on board, and the French vessels *Aiquille*, *Vigilante*, *Supérieure*, and *Poisson Volant*. In 1804 he was appointed to the command of *Leviathan*, 74 guns, and was employed in the blockade of Toulon under Lord Nelson. He shared in the pursuit of the combined French and Spanish fleets to the West Indies and back, and commanded her at Trafalgar, 1805—gold medal, the thanks of Parliament, and a

sword of honour from the Patriotic Fund. He bore the Guidon at Lord Nelson's funeral, in the water procession from Greenwich. In 1807 he took part in the expedition to Buenos Ayres. In 1811–12 he commanded the royal yacht, *Royal Sovereign*. He was promoted to Rear-Admiral in 1812, became a K.C.B. in 1815, Vice-Admiral, 1821, Admiral, 1837, and G.C.B. in 1839. He died in Bath in 1840.

(2) Captain E. Mounsher was promoted to Lieut. in 1796. Served as 1st Lieut. of the *Leviathan* at Trafalgar, 1805, and was the first man to board the Spanish 74, *San Augustin*—promoted Commander. Served in the *Drake* at the destruction of a privateer in 1810, and at the capture of Tilsit, 1811. Captain, 1813. Died in 1836, aged 65 years.

(3) Commander J. Harding was promoted to Lieut. in 1802. Served as Lieut. in the *Leviathan* at Trafalgar, 1805. Retired Commander, 1835. Died in 1839.

(4) Captain J. Baldwin was promoted to Lieut. in 1803. Served as Lieut. in the *Leviathan* at Trafalgar, 1805, and was one of those who boarded the Spanish 74, *San Augustin*. Lieut. in the *Astræa*, with the squadron under Captain C. M. Schomberg, in the action with, and capture of, the French ships *Renommée* and *Néréide*, 1811—wounded, promoted Commander. Captain, 1819. Died in London in 1840.

(5) Commander A. B. Howe, a son of Alexander Howe of Nova Scotia, was born in 1783, and entered the service in 1795. Served in the *Africa* in the unsuccessful attack on Leogane, St. Domingo, in 1796. Was wrecked in the *America* on the Formigar rocks in 1800. Lieut., 1803. Served in the *Leviathan* at Trafalgar, 1805. Lieut. in the *Renown* at the blockade of Rochefort, 1806. Present at the destruction of the *Robuste* and *Lion* off Crete, 1809. Retired Commander, 1849. Medal and clasp. Died in 1864–65.

(6) Commander F. Baker was promoted to Lieut. in 1804. Served as Lieut. in the *Leviathan* at Trafalgar, 1805. Commander, 1814. Died in 1823–24.

(7) Admiral J. Carter was the second son of Thomas Carter, of Castle Martin, Co. Kildare, and Catherine, daughter of the

Hon. John Butler.   Born in 1785, he entered the service in 1798. Was present in the *Brilliant* in her escape from the two 44-gun French frigates off Santa Cruz, 1798.   In the *Penelope* assisted in the night actions with and subsequent capture of *Gillaume Tell*, 1800; and took part in the expedition to Egypt, 1801. Acting Lieut. in the *Leviathan* in pursuit of combined fleets to West Indies and back, and at Trafalgar, 1805.   Lieut., 1805. Commander, 1809.   Captured the French privateer *L'Emile* off St. Valery, 1814.   Captain, 1815.   Supt. Haslar Hospital and Clarence Victualling Yard, 1841–46.   Rear-Admiral, 1851.   Vice-Admiral, 1857.   Admiral, 1862.   Medal and three clasps.   Died in 1863, aged 77.

(8) Commander J. W. Trotter was appointed Master, R.N., in 1797.   Served as Master of the *Leviathan* at Trafalgar, 1805. Retired Commander, 1846.   Medal with two clasps.   Died in 1851.

(9) Lieut. J. W. Boham was born in London.   Served as Master's Mate in the *Leviathan* at Trafalgar, 1805.   Lieut., 1809. Died in 1840.

(10) Lieut. J. Cumming was born in Edinburgh.   Promoted Master's Mate, 1804.   Served in that capacity at Trafalgar, 1805—promoted Lieut.   Not traced after 1809.

(11) Lieut. G. Dunsford was born in ·Exeter.   Served as Mid. in the *Leviathan* at Trafalgar, 1805.   Lieut., 1806.   Died in 1838–39.

(12) Lieut. D. Thomas was born in London.   Served as Mid. in the *Leviathan* at Trafalgar, 1805.   Lieut., 1806.   Not traced after 1811.

(13) Mid. J. W. Watson served in that capacity in the *Leviathan* at Trafalgar, 1805—wounded.   Served as Mid. in the *London* at the capture of the French ship *Marengo*, 1806— wounded.   Not traced farther.

(14) Mr. A. Smith was born in Sheerness.   Served as Mid. in the *Leviathan* at Trafalgar, 1805.   Master's Mate, 1806. Master's Mate in the *Alexandria* at the cutting out of two Spanish vessels in the Rio de la Plata, 1806.   Died from the effects of his wounds on the 10th September 1806.

N

(15) Lieut. G. Crisp was born in Cork in 1770. Is believed to have been present at the battle of the Nile in 1798, and Copenhagen in 1801. Mid., 1804. Served as Mid. in the *Leviathan* at Trafalgar, 1805. Lieut., 1815. Died in Dublin in 1831.

(16) Commander H. F. Spence was born in London, and entered the service as Volunteer 1st Class in 1804. Served in the *Leviathan* at Trafalgar, 1805. Served in the *Pompée* at the capture of Martinique, 1809; and in the *Belleisle* in the expedition to Walcheren, 1809. Lieut., 1812. Commander, 1854. Medal with two clasps. Died in Plymouth in 1856, aged 66.

(17) Mr. R. Mowbray, rated as a boy, served as Volunteer 1st Class at Trafalgar, 1805; and received the medal and clasp in 1848.

(18) Lieut. A. Shakespear was born in Jamaica in 1788, and entered the service in 1804. Served as a Volunteer in the *Leviathan* at Trafalgar, 1805. Served in the *Thetis* in 1806–8, and was wounded on one occasion in boarding a French privateer. Served in the *Avon* in her action with the French 40-gun frigate *Néréide*, 1810—wounded. Lieut., 1810. Died in 1847.

(19) Surgeon W. Shoveller was appointed Surgeon, R.N., in 1794. Served as Surgeon of the *Leviathan* at Trafalgar, 1805. Retired, 1827. Died in Brighton in 1840, aged 67.

(20) Surgeon M. Capponi served as Surgeon's Mate in the *Leviathan* at Trafalgar, 1805. Surgeon, 1815. Died in 1830 when Surgeon of the *Blonde*, in the Mediterranean.

(21) Mr. S. Rickards was appointed Paymaster and Purser, R.N., in 1795. Served in the *Leviathan* at Trafalgar, 1805. Died in 1823.

(22) Mr. R. Chien served as Coxswain in the *Leviathan* at Trafalgar, 1805. Afterwards promoted to Gunner. Served as Gunner in boats of the Squadron at the destruction of twenty-seven American vessels at Connecticut, 1814. Naval medal with two clasps.

(23) Major-General G. P. Wingrove was appointed 2nd Lieut., R.M., 1793. First Lieut., 1794. Served on shore at the taking of the Cape of Good Hope, 1795. Captain, 1801. Senior marine

officer in the *Leviathan* at Trafalgar, 1805. Major, 1813. Present at the taking of Genoa, 1814; and in the *Boyne*, 98, the same year, in an engagement on the 5th November with three French ships of the line and three frigates off Toulon. Served in the *Hercule* in the action off Cape Nichola Mole. Lieut.-Colonel, 1826. Brevet Colonel, 1831. Commandant Woolwich Division, 1837–39. Retired, 1839. Major-General (retired), 1841. Medal and clasp. Died in 1850.

(24) Lieut.-Colonel N. Cole was appointed 2nd Lieut., R.M., 1796. Served in the *Valiant* at the destruction of the French frigate *Harmonie* off St. Domingo, 1797. First Lieut., 1798. Was wrecked in the *Meleager* in the Gulf of Mexico, 1801. Served in the *Leviathan* in the pursuit of the combined fleets to the West Indies and back, and at Trafalgar, 1805, and was one of the boarders of the Spanish 74, *San Augustin*. Captain, 1806. Served in the *Northumberland* at the destruction of two French frigates, 1812. Served in the American War, 1814–15, including the capture of Washington, and the battle of Baltimore. Brevet Major, 1819. Major, 1832. Brevet Lieut.-Colonel, 1837. Died in 1837.

(25) Lieut. T. J. W. Tane entered the Royal Navy as a Volunteer in 1797. Served in the *Mars* at the capture of the French 74, *L'Hercule*, 1798. Was appointed 2nd Lieut., R.M., 1803. First Lieut., 1805. Served in the *Leviathan* at Trafalgar, 1805. Also at taking of Isle de Passe, 1810. Retired, half-pay, 1814. Medal and two clasps.

XX

H.M.S. *BELLEROPHON*, 74 GUNS

Captain . . .	John Cooke (1). *Killed*.
Lieutenants. .	William Price Cumby (2).
	Edmund Fanning Thomas (3).
	David Scott (4). *Wounded*.
	John Alexander Douglas (5).
	George Lawrence Saunders (6).
Master . . .	Edward Overton (7). *Killed*.
Master's Mates.	James Sheil.
	Edward Hartley (8). *Wounded*.
	Daniel James Woodriff (9).
Midshipmen	George Thompson.
	Daniel Charles.
	James Campbell,
	John Franklin (10).
	James Stone. *Wounded*.
	William Watford (11).
	William Nunn Jewell (12). *Wounded*.
	William Fairweather.
	John Jervis White (13).
	William Sanders.
	Hugh Patton (14).
	Thomas Bant (15). *Wounded*.
	Mark White (16).
	John Simmons (17). *Killed*.
	Henry Walker (18).
	Robert Patton (19).
Volunteers 1st	John Tucker (20).
Class	William Pilch (21).

Volunteers 1st Cl.	John Edward Markland (22).
(continued)	George Pearson (23) *Wounded.*
	*Hugh Robert Entwisle (24).
	*George William Hughes (25).
Surgeon . . .	Alexander White (26).
Assistant - Surgeon	} William Engleheart (27).
Purser . . .	Thomas Jewell (28).
Clerk	Samuel Willcocks (29).
Gunner . . .	John Stevenson.
Boatswain . .	Thomas Robinson (30). *Died of Wounds.*
Carpenter . .	Russell Mart.
Captain, Royal Marines	} James Wemyss (31). *Wounded.*
1st Lieut., Royal Marines	} Peter Connolly (32).
2nd Lieuts., Royal Marines	{ Luke Higgins (33). John Wilson (34).

The *Bellerophon*, one of the small class of seventy-fours, was launched from the private building-yard of Graves & Co., at Frindsbury, near Rochester, in 1786, having been built from the design of Sir Thomas Slade, Knight, Surveyor of the Navy. She was first commissioned on the 19th July 1790. She carried the broad pennant of Commodore, afterwards Sir Thomas Pasley, Bart., in 1793, and sailed from St. Helen's with the Channel Fleet under Lord Howe; but being damaged by colliding with the *Monarch*, 74, was sent back to port the next day. However, she was with the fleet again in October, and played a great part in the indecisive actions which led up to Lord Howe's glorious victory of the following year; one day attacking the French 100-gun ship *Révolutionnaire*, and she only a small 74-gun ship herself, sustaining the fight alone for an hour and a half,

---

* Rated as A.B.

enabling three other British ships to come up and complete the fight, and putting over four hundred of the *Révolutionnaire's* men *hors de combat*. In the actual battle of the 1st June 1794, she flew the flag of Rear-Admiral Thomas Pasley, and was closely engaged with the French 74, *Eole*, joined later by the *Trajan*. About two hours after the beginning of the fight Admiral Pasley had his leg injured by a shot, and the command devolved upon Captain Hope, who followed the *Eole* closely until the latter had had enough of it, and she herself so damaged aloft that she had to signal for assistance to the *Latona*. She lost thirty-one killed and wounded, all her boats were shot away, she lost her fore and main topmasts, her mainmast was badly damaged, and the rigging cut to pieces. Both Rear-Admiral Pasley and Captain Hope received gold medals as having particularly distinguished themselves.

She witnessed the lamentable loss of the *Boyne*, 98, which took fire and blew up at Spithead on the 1st May 1795, and succeeded in saving twelve men. Under Captain Lord Cranstoun, she was with Vice-Admiral Lord Cornwallis's squadron which captured eight out of a convoy of thirteen merchant ships near Belleisle, on the 8th June 1795 ; and in the Admiral's brilliant repulse of a French squadron under Villaret four times his superior on the seventeenth of the same month. Under Captain Henry d'Esterre Darby she joined Nelson's flying squadron in 1797, and was in the battle of the Nile on the 1st August 1798, being the last ship but two in the line, and the greatest sufferer of all the British ships, for to her it fell to engage the 120-gun French flagship *Orient*. The battle engaged just before seven o'clock at night, and by eight, so destructive was the fire of her antagonist that the *Billy Ruffian*, as the bluejackets generally called her, had lost her mizen-mast, which was quickly followed by her mainmast. Disabled, with nearly a third of her crew killed and wounded, the foremast tottering to its fall, nothing was left for Captain Darby to do but to cut his cable, set his spritsail, and drift along the rear of the French line. As she went, the French 80, *Tonnant*, poured a broadside into her, but the *Swiftsure* and *Alexander* were on the track of the *Orient*, and the work that the *Bellerophon* had so courageously begun, culminated an hour and a half later in the awful explosion that sent the *Orient* and the greater part of her crew into the air. Fifteen of the *Bellerophon's* guns were put out of action before she cut her cable; the captain and master alike were wounded; three lieutenants were killed. It was a red day in the history of the ship. Her total losses amounted to 193 killed and wounded. She was totally dismasted, her hull was damaged by shot, and 450 hammocks were destroyed.

Still under Captain Darby, in 1799 the *Bellerophon* was in the Mediterranean with Lord St. Vincent's squadron and with Lord Nelson off Sicily. In 1801–2 she was in the Channel Fleet under Captains Viscount Garlies, afterwards Earl of Galloway, and John Loring. In 1802–3 she was in the West Indies and in the Channel Fleet, made several captures, including that of the French 74-gun ship *Duquesne* off St. Domingo, on the 25th July 1803, was at the surrender of Cape François, and the capture of the 38-gun frigate *Clorinde* and the schooner *L'Oiseau*.

She bore a distinguished part in the great victory of Trafalgar on the 21st October 1805, when her captain, the gallant John Cooke, was killed almost at the same time and in the same way that Lord Nelson met his death. In the disposition of the ships for battle, the *Bellerophon* formed one of the lee division under Collingwood. When the signal was made out in the *Victory*, " England expects that every man will do his duty," Captain John Cooke went below and visited the guns' crews on each deck, giving them Nelson's message. The men's reply was to chalk on their guns four words, " *Bellerophon ;* death or glory." By the carelessness of a midshipman, a gun was fired on board the *Bellerophon* prematurely, which brought down on her the fire of many of the enemy. But though she lost her main and mizen topmasts, she compelled the *Monarca*, a Spanish 74-gun ship, to strike to her, and she repelled three attempts at boarding made by the crew of the French 74, *Aigle*. Her losses in the battle amounted to 132, including twelve officers, killed and wounded. Her main and mizen topmasts were shot away, all her lower yards badly injured, and her hull torn to pieces. Under command of Captain E. Rotherham and in company with the *Belleisle*, she escorted the *Victory*, with the body of Nelson, to England.

In 1806–9 the *Bellerophon* served in the Channel and in the Baltic, bearing the flag of Rear-Admiral Sir Albemarle Bertie in 1807–8, and that of Rear-Admiral Alan Hyde Gardner in 1808–9. In the latter year, with Captain Samuel Warren, her boats cut out and boarded three Russian vessels near Stango, on the coast of Finland on the 19th June ; and on the 7th July, in conjunction with those of others, her boats captured six Russian gunboats and a convoy in Baro Sound on the same coast, at a cost of fourteen killed and wounded. In 1815, after Napoleon's escape from Waterloo, she was employed under Captain Frederick Lewis Maitland in watching his movements at Rochefort, and effectually frustrated his plan of escape by sea. Finding he had no chance of escape, the ex-Emperor surrendered himself to Captain Maitland on the 15th July, and was con-

ducted to the *Bellerophon* in her barge, being received on
board by a guard of honour of marines. He was conveyed first to Torquay, and then to Plymouth. On the
7th August he was transferred to the *Northumberland* for
removal to St. Helena, the great man bowing and taking
off his hat to the officers and ship's company of the
Bellerophon. A fine representation of Napoleon aboard
the *Bellerophon* was painted by the late Sir William
Orchardson, R.A. The *Bellerophon* was shortly afterwards paid off, and, after having carried the British flag
with honour for more than a quarter of a century, was
degraded into a convict hulk, being employed in 1816-24
as such at Sheerness, and at Plymouth in 1824-26. In
the latter year she was renamed the *Captivity*, under which
name she existed until 1834, when she was broken up
at Plymouth, after an existence of forty-eight years, and
having earned the naval war medal with five clasps. Her
figure-head is preserved in Portsmouth Dockyard.

(1) Captain J. Cooke was the son of Francis Cooke, a cashier
under the Admiralty. He was born in 1763, and entered the
service in 1776. As a Midshipman he served during the War of
American Independence, and was in the *Eagle* in the attack on
Rhode Island, 1776. Was promoted to Lieut. in 1779. Served
as Lieut. in the *Duke* in Lord Rodney's defeat of the French
under De Grasse off Dominica, in 1782. Promoted to Commander, 1793. Commanded the *Incendiary*, fireship, in Lord
Howe's victory of the 1st June 1794—promoted Captain.
Captain of the *Nymphe* at the capture, in conjunction with the
San Fiorenzo, of the French frigates *Resistance* and *Constance*,
1797. Was in command of the *Nymphe* at the time of the
mutiny of the fleet at the Nore in 1797, when his crew mutinied
and put him on shore. Captain of the *Amethyst*, 38, in the
expedition to Holland in 1799, and took out H.R.H. the Duke
of York and his staff. Commanded her in the operations under
Lord Bridport near Quiberon, and in the expedition to Ferrol

under Rear-Admiral Sir J. B. Warren in 1800. On the 29th July 1800, her boats, in conjunction with others, captured the French *Cerbère*, and on the 29th August in the same year cut out the French 18-gun ship *Guêpe*. In the same year he captured the French corvette *Vaillante*. In 1801, still in command of the *Amethyst*, he captured in the Channel the French frigate *La Dédaigneuse*, and the Spanish ship *Général Brune*. Commanded the *Bellerophon*, 74, in the battle of Trafalgar, 1805, when she formed one of the lee division under Collingwood, and greatly distinguished herself. When the signal, "England expects that every man will do his duty," was made out on the *Victory*, Captain Cooke went below and visited the guns' crews on each deck, giving them Nelson's message. She soon after came under fire; the fighting was fast and furious; and men were falling all round him. The first lieutenant, Cumby, pointed out to him that he was wearing his epaulettes and was marked out by the men in the enemy's tops. "It is too late to take them off," he replied; "I see my situation, but I will die like a man." A few minutes later, when in the act of reloading his pistols, he fell with two musket balls in the breast. The quartermaster asked if he should take him below. "No; let me lie quietly one minute," was the reply. He died at eleven minutes past one, saying with his last breath, "Tell Lieut. Cumby never to strike." There is a monumental tablet to Captain Cooke's memory in St. Paul's Cathedral, and another in the church of Dunhead, Wilts. His widow received the gold medal for the battle, and a handsome silver vase from the Patriotic Fund.

(2) Captain W. P. Cumby, C.B., was the son of Captain David Price Cumby, R.N., by Susannah, daughter of Robert Marsh, of Yarmouth. Was promoted to Lieut. in 1793. Served as 1st Lieut. of the *Bellerophon* at Trafalgar, 1805, and succeeded to the command of the ship on the death of Captain Cooke—promoted Captain. Commanded the *Polyphemus* when her boats cut out French schooner *Colibri* from St. Domingo Harbour, 1808; and had charge of a squadron at capture of St. Domingo, 1809. C.B., 1831. Supt. Pembroke Dockyard, 1837; and died there the 27th September 1837.

(3) Commander E. F. Thomas was promoted to Lieut. in 1798. Served as second Lieut. in the *Bellerophon* at Trafalgar, 1805, and acted as 1st after the death of Captain Cooke. Retired Commander, 1830. Died at Cleethorpes, near Grimsby, the 28th April 1842.

(4) Rear-Admiral D. Scott entered the service in 1793. Served as Mid. of *Gorham*, brig, and on shore at reduction of St. Domingo, 1794—severely wounded. Acting Lieut. in the *Endymion* in her action with the Dutch ship *Brutus*, 1797. Lieut., 1800. Wrecked in the *Circe*, in North Sea, 1803. Lieut. in *Bellerophon* at Trafalgar, 1805—wounded. First Lieut. of *Bedford* escorting Royal Family of Portugal to the Brazils, 1807 (Order of Tower and Sword). Acting Flag Lieut. and doing duty in *Venerable* and *Pallas*, and afterwards in *St. Domingo* in Walcheren expedition, including the capture of Flushing, 1809. Commander, 1811. Captain, 1814. Retired Rear-Admiral, 1850. Medal and clasps. Died at Berrydon House, N.B., 1852.

(5) Lieut. J. H. Douglas was promoted to Lieut. in 1802. Served as Lieut. in the *Bellerophon* at Trafalgar, 1805. Not traced after 1809.

(6) Commander G. L. Saunders was promoted to Lieut. in 1802. Served as Lieut. in the *Bellerophon* at Trafalgar, 1805. Commander, 1814. Died in 1834.

(7) Mr. E. Overton was appointed Master, R.N., in 1794. Was killed in action when serving as Master of the *Bellerophon* at Trafalgar, the 21st October 1805.

(8) Lieut. E. Hartley served as Master's Mate in the *Bellerophon* at Trafalgar, 1805—wounded, promoted Lieut. Not traced after 1813.

(9) Captain D. J. Woodriff was the eldest son of Captain Daniel Woodriff, C.B., R.N., who died in 1842. Was born at Greenwich. Mid., 1802. Master's Mate in the *Bellerophon* at Trafalgar, 1805. Lieut., 1807. Lieut. in the *Solebay* at the reduction of Senegal, and was wrecked in her, 1809. Commander, 1822. Retired Captain, 1856. Medal and clasp. Died at Old Charlton, in Kent, in 1860.

(10) Captain Sir John Franklin, Kt., K.C.H., F.R.S., D.C.L., was the twelfth and youngest son of Willingham Franklin, of Spilsby, Lincolnshire, where young Franklin was born in 1786. He served in the *Polyphemus* at the battle of Copenhagen, 1801. Mid., 1801. When on passage home from China in the East India Company's ship *Earl Camden* was in the engagement with Linois, and took charge of the signals, 1804. Served as Mid. in the *Bellerophon* at Trafalgar, 1805, and was in charge of the signals. Lieut., 1808. Lieut. in the *Bedford* in expedition to New Orleans, 1814, and served in her boats at capture of American vessels at Lake Borgue, 1814—wounded; mentioned in despatches. His Arctic experiences commenced when he commanded the *Trent*, hired brig, in 1818. Commanded an exploration expedition to North America, 1819–22. Commander, 1821. Created an F.R.S., 1822. Captain, 1822. Commanded the Arctic Expedition, 1825–27, which was rich in geographical results. Knighted, 1829. D.C.L., Oxford, 1829. Commanded the *Rainbow*, frigate, on the coast of Greece, 1830–33, for which services he received the order of the Redeemer of Greece, and the K.C.H. in 1836. Lieut.-Governor of Van Diemen's Land, 1836–44. Was in command of the Arctic expedition, consisting of the *Erebus* and *Terror*, which left England in 1845, and during which he discovered the North-West Passage, but lost his life. After gloomy anticipations in England at the non-return and absence of news of the expedition, a series of search expeditions were organised in England and America between 1847 and 1859, and it was not until the latter year that distinct traces of the lost expedition were come upon. During his absence and supposed existence, he was promoted Rear-Admiral the 26th October 1852; but he had died on the 11th June 1847, aged 61, fortunately before the terrible fate which befell his companions, every one of whom perished miserably. The naval medal with three clasps and the first Arctic medal were presented to his family, and are now in possession of Mr. Lefroy, Blackheath. A monument has been erected to him in Westminster Abbey, and a statue in Waterloo Place.

(11) Commander W. Walford was born at Rushmere, Suffolk,

in 1788. Entered service, 1802. Served as Mid. in the *Bellerophon* at Trafalgar, 1805. Lieut., 1810. Lieut. in the *Skylark*, and assisted in the action with Boulogne flotilla, and the capture of a gun-brig, the 11th November 1811. Wrecked in the *Skylark*, 1812. Lieut. in the *Bellerophon* when Napoleon surrendered on board off Rochefort in 1815. War medal and two clasps. Retired Commander, 1850. Died in 1859.

(12) Lieut. W. N. Jewell was born in Brompton, Kent, and entered the service in 1796. Mid. in the *Bellerophon* at Trafalgar, 1805—wounded. Served in the *Bedford*, which conveyed the Royal Family of Portugal to the Brazils in 1807. Lieut., 1812. Died in Great Warley, Essex, in 1847. Entitled to medal and clasp.

(13) Mr. J. J. White was born in Hampshire. Served as Mid. in the *Bellerophon* at Trafalgar, 1805. Appointed Master, R.N., 1806. Master of the *Tartar* in a cutting-out expedition off Bergen, 1808. Died in 1829.

(14) Admiral H. Patton, son of Colonel Patton, Governor of St. Helena; was cousin to Admiral Robert Patton who served in the *Bellerophon* at Trafalgar; was born in St. Andrews, N.B., 1790. Entered service, 1804. Mid. of *Bellerophon* at Trafalgar, 1805. Lieut., 1811. Commander, 1813. In *Astræa* in action with French frigate *Etoile*, near Cape Verde Islands, 1814. Captain, 1819. Retired, 1846. Retired Rear-Admiral, 1852. Retired Vice-Admiral, 1857. Retired Admiral, 1803. Medal and clasp. Died in Cockspur Street, London, S.W., in March 1864, aged 73.

(15) Mr. T. Bant was born in Stoke Damerel, Devonport, in 1786. Served as Mid. in the *Bellerophon* at Trafalgar, 1805—wounded. Not traced farther.

(16) Commander M. White was born in Gillingham, Kent, in 1788. Entered the service in 1803. Served as Mid. in the *Bellerophon* at Trafalgar, 1805. Served in the boats of the *Melpomène* at the capture and destruction of gunboats and a convoy at Hango Head, in the Baltic, the 7th July 1809. Lieut., 1810. In the *Berwick* when she drove the French frigate *Amazon* on the rocks near Barfleur, 1811; in her boats boarded the

national zebec *Fortune*, 1813 ; and commanded a division of boats at the siege of Genoa, 1814. Commander, 1815. Medal and two clasps. Died in 1849–50.

(17) Mr. J. Simmons was born in Totnes, Devonshire, in 1784. Mid., 1805. Killed in action when Mid. in the *Bellerophon* at Trafalgar, 21st October, 1805.

(18) Lieut. H. Walker was born in Manchester, and entered service in 1803. Served as Mid. in the *Bellerophon* at blockade of Brest, Rochefort, and Cadiz, and at Trafalgar, 1805. Is said to have been present at capture of the *Marengo* and *Belle Poule*, 1806. In *Néréide* at attack on Buenos Ayres, 1807. In *Cleopatra* at capture of French 40-gun frigate *La Topaze*, and reduction of Martinique, 1809. Lieut., 1810. Lieut. of *Menelaus*, and in her boats at capture of three war vessels and convoy in harbour of Corigeon, 1815. Lieut. in the *Leander* at bombardment of Algiers, 1816—wounded. Medal and three clasps. Died in Manchester in 1849.

(19) Admiral R. Patton, son of Retired Captain Charles Patton, R.N., and first cousin to Admiral Hugh Patton, who served in the *Bellerophon* at Trafalgar, was born in 1791. Entered the service in 1804. Served as Mid. in the *Bellerophon* at Trafalgar, 1805. Served in the *Niobe* at capture of French corvette *Le Néarque*, 1806. Master's Mate, 1809. Lieut., 1810. Commander, 1815. Captain, 1827. Retired, 1847. Retired Rear-Admiral, 1854. Retired Vice-Admiral, 1861. Retired Admiral, 1864. Naval medal and clasp, and Royal Humane Society's medal for saving life in 1826. Died in Fareham, Hants, in 1883.

(20) Mr. J. Tucker was born in Plymouth in 1793. Served as Volunteer 1st Class in the *Bellerophon* at Trafalgar, 1805. Not traced further.

(21) Lieut. W. Pilch was born in Norfolk, and entered service as Volunteer 1st Class in 1804. Served on the *Bellerophon* at Trafalgar, 1805. Mid. in the *Diadem* at Monte Video, 1807. In the *Defiance,* with Admiral Stopford's squadron, at the destruction of three French frigates under the batteries of Sables D'Olonne, coast of France, 1809. In the *Northumberland* was present at the destruction of the French frigates *L'Arienne* and *L'Andro-*

maque, and the brig *Mamelouck*, 1812.   Lieut., 1814.   In Coastguard, 1827–48.   Naval Knight of Windsor, 1848.   Medal and
two clasps.   Died in Broadstairs in 1863.

(22) Mr. J. E. Markland was a relation of Captain John Cooke,
who was killed in command of the *Bellerophon* at Trafalgar, and
of Commander H. R. Entwisle, who was also present in her.   He
was born in Leicestershire in 1792.   Served as a Volunteer in
the *Bellerophon* at Trafalgar, 1805.   Not traced farther.

(23) Lieut. G. Pearson was born in Somersetshire, was son of
the Rev. T. H. Pearson, and brother of Lieut.-General Sir
Thomas Pearson, Kt., K.C.H., C.B., Colonel of the 85th Regiment.   He served as a Volunteer 1st Class in the *Bellerophon*
at Trafalgar, 1805—severely wounded.   Lieut., 1811.   Died in
1816.

(24) Commander H. R. Entwisle, D.L., J.P. of Llanbethian,
Gloucestershire, was the son of John Markland, of Foxholes,
Rochdale, who assumed the name of Entwisle.   He entered the
service in 1799.   Served in the *Amethyst*, commanded by his
relative, Captain John Cooke, at the capture of *La Dédaigneuse*
and *Le Général Brune*, 1801.   Rated as A.B., he served as
Volunteer in the *Bellerophon* at Trafalgar, 1805, and was one of
the party, which took' possession of the Spanish 74, *Bahama*.
Lieut., 1806.   Lieut. in the *Paulina* in the expedition to Copenhagen, 1807; and in the *Bucephalus* in the operations against
New Orleans, 1814.   Retired Commander, 1839.   Medal and
clasp.   Died in 1867.

(25) Admiral G. W. H. D'Aeth, J.P., formerly Hughes, was
the son of William Hughes of Betshanger, Kent, and Harriet,
daughter of Joseph Hardy, H.M. Consul at Cadiz.   Born in
London in 1786, he entered the service as a boy in 1799.   He
served in the *Amethyst* at the capture of the French frigate
Aventurier in 1799, the capture of the French corvette *Vaillante*
in 1800, and of the French frigate *La Dédaigneuse* and the
Spanish privateer *Le Général Brune*, in 1801.   Rated as A.B., he
served as a Volunteer, and did excellent service in the *Bellerophon*
at Trafalgar, 1805—promoted to Mid. and Lieut.   Served as
Lieut. in the *Resolution* in the expedition to Copenhagen, 1807.

Acting Commander of the *Swallow* at the defence of Messina; and commanded a gunboat in the attack on the enemy's flotilla under the batteries of Scylla and Reggio, 1810. Acting Commander of the *Termagant* during the blockade of Barcelona, 1811. Commander, 1811. Commander of the *Bucephalus*, troopship, and served on shore at the attack on New Orleans, 1814. Captain, 1815. Assumed name of D'Aeth, 1808, on succeeding to the estates of his cousin, Sir Narborough D'Aeth, 3rd Baronet, of Knowlton Court, Kent. Retired, 1846. Retired Rear-Admiral, 1850. Retired Vice-Admiral, 1857. Retired Admiral, 1862. Medal and clasp. J.P. for Kent. Died in 1873.

(26) Surgeon A. Whyte was appointed Surgeon, R.N., in 1796. Served as Surgeon of the *Bellerophon* at Trafalgar, 1805. Retired, 1824. Died in 1838.

(27) Assistant-Surgeon W. Engleheart was appointed Surgeon's Mate, R.N., in 1804. Assistant-Surgeon, 1805. Served in the *Bellerophon* at Trafalgar, 1805. Not traced further.

(28) Mr. T. Jewell was appointed Paymaster and Purser, R.N., in 1778. Served in the *Bellerophon* at Trafalgar, 1805. Died in 1821.

(29) Mr. S. Willcocks was born in Plymouth in 1788. Served as Clerk in the *Bellerophon* at Trafalgar, 1805. Appointed Paymaster and Purser, R.N., in 1808. Medal and clasp. Died in 1848.

(30) Boatswain T. Robinson died in Gibraltar Hospital, the 2nd November 1805, of wounds received in the *Bellerophon* at Trafalgar.

(31) Lieut.-Colonel J. Wemyss was appointed 1st Lieut., R.M., 1782. Captain, 1796. Served with marine battalion at capture of Malta, 1800. Senior marine officer in the *Bellerophon* at Trafalgar, 1805—wounded. Major, 1812. Lieut.-Colonel, 1814. Retired, 1814. Died in 1823.

(32) Lieut. P. Connolly was appointed 2nd Lieut., R.M., 1801. First Lieut., 1805. Served in the *Bellerophon* at Trafalgar, 1805. Placed on half-pay, 1816. Died in 1835.

(33) Lieut. L. Higgins was appointed 2nd Lieut., R.M., 1804. Served in the *Bellerophon* at Trafalgar, 1805. First Lieut., 1806.

Placed on half-pay, 1807. There was a Luke Higgins appointed Ensign, 92nd Gordon Highlanders, 1808, and resigned, 1813.

(34) Possibly Major J. Wilson, who was appointed 2nd Lieut., R.M., 1804. First Lieut., 1807 ; Brevet Captain, 1827. Captain, 1828. Retired full-pay, 1837. The official Navy List gives him as an Hon. Major of 1854 on the retired list, and as being in possession of the medal, but he is not on the Admiralty medal roll. The only John Wilson appearing in the medal roll of the *Bellerophon* is an ordinary.

Boulton's Medal—Reverse.

XXI

H.M.S. *ORION*, 74 GUNS

Captain . . .	Edward Codrington (1).
Lieutenants .	John Croft (2).
	John Julian (3).
	Edward Elers (4).
	John Roberts.
Midshipmen .	Richard Cole.
	Francis Medhurst.
	Elias Symes.
	Robert Small.
	Alexander McKenzie.
	Thomas Townsend.
	John Hudson (5).
	John Christian Chesnaye (6).
	John Nicholas.
	James Carle.
	Francis Gray (7).
	John Lechmere (8).
	John Anderson.
	John King.
Volunteers 1st	George Barker (9).
Class	*Hon.* George James Perceval (10).
	Henry Molyneux.
	Thomas William Holburne (11).
	James Robins (12).
	Abraham Filmore.
	* *George Starr* (13).
Master . . .	Cass Halliday (14).

* Served as Ordinary Seaman.

2nd Master . .   Barnard Turner (15).
Master's Mates   Charles Cable. *Wounded.*
                  Charles Hall (16).
                  Richard Sauce (17). *Wounded.*
Chaplain . .   Rev. George Outhwaite.
Surgeon . . .   Thomas Johnston (18).
Assistant - Sur- {Robert Henry Bolton (19).
  geons . .   {Charles Linton (20).
Purser . . .   William Bowman Murray (21).
Gunner . . .   John Filmore.
Boatswain . .   Joseph Marshall.
Carpenter . .   John Mills.
Captain, Royal   }Heneage William Creswell (22).
  Marines . . }
2nd Lieuts., .   {Samuel Collins (23).
'Royal Marines   {Stephen Bridgeman (24).

The *Orion,* a ship with a very distinguished career,
was built on the Thames in 1787 from the design of
William Bateley. On the commencement of the war of
the French Revolution in 1793 she was commissioned by
Captain John Thomas Duckworth, and in the following
year joined the Channel Fleet under Lord Howe. She
does not appear to have come under fire in the partial
action of the 28th May; but she took part in that of the
29th May, when she was engaged for a short time with
the French 80, *Indomptable.* She lost three men killed,
and had her mizen-yard shot in two, mainmast and
main-topmast, mizen-topmast, and spanker-boom shot
through. On the glorious 1st June she was the seventeenth in the line of battle, and engaged the *Northumberland* and *Patriote* until they bore up, when she hauled up
as well as she could in support of the *Queen Charlotte.*
She lost her main-topmast, main-top and main-yard, and
had five seamen killed and twenty-four seamen and
marines wounded. Captain Duckworth had the satis-

faction of receiving the gold medal as having particularly signalised himself.

On the 12th June 1795, with Captain Sir James, afterwards Lord, Saumarez in command, she accompanied the Channel Fleet from Spithead under Lord Bridport, and took part in his action off Isle Groix on the 23rd June. She was a good deal engaged with, amongst other ships, the *Alexandre*, 74, which had been captured the previous year from the British. Her losses in the battle amounted to twenty-four killed and wounded. For the next eighteen months she was employed in the blockade of Brest and Rochefort, and on the 19th January 1797, was detached under Rear-Admiral William Parker to join Lord St. Vincent. She joined him a few days before the battle of St. Vincent, fought on the 14th February, in which she had a brilliant share, though her losses were small—nine wounded. She was engaged with the two Spaniards, *San Ysidro* and *Salvador del Mundo*, and later with the *Santisima Trinidad* and the ships covering her.

Continuing with Lord St. Vincent off Cadiz until May 1798, she joined Lord Nelson in the Mediterranean at the time of Napoleon's expedition to Egypt, and was enabled to participate in his victory of the Nile, the 1st August 1798. Early in the action she engaged the *Sérieuse*, into which she poured her starboard broadside, dismasted, cut her cable, and reduced to a sinking condition. She then occupied herself with the *Peuple Souverain* and the *Franklin*. Her losses amounted to thirteen killed and twenty-nine wounded, her captain being amongst the latter. She had her fore and mizen masts shot through in several places, her yards and rigging greatly disabled, her stern boat shot away, and had a narrow escape from more imminent danger from one of the enemy's fire rafts. The *Orion* afterwards went to Gibraltar and Malta, and thence to Plymouth, where, being in need of repair, she was paid off.

In May 1805, she was commissioned by Captain Edward Codrington, and was employed in the blockade of Cadiz by Lord Collingwood. In the weather column she took part in the great victory of Trafalgar, on the 21st October 1805. She fought the French 74, *Intrépide*, which she forced in quarter of an hour to haul down her colours, and assisted in the submission of the French *Swiftsure*. Her losses amounted to twenty-four killed and wounded; she had several spars injured, and her main-topsail yard shot away. She continued attached to the fleet under Codrington until December 1806, when she returned home. On the 26th July 1807, under Captain Sir Archibald Collingwood Dickson, Bart., she sailed from Yarmouth Road with the fleet under Admiral James Gambier in command of the expedition to Copenhagen. She took part in the subsequent operations resulting in the surrender of the Danish fleet. In 1808–9 she was in the expedition to the Baltic under Vice-Admiral Sir James Saumarez, which was her last service of any importance; and she was broken up at Plymouth in June 1814, after an unusually distinguished career of twenty-six years, and having earned the war medal with five clasps.

(1) Admiral Sir E. Codrington, G.C.B., G.C.M.G., F.R.S., was the third son of Edward Codrington, of Dodington Park, Gloucestershire, and grandson of Sir William Codrington, 1st Bart., of Dodington, and was born in 1770. Educated at Harrow, he entered the service in 1783 as Midshipman. Promoted to Lieut., 1793. Lieut. in the *Queen Charlotte*, flagship of Lord Howe, in 1793–94, including the pursuit of the French fleet under Van Stabel in 1793, the actions of the 28th and 29th May, and that of the glorious 1st June 1794. Was sent home by Lord Howe with the duplicate despatches announcing the safe arrival

of the fleet and the prizes off the Isle of Wight—promoted Commander. Appointed to the *Comet*, fireship, to accompany Lord Howe in his unexpected battle with the French fleet in October 1794. Captain, 1795. Commanded *La Babet*, frigate, in Lord Bridport's action with the French fleet off Isle Groix, the 23rd June 1795—received thanks of Parliament. Commanded the *Druid*, 32, in company with the frigates *Unicorn* and *Doris*, at the capture of the *Ville de l'Orient*, a troopship of the French squadron intended to invade Ireland. Captain of the *Orion*, 74, in 1805–6, including the blockade of Cadiz under Lord Collingwood, and the battle of Trafalgar, the 21st October 1805—received the gold medal, the thanks of Parliament, and a sword of honour from the Patriotic Fund. Captain of the *Blake*, 74, flagship of Lord Gardner, in the Walcheren expedition, 1809, and was specially mentioned in despatches for his services at the forcing of the Scheldt, when the *Blake* was twice set on fire by red-hot shot, and aground for nearly three hours under fire of the batteries. Next year she was sent to the coast of Portugal and Spain, and took part in the defence of Cadiz. In 1811–13 he commanded a squadron on the coast of Spain, and performed valuable service at the defence of Tarragona, the defeat of the French near Villa Succa, and on other occasions. Appointed Colonel, Royal Marines, 1813. Rear-Admiral, 1814. Captain of the *Tonnant* and Captain of the fleet under Sir Alex. Cochrane, in the American War, 1814–15, including the capture of Washington, the destruction of the American fleet on the Penobscot, the capture of Alexandria, the expedition against Baltimore, and the attack on New Orleans—mentioned in despatches, thanks of Parliament, and K.C.B. Promoted to Vice-Admiral, 1821. Commander-in-Chief in the Mediterranean in 1826–28, with his flag in the *Asia*, and commanded the British, French, and Russian squadrons employed in the pacification of Greece, and at the battle of Navarino, the 20th October 1827, for which services he received the G.C.B., the St. Louis and Legion of Honour of France, the St. George of Russia, and the Redeemer of Greece. Commanded the Evolutionary Squadron in the Channel in 1831. Admiral, 1837. Commander-in-Chief, Portsmouth, 1839–42.

M.P. for Devonport, 1832–40. Good service pension, 1847. War medal and four clasps. His eldest son, Edward, a Midshipman, R.N., was drowned at sea. He was father also of General Sir William Codrington, Commander-in-Chief in the Crimea, who died in 1884, and of Admiral of the Fleet Sir Henry John Codrington, K.C.B., who died in 1877. Died in Eaton Square, London, 1851, and was buried in St. Peter's, Eaton Square.

(2) Commander J. Croft was promoted to Lieut. in 1797. Served as 1st Lieut. of the *Orion* at the blockade of Cadiz and in the battle of Trafalgar, 1805—promoted to Commander. Died in Abany, Hungary, in June 1808.

(3) Commander J. Julian was born in Plymouth in 1778. Promoted Mid., 1793. Lieut., 1799. Was wrecked in the *Havik*, 16, off Jersey, 1800. Served as Lieut. in the *Orion* at Trafalgar, 1805. Commanded the gun-brig *Teaser* in her action with and escape from the French frigate *Arethusa* after a chase of two nights and three days in 1812. Commander, 1814. Died in Kingsbridge, Devonshire, when serving in the Coastguard, 1828.

(4) Lieut. E. Elers was promoted to Lieut. in 1801. Served as Lieut. in the *Orion* at Trafalgar, 1805. Died in Stoke, near Devonport, in 1815.

(5) Lieut. J. Hudson entered the service in 1803 as A.B. Promoted to Mid., 1805. Served as Mid. in the *Orion* at Trafalgar, 1805, the expedition to Copenhagen, 1807, and in the expedition to Walcheren, including the forcing of the Scheldt, 1809. Lieut., 1813. Commanded a Revenue vessel in Ireland, 1828–31. Medal and clasp. Died in Portsea in 1848.

(6) Lieut. J. C. Chesnaye was born in 1791, and entered the service as Volunteer 1st Class in 1803. Promoted to Mid., 1805. Served as Mid. in the *Orion* at Trafalgar, 1805. Mid. in the *Endymion* at the passage of the Dardanelles, and the investment of Rosetta, 1807. Served in the *Kent*, 74, at capture of coasting vessels at Noli, 1808. Sub-Lieut., 1810. Sub-Lieut. in the *Sylvia*, 10, in the East Indies, took part in several captures— once wounded—including that of the Dutch brig *Echo* in the

Straits of Sundy, 1810. Lieut., 1813. Served in the Coastguard, 1828–32. Medal and two clasps. Died in 1854.

(7) Lieut. F. Gray, one of four brothers in the navy, all of whom attained the rank of Lieutenant, entered the service in 1803 as a 1st Class Boy. Promoted to Mid., 1805. Served as Mid. in the *Orion* at Trafalgar, 1805, as A.D.C. to his Captain, and in the expedition to Copenhagen, 1807, and to Walcheren, including the siege of Flushing, 1809. Served in the *Venerable*, 74, at the capture, off Madeira, of the French frigates *Iphigénie* and *Alcmène*, the 16th January 1814. Lieut., 1814. In charge of Police Department, Chatham Dockyard, 1834–35. Medal and two clasps. Died in 1851.

(8) Commander J. Lechmere, D.L., J.P., was the son of Vice-Admiral William Lechmere, of Steeple Aston, Wilts., and Elizabeth, daughter of Sir John Dashwood King, Bart., of West Wycombe, Bucks. Born in 1793, he entered the service as Mid. in 1805. Mid. in the *Thunderer* in Sir Robert Calder's action, 1805. Mid. in the *Orion* at Trafalgar, 1805. Served in the *Royal George* at the passage of the Dardanelles, 1807. Was in the *Grasshopper*, which surrendered, to avoid being lost, to the Dutch fleet in the Texel, 1811, and remained a prisoner until 1814. Lieut., 1815. Retired Commander, 1860. Medal and clasp. Died in 1867–68.

(9) Lieut. G. Barker, who was born in 1789, entered the service in 1805 as Volunteer 1st Class. Served in the *Orion* at Trafalgar, 1805. As Mid. in the *Tigre* witnessed the surrender of Alexandria, 1807. Mid. in the *Blake*, 74, in the Walcheren expedition, 1809, and served with the army on shore during the operations against Flushing. Was afterwards at the defence of Tarragona. Lieut., 1814. Medal and clasp. Died in 1853.

(10) Admiral G. J., 6th Earl of Egmont, was the eldest son of Charles George, Lord Arden, and Mary Elizabeth, daughter of Sir Thomas Spencer Wilson, Bart., of Charlton, Kent, and grandson of the 2nd Earl. Born in 1794. Served as Volunteer in the expedition to Egypt, 1801; and in the *Orion* at Trafalgar, 1805. Commanded a boat of the *Tigre*, 74, at the capture of

the French *Lamproie* and other armed vessels in the Bay of Rosas, 1809. Lieut., 1813. Lieut. in the *Tenedos*, 38, in the American War, 1813–14, including the expedition up the Penobscot, and commanded a boat at the capture and destruction of the U.S. ship *Adams*, 26, in 1814. Commander, 1815. Commanded the *Infernal*, bomb, in the battle of Algiers, 1816. Captain, 1818. M.P. for West Sussex, 1837–40. Succeeded as Baron Arden, 1840, and as 6th Earl of Egmont, 1841. Rear-Admiral, 1851. Vice-Admiral, 1857. Admiral, 1863. Medal with four clasps. Died in Epsom in 1874.

(11) Commander Sir T. W. Holburne, 5th Bart., of Menstrie, near Edinburgh, was the son of Sir Francis Holburne, 4th Bart., and Alicia, daughter of Thomas Brayne, and grandson of Admiral Francis Holburne, M.P., Governor of Greenwich Hospital. Entered the service as Volunteer 1st Class, 1805. Served in the *Orion* at Trafalgar, 1805, and at blockade of Toulon, 1806. Mid., 1807. Mid. in the *Tonnant* in Sir John Duckworth's pursuit of the French squadron from Rochefort to the West Indies, 1808; and assisted in the embarkation of the army after Corunna, 1809. Lieut., 1813. Succeeded to the baronetcy, 1820. Retired Commander, 1867. Medal and clasp. Died in Bath in 1874.

(12) Mr. J. Robins served as Volunteer 1st Class in the *Orion* at Trafalgar, 1805. He received the medal and clasp in 1848.

(13) Mr. G. Starr served as an Ordinary Seaman in the *Orion* at Trafalgar, 1805. Appointed Clerk, R.N., 1805. Served in the *Alfred* in the expedition to Copenhagen, and the blockade of Lisbon, 1807; in the expedition to Walcheren, 1809, and the capture of Guadeloupe, 1810. Paymaster and Purser, 1811. Served in the *Rosario* in her action with a French flotilla off Dieppe, when three brigs were captured and two driven ashore, 1812. Medal and three clasps. Died in 1862.

(14) Mr. C. Halliday was appointed Master, R.N., in 1794. Served as Master in the *Orion* at Trafalgar, 1805. Died in 1818.

(15) Lieut. B. Turner served as Second Master of the *Orion* at Trafalgar, 1805. Lieut., 1809. Died in 1830.

(16) Captain C. Hall entered the service as A.B. in 1804, having been impressed from mate of a West Indiaman. Appointed Master's Mate in the *Orion* in 1805, and served in her at Trafalgar, 1805, and in the expedition to Copenhagen in 1807. Commanded the cutter of the *Prometheus* at the destruction of a French privateer in the Baltic, 1810. Lieut., 1815. Commander, 1841. Captain, 1853. Greenwich Hospital pension, 1862. Medal and clasp. Died in 1863.

(17) Mr. R. Sauce was the son of Commander Robert Sauce, R.N., who died in 1817. Promoted Master's Mate, 1805. Served in that capacity in the *Orion* at Trafalgar, 1805—severely wounded. Died in London from the effects of the wound, on the 6th March 1807.

(18) Surgeon T. Johnston was appointed Surgeon, R.N., in 1793. Served as Surgeon in the *Orion* at Trafalgar, 1805. Retired, 1815. Died in 1830.

(19) Surgeon R. H. Bolton, M.D., served as Assistant-Surgeon in the *Orion* at Trafalgar, 1805. Became Hospital Assistant in the Army, 1807, and was present at the battles of Roleia and Vimiero in the Peninsula in 1808. Assistant-Surgeon, 62nd Regiment, 1809. Surgeon, Medical Staff, 1813. Surgeon, 78th Highlanders, 1823. Retired, half-pay, 1826. Naval medal and clasp, and Peninsula medal with two clasps. Died in 1866.

(20) Surgeon C. Linton served as Assistant-Surgeon in the *Orion* at Trafalgar, 1805. Appointed Surgeon, R.N., 1807. Surgeon, Jamaica Hospital, 1829. Retired, 1839. Medal and clasp. Died in September 1853.

(21) Mr. W. B. Murray was appointed Purser, R.N., 1796. Served as Purser in the *Ambuscade*, 32, in her unfortunate action with, and capture by the 24-gun brig *Bayonnaise*, 1798, on which occasion, on the death or disablement of the other officers, the command devolved on him. Served as Purser of the *Orion* at Trafalgar, 1805; in the expedition to Copenhagen in 1807, and the expedition to the Baltic under Saumarez in 1809. Died in 1830.

(22) Major H. W. Cresswell became 1st Lieut., R.M., 1795.

Captain, 1804. Served in *Orion* at Trafalgar, 1805. Brevet-Major, 1814. Died in 1826.

(23) Second Lieut. S. Collins became 2nd Lieut., R.M., 1805. Served in *Orion* at Trafalgar, 1805. Not in Navy List after 1806.

(24) Lieut. S. Bridgeman became 2nd Lieut., R.M., 1805. Served in *Orion* at Trafalgar, 1805. First Lieut., 1808. Retired, half-pay, 1814. Died in 1833.

Naval General Service Medal.

XXII

H.M.S. *SWIFTSURE*, 74 GUNS

Captain . . .	William Gordon Rutherford (1).
Lieutenants .	James Lilburne (2).
	Thomas Sykes (3).
	Robert Carter (4).
	Thomas Read (5).
	Robert Heriot Barclay (6).
Master . . .	George Forbes (7).
Master's Mates	A. M. Hemsworth (8).
	Henry Weekes (9).
	John Harry Sanders (10).
	Richard Davis.
Midshipmen .	A. A. Cruikshanks.
	Frederick Fossett.
	Warwick Richardson.
	Samuel McCrea.
	Robert Contart McCrea (11).
	William Scott.
	Edward Townsend.
	Charles Henry Marshall (12).
	George Alexr. Barker (13).
	Charles Cowling Robinson (14).
	Patrick Deuchar (15).
	George Burt (16).
	Thomas Bartholomew (17).
	Miller Worsley (18).
	Henry John Ogden.
	Alexander Bell Handcock. *Wounded.*

Volunteers 1st Class	James Benson.
	James Cockrell.
	John Lihou (19).
	William Millikin.
	George Norris.
Chaplain . .	*Rev.* Timothy Myers.
Acting Surgeon	Peter Suther (20).
Surgeon's Mates	{James Osmand (21).
	{Robert Hilton.
Purser . . .	James Robinson (22).
Clerk	David Walker.
Gunner . . .	John McPhail.
Boatswain . .	Andrew Bell.
Carpenter . .	Thomas Evans.
2nd Lieuts., Royal Marines	{William Gibbons (23).
	{Robert Gordon (24).
	{Henry Miller (25).

The *Swiftsure,* of 74 guns, was built at Bucklershard, Southampton. She is frequently confounded with a 74 of the same name, which after a distinguished career, including the battle of the Nile, 1798, and the operations on the coast of Egypt, 1801, was, after a gallant fight, captured by a French squadron under M. Gantaume, off the coast of Barbary, on the 24th June 1801, and fought against us at Trafalgar. The British *Swiftsure* of Trafalgar fame was launched in 1804, and commissioned by Captain Mark Robinson. After cruising on the coast of Spain, she joined Lord Nelson on Christmas Day at Toulon. She took part in the pursuit of the combined fleets to the West Indies and back, and was present, under command of Captain William Gordon Rutherford, in the lee column at Trafalgar, on the 21st October 1805. She engaged the French *Achille,* which, in about forty minutes, having had her mizen-mast and foreyard shot away, and having caught fire, ceased

firing, and waved a Union Jack at her starboard cathead ;
she afterwards blew up. The *Swiftsure* had her own
mizen-topmast shot away and mizen-mast badly damaged,
and lost seventeen killed and wounded, including a
midshipman. After the battle she took in tow the
French 74, *Redoutable*, one of the prizes ; but when
the latter was found to be sinking, the *Swiftsure* cut
herself loose. It was a dreadful night of wind,
rain, and lightning, but she sent her boats and succeeded in saving 170 of the *Redoutable's* crew, but five
of her own men unfortunately went down in the
wreck.

There is nothing particular to record of her for the
next few years, until the 26th November 1813, when,
under the command of Captain Edward Stirling Dickson,
off Cape Rousse, island of Corsica, her boats, under
Lieut. William Smith, chased and captured the French
privateer-schooner *Charlemagne*, of eight guns and ninety-
three men. The *Charlemagne* tried to make off by using
her sweeps, but on the approach of the boats made every
preparation for resistance. She reserved her fire till the
boats had opened theirs, when the schooner returned it
in the most determined manner for some minutes, until
the boats got close alongside. The British then boarded
the privateer on the bow and quarter, and instantly
carried her, but not without a loss of one midshipman
and four men killed, two lieutenants, a lieutenant of
marines, a midshipman, and eleven men wounded—in all
twenty *hors de combat*. In 1814 she flew the flag of Vice-
Admiral John Langhorne in the Mediterranean, and in
the two following years was in the West Indies under
Captain William Henry Webly. Returning to Portsmouth in 1816, she remained there on harbour service
as a receiving hulk until 1845. She was then used for a
short time as a target, until sold in October of the same

year for £1050.   She earned the war medal with one clasp.

(1) Captain W. G. Rutherford, C.B., was the son of John Rutherford, of Bowland Stow, near Edinburgh, and Frances, widow of Gabriel Johnson, Governor of North Carolina. He was born in North Carolina in 1764; educated in Edinburgh and St. Andrew's University, and entered the service as a boy in 1778. He served as Acting Lieut. in the *Boyne*, 98, flagship of Vice-Admiral Sir John Jervis, in the West Indies, 1793. Promoted to Lieut., 1794. Accompanied the combined naval and military expedition for the capture of Martinique, and greatly distinguished himself on shore with a division of bluejackets, 1794—mentioned in despatches, promoted to Commander. Promoted to Captain, 1796. Took part in the capture of the island of Curaçoa, September 1800. Continued on the West Indian station until 1804, in command successively of the *Nautilus*, *Adventure*, *Dictator*, *Brunswick*, and *Decade*. Commanded the latter, a 36-gun frigate, at the blockade of Cherbourg in 1804. In 1805 was appointed to the *Swiftsure*, 74, which he commanded at Trafalgar, 1805—received the thanks of Parliament, a gold medal, and a sword of honour from the Patriotic Fund. Captain of Greenwich Hospital, 1814. Created a C.B., 1815. Died in Greenwich Hospital, 1818, and was buried in St. Margaret's, Westminster, where a tablet was erected to his memory.

(2) Commander J. Lilburne was promoted to Lieut. in 1798. Served as 1st Lieut. of the *Swiftsure* at Trafalgar, 1805—promoted to Commander. In command of the *Goshawk*, 16, assisted in the action with the *Amazone*, 40, near Barfleur, which ended in her destruction, 1811. With the *Barbados* was in action with seven French gun-brigs off Calvados, 1811. Was killed in action when commanding the boats of the *Goshawk*, in an engagement with a flotilla of Genoese privateers under the famous Giuseppe Bavastro, by the mole of Malaga, the 29th April 1812.

(3) Captain T. Sykes entered the service as A.B. in 1789. Promoted to Lieut., 1799. Lieut. in the *Hannibal* at defeat of seventeen Spanish gunboats near Gibraltar; and was taken

prisoner in the action between Sir James Saumarez and Admiral Linois near Algeciras, 1801, but was present in action of 12th July following, in command of the *Calpe*. Second Lieut. in the *Swiftsure*, 74, at Trafalgar, 1805, and did good service in rescuing the crew of the French *Redoutable*. Senior Lieut. in the *Tartar*, frigate, 1808–11 ; commanded the pinnace in an action with six gunboats off coast of Norway in 1808, and the boats of the *Tartar* at the capture, off the coast of Courland, of a Danish privateer, 1809—twice mentioned in despatches. Commander, 1813. Commanded the *Recruit* and *Fantome* during the American War, 1813–14, and was wrecked in the *Fantome*, 18, while on passage from Brunswick to New Halifax, 1814. Retired Captain, 1851. Medal and two clasps. Died in 1855.

(4) Lieut. R. Carter entered the service as Volunteer 1st Class in 1795. Served as Mid. in the *Royal George*, 100, in Lord Bridport's action with the French fleet off Ile Groix, 1795. Mid. in the *Mermaid*, 32, in her gallant action with the French frigate *Loire*, 40, off Ireland, 1798. Lieut., 1801. Third Lieut. in the *Swiftsure*, 74, in the pursuit of the combined fleets to the West Indies and back, and at Trafalgar, 1805. Appointed a Naval Knight of Windsor, 1834. Died, 1845.

(5) Commander T. Read entered the service in 1797. Said to have been present in the battle of the Nile, 1798; was Mid. in the *Elephant*, Lord Nelson's flagship, in the battle of Copenhagen, 1801. Lieut., 1805. Lieut. in the *Swiftsure*, 74, at Trafalgar, 1805, and was placed in charge of the French prize, *Redoutable*, 74, until she went down in the gale that followed. Commander, 1829. Was several times wounded, and was awarded a pension for wounds in 1814 of £91, 5s. per annum. Was presented with swords of honour by Admirals Sir George Montagu and Sir Isaac Coffin. Commander of Greenwich Hospital, 1843. Medal and three clasps. Died at Fishbourne, near Chichester, in 1850.

(6) Captain R. H. Barclay was the son of the Rev. Peter Barclay, D.D., Minister of Kettle, Fifeshire, N.B. He was born at Kettle in 1786, and entered the service in 1798. Served as Mid in the *Anson*, 44, in Sir John Borlase Warren's defeat of

the French squadron under Bompart off Ireland, 1798, and at the capture of the French *Loire*, 40, in the same month. Lieut., 1805. Lieut. in the *Swiftsure* at Trafalgar, 1805, and did good service in saving some of the crew of the French prize, *Redoutable*. Lost his right arm in an attack on a French convoy near Rochefort, in 1808, for which he received a pension. Acting Commander, and commanded a British flotilla during the American War, and in the action with a superior American squadron under Commodore Perry on Lake Erie in September 1813, when he was severely wounded in the thigh and in his left and only arm, and taken prisoner. He was tried by court martial for the loss of his flotilla, but was "most fully and honourably acquitted"; and was promoted to Commander, and presented with a service of plate by the inhabitants of Quebec. Promoted to Captain, 1814. Died in Edinburgh in 1837.

(7) Mr. G. Forbes was appointed Master, R.N., in 1796. Served as Master of the *Swiftsure*, 74, at Trafalgar, 1805. Died in 1821.

(8) Mr. A. M. Hemsworth was born in London in 1783. Was promoted from Mid. to Master's Mate in 1804. Served as Master's Mate in the *Swiftsure* at Trafalgar, 1805. Not traced further.

(9) Lieut. H. Weekes was born in Woolwich in 1783. Was promoted from Mid. to Master's Mate in 1805. Served as Master's Mate in the *Swiftsure* at Trafalgar 1805. Lieut., 1805. Not in Navy List after 1814.

(10) Lieut. J. H. Sanders was born in Herts. Promoted to Master's Mate in 1804. Served as Master's Mate in the *Swiftsure* in the pursuit of the combined fleet to the West Indies and back, and at Trafalgar, 1805. Lieut., 1806. Not traced after 1808.

(11) Admiral R. C. McCrea was born in Guernsey in 1793. Entered the service in 1803 as Volunteer 2nd Class. Served in the *Décade*, frigate, at the blockade of Cherbourg in 1804. Mid., 1805. Served as Mid. in the *Swiftsure* in the pursuit of the combined fleets to the West Indies and back, and at Trafalgar, 1805. Served in the *Salsette*, 36, in the Walcheren expedition, including the bombardment of Flushing, 1809. Lieut., 1812. Lieut. in the *Amphion*, 32, in 1813-15, including the capture of the

P

islands of Schouwen and Tholen in 1813.   Flag-Lieut. to Admiral
Sir James Saumarez, Commander-in-chief, Plymouth, 1824—
promoted to Commander.   Captain, 1837.   Captain of the
Zebra, 16, in action with Malays in 1837, and took the ex-Rajah
of Quedah prisoner.   For this service he was presented with a
piece of plate, value 100 guineas, by the Hon. East India Company.   Rear-Admiral, 1857.   Vice-Admiral, 1863.   Admiral,
1868.   Medal and clasp.   Died in 1874.

(12) Lieut. C. H. Marshall was born in Portsmouth.   Became Mid., 1804.   Served as Mid. in the *Swiftsure*, 74, at
Trafalgar, 1805.   Lieut., 1813.   Chief Officer of Coastguard,
1828–35.   Died at Larne, County Antrim, Ireland, in 1835.

(13) Lieut. G. A. Barker became Mid. in 1804.   Served as
Mid. in the *Swiftsure* at Trafalgar, 1805.   Lieut., 1811.   First
Lieut. of the *Badger*, 10, on the West India station, 1811–15, including the reduction of Guadeloupe in the latter year.   Not
traced after 1817.

(14) Commander C. C. Robinson was a son of Commander
Charles Robinson, R.N., and was born in Hampshire in 1790,
and entered the service as Volunteer 1st Class, 1803.   Promoted
Mid., 1804.   Served as Mid. in the *Swiftsure*, 74, in the pursuit
of the combined fleets to the West Indies and back, and at Trafalgar, 1805.   Lieut., 1812.   Medal and clasp.   Died in 1850.

(15) Commander P. Deuchar was born in Edinburgh in 1785,
and entered the service in 1804 as ordinary, having previously
served an apprenticeship of four years in the merchant service.
Mid., 1805.   Served as Mid. in the *Swiftsure*, 74, in the pursuit of
the combined fleets to the West Indies and back, and at Trafalgar,
1805.   Mid. in the *Seahorse*, 38, in the operations off Cadiz in
1806 ; and in the *Moselle*, 18, at the attack on Rosetta in 1807.
Master's Mate, 1808.   Master's Mate in the *St. Domingo* in the
Walcheren expedition, 1809, including the bombardment of
Flushing.   Lieut., 1813.   Commanded a portion of the Cadiz
flotilla, 1813–14.   Retired Commander, 1856.   Medal and clasp.
Died in 1869.

(16) Lieut. G. Burt was born in Dublin.   He served as Mid.
in the *Swiftsure*, 74, at Trafalgar, 1805.   Mid. in the *Dreadnought*,

98, and took part in her boats in the unsuccessful attempt to cut out a French ship off Ushant, 1810—wounded. Senior Lieut. in the *Sylph*, 16, and was drowned when she was wrecked on Southampton Bar, North America, the 17th January 1815.

(17) Mr. T. Bartholomew was born in Dorking in 1792. Served as Mid. in the *Swiftsure*, 74, at Trafalgar, 1805. He was killed by a fall in the *Swiftsure* on the 27th November 1805, aged 14.

(18) Commander M. Worsley was born in the Isle of Wight. Served as Mid. in the *Swiftsure*, 74, at Trafalgar, 1805. Lieut., 1813. Served during the American War in 1813–14. Commanded the schooner *Nancy* up the Nattawassaga, which, under cover of a blockhouse, was attacked and blown up, after a smart defence, by an American squadron under Captain Sinclair, U.S.N. With a party in boats performed a very gallant action in boarding and capturing the American schooners *Tigress* and *Scorpion* on Lake Huron, the 3rd and 6th September 1814. Commander, 1815. Inspecting-Commander of Coastguard, 1832–34. Died in 1835.

(19) Captain J. Lihou was a son of Peter Lihou, of Guernsey, and Carteret, fourth daughter of Matthew de Saumarez, who was father of Admiral James, 1st Lord de Saumarez, G.C.B. He was born in Guernsey. He served as a Volunteer 1st Class in the *Swiftsure*, 74, at Trafalgar, 1805. Lieut., 1811. Senior Lieut. in the *Pique*, 42, in Jamaica, 1816. Commander, 1827. Sup. Commander of the *Victory*, 101, in 1832–33. Captain, 1833. Invented a rudder which was adopted by the Admiralty. Died in Guernsey in 1840.

(20) Mr. P. Suther was appointed Surgeon, R.N., in 1805. Served as Surgeon in the *Swiftsure*, 74, in pursuit of the combined fleets to the West Indies and back, and at Trafalgar, 1805. Surgeon of the *Eurydice* at the capture of Martinique, 1809. Assistant-Surgeon, Portsmouth Dockyard, 1838–39. Surgeon, royal yacht, *William and Mary*, 1839–41. Surgeon, Woolwich Dockyard, 1841–49. Surgeon, Chatham Dockyard, 1849–55. Deputy-Inspector of Hospitals and Fleets, 1855. Greenwich Hospital pension, 1866. Medal and two clasps. Died in 1877.

(21) Mr. J. Osmand served as Surgeon's Mate in the *Swift-sure*, 74, at Trafalgar, 1805. Surgeon, 1809. Surgeon of the *Beelzebub* in the battle of Algiers, 1816. Retired, 1839. Medal and two clasps. Died in 1848.

(22) Mr. J. Robinson was appointed Paymaster and Purser, R.N., 1779. Served as Purser of the *Swiftsure*, 74, at Trafalgar, 1805. Died in 1825.

(23) Second Lieut. W. Gibbons became 2nd Lieut., R.M., in 1804. Served in the *Swiftsure*, 74, at Trafalgar, 1805. Not in the corps after 1807.

(24) Major R. Gordon became 2nd Lieut., R.M., in 1804. Served in the *Swiftsure*, 74, at Trafalgar, 1805. First Lieut., 1806. Captain, 1827. Brevet-Major, 1841. Retired full pay, 1842. Medal and clasp. Died in 1849.

(25) Lieut. H. Miller became 2nd Lieut., R.M., in 1804. Served in the *Swiftsure*, 74, at Trafalgar, 1805. First Lieut., 1806. Served with the 2nd Marine Battalion in the American War, 1813–14. Retired, half-pay, 1814. Medal and clasp. Died in 1849.

XXIII

H.M.S. *AJAX*, 74 GUNS

Acting Captain	Lieut. John Pilford (1).
Lieutenants .	Jeremiah Brown (2).
	Thomas Prowse (3).
	Peter Mitchell (4).
	Thomas Dobbins Barker (5).
	Charles Wood (6).
	Henry Nathaniel Rowe (7).
Midshipmen .	Charles Wallis (7a).
	George Benjamin Roper (8).
	Daniel Guerin (9).
	William Nicholl.
	William Lowcay (10).
	Robert Saunders (11).
	William Smith (12)
	George Walker.
	William Hood.
	Richard Owens.
	James Face.
	Henry Symes.
	Robert Harvey (13).
	James Waring (14)
	Hugh Reculist.
	Benjamin Danford (15).
	John Phepoe (16).
Volunteers 1st Class	Adam Gordon (17).
	Joseph Gape (18).
	John Milligan Dacres.
	Benjamin Rundell.

Volunteers 1st Cl.	James Bundock.
(*continued*) .	Hugh Dyke Acland (19).
	Robert Hemer (20).
Master . . .	David Donaldson (21).
Master's Mates	John Callan.
	Henry Loney (22).
	Richard Hames.
Surgeon . . .	William Mustard (23).
Assistant - Surgeons . . .	{ Thomas Reynolds (24).
	{ Launcelot Armstrong (25).
Purser . . .	William Bundock (26).
Clerk	William Garn Mason (27).
Gunner . . .	John Dunnett (28).
Boatswain . .	John Turner.
Carpenter . .	Thomas Prior.
Captain, Royal Marines .	} David Boyd (29).
2nd Lieuts., Royal Marines	{ Samuel Burdon Ellis (30).
	{ Joseph Cinnamond (31).

The *Ajax* was launched from Randall's Yard, Rotherhithe, in 1798, in which year she was first commissioned. In February 1799, Captain Hon. Alexander Cochrane was appointed to her, and she soon afterwards joined Lord Bridport off Brest. In June she was with the blockading force off Rochefort, under Rear-Admiral Hon. G. C. Berkeley; in the following month, participating in Rear-Admiral Sir Charles Morice Pole's action with the Spanish in Basque Roads. In 1800, in addition to capturing the French privateer *Avantageur*, she was with Earl St. Vincent off Brest; and in June was detached with the squadron under Captain Sir Edward Pellew, co-operating with the insurgent French Royalists in the Morbihan. In 1801, still under Captain Cochrane, she took part in the expedition to Egypt under Lord Keith; and when the British army landed at Aboukir

Bay on 8th February, the boats employed were under the direction of Captain Cochrane. Her launch, with the others of the squadron, assisted in the taking of Marabout in June.

In 1805 she was under the command of Captain William Brown, and under him fought in Sir Robert Calder's action of the 22nd July, when she suffered rather severely, losing eighteen in killed and wounded, and having her main-yard and driver boom shot away. She joined Lord Nelson's fleet at Plymouth on the 18th October, and in the absence of Captain William Brown, who had gone home as a witness in Sir Robert Calder's trial, was temporarily commanded by the 1st Lieutenant, John Pilfold. Under him she fought in the weather column at Trafalgar, and was a good deal engaged with Dumanoir's division, losing eleven killed and wounded.

Under Captain Hon. Henry Blackwood she joined the expedition to the Dardanelles under Sir John Duckworth in 1807. This was her last service. On the evening of the 14th February, while the squadron lay wind-bound off Cape Janissary, and just as Captain Blackwood had retired to rest, the officer of the watch ran into the cabin with an alarm of fire in the after part of the ship. Signals of distress were immediately made and enforced by guns. The fire had broken out in the after cockpit, and in the course of ten minutes, notwithstanding every attempt to stifle it, the smoke became so dense that, although the moon shone bright, the officers and men on the upper deck could only distinguish each other by speaking or feeling; all attempts, therefore, to hoist out the boats, except the jollyboat, were ineffectual. The flames burst up the main hatchway, thereby dividing the fore from the after part of the ship; and with the greatest difficulty the captain and about 381 of the officers, seamen, and marines effected their escape, chiefly by jumping overboard from the bowsprit, or by dropping into the few boats of the squadron that were enabled to approach. Captain Blackwood leaped from the spritsail yard, and after being about half an hour in the water was picked up, much exhausted, by one of the boats of the *Canopus*. The *Ajax* burnt during the whole night, and, the wind blowing fresh from the north-east, she drifted on the island of Tenedos ; where at 5 A.M. on the following day, the 15th, she blew up with an awful explosion. Her net complement of men and boys was about 633 ; therefore, admitting all to have been on board at the commencement of the disaster, 250 persons must have perished. Among the sufferers were two merchants of Constantinople and two women ; a third saved herself by following her husband, with a child in his arms, down a rope from the jib-boom end. Captain Blackwood and the surviving officers and crew were honourably acquitted of all blame for the loss of the ship, which was attributed either to carelessness or to the spontaneous combustion of some coal. The *Ajax* was the shortest lived of the Trafalgar ships, having existed for a little over seven years.

(1) Captain J. Pilfold, C.B., was the second son of Charles Pilfold, of Horsham, Sussex, and Bathia, daughter of William White, of Horsham. He entered the service in 1788. He served as Master's Mate in the *Brunswick*, 74, in Lord Howe's victory of the 1st June 1794—promoted Lieut. Lieut. in the *Russell*, 74, in Lord Bridport's action of Groix, 1795. As Lieut. in the *Kingfisher*, sloop, assisted in the capture of several privateers in 1796 ; and behaved very pluckily on the occasion of a mutiny on board. Lieut. in the *Impétueux*, 78, with the squadron co-operating with the insurgent French Royalists in the Morbihan in 1800 ; commanded a division of boats which captured and destroyed the French 18-gun corvette *Insolante*, carried off several small craft and prisoners, destroyed

some guns, and blew up a magazine. Served as 1st Lieut. of the *Ajax*, 74, in Sir Robert Calder's action of the 22nd July 1805; and, in the absence of the Captain, commanded her at Trafalgar, 1805, for which he received the gold medal, the thanks of Parliament, a sword of honour from the Patriotic Fund, and an hon. augmentation to his arms. Created a C.B., 1815. Captain of the Ordinary at Plymouth, 1828–31. Died in Stonehouse, Devon, 1834.

(2) Lieut. J. Brown was promoted to Lieut., 1801. Acting 1st Lieut. of the *Ajax* at Trafalgar, 1805. Died in 1817.

(3) Commander T. Prowse was promoted to Lieut., 1801. Lieut. in the *Ajax* in Sir Robert Calder's action, 1805, and at Trafalgar, 1805. Commander, 1806. Commanded the *Martin*, 16, which was lost in the Atlantic, when he and all hands were drowned, in September 1806.

(4) Lieut. P. Mitchell was promoted to Lieut., 1801. Lieut. in the *Ajax* at Trafalgar, 1805. Lost his life in her, the 14th February 1807.

(5) Lieut. T. D. Barker was promoted to Lieut., 1801. Lieut. in the *Ajax* at Trafalgar, 1805. Not in Navy List after 1806.

(6) Lieut. C. Wood was promoted to Lieut., 1804. Lieut. in the *Ajax* at Trafalgar, 1805. Died in 1819–20.

(7) Captain H. N. Rowe was the son of Rev. Henry Rowe, LL.B., of Padnall Hall and Toby Priory, Essex, Rector of Rings-hall, Co. Suffolk, and Harriett, daughter of Rev. Thomas Bland, Vicar of Sittingbourne, Kent. Entered service as Leading Man, 1798. Mid. of *Wolverene* in the expedition to Holland, 1799. Master's Mate, 1801. Sub-Lieut., 1805. Lieut., 1805. Lieut. in the *Ajax* in Sir Robert Calder's action, and at Trafalgar, 1805; and was serving in her at the time of her destruction by fire, but escaped, 1807. Volunteer in the *Windsor Castle*, 98, at the passage of the Dardanelles, 1807. Lieut. in the *Valiant*, 74, in the expedition to Copenhagen, 1807—severely wounded, leg amputated; pension for wounds of £200 per annum. Acting Commander of the *Rosamond* at the reduction of Guadeloupe, 1810. Retired Captain, 1840. Medal and two clasps. Died in 1860.

(7a) Mr. C. Wallis was a son of Ralph Wallis of Knaresdale, Northumberland.

(8) Lieut. G. B. Roper served as Mid. in the *Ajax* at Trafalgar, 1805. Lieut., 1809. As Lieut. in the *Diana*, 38, commanded a boat in cutting out some French merchantmen in the mouth of the Gironde, 1811. Died, 1815.

(9) Lieut. D. Guerin served as Mid. in the *Ajax* at Trafalgar, 1805. Lieut., 1808. Died, 1825.

(10) Captain W. Lowcay was the son of Mr. Henry Lowcay, Master's Mate, R.N., who died in 1827. He had four brothers in the navy and one in the marines. He was born in Chatham in 1787. Entered the service as Volunteer 2nd Class, 1796. Served as Mid. in the *Ajax* at Trafalgar, 1805. Sub-Lieut. in the *Contest*, brig, in an attack on a French convoy, 1807— wounded. Lieut., 1809. Lieut. in the *Princess of Orange*, 74, in Walcheren expedition, 1809. In Coastguard, 1820–33. Retired Commander, 1847. Retired Captain, 1849. Medal and clasp. Died in Weymouth in July 1852.

(11) Mr. R. Saunders served as Mid. in the *Ajax* at Trafalgar, 1805. Master's Mate, 1806. Lost his life in her, the 14th February 1807.

(12) Mr. William Smith served as Mid. in the *Ajax* at Trafalgar, 1805. Received the medal and clasp in 1848.

(13) Lieut. R. Harvey was born in Liskeard, Cornwall. Served as Mid. in the *Ajax* at Trafalgar, 1805. Lieut., 1806. When Lieut. in the *Superb*, 74, was killed in action in a boat attack on two Danish vessels at Nyborg in Fünen, in the Baltic, the 9th August 1808.

(14) Lieut. J. Waring served as Mid. in the *Ajax* at Trafalgar, 1805. Lieut., 1808. Lieut. in the *Royalist*, 16, at the capture of the Franco-Batavian frigate *Weser*, 40, off the Texel, 1813— wounded. Died in 1832.

(15) Mr. B. Danford served as Mid. in the *Ajax* at Trafalgar, 1805. Lost his life in her, the 14th February 1807.

(16) Commander J. Phepoe was the son of Colonel John Phepoe, of Dublin, who commanded one of the corps of Irish Volunteers in 1782. He was born in 1786, and entered the

service in 1801. Mid., 1803. Mid. in the *Ajax* at Trafalgar, 1805. Was in her when she caught fire in 1807, and narrowly escaped drowning. Mid. in the *Thunderer*, 74, at the forcing of the Dardanelles, and in the expedition to Egypt, 1807. Lieut., 1809. Served in the Walcheren expedition, 1809. Served in the boats of the *Armide*, 38, at the destruction of a convoy at Ile de Ré, and at the capture of the American schooner *Trojan*, 18, both in 1811. Retired Commander, 1848. Medal and clasp. Died in Clifton in 1862.

(17) Lieut. A. Gordon, Viscount Kenmure, D.L., J.P., was the son of Hon. Adam Gordon and Harriet Davies, and nephew of the 10th Viscount Kenmure. Born at Drungan Lodge, Dumfries, N.B., in 1792, and entered the service in 1804 as Volunteer 1st Class. Served in the *Ajax* in Sir Robert Calder's action, and in the battle of Trafalgar, 1805. Mid. in the *Seahorse*, 42, at the capture of the Turkish frigate *Badere i Zaffer*, 44, in the Archipelago, 1808; at the reduction of the islands of Gianuti and Pianosa, and in a boat action on the coast of Italy, 1809— wounded. Taken prisoner in a prize off Sardinia in 1809 and detained at Verdun until 1814. Served on the Canadian lakes, 1814–16. Lieut., 1815. Succeeded as 11th Viscount Kenmure, 1840. Medal and two clasps. Died at Kenmure Castle, Kirkcudbright, N.B., 1847.

(18) Vice-Admiral J. Gape was the son of the Rev. W. C. Gape, J.P., of St. Albans, Herts. Entered the service, 1803, as Volunteer 1st Class. Served in the *Ajax* in Sir Robert Calder's action, and in the battle of Trafalgar, 1805. Mid. in the *Amphion*, 32, and served in her in an action with a French frigate in the Bay of Rosas, 1808; in her boats at the destruction of a battery, and the capture of six gunboats and a convoy at Cortellazzo, near Trieste, 1809; the capture of a convoy of twenty-five vessels at Grao, 1810; and in Sir William Hoste's action with and capture of frigates off Lissa, 1811. Lieut., 1811. Commander, 1814. Inspecting Commander of Coastguard, 1837–41. Captain, 1841. Retired Rear-Admiral, 1862. Retired Vice-Admiral, 1867. Medal and four clasps. Died in 1875.

(19) Mr. H. D. Acland was the son of Sir Thomas Dyke

Acland, 9th Bart., and Henrietta Anne, only daughter of Sir Richard Hoare, Bart. Born in 1791. Served as a Volunteer 1st Class in the *Ajax* at Trafalgar, 1805. Left the service shortly afterwards. Died, 1834.

(20) Commander R. Hemer was born in Exeter, and entered the service as Volunteer 1st Class, 1805. Served in that capacity in the *Ajax* at Trafalgar, 1805. Mid., 1806. Mid. in the *Dreadnought*, 98, was taken prisoner in attempting to cut out a brig in the Ile d'Aix, and detained till 1814. Lieut., 1815. Afterwards in command of a Revenue cruiser, and in the Coastguard. Commander retired half-pay, 1859. Medal and clasp. Died in 1862.

(21) Mr. D. Donaldson was appointed Master, R.N., 1795. Served as Master of the *Ajax* at Trafalgar, 1805. Lost his life in her in 1807.

(22) Lieut. H. Loney was born in Plymouth. Served as Master's Mate in the *Ajax* at Trafalgar, 1805—promoted Lieut. Died in 1827.

(23) Surgeon W. Mustard was appointed Surgeon, R.N., in 1795. Served as Surgeon of the *Ajax* in Sir Robert Calder's action, and at Trafalgar, 1805. Died in 1829.

(24) Mr. T. Reynolds served as Assistant-Surgeon in the *Ajax* at Trafalgar, 1805. Lost his life in her, 1807.

(25) Surgeon L. Armstrong was appointed Assistant-Surgeon, R.N., 1805. Served as Assistant-Surgeon in the *Ajax* at Trafalgar, 1805. Surgeon, 1807. Surgeon of the *Ajax* in the expedition to Dardanelles, and was in her when she caught fire, and narrowly escaped drowning, 1807. Died at Canonbie, Dumfriesshire, N.B., in 1848.

(26) Mr. W. Bundock was appointed Paymaster and Purser, R.N., in 1791. Served as Purser of the *Ajax* at Trafalgar, 1805. Died at Totnes in 1841.

(27) Mr. W. G. Mason served as Clerk in the *Ajax* at Trafalgar, 1805. Purser, 1806. Served in *President* at capture of Java, 1811; and in the *Princess Charlotte* in the operations on the coast of Syria, 1840, including the bombardment of Acre. Naval medal and three clasps, and Turkish medal for Syria. Died in 1857.

(28) Mr. J. Dunnett served as gunner of the *Ajax* at Trafalgar, 1805. Lost his life in her, 1807.

(29) Captain D. Boyd was appointed 2nd Lieut., R.M., 1782. First Lieut., 1793. Captain, 1800. Senior marine officer in the *Ajax* in Sir Robert Calder's action, and at Trafalgar, 1805. Lost his life in her in 1807.

(30) Lieut.-General Sir S. B. Ellis, K.C.B., one of four brothers in the Royal Navy and Marines, was the son of Lieut. John Ellis, R.N., who died in 1798. Was appointed 2nd Lieut., R.M., 1804. Served in the *Ajax* in Sir Robert Calder's action, and at Trafalgar, 1805 ; and was in her when she was destroyed by fire in 1807. In the *Lavinia*, 44, in the Walcheren expedition, including the forcing of the mouth of the Scheldt, 1809. Was also at the capture of Guadeloupe, January–February 1810. Present at the storming of the batteries of Cassis, between Marseilles and Toulon, 1813—mentioned in despatches. In the *Pomone*, 38, was engaged with the U.S. frigate *President*, 44, which was subsequently captured by the *Endymion*, 1815. Captain, 1826. Served in the *Wellesley*, 72, in the operations in Scinde and in the Persian Gulf, 1839, including the capture of Fort Munora and Kurrachee. In the *Wellesley*, served as senior marine officer in the first China War, 1840-42, including the capture of Chusan, battle of Chuenpee, storming and capture of the heights above Canton, second capture of Chusan, capture of Chunhae, &c.—three times mentioned in despatches, brevets of Major and Lieut.-Colonel, C.B., and medal. Lieut.-Colonel, 1846. Colonel, 1851. Commandant, Woolwich Division, 1852-1855. Major-General, 1855. Lieut.-General, 1857. K.C.B. Naval medal and two clasps. Died in Charlton, Kent, 1865.

(31) Lieut. J. Cinnamond was born in Ballenderry, Co. Antrim, 1779. Appointed 2nd Lieut., R.M., 1803. Served in the *Ajax* at Trafalgar, 1805, and was in her when she was destroyed by fire in 1807. First Lieut., 1806. Served in the *St. George* at the passage of the Dardanelles, 1807. Retired, half-pay, 1815. Medal and clasp. Died in Belfast in 1861.

XXIV

H.M.S. *THUNDERER*, 74 GUNS

Captain . . .	Lieut. John Stockham (acting) (1).
Lieutenants .	William Norman (2).
	John Clark (3).
	Thomas Carter (4).
	Thomas Colby (5).
Master . . .	Robert Cock (6).
Master's Mate .	Thomas Slade.
Midshipmen .	Robert Cock (7).
	John Coxetter Snell (8). *Wounded*.
	John Jane (9).
	Alexander Gallaway (10). *Wounded*.
	Alexander Fife.
	John Strike.
	Benjamin Tropshaw.
	William Owen Tudor.
	John Ellard.
Volunteers 1st Class	John Treffry.
	John Fletcher Herbert (11).
	John Harvie.
	James Suttor Britton (12).
Chaplain . .	*Rev.* John Holmes.
Surgeon . . .	John Stokoe (13).
Assist.-Surgeon	James Marr Brydone (14).
Purser . . .	Henry Wells (15).
Clerk	Michael Gould.
Gunner . . .	William Watt.
Boatswains . .	{Richard Keefe.
	James Samuel Simpson (Supy. for Victuals).

* Rated as A.B.

Carpenter . . Edward Trego.

Captain, Royal } Gilbert Elliot (16).
Marines . . }

Lieuts., Royal { William Hockly (17).
Marines . . { John Lister (18).

The *Thunderer* of Trafalgar fame, not to be confounded with a 74 of a similar name which was lost in
a hurricane in the West Indies three years before, was
built on the Thames in 1783. There is nothing interesting
to relate of her until the commencement of the war
of the French Revolution in 1793, shortly after which she
was commissioned by Captain Albemarle Bertie, and
employed with the Channel Fleet under Lord Howe.
She was in the action of the 28th May 1794, and was
engaged with the rear ships of the French fleet; and
participated in the glorious victory on the 1st June, but
had no opportunity of distinguishing herself. She was
with the British fleet under Lord Bridport in his action
with the French, and the capture of three sail of the line
on the 23rd June 1795. She then accompanied the
expedition to Quiberon. Under command of Captain
William Ogilvy she was with Vice-Admiral Sir Hyde
Parker at Jamaica in 1797, and in company with the
Valiant, drove ashore and caused the destruction of the
French 44-gun frigate *Harmoine*, off San Domingo, on
the 16th April in that year.

On the recommencement of war with France in
1803 she was serving with the Channel Fleet, William
Bedford being her captain. Under him, on the 28th
May, she took part with the *Minotaur* and *Albion* in the
chase and capture of the French 40-gun frigate *Franchise*,
which was on her way home from San Domingo. On
the 26th July following, whilst blockading L'Orient, she
pursued and captured the French *Venus*, 16, a very

fast Bordeaux privateer manned by 150 men. At the end of the year she was off Ireland, and underwent a terrible experience during the heavy gale on the night of the 10th December, but arrived safely in Bantry Bay. Captain William Lechmere was appointed to her early in 1805, and he commanded her in Sir Robert Calder's action off Ferrol on the 22nd July, on which occasion she lost nineteen killed and wounded. Her rigging, &c., was much cut, her mizen-mast, foreyard, and main topsail-yard and head shot through. When Captain Lechmere was ordered home to attend the court-martial on Sir Robert Calder, the command of the *Thunderer* devolved upon Lieut. John Stockham ; and under his acting command she joined Lord Nelson at Plymouth on the 18th September, and was present in the lee column in the great victory of Trafalgar, the 21st October 1805. In the battle she was of some assistance to the *Revenge*, and subsequently was engaged with the Spanish 112, *Principe de Asturias*, and the French 84, *Neptune*. Her losses amounted to sixteen killed and wounded, including three officers. Shots were found in her main and mizen-masts and bowsprit, but otherwise her damages were not material.

In 1806–7, under Captain John Talbot, she was with Lord Cornwallis watching Cadiz, and in the defence of Gaeta. She then joined Sir J. T. Duckworth's squadron, and was at the passage of the Dardanelles on the 19th February 1807. She distinguished herself at the destruction of a Turkish squadron lying within the forts of the Dardanelles, in which affair and in the subsequent operations against the Turks by the squadron she lost thirty-four killed and wounded. In the following year she was with Sir Richard Strachan's squadrons watching Allemand's Rochefort squadron. She performed no other important service, and was broken up at Chatham in 1814, after earning the naval medal with three clasps.

(1) Captain J. Stockham was promoted to Lieut. in 1797. Served as 1st Lieut. of the *Thunderer* in Sir Robert Calder's action in July 1805, and when Captain Lechmere was sent home to attend the court martial, acted as her captain at Trafalgar, 1805—promoted Captain, gold medal, thanks of Parliament, and a sword of honour from the Patriotic Fund. Died in Exeter, 1814.

(2) Commander W. Norman, one of four brothers in the Royal Navy, two of whom were killed in action, was promoted to Lieut., 1799. Commanded the *Biter*, gun-brig, at the capture of the French frigate *Désirée* and other vessels in Dunkerque Road, the 8th July 1800. Lieut., and acted as First, at Trafalgar, the 21st October 1805. Lieut. in the *Sirius* at the capture of *Réunion* or *Bourbon*, 1810. Commanded her boats at destruction of a French schooner off Mauritius, same year; and was killed in action, shot through the heart, when in command of the boats at the capture of the Ile de la Passe, the 13th August 1810. He had been promoted to Commander, but died before the announcement reached him.

(3) Commander J. Clark was born in 1777, and entered the service from Christ's Hospital, 1794. Mid., 1795. Served as Mid. in the *Russell*, 74, in Lord Bridport's action with the French fleet, 1795. In the *Indefatigable*, 46, in the expedition to Ferrol, and the capture of the French *Venus*, 52, in 1800. Mid. in the *Theseus*, 74, at the capture of a French cutter and thirteen merchant vessels at Port Jeremiah, St. Domingo, 1802. In the *Hercule*, 74, at the attack on Curaçoa, 1804. Lieut., 1805. Lieut. in the *Thunderer*, 74, in Sir Robert Calder's action, and in the battle of Trafalgar, 1805, the siege of Gaeta, 1806, the passage of the Dardanelles, 1807, and the expedition to Egypt, 1807. Commanded a gunboat, and afterwards a flotilla of gunboats in the expedition to Walcheren, 1809. Retired Commander, 1837. Medal and two clasps. Died, 1849–50.

(4) Lieut. T. Carter was promoted to Lieut., 1805. Served as Lieut. in the *Thunderer*, 74, in Sir Robert Calder's action, and at Trafalgar, 1805. Not in Navy List after 1810.

(5) Captain T. Colby was the son of Dr. Thomas Colby, of Great Torrington, Devonshire, and was born in 1782. Entered the service as Mid., 1797. Served as Mid. in the *Bedford*, 74, in the battle of Camperdown, 1797. Mid. in the *Foudroyant*, 80, in Sir John Borlase Warren's action with the French on the coast of Ireland, 1798. Mid. in the *Centurion*, 50, in her action with the French *Marengo*, 80, and the *Atalante* and *Sémillante*, frigates, in Vizagapatam Roads, 1804. Lieut., 1805. Lieut. in the *Thunderer*, 74, in Sir Robert Calder's action, and in the battle of Trafalgar, 1805; the defence of Gaeta, 1806; the passage of the Dardanelles, 1807—wounded; and in her boats at the boarding and destruction of a Turkish squadron at Point Pesquies; and in the expedition to Egypt, 1807. Lieut. in the *Cadmus*, 10, and in her boats cut out a French armed transport in Quiberon Bay, 1809. Senior Lieut. in the *Prince of Wales*, 98, at the reduction of Genoa, 1814. Commander, 1814. Commander of Greenwich Hospital, 1850. Retired Captain, 1864. Medal and five clasps. Died in Great Torrington, Devonshire, in 1864.

(6) Mr. R. Cock was appointed Master, R.N., 1794. Served as Master of the *Thunderer*, 74, in Sir Robert Calder's action, and in the battle of Trafalgar, 1805. Not in Navy List after 1809.

(7) Commander R. Cock entered the service as Volunteer 1st Class, 1796. Served in *Thalia*, 36, at the capture of the French corvette *L'Espoir*, 1797. Mid., 1802. Mid. in the *Thunderer*, 74, in Sir Robert Calder's action, and in the battle of Trafalgar, 1805; in the passage of the Dardanelles, and the destruction of a Turkish squadron near Point Pesquies, 1807. Master's Mate in the *Aurora*, 28, at the capture of Guadeloupe, January-February 1810. Served in boats of *Quebec* at the capture of three Danish gun-brigs in the river Jahde, 1811. Lieut., 1811. Retired Commander, 1852. Medal and three clasps. Died in 1855.

(8) Lieut. J. C. Snell was a brother of Commander William Snell, who served in the *Britannia* at Trafalgar, and was born in Greenwich. He served as Mid. in the *Thunderer* at Trafalgar, 1805—wounded. Lieut., 1808. Died in 1838.

(9) Lieut. J. Jane served as Mid. in the *Thunderer* at Trafalgar, 1805. Lieut., 1815. Died in 1835.

(10) Commander A. Gallaway, the son of a boatswain, R.N., was born at Gisborough, Yorkshire, in 1792. Entered the service as a boy, 1800. Volunteer 1st Class, 1801. Mid., 1805. Served as Mid. in the *Thunderer* in Sir Robert Calder's action, and at Trafalgar, 1805—wounded ; at the siege of Gaeta, 1806 ; the passage of the Dardanelles, 1807—wounded ; and the expedition to Egypt, 1807. Served in the *Cordelia* in the Walcheren expedition, 1809. Lieut., 1812. Afterwards employed in the merchant service. Retired Commander, 1854. Greenwich Hospital pension, 1856. Medal and clasp. Died in 1873.

(11) Lieut. J. F. Herbert entered service in 1805 as Volunteer 1st Class. Served in the *Thunderer* in Sir Robert Calder's action, and at Trafalgar, 1805 ; the passage of the Dardanelles, and the destruction of the Turkish squadron near Point Pesquies, 1807. Mid., 1808. Lieut., 1819. Died in 1847.

(12) Commander J. S. Britton was born at Charleston, North America, in 1781, and was impressed into the service, 1800. Rated as A.B., served as a Volunteer in the *Thunderer* in Sir Robert Calder's action, and at Trafalgar, 1805 ; the defence of Gaeta, 1806 ; and the passage of the Dardanelles, 1807. Wrecked in the *Wildboar*, 10, near Land's End, 1810. Master's Mate, 1810. Lieut., 1815. Retired Commander, 1860. Medal and clasp. Died in 1860.

(13) Surgeon J. Stokoe was promoted to Surgeon, R.N., 1800. Served as Surgeon in the *Thunderer* at Trafalgar, 1805. Surgeon of the *Conqueror*, 74, guarding Napoleon, at St. Helena, 1818–19. Died there in 1819.

(14) Surgeon J. M. Brydone was born in Selkirk, N.B., in 1779. Appointed Assistant-Surgeon, R.N., 1804. Assistant-Surgeon in the *Thunderer* at Trafalgar, 1805, and at the siege

of Gaeta, 1806. Surgeon, 1806. Retired, 1839. Medal and clasp. Was Land Steward to the Earl of Leaconfield from 1847 until his death. Died at Petworth, Sussex, in 1866.

(15) Mr. H. Wells served as Clerk in the *Russell* in Lord Howe's victory of the 1st June 1794—wounded; and in Lord Bridport's action with the French fleet, 1795. Paymaster and Purser, 1797. Served as Purser of the *Thunderer* in Sir Robert Calder's action, and at Trafalgar, 1805; at the siege of Gaeta, 1806; and the forcing of the Dardanelles, 1807. Retired, 1843. Medal and three clasps. Died in 1849.

(16) Major G. Elliot was appointed 2nd Lieut., R.M., 1795. First Lieut., 1796. Captain, 1805. Served in the *Thunderer* in Sir Robert Calder's action, and at Trafalgar, 1805. Brevet-Major, 1819. Died in 1820.

(17) Lieut. W. Hockly was appointed 2nd Lieut., R.M., 1805. Served in the *Thunderer* at Trafalgar, 1805. First Lieut., 1808. Served in the *Havannah*, 42, and performed good service at the capture of French vessels near the town of Vasto, and Fortose, in the Adriatic, 1813; also took part in the capture of the fortress of Zara, 1814. Half-pay, 1817. Not in Navy List after 1823.

(18) Lieut. J. Lister was appointed 2nd Lieut., R.M., 1805. Served in the *Thunderer* at Trafalgar, 1805; at the siege of Gaeta, 1806; and at the forcing of the Dardanelles, 1807. First Lieut., 1808. Reserved, half-pay, 1825. Medal and clasp. Died in 1862.

XXV

H.M.S. *POLYPHEMUS*, 64 GUNS

Captain . . .	Robert Redmill (1).
Lieutenants .	George Moubray (2).
	William Sandey (3).
	Charles Squarey (4).
	John Medlicott (5).
	Robert Mayne (6).
Master . . .	Robert Louthean (7).
Master's Mates	David Hunter (8).
	Samuel Wise.
	John Perkins.
Midshipmen .	Thomas Darby.
	Thomas Woodyatt (9).
	William Rule (10).
	John Newell (11).
	George Edward Cocksedge (12).
	George Cordry (13).
	John Matthews.
	Thomas Simmonds.
	Joseph Mason (14).
	Andrew Dalzell.
Surgeon . . .	James Corbet (15).
Surgeon's Mate	William Sealey.
Purser . . .	James Steward (16)
Clerk . . .	John Melwood.
Boatswain . .	George Bruce.
Carpenter . .	John Roaf.
Captain, Royal Marines .	Michael Perceval (17).
2nd Lieuts., Royal Marines	John Mackintosh (18). Charles Almond Trusson (19).

The *Polyphemus*, a third-rate, was launched at Sheerness in 1782. Her first prominent service occurred during the war of the French Revolution. She was commissioned in 1794 by Captain George Lumsdaine, under whom, on the 22nd October 1795, she captured the Dutch 74, *Overijssel*, off Queenstown. In March 1796, Vice-Admiral R. Kingsmill hoisted his flag in her, and she was employed off Ireland during the ill-fated French expedition in 1796–97; on the 30th December 1796, she made another successful capture in the *Tortue*, 40, after a running fight of four hours. In March 1801, under Captain John Lawford, she accompanied Admiral Sir Hyde Parker's expedition to the Baltic, afterwards forming one of Nelson's squadron in the battle of Copenhagen, on the 2nd April 1801, in which she lost thirty-one killed and wounded. She was originally intended to have been the most northward ship of the British line; but, in consequence of some mishap to the *Agamemnon*, she took her place and followed the lead of the *Edgar*. She thus became the most southward ship, and was one of those principally engaged, especially with the *Provesteen*.

On the recommencement of war in 1803, she was again to the fore. On the 7th December 1804, when, under Captain John Lawford, she was cruising off Cape St. Mary in conjunction with the *Lively*, she fell in with and captured the Spanish 36, *Santa Gertrudis*, with stores and specie. Captain Robert Redmill was appointed to her in the summer of 1805, and under him she fought in the lee column at Trafalgar, on the 21st October 1805, losing six killed and wounded. She engaged the French 84, *Neptune*, and the *Achille*, 74, only quitting the latter when she saw a Union Jack being waved from the French ship's starboard cathead. After the battle, and during the gale that followed, she performed good service in regaining possession of the Spanish 80, *Argonauta*, which she delivered over to Lord Collingwood at Cadiz. She afterwards took in tow the *Victory*, with the body of Nelson on board, and conducted her to the mouth of the Straits of Gibraltar. In December of the same year, when escorting, with the *Sirius*, a convoy from Gibraltar, she was chased by the French squadron under Willaumez, and lost one of her transports.

On the 16th July 1806, when cruising off Rochefort with Commodore Sir Samuel Hood's squadron, her boats, in conjunction with others, performed distinguished service in the cutting out and capture in the Gironde of the French 16-gun corvette *César;* and in September she witnessed the surrender to Hood's squadron of four French frigates from Rochefort. In 1806, Rear-Admiral George Murray hoisted his flag in her, and in the next assumed the naval command of the expedition to Buenos Ayres, Captain Peter Heywood going with him as Flag-Captain; and she witnessed Major-General Whitelock's disastrous attack. In May 1808, Captain William Pryce Cumby, a Trafalgar officer, was appointed to her, and she became the flagship of Vice-Admiral B. S. Rowley, Commander-in-Chief at Jamaica. In one of her cruises, on the 14th November 1808, her boats cut out the French war steamer *Colibri* from the harbour of San Domingo, with the loss of only one killed. In April 1809, she witnessed the action resulting in the capture of the French 74-gun flagship *d'Hautpoult;* and in June she took part in the combined operations for the capture of San Domingo. With eight small craft she blockaded the city on the seaward side, and landed eight of her lower-deck guns for service in the batteries: San Domingo surrendered on the 6th July. She returned home and was paid off in November 1812. From 1816 to 1832, she was employed as a powder ship at Chatham, when she was broken up, after a service of half a century, and having earned the naval war medal with three clasps. Her figure-head is preserved in Chatham Dockyard.

(1) Captain R. Redmill, C.B., entered the service at an early age, and was promoted to Lieut. in 1783. He was promoted to Commander in 1795. Commanded the *Comet*, 14, fireship, in 1795–96, including Hotham's action with the French in July 1795. Promoted to Captain in 1796. He commanded the *Delft*, 64, in 1799–1802, including the operations on the coast of Egypt in 1801, for which he received the Turkish gold medal. Captain of the *Polyphemus*, 64, in 1805–6, including the battle of Trafalgar, 1805—gold medal, thanks of Parliament, and a sword of honour from the Patriotic Fund. Relieved on account of ill-health in 1806. Created a C.B., 1815. Died in March 1819.

(2) Captain G. Moubray was the son of George Moubray, of Cockardine, Fifeshire, and was born in 1773. He entered the service in 1789. Served as Master's Mate in the *Juno* in her escape from Toulon in 1794. Master's Mate in the *Victory* at the siege of St. Fiorenzo and Bastia, Corsica, 1794—promoted Lieut. Senior Lieut. in the *Moselle* in Vice-Admiral Hotham's action with the French fleet and capture of two sail of the line, 1795. First Lieut. of the *Polyphemus*, 64, at Trafalgar—promoted to Commander. Succeeding to the command immediately after the action, owing to the serious illness of the Captain, did good service in recovering the Spanish *Argonauta*, 80, during the gale that followed ; afterwards towing the *Victory*, with Nelson's body on board, to the mouth of the Straits of Gibraltar ; and conducting the French *Swiftsure* from Cadiz to Gibraltar. Served in the *Rhodian* and *Moselle* for the protection of the Bahamas, 1809–13. Captain, 1812. Captain of the *Victory*, 104, 1844–1846. Captain of Greenwich Hospital, 1846. Naval medal and two clasps. Died in 1856.

(3) Lieut. W. Sandey was promoted to Lieut. in 1801. Served as Lieut. in the *Polyphemus* at Trafalgar, 1805. Died in 1832.

(4) Lieut. C. Squarey was promoted to Lieut. in 1801. Served as Lieut. in the *Polyphemus* at Trafalgar, 1805. Died in 1820.

(5) Commander J. Medlicott served during the operations on the coast of Egypt in 1801. Was promoted to Lieut., 1802. Served as Lieut. in the *Polyphemus* at Trafalgar, 1805. Commander, 1814. Died in 1831.

(6) Commander R. Mayne was born in 1783, and entered the service as Volunteer 1st Class in 1798. Served as Mid. in the *Polyphemus* in the battle of Copenhagen, 1801. Lieut., 1804. Lieut. in the *Polyphemus* at Trafalgar, 1805; and in the expedition to Copenhagen in 1807, when he served on shore with the Naval Brigade. Commanded a signal station at Cork, 1808–13. Transport Agent, 1813–16. Retired Commander, 1842. Died in Jersey, in January 1846.

(7) Mr. R. Louthean was appointed a Master, R.N., in 1795. Served as Master of the *Polyphemus* at Trafalgar, 1805. Died in 1836.

(8) Lieut. D. Hunter was born in Dundee, Forfarshire. He served as Master's Mate in the *Polyphemus* at Trafalgar, 1805. Lieut., 1806. Not traced after 1809.

(9) Lieut. T. Woodyat was born in Herefordshire. Entered the service as Volunteer 1st Class in 1804. Mid., 1805. Served as Mid. in the *Polyphemus* at Trafalgar, 1805. Lieut., 1811. Died in 1841.

(10) Lieut. W. Rule was born in the Isle of Wight in 1787. Entered the service as Boy, 3rd Class, 1803. Mid., 1803. Served as Mid. in the *Minotaur* at the capture of the French 36, *La Franchise*, 1803; and in the *Polyphemus* at the capture of the Spanish 36, *Santa Gertrudis*, 1804. Mid. in the *Polyphemus* at Trafalgar, 1805; witnessed the surrender of the French frigates from Rochefort, 1806; the unsuccessful attack on Buenos Ayres, 1807; and the blockade and reduction of San Domingo, 1809. Served in the *Bedford* at the capture of six gunboats and a sloop on the north coast of America, 1814; and in the attack on New Orleans. Lieut., 1815. Medal and two clasps. Died in Peckham, London, S.E., in 1850.

(11) Mr. J. Newell was son of John Newell, of Shepston. Entered the service in 1804. Mid., 1805. Served as Mid. in the *Polyphemus* at Trafalgar, 1805. Not traced farther.

(12) Lieut. G. E. Cocksedge was born in Suffolk. Entered the service as Volunteer 1st Class in 1798. Served in the *Plantagenet* at the capture of the corvette *L'Atalante*, 22, in 1803. Mid., 1805. Mid. in the *Polyphemus* at Trafalgar, 1805 ; and witnessed the unsuccessful attack on Buenos Ayres, 1807. Lieut., 1816. Retired, 1851. Medal and clasp. Died in 1860.

(13) Lieut. G. Cordry was born in London, and entered the service in 1803 as A.B. Mid., 1804. Served as Mid. in the *Polyphemus* at Trafalgar, 1805. Was captured the same year, and kept a prisoner until 1814. Lieut., 1815. Medal and clasp. Died in 1854.

(14) Mr. J. Mason was born in London, in 1789, and was brother of Vice-Admiral Sir Francis Mason, K.C.B. He was promoted to Mid. in 1804. Served as Mid. in the *Rattler*, 24, in action with the enemy's flotilla off Flushing and Ostend in 1804–5. Mid. in the *Polyphemus* at Trafalgar, 1805. Mid. in the *Daphne* at the capture of Monte Video, 1807. Became Paymaster and Purser, 1808. Served in the *Heroine* in the Walcheren expedition, 1809. Retired, 1852. Medal and clasp. Died in Titchfield, Hants, in 1863.

(15) Surgeon J. Corbet was appointed Surgeon, R.N., in 1794. Served as Surgeon in the *Polyphemus* at Trafalgar, 1805. Died in 1830.

(16) Mr. J. Stuart, or Steward, as it was sometimes spelt, served as Purser of the *Polyphemus* in 1804–6, including the battle of Trafalgar, 1805. Not in Navy List after 1809.

(17) Captain M. Perceval became 2nd Lieut., R.M., in 1793. First Lieut., 1794. Captain, 1803. Senior officer of marines in the *Polyphemus* at Trafalgar, 1805. Placed on half-pay, 1815. Died in 1830.

(18) Lieut. J. Mackintosh was born in 1786, and served as Mid. in the *Elephant* at the battle of Copenhagen, 1801. Became 2nd Lieut., R.M., in 1803. First Lieut., 1805. Served in the *Polyphemus* at Trafalgar, 1805 ; and in her boats at the

cutting out of the French corvette *César*, 1806. Placed on reserved half-pay, 1823. Appointed Paymaster, 6th (Royal Warwickshire) Regiment, 1846. Medal and three clasps. Died in King William's Town, South Africa, 1850.

(19) Second Lieut. C. A. Trusson became 2nd Lieut., R.M., 1804. Served in the *Polyphemus* at Trafalgar, 1805. First Lieut., 1807. Not in Marine or Navy Lists after 1809.

XXVI

H.M.S. *AFRICA*, 64 GUNS

Captain . . .	Henry Digby (1).
Lieutenants. .	John Smith (2).
	George Macrae (3).
	George William Bourn (4).
	John Street Pearce (5).
	Matthew Hay (acting) (6). *Wounded.*
Master . . .	William Ottey (7).
Master's Mates	John Sheals.
	James Taylor (8).
	Henry West (9). *Severely wounded.*
2nd Master and Pilot . . . }	Abraham Turner. *Wounded.*
Midshipmen .	John Page Bailey (10). *Wounded.*
	Charles Beekman.
	Duncan Campbell.
	Philip James Elmhurst (11). *Wounded.*
	James Gordon.
	William Frazier.
	Charles Frazier.
	Joshua Ford.
	John Clark.
	Thomas Blease.
	Andrew H. Winterscale.
Volunteers 1st Class	John Chancellor.
	James Fynmore (12).
	James Wightman.
	John T. Kirkup.
	Frederick Lea-White (13). *Wounded.*
	*Francis Bender (14). *Wounded.*

* Rated as Boy, Royal Marines.

Chaplain . .	Rev. William Williams.	
Surgeon . . .	David Gardner (15).	
Assist.-Surgeon	John Mortimer (16).	
Purser . . .	William Holman (17).	
Gunner . . .	William Shepherd.	
Boatswain . .	William Sarth.	
Carpenter . .	Thomas Coats.	

Captain, Royal Marines . } James Fynmore (18). *Wounded.*

1st Lieut., Royal Marines } Thomas Norcross Brattle (19).

The *Africa* was built on the Thames in 1781. Her first serious service seems to have been in 1783, when she was employed with the fleet under Vice-Admiral Sir Edward Hughes, co-operating with the army in the siege of Cuddalore. She took part in his fifth and last battle with the French squadron under M. de Suffren on the 20th June, in which she suffered a loss of thirty killed and wounded.

Nothing further of consequence is recorded of her until the war of the French Revolution. We find her, under command of Captain Roddam Home, participating in the bombardment of Fort Leogane, San Domingo, on the 21st March 1796, on which occasion her losses were recorded as eight killed and wounded. Her masts and yards were so damaged by the guns on shore that she had to proceed to Jamaica to refit. She was with Nelson watching Cadiz in 1805, and under Captain Henry Digby bore a conspicuous part in the battle of Trafalgar on the 21st October. She appears to have lost sight of the fleet in the course of the night before the battle, and, when the firing began, was broad on the *Victory's* port beam, and nearly also broad on the port beam of the leading ship of the allied van. Nelson signalled to her to make all possible sail; but Digby seems to have misunderstood the order—which was intended to keep him out of danger—as meaning that he was to lose no time in closing with the enemy. He therefore made the best of his way along the Franco-Spanish van, exchanging broadsides with it, and at length bore down ahead of the Spanish 140, *Santisima Trinidad*. Judging from her appearance that that vessel had surrendered, Digby sent his first lieutenant to take possession of her. This officer reached her quarter-deck ere he learned that the Spaniard had not surrendered, and as he was not in a position to coerce her, he withdrew, no one, strange to say, making an effort to stop him. The *Africa*, then, at about 3.20 P.M., very gallantly brought to action the French 74, *Intrépide*, and for about forty minutes fought her steadily, until the arrival of the British *Orion* upon the Frenchman's starboard quarter relieved her before she was silenced. She had her main-topsail-yard shot away, and her bowsprit and three lower masts so badly injured that none of the latter could afterwards stand. Her remaining masts and yards were also more or less damaged ; her rigging and sails cut to pieces ; while her hull, besides its other serious damage, received several shots between wind and water. Her losses in killed and wounded amounted to sixty-two, including seven officers.

Under Captain John Barrett she accompanied the expedition to the Baltic in 1808; and was with the Anglo-Swedish fleet at the blockade of the port of Roggersvick in August-September 1808. On the 20th October of the same year, while escorting a convoy, she was attacked in a dead calm by twenty-five Danish gun- and mortar-boats off the island of Amager, in the Sound, and lost sixty-two killed and wounded. Her masts and yards were badly injured, her boats disabled or destroyed, and her running rigging cut to pieces,

Indeed, had not the enemy withdrawn at nightfall, the *Africa* was in such a state that with a continuance of the fighting she must have struck. In April 1810, when commanded by Captain George Frederick Ryves, one of her boats destroyed a Danish privateer on Falstubo reef. Two years later we find her, under Captain John Bastard, bearing the flag of Vice-Admiral Herbert Sawyer on the Halifax station. She formed part of the squadron under Captain Philip B. V. Broke, of the *Shannon*; and took part, on the 16th and 17th July 1812, in the pursuit of the American 44-gun frigate *Constitution*, known as "Old Ironsides." On the 14th August in the same year, her tender, the *Hope*, captured the American schooner *Lewis*, of six guns and thirty men, off Halifax. She returned home shortly after this, was paid off at Portsmouth in March 1813, and broken up, after a service of thirty-three years.

(1) Admiral Sir H. Digby, G.C.B., a grandson of the 1st Earl of Digby, was the son of the Very Rev. the Hon. William Digby, D.C.L., Dean of Durham, and Chaplain to George III., by his marriage with Charlotte, daughter of Joseph Cox. Born at Bath in 1770, he entered the service in 1783. He was promoted to Lieut. in 1790. In 1795, when Lieut. in the *Pallas*, he performed valuable service on the occasion of the loss of the *Boyne*. Promoted to Commander in 1795. In command of the *Incendiary*, sloop, and the *Aurora*, frigate, he made several valuable captures in 1796, including a Spanish frigate, a French corvette, and a privateer, and seven others, with forty-eight sail of merchantmen. He was promoted to Captain in 1796; and in 1798 commanded the *Leviathan*, bearing the broad pennant of Commodore Duckworth, at the reduction of Minorca. In 1799 he was appointed to the *Alcmène*, frigate, in command of which he cruised between the coast of Portugal and the Azores, making numerous important captures, including the French privateer *Courageux*, 28; and assisted in that of the rich Spanish

treasure-ship, *Santa Brigada*, of thirty-six guns, having aboard over a million dollars. A curious story is related of his encountering this ship. On three occasions he was awakened from sleep by fancying he heard someone calling him by name and advising him to change his course. So much impressed was he by the dream that he did alter his course, and thereby intercepted the *Santa Brigada*. It was calculated that he had by this time acquired some £60,000 in prize money. In command of the *Resistance*, frigate, in 1801, he captured the French *Elizabeth* on the way to North America.

In command of the *Africa*, 64, he took a leading part in the battle of Trafalgar, 1805, in which his ship was seriously engaged. He received the gold medal, the thanks of Parliament, and a sword of honour from the Patriotic Fund. He was created a C.B. in 1815, was promoted to Rear-Admiral in 1819, Vice-Admiral in 1830, and Admiral in 1841. He was advanced to K.C.B. in 1831, and G.C.B. in 1842, and was Commander-in-Chief at Sheerness in 1840–41. He died at Minterne, Dorsetshire, 1842.

(2) Captain J. Skene, C.B., formerly Smith, was promoted to Lieut. in 1794. Served as Master of the *Egmont* in the battle of St. Vincent, 1797. First Lieut. of the *Africa* at Trafalgar, 1805 —promoted Commander. Commanded the *Beagle*, sloop, at the reduction of St. Sebastian, 1813—promoted Captain. C.B., 1815. Assumed name of Skene, in lieu of Smith, 1830. Died at Ben Rock, Cardy, Forfarshire, N.B., in 1833.

(3) Lieut. G. Macrae was promoted to Lieut. in 1800. Served as Lieut. in the *Africa* at Trafalgar, 1805. Died in 1823.

(4) Commander G. W. Bourn was promoted to Lieut. in 1801. Served as Lieut. in the *Africa* at Trafalgar, 1805. Retired Commander, 1840. Died in 1844.

(5) Lieut. J. S. Pearce was promoted to Lieut. in 1800. Served as Lieut. in the *Africa* at Trafalgar 1805. Not in Navy List after 1809.

(6) Lieut. M. Hay served as Acting Lieut. in the *Africa* at Trafalgar, 1805—wounded, promoted Lieut. Not in Navy List after 1821.

(7) Mr. W. Ottey was appointed Master, R.N., in 1793. Served as Master in the *Africa* at Trafalgar, 1805. Died in 1806.

(8) Mr. J. Taylor served as Master's Mate in the *Africa* at Trafalgar, 1805. He received the medal and clasp for the battle in 1848.

(9) Captain H. West, D.L., J.P., was son of Rev. Edward Matthew West, Rector of Clifton Mabank, and Vicar of Bradford Abbas, Dorsetshire, and Ann, daughter of Rev. Edward Cotes, Vicar of Sherbourne, Dorsetshire. Born in Bradford, Dorset, in 1787, and entered service as Volunteer 1st Class, 1801. Mid., 1801. Was wrecked in the *Resistance*, 38, near Cape St. Vincent, 1803. Served in the *Amphion*, 32, at capture of Spanish transports off Cape St. Mary, 1804, and in the pursuit of the combined fleets to the West Indies and back. Master's Mate, 1805. Master's Mate in the *Africa* at Trafalgar, 1805—severely wounded. Master's Mate in the *Lavinia*, 40, and was taken prisoner by a Spanish corvette when in charge of a prize, 1807; escaped, 1808. Lieut., 1808. Lieut. in the *Lavinia* in the Walcheren expedition, 1809, including the bombardment of Flushing. Senior Lieut. of the *Jaseur*, sloop, in the American War, 1814–15; in a single boat cut out the American privateer *Grecian*, on the Chesapeake—thanked by the Commander-in-Chief—and assisted in other captures. Commander, 1831. Retired Captain, 1856. Medal and clasp. Died at Jesmond, near Newcastle-on-Tyne, in 1861.

(10) Mr. J. P. Bailey, Purser, R.N., was born in 1784, and entered the service as Clerk. Became Mid., 1805. Served as Mid. in the *Africa* at Trafalgar, 1805—wounded. Appointed Paymaster and Purser, 1807. Purser of the *Néréide* at the capture of the *Caroline* and the taking of the island of Bourbon, and Belle Poule, 1806. Served on shore at the destruction of batteries in the Gironde. Naval Commissary in the operations against New Orleans, 1814. Medal and clasp. Died in Stonehouse, Devonport, 1855.

(11) Commander P. J. Elmhurst was born in Lincolnshire, and entered the service in 1805 as A.B. Mid., 1805. Served as Mid. in the *Africa* at Trafalgar, 1805—wounded. Master's Mate, 1806. Served in the *Magnificent* at the reduction of Zante and Cephalonia,

R

&c., 1809–10; and co-operating with the patriots on the north coast of Spain, 1812. Lieut., 1814. First Lieut. of the *Thistle*, 12, in the attack on New Orleans, 1814. Retired Commander, 1857. Medal and clasp. Died in 1865–66.

(12) Lieut.-Colonel J. Fynmore, R.M., was the son of Major James Fynmore, R.M., senior officer of marines in the *Africa* at Trafalgar (see No. 18). He entered the service as Volunteer 1st Class. Served in that capacity in the *Africa* at Trafalgar, 1805. Was also in the expedition to Buenos Ayres in 1807. Was appointed 2nd Lieut., R.M., 1808. Served in the *Vanguard*, and commanded a gunboat in the Great Belt protecting convoys, 1809–10, and in cutting out three merchantmen, 1810. Served in the *Hebrus* in the battle of Algiers, 1816. First Lieut., 1822. Captain, 1836. Major, 1846. Lieut.-Colonel, 1854. Retired, full pay. Medal and two clasps. Died, 1887.

(13) Commander F. Lea-White was born in Norwich in 1792, and entered the service as Volunteer 1st Class, 1805. Served in that capacity in the *Africa* at Trafalgar, 1805—wounded, promoted Mid., 1805. In the *Orestu* in the expedition to Copenhagen, 1807 ; and in the *Cossack* assisting patriots on the north coast of Spain, 1808, and embarking troops after Corunna, 1809. Lieut., 1812. In the *Rinaldo* escorting the allied Sovereigns to England, 1814. Stipendiary Magistrate in Jamaica, 1833–35. Served in Coastguard, 1837–41. Admiralty Agent, 1841–43. Commander, 1846. Greenwich Hospital pension, 1852. Medal and clasp. Died in 1859.

(14) Mr. F. Bender was borne on the ship's books as a Boy, Royal Marines, but he served as Mid. in the *Africa* at Trafalgar, 1805—severely wounded. Died from the effects, the 23rd October 1805.

(15) Mr. D. Gardner was appointed Surgeon, R.N., in 1781. Served as Surgeon of the *Africa* at Trafalgar, 1805. Died in 1810.

(16) Mr. J. Mortimer, Inspector-General of Hospitals and Fleets, served as Assistant-Surgeon in the *Africa* at Trafalgar, 1805. Surgeon, 1806. Deputy-Inspector-General of Hospitals and Fleets, 1840. Inspector-General, &c., 1846. Medal and clasp. Died in Gosport in 1856.

(17) Mr. W. Holman, Purser, R.N., was appointed Paymaster and Purser, 1795. Served as Purser of the *Africa* at Trafalgar, 1805. Retired, 1843. Medal and clasp. Died in 1857.

(18) Major J. Fynmore was the father of Lieut.-Colonel J. Fynmore (see No. 12), and was appointed 2nd Lieut., R.M., 1778. First Lieut., 1780. Placed on half-pay, 1783. Re-appointed 1st Lieut., 1793. Served in *Carysfort* at capture of 32-gun French frigate *Castor* off Land's End, 1794. Capt.-Lieut., 1800. Captain, 1803. Served as senior officer of marines in the *Africa* at Trafalgar, 1805. Brevet-Major, 1812. Placed on half-pay, 1814. Died in 1824.

(19) Lieut. T. N. Brattle was appointed 2nd Lieut., R.M., 1803. First Lieut., 1805. Served in the *Africa* at Trafalgar, 1805; in the expedition to Monte Video, 1807; and in the action with a flotilla of Danish gunboats near the island of Amag, near Copenhagen, 1808—wounded, reward from Patriotic Fund. Served in the *Audacious* in the Walcheren expedition, 1809, including the bombardment of Flushing. Was wrecked in the *Barbados* on Sable Island, 1812. Served in the *Magicienne* at the capture of St. Sebastian, 1813. Retired on half-pay, 1814. Medal and two clasps. Died in Southampton in 1864.

XXVII

H.M.S. *AGAMEMNON*, 64 GUNS

Captain . . .	*Sir* Edward Berry, *Bart.* (1).
Lieutenants. .	Hugh Cook (2).
	Samuel Clark (3).
	William Coote (4).
	Thomas Pinto (5).
	Stewart Blacker (6).
Master . . .	Thomas Webb (7).
Master's Mates	John Thomas Sadler (8).
	Thomas Bagnall.
	John Reeve (9).
	Charles Ross.
Midshipmen .	Joseph Chappell Woolnough (10).
	Thomas Jackson.
	James Emery (11).
	John Charles Cozens (12).
	Rodger Judson.
	William Read (13).
	Robert Jeffry.
	Charles Stewart.
	James Robb.
	Charles Lamb.
	Charles Alexander Johnson (14).
	Alexander Forsyth Parr (15).
Volunteers 1st Class	Henry Paget Bailey Ross (16).
	James St. Quintin (17).
	William Weaver (18).
Surgeon . .	John Jameson (19).

Assistant-Sur- { William Mcallin.
   gcons . .   { Henry B. Moulter.
Purser . . .   Charles Ross (20).
Clerk. . . .   James Henry Eden.
Gunner . . .   Archibald Freeburne.
Boatswain . .   Thomas Needham.
             * *Samuel Tallence* (21).
Carpenter . .   George Robins.
Captain, Royal } Henry Bowles Downing (22).
   Marines . . }
2nd Lieuts.,   { Herbert Raban (23).
   Royal Marines { Donald Campbell (24).

With the exception of the *Victory*, no ship has such
intimate association with the career and name of Nelson
as the *Agamemnon*, which he considered "without exception the finest 64 in the service." She was built at
Bucklershard, that one-time famous shipbuilding establishment at the head of Southampton Water, where
another Trafalgar fighter, the *Euryalus*, was also built.
She was launched in 1781, and commissioned in the
same year by Captain Benjamin Caldwell, under whom
she was under fire in the West Indies, when Rear-
Admiral Richard Kempenfelt encountered De Guichen
on the 12th–13th December 1781, and captured fifteen
of his convoy, laden with naval and military stores of
great value. She was also in Rodney's famous victory
over De Grasse in April 1782, off Dominica, on which
occasion her losses were returned at twenty-eight killed
and wounded.

On the commencement of the war of the French
Revolution in 1793, Nelson was appointed to her, and
under him the *Agamemnon* and her crew performed
many doughty deeds. She was a particular favourite
of his. In her he first gathered round him a band of

* Served as A.B.

brothers. He was, as Admiral Mahan says, one in purpose and spirit with her officers and seamen; sharing personally their hopes, their dangers, and their triumphs, quickening them with his own ardour, moulding them into his own image, until vessel and crew, as one living organism, reflected in act the heroic and unyielding energy that inspired his feeble frame. Under Nelson she was with Hood's squadron in the Mediterranean, was engaged in the blockade of Toulon, and was associated with the missions to Naples and Tunis; Nelson on his way encountering, on the 22nd October, and chasing a French squadron of four large frigates and a brig, until the *Agamemnon* ran into a calm. Though without decisive results, Nelson was satisfied with his own conduct in this affair, as was also Lord Hood when it came to his knowledge. The *Agamemnon*, as is well known, played a leading part in the reduction of Corsica in 1794. At the siege of Bastia her crew helped to drag guns up heights that seemed unscalable; and what the army failed to do, they did, forcing 4500 men to lay down their arms to 1200 seamen and soldiers serving as marines. The town and citadel of Bastia contained 77 pieces of ordnance, with an incredible amount of stores. From Bastia the *Agamemnons*, as Nelson called them, proceeded to the siege of Calvi, which was also taken; but Corsica, as Nelson himself said in a letter, cost him £300, an eye, and a cut across the back. After this the fleet was, fortunately, removed from the pestilential coast, for the *Agamemnon's* crew had suffered severely. "My ship's company are all worn out," wrote Nelson at one time, when one hundred and fifty of them were on their backs.

After refitting at Leghorn, the *Agamemnon* sailed, in 1795, with Hotham; and when he chased the French fleet in March, it was she that first got into touch with the enemy. On the 13th, after three days' hunt, she was so far ahead of her consorts that Nelson, looking round, saw no ship of the line within several miles to support him, yet he attacked the *Ça Ira*, a ship of 100 guns, which he said was "absolutely large enough to take the *Agamemnon* in her hold." By his clever handling of the *Agamemnon* he reduced his huge adversary to an unmanageable hulk, but other ships of the enemy were coming to her support. Hotham was not yet near enough to help the *Agamemnon*, and so for once the signal of recall was obeyed. In the battle which took place the next day the fighting was indecisive, and the *Agamemnon* did not play a large part. Four months later she once more got in touch with the enemy, when she was detached with some smaller vessels under Nelson to co-operate with the Austrians. On the 13th July he fell in with the French fleet of seventeen of the line, narrowly escaping capture himself in doing so ; but again only a partial action resulted. On the 26th August the *Agamemnon* with the rest of Nelson's squadron, under his personal direction, cut out of the bays of Alassio and Langueglia, near Vado, two French gunbrigs, two five-gun galleys, and five vessels laden with stores, and destroyed two other vessels, without losing a man. After participating with the squadron in the operations on the Riviera in 1795–96, and sharing in the cutting out from under the French batteries the vessels carrying Napoleon's siege train and their escort, she severed her long and affectionate connection with Nelson. The old battered ship anchored at San Fiorenzo in June ; and soon afterwards sailed for England to be refitted at Chatham, for she was sadly in want of repair, and had been wrapped with hawsers to hold her together. In the following year, 1797, she was unfortunately implicated in the mutiny of the Nore ; but she was soon again doing good service with the Channel

Fleet. Under Captain Robert Devereux Fancourt she was with Nelson at Copenhagen in 1801, but in the battle of the 2nd April was unfortunately so anchored as to be unable to get into action. Her next important service was under Captain John Harvey in Sir Robert Calder's action off Finisterre on the 22nd July 1805, when she had her fore topsail-yard and mizen topmast shot away, her fore and main-yards and main topmast injured, and lost three men wounded. On the 13th October she joined Lord Nelson off Cadiz with Sir Edward Berry, Bart., as captain, and, during the pursuit of the enemy, very nearly fell into their hands. On the morning of the 20th, the day before the great battle, with a prize—a heavy French merchant brig—in tow, she was unconsciously running into the midst of the enemy's ships, but eventually got clear. In the weather column she fought at Trafalgar, and was a good deal engaged with Dumanoir's division. Her losses amounted to ten killed and wounded, and she received a nasty wound under the quarter, which kept her pumps constantly going. After the battle she was detached with the squadron under Rear-Admiral Sir Thomas Louis at Cadiz until the raising of the blockade, when she joined Sir John Duckworth in the West Indies. She was present in his action of the 6th February 1806, off Domingo, when she lost fourteen killed and wounded; and on the 29th March, in conjunction with the *Heureux*, 16, she effected the capture of the notorious French privateer, *Dame Ernouf*, of 16 guns, off Barbados.

At the end of the year she was put out of commission, but was again in active employment in the West Indies in 1807, under the command of Captain Jonas Rose. In conjunction with the *Carysfort* she effected the capture, on the 24th March, of the French *Lutine* in the Leeward Islands; and in the summer joined Cochrane's squadron off Martinique. After escorting a large British convoy, she took part in the expedition against Copenhagen under Admiral Gambier, including the second bombardment, and the surrender of the Danish fleet ; after which she returned home. She left Portsmouth on 6th December 1807, and joined Sir William Sidney Smith in the blockade of Lisbon. On the 13th March 1808, she sailed for the Brazils, where her bones rest ; for, on the 28th June 1809, she grounded on a shoal in Maldonado Bay, at the entrance of the river Plate, and was lost after nearly thirty years of service. Her end was pathetic. The British squadron were making for the bay to shelter from the stormy weather, when two miles off, signal was made, "Ships indiscriminately to put into port." Captain Jonas Rose, of the *Agamemnon*, who thought he knew Maldonado Bay well, set topsails and took the lead, boldly rounding Goretta Island to make for the anchorage, when, in the laconic words of an officer of the *Foudroyant*, "her way was deadened ; she stood still. For some moments her canvas remained stiff as boards. Then we saw it hurriedly clewed up and left anyhow in great disorder. Down came her ensign, to be immediately rehoisted upside down, the signal of distress." The old ship was hard on the sand and filling, for she had dragged one of her anchors under her, till it caught her keel and broke through the bottom abreast of the fore chains. Officers and men left her, after an affecting scene, in which Rose bade the ship farewell. An old boatswain's mate who had fought in her with Nelson tried to cheer the captain, but ended "with a mournful shaking of the head as he brushed his rough hand across his eyes and drew back among his shipmates," many of whom had been in the *Agamemnon* during Nelson's command. Her gunner has left it on record that some of the men cried like children when they were ordered to abandon the old ship.

(1) Rear-Admiral Sir Edward Berry, Bart., K.C.B., was the son of a London merchant, and was born in 1768. He entered the service in 1779 as a Volunteer, and served in the *Burford* in that capacity, and as a Midshipman, during the war of American Independence in 1779-83, including the five fleet actions between Suffren and Hughes in the East Indies in 1782-83. He was promoted to Lieut. in 1794 as a reward for his gallantry in boarding a French ship of war, and is said in a vague way to have distinguished himself in Lord Howe's victory of the 1st June. He served as 1st Lieut. of the *Agamemnon* under Nelson in 1795, and followed him into the *Captain* in 1796; performing such good service as to be mentioned in despatches and promoted to Commander. He served as a Volunteer in the *Captain* in the battle of St. Vincent, 1797; was the first man to board the *San Nicolas*, and assisted Nelson into the main chains of the *San Josef*—promoted to Captain. He was Nelson's flag-captain in the *Vanguard* in the battle of the Nile, 1798, and when Nelson was wounded he caught him in his arms; and was sent off in the *Leander* with the despatches, but was unfortunately captured by the French *Généreux* after a stout resistance, in which he was severely wounded. He was released on parole, and on arrival in England was knighted and presented with the freedom of the City of London. He also received the gold medal. As captain of the *Foudroyant* he assisted at the capture of his old enemy the *Généreux* in 1799, was at the blockade of Malta, and helped to take the *Guillaume Tell* in 1800. He also conveyed the Queen of Naples from Palermo to Leghorn in the same year, for which service he was presented with a gold box set with diamonds and a diamond ring. He commanded the *Agamemnon* in the victory of Trafalgar, 1805—gold medal, the thanks of Parliament, and a sword of honour from the Patriotic Fund. The *Agamemnon* joined the fleet on the 13th October, and when his approach was reported to Nelson he gleefully exclaimed, "Here comes Berry! Now we shall have a battle," for Berry, having been

in more fleet actions than any captain in the service, had a proverbial reputation for such luck, and the event did not belie the prediction. He again commanded the *Agamemnon* in the battle of San Domingo, 1806—gold medal, the thanks of Parliament, a valuable sword and vase from the Patriotic Fund, and was created a baronet. He is believed to have been the only officer in the navy of his time, except Lord Collingwood, who received three gold medals. He was in eight general actions, besides numerous incidental skirmishes. He commanded the *Royal Sovereign* and *Royal George* yachts in 1813–15, and was appointed a K.C.B. in the latter year. Became Colonel, Royal Marines, 1819, and Rear-Admiral in 1821. He died in Bath in 1831. His portrait is in the Painted Hall, Greenwich.

(2) Captain H. Cook entered the service in 1784, and was promoted to Lieut. in 1793. He served as Lieut. in the *Prince* in Lord Bridport's action off Groix, 1795; and in the *Brunswick*, landed in command of a detachment from the British squadron to defend the port of Irois, Circasse Bay, San Domingo, 1797. Served as 1st Lieut. of the *Agamemnon* in Sir Robert Calder's action in July, and at Trafalgar, 1805—promoted to Commander. Captain, 1806. Died in 1834.

(3) Commander S. Clark was promoted to Lieut. in 1801. Served as Lieut. in the *Agamemnon* in Calder's action in July 1805, at Trafalgar, 1805, and in the battle of San Domingo, 1806 —promoted Commander. In command of the *Rolla*, sloop, captured the French privateer *Espoir* off Fecamp, 1811. Died in 1834.

(4) Commander W. Coote was the son of the Rev. Charles Coote, of Dublin, and entered the service in 1794. Served as Mid. in the *Royal George* in Lord Bridport's victory off Groix, 1795; and in the *Edgar* in the battle of Copenhagen, 1801. Lieut., 1802. Lieut. in the *Agamemnon* in Calder's action, and at Trafalgar, 1805; and in the battle of San Domingo, 1806— wounded. Lieut. in the *Cerberus*, 32, and commanded her boats in the cutting out and capture of a French privateer near Pearl Rock, Martinique, the 2nd January 1807—severely wounded, losing the sight of both eyes, pension for wounds, and gratuity

from Patriotic Fund, mentioned in despatches, and promoted to Commander. Retired Commander, 1840. War medal with five clasps. Died in Cheltenham in 1857.

(5) Captain T. Pinto was born in 1772, and entered the service as A.B. in 1795. He served as Mid. in the *Irresistible* in the battle of St. Vincent, 1797, and at the capture of two Spanish frigates in 1798. Was Mid. in the *Minerva* in the expedition to Ostend. Mid. in the *Northumberland* at the capture of the *Généreux*, 1799, and the *Diana*, 1800; the blockade of Malta; and Master's Mate in her in the operations on the coast of Egypt in 1801. Lieut., 1805. Lieut. in the *Agamemnon* in Sir Robert Calder's action, 1805; the battle of Trafalgar, 1805; and the battle of San Domingo, 1806. Commander, 1808. Commanded the *Achates*, 14, at cuttting out of the *Nisus* at Guadeloupe, 1809, and at the capture of Guadeloupe, 1810, and when she was unfortunately lost shortly afterwards. Naval medal with six clasps. Retired Captain, 1840. Died in 1851.

(6) Captain S. Blacker was born in Armagh. Served as Lieut. in the *Agamemnon* in the battles of Trafalgar, 1805, and San Domingo, the 6th February 1806. Lieut. in the *Dreadnought* in the cutting out of a vessel off Ushant, 1810—wounded. Commander, 1812. Captain, 1821. Died in Dublin, 1826.

(7) Mr. Thomas Webb was appointed Master, R.N., in 1799. Served as Master of the *Agamemnon* in the battles of Trafalgar, 1805, and San Domingo, 1806. Died in 1823.

(8) Lieut. J. T. Sadler was born in Cornwall. Served as Master's Mate in the *Agamemnon* in the battle of Trafalgar, 1805 —promoted to Lieut. Not in Navy List after 1807.

(9) Rear-Admiral J. Reeve was born in London, and entered the service as Volunteer 1st Class in 1799. Served as Master's Mate in the *Agamemnon* in the battles of Copenhagen, 1801; Trafalgar, 1805; and San Domingo, 1806. Lieut., 1808. Lieut. in *L'Aimable*, and served in her boats at the capture and destruction of the fort of Bremerlé, Cuxhaven, 1809. Commander, 1830. Captain, 1851. Retired Rear-Admiral, 1867. Naval medal and four clasps. Died in 1868.

(10) Commander J. C. Woolnough, K.H., was the son of

Surgeon Joseph Chappell Woolnough, R.N., and Ruth Cator, daughter of William Clark, of Stubbs, Norfolk. He was born in 1786, and entered the service in 1800. Became Mid., 1803. Served as Mid. in the *Bloodhound* at the blockade of Boulogne, 1803-4; and as Mid. in the *Agamemnon* in Sir Robert Calder's action, 1805; and in the battles of Trafalgar, 1805, and San Domingo, the 6th February 1806; and the blockade of the Tagus, 1807; and was serving in her when she was lost in 1809. Lieut., 1811. Lieut. in the *Blazer*, sloop, at Cuxhaven, and the capture of the fortress of Gluckstadt, 1814—4th class of St. Wladimir of Russia. Commander, 1828. K.H., 1834. Died in Twickenham, in 1839.

(11) Lieut. J. Emery was born in Portsmouth. He served as Mid. in the *Agamemnon* in the battles of Trafalgar, 1805, and San Domingo, 1806. Lieut., 1808. Not in Navy List after 1810.

(12) Mr. J. C. Cozens served as Mid. in the *Agamemnon* in the battles of Trafalgar, 1805, and San Domingo, 1806. He received the naval war medal with two clasps in 1848.

(13) Mr. W. Read served as Mid. in the *Agamemnon* in the battle of Trafalgar, 1805. He received the naval medal and clasp in 1848.

(14) Captain C. A. Johnston was the son of Lieut. Charles Johnston, R.N., who died in 1804. He was born in Portsmouth, and entered the service as Volunteer 2nd Class in 1803. Mid., 1805. Served as Mid. in the *Agamemnon* in the battles of Trafalgar, 1805, and San Domingo, 1806, the capture of the French *Lutine*, 1807, the expedition to Copenhagen, 1807, and was in her when she was wrecked and lost in 1809. Lieut., Coast Blockade, 1825-31, and in the Coastguard, 1831-44. Commander, 1844. Retired Captain, 1860. Naval medal and two clasps. Died in 1861.

(15) Lieut. A. F. Parr, one of four brothers in the Royal Navy, was born in Portsmouth in 1786, and entered the service in 1796. He served as Mid. in the *Swiftsure* in the battle of the Nile, 1798; and in the operations on the coast of Egypt in 1801. Served as Mid. in the *Agamemnon* in the battles of Trafalgar,

1805, and San Domingo, 1806—promoted Lieut.; at the capture of the French *Lutine*, and in the expedition to Copenhagen in 1807; and was in the *Agamemnon* when she was lost in 1809. Lieut., Royal Naval Hospital, Haslar, 1831. Naval medal with four clasps. Died in Haslar Hospital in 1856.

(16) Mr. H. P. B. Ross served as a Volunteer in the *Agamemnon* in the battles of Trafalgar, 1805, and San Domingo, 1806. Received the naval medal with two clasps in 1848.

(17) Commander J. St. Quintin was born in Norwich in 1791, and entered the service as Volunteer 1st Class in 1805. Served as Orderly Officer to his captain, Sir Edward Berry, in the battle of Trafalgar, 1805—promoted to Mid.; was also in the battle of San Domingo, 1806, and in the expedition to Copenhagen in 1807, and was in the *Agamemnon* when she was lost in 1809. Commanded the barge of the *Barfleur* in an attack on the batteries at Cassio, 1813. Lieut., 1814. Retired Commander, 1856. Naval medal with two clasps. Died in 1864–65.

(18) Commander W. Weaver was born in Dublin in 1795, and entered the service as Volunteer 1st Class in 1805. Served in the *Agamemnon* in the battles of Trafalgar, 1805, and San Domingo, 1806, the capture of the French *Lutine*, and in the expedition to Copenhagen in 1807. Was in the *Agamemnon* when she was lost in 1809. As Acting Master of the *Pilot* assisted in the defeat of the French corvette *Legère* off Cape Corse, 1815—mentioned in despatches, promoted to Lieut. Retired Commander, 1861. Naval medal with three clasps. Died in Cheltenham in 1864.

(19) Sir John Jameson, Kt., M.D., was appointed Surgeon, R.N., in 1799. Served as Surgeon of the *Agamemnon* in the battles of Trafalgar, 1805, and San Domingo, 1806. Appointed Physician, R.N., 1807. Physician to the Baltic Fleet, 1807. Knighted, 1813. Knight of the Order of Vasa. Appointed Inspector of Hospitals and Fleets. Died in New South Wales in 1844.

(20) Mr. C. Ross was appointed a Purser, R.N., in 1777. Served in the *Agamemnon* in that capacity in the battles of Trafalgar, 1805, and San Domingo, 1806. Died in 1816.

(21) Mr. S. Tallence served as A.B. in the *Agamemnon* in the battles of Trafalgar, 1805, and San Domingo, 1806. Boatswain, 1807. Boatswain of *Pelorous* at the capture of Martinique, 1809, and Guadeloupe, 1809. Boatswain of the *Mutine* in the battle of Algiers, 1816. Received medal with five clasps in 1848.

(22) Captain H. B. Downing was appointed 2nd Lieut., R.M., in 1795. First Lieut., 1796. Captain, 1805. Senior marine officer in the *Agamemnon* in the battles of Trafalgar, 1805, and San Domingo, 1806. Retired on half-pay, 1806. Died in 1833.

(23) Second Lieut. H. Raban was appointed 2nd Lieut., R.M., in 1804. Served in that capacity in the *Agamemnon* in the battles of Trafalgar, 1805, and San Domingo, 1806. Not in the Navy List after 1807.

(24) Lieut. D. Campbell was appointed 2nd Lieut., R.M., in 1804. Served in that capacity in the *Agamemnon* in the battles of Trafalgar, 1805, and San Domingo, 1806. Was present at the destruction of shipping in the Basque Roads, 1809. Resigned, 1813. Received naval medal with three clasps in 1848.

XXVIII

H.M.S. *EURYALUS*, 36-GUN FRIGATE

Captain . . .	*Hon.* Henry Blackwood (1).
Lieutenants .	Kempthorne Charles Quash (2).
	John Poulton Williams (3).
	Walter Pike (4).
Master . . .	Frederick Ruckert (5).
Master's Mates {	Thomas Gardner.
	William Fotheringham.
Midshipmen .	Hercules Robinson (6).
	Jeremiah Parrott.
	James Bayly (7).
	Richard Keen.
	Henry William Bruce (8).
	Archibald Crail.
	Thomas Keating.
	Alexander Koolomsin (Russian).
—	**Joseph Henry Moore* (9).
—	**Jacob Richards* (10).
Surgeon . . .	Edward Owen.
Assist.-Surgeon	Alexander Ross (11).
Purser . . .	Jonas Toby (12).
Clerk . . .	Samuel Armstrong (13).
Gunner . . .	Peter Richards.
Boatswain . .	William Phillips (acting).
Carpenter . .	Thomas Parrott.
Lieut., Royal Marines }	John Sandford (14).
2nd Lieut., Royal Marines }	William Tell Paschoud (15).

* Rated and served as Boy 3rd Class.

The *Euryalus*, of which there is a good model at Greenwich, was launched in 1803 at Adam's Yard, Bucklershard ; having been built from the design of Sir William Rule, Surveyor of the Navy. She was commissioned in the same year by Captain Hon. Henry Blackwood, and was employed on the coast of Ireland under Lord Gardner, and under Lord Keith watching Boulogne. In 1805 she was with Lord Collingwood, and when Villeneuve's squadron arrived at Cadiz in August she was sent home with the news. On the 15th September, in company with the *Victory* with Nelson on board, she sailed from Spithead, joined the blockading fleet off Cadiz, and was employed under Captain Blackwood, with his squadron of frigates, on the important duty of keeping watch on the harbour mouth during the three weeks which preceded the battle of Trafalgar. It was from the deck of the *Euryalus* that the first signs of a movement on the part of the Franco-Spanish fleets were detected, three days before the battle ; and from that time Nelson's "Watch Dog"—as she was eventually nicknamed—and her five consorts never lost sight of the enemy, at times being so close during the thick weather that she had some difficulty in keeping out of danger.

All through the long, dark, and unsettled night preceding the battle the frigate kept vigil, and dogged the enemy's movements. At each tack of the enemy she fired a signal gun : at every hour, to show the Admiral that she was still watching, a blue light was burned. Two frigates a little farther off took up the signals, and a chain of battleships communicated with the *Victory*. At six o'clock on the memorable twenty-first, when daylight had shown the enemies to each other, Blackwood was summoned by Nelson on board the *Victory*, and personally thanked for the very valuable services the

s

Euryalus had rendered. She was present in the battle, to windward of the weather column, and, though not actually engaged, continued her valuable services; for after Nelson was wounded, and the *Royal Sovereign* had lost her masts except the tottering foremast, the *Euryalus* was sent for by Collingwood, and lying within hail made his signals during the continuance of the fight. She was at one time fired upon by the enemy's van, and had her main and topmast rigging and backstays shot away. After the battle Collingwood shifted his flag to her, and she towed the *Royal Sovereign* out to seaward.

On the 16th June 1808, we hear of her boats with those of the *Cruiser* capturing a Danish gun-vessel in the Great Belt. Under Captain Hon. George H. L. Dundas she took part in the ill-fated expedition to Walcheren in 1809, and was at the forcing of the mouth of the Scheldt on the 11th August; while, in November of the same year, she captured the French *Etoile*, of 14 guns, off Cherbourg. In July 1810, when with a division of the British fleet at Toulon under her old captain, Blackwood, she took part in the chase of a convoy of French coasters into the port of Bandol, in which service she exchanged some broadsides with a French 74. In 1813, Captain (afterwards Admiral) Sir Charles Napier was appointed to her, and she was employed in the blockade of Toulon. On the 16th May we find her boats, with those of the *Berwick*, capturing the national zebec *La Fortune*, of 10 guns, with twenty merchant vessels, in Cavalarie road; while she effected the capture seven months later of a French 22-gun storeship, and nearly made a prize of the French schooner *Undaunted*. After refitting at Halifax she served during the American War; was with Sir Alexander Gordon's little squadron in the successful expedition up the Potomac, the destruction of Fort Washington, and the capture of Alexandria on the

17th August 1814. In the expedition, which lasted twenty-three days, she had thirteen killed and wounded —her captain being amongst the latter. While in the Potomac she was in a tremendous squall which carried away her bowsprit, the head of her foremast, and the heads of all her topmasts; but in twelve hours she was again ready for work. She was also present in the operations against Baltimore. At the peace in 1815 she was brought home by Captain Napier and paid off at Chatham.

The *Euryalus* was commissioned for a tour in the West Indies in 1818–21 under command of Captain Thomas Huskisson, and again in the Mediterranean in 1821–25 under Captain A. W. J. Clifford; she was then paid off at Chatham. She ended her career as a convict ship, first at Chatham from 1826 to 1844, and finally from 1845 to 1859 at Gibraltar, where she was sold to Mr. Recano for £337, 6s. 8d. She earned the naval medal with two clasps.

(1) Vice-Admiral the Hon. Sir Henry Blackwood, Bart., G.C.H., K.C.B., was the fourth son of Sir John Blackwood, 2nd Bart., of Ballyliddy, Co. Down, by his marriage with Dorcas, Baroness Dufferin and Claneboye. Born in 1770, he entered the service in 1781, and is said to have served as a Volunteer in the *Artois* in the battle of the Doggerbank the same year. He was Signal Midshipman of the *Queen Charlotte*, flagship of Lord Howe, in 1790, and was promoted to Lieutenant the same year. He served as 1st Lieut. of the *Invincible*, 74, in Lord Howe's battle of the 29th May, and in his victory of the 1st June 1794, and he took possession of the French 84 *Le Juste*— mentioned in despatches, promoted to Commander. He was promoted to Captain in 1795; he commanded the *Megæra*, 14, fireship, in Lord Bridport's action off Groix, 1795; and in command of the *Brilliant*, frigate, captured the *Nonsuch*, of 64 guns, in 1796. In the following year she was implicated in the

mutiny of the Nore, and he was compelled by the mutineers to moor her across the river to obstruct the passage. In 1798, in command of the *Brilliant*, after compelling a Spanish vessel of superior force to take refuge under the batteries of Teneriffe, he sustained a plucky action with, and effected his escape from, two French ships of war, each mounting 36 guns. He commanded the *Penelope*, 36 guns, in the Mediterranean in 1799–1802, including the capture of the Spanish *N.S. del Carmen*, 16, and the blockade of Malta. He particularly distinguished himself on the occasion of the capture of the *Guillaume Tell*, of 86 guns and 1000 men, 1800. When the latter came out of Malta, it was the *Penelope* which first sighted her, engaged her, and shot away her main and mizen topsails, afterwards holding on to the Spaniard until the *Lion* and *Foudroyant* were able to come up; for this service he was specially mentioned by Nelson. He was also present, in command of the *Penelope*, in the operations on the coast of Egypt in 1801, for which he received the Turkish gold medal. In 1803 he was appointed to the command of the frigate *Euryalus*, in which he served on the coast of Ireland, in watching Boulogne, and at Cadiz. With his squadron of frigates he performed most valuable services in watching the combined fleet during the three weeks preceding the battle of Trafalgar. Summoned to the *Victory* on the morning of the battle, he was personally thanked by Lord Nelson for his very valuable services; and was a witness, with Hardy, to the codicil of the will in which Nelson bequeathed Lady Hamilton and the child Horatia to the care of the nation. Although not actually engaged, the *Euryalus* performed valuable service during the battle, and made Collingwood's signals after the *Royal Sovereign* was disabled. He was sent home with despatches, and in charge of the French Admiral; and at the funeral of Lord Nelson acted as Train-bearer to the Chief Mourner, Sir Peter Parker, the aged Admiral of the Fleet. He received the gold medal, the thanks of Parliament, and a testimonial from the Patriotic Fund. In 1806 he was appointed to the *Ajax*, 80 guns, and commanded her in Sir John Duckworth's expedition to the Dardanelles in 1807, and on the occasion of her destruction by fire, when he was nearly drowned. He was tried by court martial and acquitted. He then served as a Volunteer in the *Royal George*, bearing Sir John Duckworth's flag, during the remainder of the expedition, including the forcing of the passage of the Dardanelles; and was specially mentioned in the Admiral's despatches. He commanded the *Warspite* from 1807 to 1813, including the blockade of Toulon in 1810–12, and was in charge of the inshore squadron in the action with six sail of the enemy's fleet—received the thanks of the Commander-in-Chief, Sir Charles Cotton; and in 1813 captured three letters of marque. He was Captain of the Fleet at Spithead under H.R.H. the Duke of Clarence on the occasion of the visit of the Allied Sovereigns to England in 1814, in which year he was created a baronet. He was promoted to Rear-Admiral in 1814, and created a K.C.B. in 1819. He was Commander-in-Chief in the East Indies from 1819 to 1822, Groom of the Bedchamber to William IV. from 1824 to 1832; promoted to Vice-Admiral in 1825, and was Commander-in-Chief at the Nore from 1827 to 1830. He was also a G.C.H. and a Knight of St. Ferdinand and Merit. He died at Ballyliddy, co. Down, in December 1832. His bust is in the Painted Hall, Greenwich.

(2) Captain K. C. Quash was promoted to Lieut. in 1801. Served as 1st Lieut. of the *Euryalus* in the battle of Trafalgar, 1805. Commander, 1806. Captain, 1811. Died, 1816–17.

(3) Lieut. J. P. Williams was promoted to Lieut. in 1802. Served as Lieut. in the *Euryalus* at Trafalgar, 1805. Was killed in action, when Lieut. in her, in an attempt to cut out a merchant ship at Toulon, the 30th July 1809.

(4) Commander W. Pike was born in 1785, and entered the service in 1798 as A.B. Promoted to Lieut., 1805. Served as Lieut. in the *Euryalus* at Trafalgar, 1805. Lieut. in the *Achates* in action with the French 44-gun frigate *La Trave*, 1813; and at the capture of the French frigate *Clorinde*, 1814, off the coast of France. Retired Commander, 1840. Medal with two clasps. Died in 1849–50.

(5) Mr. F. Ruckert was appointed Master, R.N., in 1797. Served as Master of the *Euryalus* at Trafalgar, 1805. Afterwards

Master-Superintendent, Sheerness ; and Master of the Royal Yacht, *William and Mary*, 1818–20. Died in 1833.

(6) Admiral H. Robinson, D.L., J.P., was the second son of the Rev. Christopher Robinson, M.A., Rector of Granard, by Elizabeth, second daughter of the Right Hon. Sir Hercules Langrishe, Bart., M.P., and father of the Right Hon. Sir Hercules Robinson, first Lord Rosmead. He was born in Dublin in 1789, and entered the service in 1800 as Volunteer 1st Class. Served as Mid. of *Euryalus*, frigate, at Trafalgar, 1805. Lieut., 1807. Commander, 1809. In command of *Prometheus*, sloop, captured two Dutch privateers in the Baltic, and destroyed French schooner, *La Messalina*, 1810; and captured American schooner, *Lizard*, off Nova Scotia, 1814. Promoted to Captain, 1814. Employed as Arbitrator in Labrador Fisheries, 1820. Retired, 1846. Retired Rear-Admiral, 1849. Retired Vice-Admiral, 1856. Retired Admiral, 1862. Naval medal and clasp. Author of *Sea Drift*, and other publications. D.L. and J.P. for Westmeath. Died at Southsea, in 1864.

(7) Captain J. Bayly, one of five brothers in the navy and army, was the son of the Rev. Henry Bayly, Rector of Nenagh and Nigh, Co. Tipperary. Born at Nenagh, and entered the service in 1799 as a Volunteer. Served in *Penelope* at blockade of Malta, and at the capture of the *Guillaume Tell*, 1800; and in the expedition to Egypt in 1801. Served as Mid. of *Euryalus* at Trafalgar, 1805—promoted to Lieutenant. Lieutenant of the *Ganges* at capture of the French frigate *Le Président*, 1806; and in the expedition to Copenhagen, 1807. Did good service in rescuing the *Euryalus* and *Shearwater*, brig, from six of the enemy's ships in a gale off Toulon, 1810. Commander, 1828. Retired Captain, 1856. War medal and three clasps. Died in 1857.

(8) Admiral Sir H. W. Bruce, K.C.B., was the son of the Rev. Sir Henry Harvey Aston Bruce, Bart., of Downhill, Co. Londonderry, by Letitia, daughter of Rev. Dr. Henry Barnard. Born in Dublin, 1792. Entered service as a Boy in 1805. Mid., 1805. Served as Mid. in the *Euryalus* at Trafalgar, 1805. Mid. in the *Ajax*, 74, when destroyed by fire, 1807. Mid. of

Endymion at the forcing of the passage of the Dardanelles, 1807 ;
and at the embarkation of Sir John Moore's army at Corunna,
1809. Lieutenant, 1810. Lieutenant of *Belvedere*, and assisted
at capture of two Danish schooners on coast of Norway, 1810 :
and in the American War, 1812–14, including the action with
Commodore Roger's squadron—wounded, and assisted in several
captures. Commander, 1814. Commanded *Manley*, brig, in
operations in the Patuxent and Patopsco rivers, 1814. Captain, 1821. Rear-Admiral, 1852. Vice-Admiral, 1857. Commander-in-Chief, Portsmouth, 1860–63. K.C.B., 1861. Admiral,
1863. Good Service Pension, 1863. Naval medal and clasp.
Died at Fairfield, near Liverpool, in 1863.

(9) Lieut. J. H. Moore was born in Bath in 1791; and
entered the service in 1804 as a Boy. Served in *Euryalus* at
Trafalgar, 1805. Served in *Shamrock*, brig, at capture of batteries at Cuxhaven, 1813 ; capture of fortress of Glückstadt, 1814 ;
and commanded a division of gunboats at reduction of Ham-
burgh and Harburgh 1814—wounded ; pension for wounds of
£91, 5s. Lieut., 1815. Naval medal and two clasps. Died
in 1857.

(10) Mr. J. Richards was born at Swansea, and entered the
service, 1804. Served in *Euryalus* at Trafalgar, 1805. Mid.,
1805. Served in boats of *Euryalus* at cutting out of a Danish
gunboat, and destruction of shipping in the Great Belt, 1808.
Not traced farther.

(11) Surgeon A. Ross served as Assistant-Surgeon in the
Euryalus at Trafalgar, 1805. Promoted to Surgeon, 1809.
Died in 1819–20.

(12) Mr. J. Toby served as Clerk in the *Hind* in 1795–96,
including the pursuit by Richery's squadron. Promoted to
Paymaster and Purser, R.N., 1798. Served in the *Euryalus* at
Trafalgar, 1805. Was the author of the plan of Trafalgar which
was sent home to Lord Barham, and published in the *Naval
Chronicle*. Died in 1829.

(13) Mr. S. Armstrong served as Clerk of the *Euryalus* at
Trafalgar, 1805. Purser, 1809. Received naval medal and clasp
in 1848.

(14) Captain J. Sandford was appointed 2nd Lieut., R.M., in 1796. First Lieut., 1801. Served in *Euryalus* at Trafalgar, 1805. Captain, 1808. Retired on reduction, 1816.

(15) Second Lieut. W. T. Paschoud was appointed 2nd Lieut., R.M., in 1805. Served in the *Euryalus* at Trafalgar, 1805. Not traced after 1807.

XXIX

H.M.S. *PHŒBE*, 36-GUN FRIGATE

Captain . . .	*Hon.* Thomas Bladen Capel (1).
Lieutenants .	Thomas Paul Perkins (2).
	John Hindmarsh (3).
	Alexander Dixie (4).
	Daniel O'Hea (5).
Master . . .	James Burton (acting).
Master's Mate .	John Hobbs (6).
Midshipmen .	Prosper Ambrose (7).
	John Miller.
	Samuel George Pechell (8).
	Thomas McGill.
	Thomas Harvey.
	James W. Willis (9).
	William Henry Haswell (10).
	Hon. Robert Rodney (11).
	Charles Cobb (12).
	Charles Henry Crooke (13).
Volunteers 1st Class . .	{ Philip Chilham.
	{ James Athill.
—	**Richard Meredith* (14).
—	**Henry Forbes* (15).
Surgeon . . .	George Mackie.
Surgeon's Mate	John Sinclair.
Purser . . .	Henry Conyngham Bradford (16).
Clerk . . .	Richard Baker.
Gunner . . .	John White.
Boatswain . .	Thomas Evans.
Carpenter . .	Samuel Lovenewton (17).
1st Lieut., Royal Marines	} Mortimer Timpson (18).

* Rated as A.B.

The *Phœbe* was built at Dudman's Yard, Deptford, in 1795, from the design of Sir John Henslow, Knight, Surveyor of the Navy; she measured 926 tons. With Captain Robert Barlow in command she was employed off the coast of Ireland in 1796–97, watching the French fleet which was to convey Hoche's expedition. That expedition, as is well known, ended in failure, and most of the ships were taken or wrecked, amongst the former being the 20-gun brig *Atalante*, which was captured off Sicily by the *Phœbe* on the 10th January 1797. On the 20th December in the same year the *Phœbe* had a further stroke of luck when she gave chase in the Bay to the French *Néréide* of 36 guns. At 9 P.M. the two were near enough for the *Néréide* to open with her stern-chasers and inflict considerable damage on the *Phœbe's* masts, sails, and rigging. The *Néréide* then suddenly tacked, and the *Phœbe* shot ahead. The *Phœbe*, however, tacked as soon as she could, and seemingly the *Néréide* tacked again, for the two passed on opposite courses, exchanging fire. Finally they closed and fought at three hundred yards for three-quarters of an hour. The *Néréide* once fell on board the *Phœbe*, but the latter easily got clear. At 10.45 P.M. the French ship struck, being in a very battered condition, and having lost 75 killed and wounded. The *Phœbe's* losses amounted to three killed and ten wounded. On the institution of the naval war medal a clasp was given for this action.

On the 19th February 1801, the *Phœbe*, under Captain Robert Barlow, when east of Gibraltar discovered the French 40-gun frigate *Africaine*, Captain Saumur, steering up the Mediterranean. The *Africaine* was heavily laden, having on board, besides her crew, four hundred troops for Egypt, six field guns, and a quantity of arms and ammunition. She had parted some days previously from the similarly-freighted *Régénérée*, 16.

The *Phœbe*, steering a parallel course, quickly over-hauled her enemy, and brought her to close action. The French ship was at a great disadvantage, for her decks were crowded with troops who made a point of honour of remaining on deck during the action; and her only chance seemed to lie in boarding the *Phœbe*. But Captain Barlow was too smart to allow this. The effect of the *Phœbe's* well-directed fire made sad havoc on the crowded decks of her opponent. For two hours the fighting was furious; and not until both her senior officers were wounded, the ship on fire in several places, a foot of water in her hold, most of her guns dismantled, and 344 of her crew killed and wounded, did the gallant *Africaine* strike her flag. The losses in the *Phœbe* amounted to thirteen killed and wounded, and it was not without some difficulty she managed to carry her prize into Port Mahon. Another clasp to the naval medal commemorates this gallant action of the *Phœbe*.

Captain the Hon. Thomas Bladen Capel was ap-pointed to the *Phœbe* in August 1802, and for three full years she was employed in the Mediterranean. In 1803 we find her having a brush with some French frigates off Porquerolles. In 1805 she was with Nelson, and when he went in pursuit of the combined fleets to the West Indies she remained with the frigates watching the coast. With the *Euryalus*, *Naiad*, and *Sirius* she formed the "eyes of the fleet," and did much towards bringing the hostile fleets together, without which there could have been no victory. She was present in the battle of Trafalgar on the 21st October 1805, to wind-ward of the weather column, but took no part in the engagement. Her exertions, however, were the means of saving the French *Swiftsure*, and with the *Donegal* she afterwards brought out the *Bahama*. Her surviving officers and men received the medal and clasp in 1848.

Her next important service seems to have been under Captain James Hillyar in 1810, when, with the force under Vice-Admiral Albemarle Bertie, she assisted in the reduction of the island of Mauritius, then known as the Isle de France, which surrendered on the 3rd December 1810. With the squadron under Captain Charles Marsh Schomberg she performed gallant service on the occasion of the action with the French *Renommée*, 40, and the *Néréide*, 40 guns, off Madagascar, on the 20th and 26th May 1811. She succeeded in disabling the *Néréide*, but was herself badly cut about, and lost thirty-one killed and wounded. She then took part with the fleet under Rear-Admiral Hon. R. Stopford, in the combined expedition for the reduction of Java; was present at the capture of Cheribon, and the surrender of Java on the 18th September 1811. Early in 1814, in company with the 20-gun sloop *Cherub*, she was sent, under Captain Hillyaz, to the Pacific to try and capture the American captain, David Porter, break up the American whaling trade, and destroy their fur stations at the mouth of the Columbia. On the 28th March 1814, they fell in with the American 32-gun frigate *Essex*, commanded by Captain David Porter, near Valparaiso Bay, on the coast of Chile, and captured her after a severe fight of two hours. The *Phœbe* lost ten killed and wounded, and the *Cherub* four; while the American frigate had fifty-eight killed, sixty-six wounded, and thirty drowned. Of the latter's crew only seventy-six remained unwounded. The action was commemorated by the award of a clasp to the naval medal. Following the capture of the *Essex* came the destruction of the fur-posts in the Columbia, and what remained of the American whaling trade in the South Seas.

The *Phœbe* seems to have been uninterruptedly employed during the long war, and so successful were the efforts from time to time of her gallant crew that no

fewer than six gold medals were earned by her captains
—a record which few ships could beat, while six clasps
fell to her lot when the naval war medal was instituted
in 1848. One of her crew, at all events, Stephen Laurie,
received the medal with six clasps, commencing with
the action of the 11th December 1797, in which he
served as a boy, and ending as captain of the foretop in
that of the 28th March 1814.

The *Phœbe* was paid off at Plymouth at the peace in
1814. In 1822 she became a depot for supplying the
men and boys of the Ordinary in Hamoage with clothing,
&c., and was finally broken up at Plymouth in 1841.

(1) Admiral Hon. Sir T. B. Capel, G.C.B., was the youngest
son of William, 4th Earl of Essex, by his second wife, Harriett,
daughter of Colonel Thomas Bladen. Born in 1776, he was,
according to the fiction then in vogue, entered on board the
Phaeton, frigate, as captain's servant in 1782, but did not join
till ten years later. He was promoted to Midshipman in 1793,
and in that capacity served in the *Sans Pareil* in Lord Bridport's
action off Orient, 1795. He was promoted to Lieut. in 1797,
and in the *Vanguard* served as signal officer to Nelson at the
battle of the Nile, 1798. He was very favourably mentioned
by Nelson, appointed to the command of the brig *Mutine*, and
sent home with duplicate despatches, which, in consequence of
the capture of the *Leander*, brought the first news of the victory
to England. He was confirmed in the rank of Commander, and
promoted to Captain. In 1799–1800 he commanded the *Arab*,
frigate, in the West Indies, and from 1800 the *Meleager*, until
wrecked in the following year in the Gulf of Mexico. In August
1802, he was appointed to the command of the frigate, *Phœbe*,
in which he served in the Mediterranean for three years. He
did good service in her in watching the French and Spanish
fleets, and was present, though not actually engaged, in the
battle of Trafalgar to windward of the weather column. " The
excellent service of Captain Capel," wrote Collingwood on the
4th November, "saved the French *Swiftsure*, and his ship, the

Phœbe, together with the *Donegal*, afterwards brought out the *Bahama*." He received the gold medal, the thanks of Parliament, and a testimonial from the Patriotic Fund. On his return to England he sat on the court martial on Sir Robert Calder, and in December was appointed to the *Endymion*, 40 guns, in the Mediterranean, and took out the English ambassador to Constantinople. She was afterwards one of the fleet which, under Sir John Duckworth, forced the passage of the Dardanelles in February–March 1807. In command of the *Hague*, he served in the American War, 1811–14. He was created a C.B. in 1815; commanded the royal yacht, *Royal George*, 1821–25; was promoted to Rear-Admiral in 1825, and to Vice-Admiral and K.C.B. in 1832. He was Commander-in-Chief in the East Indies in 1834–37, was promoted to Vice-Admiral in 1837, and Admiral in 1847. He was Commander-in-Chief at Portsmouth in 1848, was promoted to G.C.B. in 1852, and received the naval war medal with three clasps. He died at Rutland Gate, Hyde Park, in 1853.

(2) Commander T. P. Perkins was promoted to Lieut. in 1797. He served as 1st Lieut. of the *Phœbe* at Trafalgar, 1805. Commander, 1810. Died, 1815.

(3) Rear-Admiral Sir J. Hindmarsh, Kt., K.H., entered the service as officer's servant in 1793. Served as a Volunteer in the *Bellerophon* in Lord Howe's victory of the 1st June 1794; in Lord Cornwallis' victory of 1795; the battle of the Nile, 1798— severely wounded, lost an eye; and at the capture of forts at Naples and Gaeta, 1799. Served in the *Spencer* in the action off Algeciras, and in Sir J. Saumarez' victory in the Gut of Gibraltar, 1801. Lieut., 1803. Lieut. in the *Phœbe* at the storming of a fort and the cutting out of a vessel near Toulon, 1805; and at Trafalgar, 1805, when he contributed to the preservation of two of the prizes, and was subsequently placed in charge of the *Fougeux* and afterwards of the *Bahama*. Served as Lieut. in the *Beagle* at the destruction of the French squadron in the Basque Roads, 1809; and the reduction of Flushing in the same year. 1st Lieut. of the *Nisus* at the capture of Mauritius, 1810, and of Java, 1811. Commander, 1814. Captain, 1831. Captain of

the *Buffalo*, and founded the colony of South Australia, of which he was first governor, 1836—created a K.H. Lieut.-Governor of Heligoland, 1840. Awarded a Good Service Pension, 1849. Knighted, 1851. Rear-Admiral, 1856. One of the only two persons who received the naval war medal with seven clasps, the greatest number that anyone succeeded in claiming. He died in 1860.

(4) Captain Sir A. Dixie, Bart., D.L., J.P., of Bosworth Park, Leicestershire, was the third son of Rev. Beaumont Dixie and Margaret, daughter of Richard Shewin. Born in 1780, he entered the service as Volunteer 1st Class in 1795. Served as Volunteer in the *Amazon*, and was wrecked and taken prisoner in the action with the French 74, *Les Droits de l'Homme*, 1797. Mid. in *La Pomone* in the expedition to Holland in 1799. Lieut., 1804. Third Lieut. in the *Phœbe* at Trafalgar, 1805. Commander, 1814. Commanded the *Saracen* at the capture and destruction of several vessels in the Chesapeake in 1814–15. Retired Captain, 1851. Naval war medal with two clasps. Died at Bosworth Park, 1857.

(5) Lieut. D. O'Hea was promoted to Lieut. in 1805. Lieut. in the *Phœbe* at Trafalgar, 1805. Distinguished himself when Lieut. in the *Swallow*, 18, in a gallant action with the French ship *Renard* near Isle St. Marguerite, 1812. Died, 1835.

(6) Lieut. J. Hobbs served as Master's Mate in the *Phœbe* at Trafalgar, 1805. Lieut., 1806. Died in 1826.

(7) Lieut. P. Ambrose entered the service as Volunteer 1st Class in 1796. Served in the *Sheerness* in the expedition to Holland in 1799. Served as Mid. in the *Phœbe* at Trafalgar, 1805; and in the *Endymion* at the passage of the Dardanelles, 1807. Acting Lieut. in the *Port d'Espagne* at the reduction of Martinique, February 1809. Lieut., 1810. Transport agent, 1814–16. In charge of the platform semaphore at Portsmouth, 1831–34 Naval medal with two clasps. Died in Portsmouth, 1848.

(8) Captain S. G. Pechell, of Bereleigh, Hants, was the son of Augustus Pechell, of Berkhampstead, Berks, Receiver-General of Post Office and Customs, by Sarah, daughter of Rev. Thomas

Drake, D.D., Rector of Amersham, and grandson of Sir Thomas Pechell, 2nd Bart. Born in London in 1786, he entered the service as Volunteer 1st Class in 1802. Mid., 1803. Served as Mid. in the *Phœbe* at Trafalgar, 1805. Lieut., 1806. Commander, 1809. Captain, 1810. Commanded the *Clorinde*, 40, in attendance upon Queen Caroline, during her visit to the Mediterranean in 1815–16. Died, 1840.

(9) Mr. J. W. Willis served as Mid. in the *Phœbe* in the battle of Trafalgar, 1805. He received the medal and clasp in 1848.

(10) Commander W. H. Haswell, the son of a naval officer, was born in London, and entered the service in 1800. He served as Mid. in the *Phœbe* at Trafalgar, 1805. When Mid. of *Endymion* he served in the Dardanelles, 1807; was taken prisoner, and while in the Turkish Admiral's ship was present in two general actions with the Russian fleet, by which he was recaptured. Lieut., 1809. Lieut. of *Revenge* in expedition to Walcheren, and bombardment of Flushing, 1809. Lieut. of *Superb* during American War, 1814–15. Commander, 1830. Inspector-Commander Coastguard, 1832–35. War medal and clasp. Commander of *Poictiers*, guard-ship at Chatham, in which he died, 1848.

(11) Captain Hon. R. Rodney was the son of George, 2nd Baron Rodney, by Anne, daughter and co-heir of Hon. Thomas Harley, and grandson of the distinguished Admiral, the first peer. Born in London in 1786, he entered the service as Volunteer 1st Class, 1801. Mid., 1805. Served as Mid. in the *Phœbe* at Trafalgar, 1805. Lieut., 1806. Commander, 1811. Captain, 1813. Died in command of the *Dryad*, frigate, 1826.

(12) Lieut. C. Cobb, one of three brothers in the Royal Navy, was the son of Benjamin Cobb, D.L., J.P., of New Romney, Kent, where he was born. He entered the service in 1802, and became Mid. in 1805. Served as Mid. in the *Phœbe* at Trafalgar, 1805. Lieut., 1807. When serving as 1st Lieut. of the *Castilian* was killed in action in an attack on the Boulogne flotilla, the 21st September 1811.

(13) Captain C. H. Crooke was the son of J. C. Crooke of Kempshot Park, Hants, and was educated at the Royal Naval

Academy, Portsmouth. He became Mid. in 1804. Served as Mid. in the *Phœbe* in a boat attack in the Mediterranean in 1805—wounded; and in the battle of Trafalgar, 1805. Commanded the boats of the *Circe* in the attack on the batteries and on the corvette *Cygne*, near St. Pierre, Martinique, 1808— severely wounded, pension for wounds, gratuity from the Patriotic Fund, and promoted to Lieut. He was also at the capture of Martinique, 1809. Served in the boats of the *Medusa* at the capture and destruction of *La Dorade* in the harbour of Arcasson, 1812. Commander, 1815. Retired Captain, 1854. Naval medal with three clasps. Died in Tuscany, 1858.

(14) Captain R. Meredith was born in Co. Kerry, Ireland, in 1789, and entered the service as a Boy in 1799. He served in the *Phœbe* at the capture of the *Africaine*, 1801; and was rated as A.B., but served as Mid. in the battle of Trafalgar, 1805, when he took possession of the Spanish 74 *Monarca*. Lieut., 1806. Lieut. in the *Endymion* at the forcing of the Dardanelles and destruction of the Turkish squadron, 1807. Lieut. in the sloop *Vulture* at the reduction of Copenhagen, 1807. Lieut. in the *Implacable* in the boat action of the 7th July 1809; and commanded a division of gunboats at capture of a convoy at Hango Head, Baltic, and at the defence of Cadiz in 1810. Commander, 1814. Captain, 1837. Medal and three clasps. Died at Torquay, 1850.

(15) Rear-Admiral H. Forbes, a member of the Skellater branch of the family, was the youngest son of General Gordon Forbes, Colonel of the 29th Regiment, of Ham Common, Surrey, and Margaret, daughter of Benjamin Sullivan, of Dromenaugh, Co. Cork. He entered the service in 1799 as a Boy. He was rated as A.B., but served as Mid. in the *Phœbe* at the cutting out of a French man-of-war brig in the Mediterranean in 1804— wounded; and in the battle of Trafalgar, 1805. Served as Acting Lieut. in the *Donegal* in the battle of San Domingo, 1806 —promoted to Lieut.; also in escorting troops to Portugal in 1808; at the destruction of three frigates under the batteries of Sables d'Olonne; and the destruction of French shipping in the Basque Roads, 1809. Commander, 1812. Captain, 1819.

T

Retired, 1846. 'Retired Rear-Admiral, 1852. Medal with three clasps. Died at Ham Common, 1855.

(16) Mr. H. C. Bradford was appointed Paymaster and Purser, R.N., in 1794. Served in the *Phœbe* in the battle of Trafalgar, 1805. Died in 1817.

(17) Mr. S. Lovenewton served as carpenter of the *Phœbe* at Trafalgar, 1805; and of the *Minden* in the battle of Algiers, 1816. Medal and two clasps.

(18) Major M. Timpson was appointed 2nd Lieut., R.M., in 1796. First Lieut., 1799. Served in the *Mermaid*, 32, in the gallant action with the French frigates, *Loire* and *Résolue*, part of Bompart's expedition to Ireland in 1798. Senior marine officer in the *Phœbe* in the battle of Trafalgar, 1805. Captain, 1808. Brevet-Major, 1825. Retired, 1826.

XXX

H.M.S. *NAIAD*, 36-GUN FRIGATE

Captain . . .	Thomas Dundas (1).
Lieutenants .	John Fordyce Maples (2).
	Thomas Francis Charles Mainwaring (3).
	Henry Le Vesconte (4).
Master . . .	Henry Andrews (5).
Master's Mates {	Hugh Montgomery (6)
	Edward Pascoe (7).
Midshipmen .	Samuel Jessop (8).
	William Gapper Agar (9).
	John Higgins (10).
	Mark Anthony (11).
	Stephen Cousins (12).
	Thomas Mockler (13).
Volunteers 1st Class	Thomas Valentine Cooke (14).
	James Watson Harvey (15).
	William Allen (16).
Surgeon . . .	John Macansh (17).
Purser . . .	Thomas Menzies (18).
Clerk	James Corbyn (19).
Gunner . . .	Robert Gallon.
Boatswain . .	John Smith.
Carpenter . .	Thomas Webb.
Lieuts., Royal Marines {	Edward Jones (20).
	Thomas Steele Perkins (21).

The *Naiad* was built at Hill's Yard, Limehouse, from the design of the celebrated architect, Sir William Rule, and was launched in April 1797; her burden in tons,

B.M., being 1020. She was commissioned at once under Captain William Pierrepoint, who commanded her for the next three years. With the *Jason*, frigate, she participated in the capture of the French gunboat *Arrogante*, 6, off Brest, on the 23rd April 1798. On the 24th August following she had a further success when, in company with the *Magnanime*, 44, she chased and captured the French 36-gun frigate, *Décade*, Captain Villeneuve. The *Naiad* first sighted her enemy at noon off Cape Finisterre, and chased her during the night. Next day the *Magnanime* joined in the pursuit. At 5 P.M. the Frenchman opened on the *Naiad*, and the two fought for about sixty minutes, when, seeing no chance of escape from so superior a force, Captain Villeneuve hauled down his flag. The prize measured 915 tons, and was added to the British Navy.

On the 15th October in the following year, 1799, the *Naiad* discovered and chased two rich Spanish 34-gun frigates from Mexico, the *Santa Brigada* and *Thetis*. Regardless of the apparent odds against her, she continued the pursuit under all sail until the 38-gun frigate *Ethalion*, and the 32-gun frigates *Alcmène* and *Triton*, joined in the chase. The two Spanish frigates then took different routes, the *Ethalion* eventually engaging and capturing the *Thetis*, and the *Santa Brigada*, after a gallant defence, falling a victim to the other three British frigates. The treasure on board the two frigates was valued at £600,000, while the share of prize-money varied from £40,738, 18s. to the captains, to £182, 4s. 7¼d. to the seamen and marines.

On the 16th May 1801, the boats of the *Naiad*, with those of the *Phaeton*, cut out the Spanish *Alcadia*, near Pontevedra. On the 29th May, 1803, under Captain James Wallis, she performed a smart act in capturing the French corvette, *Impatiente*, 10, in the Bay of

Biscay, on her way home from Senegal to Rochefort. The *Impatiente*, according to Captain Wallis's despatch, was considered one of the fastest sailers in the French fleet ; and, during the chase, she cut away her anchors and threw several of her guns overboard. In the evening of the 4th July in the same year, Captain Wallis sent the boats of the *Naiad* to cut out from among the rocks and shoals of the Saintes, near Brest, the French national schooner, *Providence*, of two guns and twenty-two men and boys, which was on her way from the foundry near Nantes to Brest, laden with heavy cannon, 36, 24, and 18 pounders, and some choice ship-timber. Notwithstanding all the difficulties which had to be encountered in the rapidity of the tide, and the number of rocks and shoals with which the French schooner was surrounded and protected, the British boats brought her safely off without the occurrence of the slightest accident.

Captain Thomas Dundas was in command of the *Naiad* in 1804-5. On one occasion she was attacked by Spanish gunboats in the Bay of Gibraltar, and in August 1805 was pursued by a French squadron of twenty-six sail of the line and ten frigates, a shot from one of which passed over her. She joined Lord Nelson on the 21st August, and was usefully employed in preventing supplies reaching the enemy's fleet coastwise. With the *Euryalus*, *Phœbe*, and *Sirius*, as the "eyes of the fleet," she did much to bring the hostile fleets together, without which there could have been no victory. She was present to windward of the weather column in the great battle of the 21st October, and, though she took no actual part in it, she rendered valuable help in rescuing officers and men from the disabled ships, and towed the *Belleisle* out of action when she became unmanageable.

In 1808 she was with the squadron blockading Rochefort. In 1811, under Captain Philip Carteret, she was

with the British squadron off Boulogne; on the 20th
September, when lying at anchor off the road, was
attacked for three hours by a division of Napoleon's
flotilla, consisting of seven 12-gun prames, ten 4-gun
brigs, and a bomb. On the following day the attack
was renewed, but they failed to drive her off the coast.
She herself did excellent service in boarding and carrying the *Ville de Lyons*, 12 ; her own losses amounting to
sixteen killed and wounded. In 1813 she returned home
and was paid off at Portsmouth, where she remained in
ordinary until 1823, when she did a three years' commission in the Mediterranean under Captain Hon. Sir Robert
Cavendish Spencer. Under him she was employed in
operations against the Dey of Algiers in 1824 ; and when
blockading the coast engaged, in company with the
Cameleon, 12, the Algerine corvette *Tripoli*, of 20 guns.
On the 23rd May following her boats very creditably
destroyed an Algerine brig of war under the fortress of
Bona, near Algiers. She was paid off at Portsmouth in
1826, and remained there in ordinary until 1846, when
she sailed for the Pacific as a depot ship. She acted
as store-ship at Valparaiso until 1851, and in the same
capacity at Callao until 1865, when she was sold to the
Pacific Steam Navigation Company. As store-ship for
that company she was afloat in Callao Harbour, retain-
ing her old lower masts, bowsprit, and figurehead work,
until as late as 1898, when she was broken up after an
existence of a hundred years, the longest lived of the
British Trafalgar ships except the *Victory*.

(1) Vice-Admiral Sir Thomas Dundas, K.C.B., entered the
service in 1778, and served during the war of American Independence. He was promoted to the rank of Lieutenant in 1793;
and for his services during the war of the French Revolution
obtained the rank of Commander in 1795, and Captain in 1798.

In command of *La Prompte*, West Indiaman, he captured the Spanish vessel *Urca Cargadora*, in 1799. In 1804 he was appointed to the command of the 38-gun frigate *Naiad*, in which he made several captures. The *Naiad*, as is well known, performed good service in tracking the enemy's fleet prior to Trafalgar, and was in the weather column, though not actually engaged in the battle. Captain Dundas commanded her with the squadron blockading Rochefort in 1808. His subsequent service was uneventful. He was promoted to the rank of Rear-Admiral in 1825, and Vice-Admiral in 1837. In 1831 he was created a K.C.B., and he died in 1841.

(2) Rear-Admiral J. F. Maples, C.B., entered the service in 1782 as captain's servant. Master's Mate, 1789. Served in the *Penelope*, 32, at the capture of the French vessels *Le Goëland*, 14, and *L'Inconstante*, 36-gun frigate, in 1793; and the blockade of Port-au-Prince, 1794. Lieut., 1794. Served in *La Magicienne* at several captures in 1794–97. Served on shore at Irois in 1798—wounded. Lieut. in the *London*, 98, and served as a Volunteer with Nelson's division in the battle of Copenhagen, 1801. First Lieut. of the *Naiad* at Trafalgar, 1805. Commander, 1810. Commanded the *Aetna*, bomb, at the defence of Cadiz, 1811. Commanded the *Pelican*, 18, and captured, after a spirited action of forty-five minutes, the American brig, *Argus*, of 20 guns, off Cork, the 14th August 1813—mentioned in despatches, promoted Captain. C.B., 1815. Retired Rear-Admiral, 1846. Died at the Priory, Kilburn, 1847.

(3) Vice-Admiral T. F. C. Mainwaring was the eldest son of Charles Henry Mainwaring, of Whitmore Hall, Co. Stafford, and Julia, daughter of Rev. Philip Wroughton. He was second cousin of Lieut. Benjamin Mainwaring, R.N., who served in the *Téméraire* at Trafalgar. Born in 1780, he entered the service from the Royal Naval Academy in 1796, as a Volunteer 1st Class. Lieut., 1800. Lieut. of *Naiad*, 1802–6, including the battle of Trafalgar, 1805. Commander, 1806. Commanded the *Tartarus*, fireship, in the expedition to Copenhagen, 1807; at the sinking of two French privateers off Pillau, 1810; and conveying the ex-King of Sweden from Riga to England, 1810.

Captain, 1810. Retired Rear-Admiral, 1846. Medal and clasp. Died in Marlborough Buildings, Bath, 1858.

(4) Commander H. Le Vesconte was son of Mr. Philip Le Vesconte, Purser, R.N., who lost a leg in Lord Howe's victory of the 1st June 1794, and died in 1807. His son, Lieut. Henry Thomas Dundas Le Vesconte, R.N., of the *Erebus*, was lost in the Arctic regions with Sir John Franklin. He entered the service in 1790 as Volunteer 1st Class. Lieut., 1800. Lieut. in the *Jamaica* at Copenhagen, 1801; and at the destruction of shipping at St. Valery, 1801—mentioned in despatches. Lieut. in the *Naiad* at Trafalgar, 1805. Commander, 1828. Medal and two clasps. Died in Canada, 1850.

(5) Mr. H. Andrews was appointed Master, R.N., 1805. Master of the *Naiad* at Trafalgar, 1805; and after the battle rendered valuable service in towing the *Belleisle* from a perilous position near the rocks, where she was drifting. Commanded a boat of the *Nymphe* at the unsuccessful attempt to cut out the French corvette *La Gavotte* in the Tagus, 1808. Placed on Reserved List, 1851. War medal and one clasp. Died in 1859.

(6) Lieut. H. Montgomery was born in Aberdeen in 1776. Appointed Master's Mate, 1804. Served as Master's Mate in the *Naiad* in the battle of Trafalgar, 1805—promoted Lieut. Died at Newton, Suffolk, in 1837.

(7) Mr. E. R. Pascoe was born in Truro, Cornwall. Became Mid., 1805. Master's Mate, 1805. Served as Master's Mate in the *Naiad* at Trafalgar, 1805. Master, R.N., 1808. Died in 1827.

(8) Lieut. S. Jessop was born in Tipperary, Ireland. Became Mid., 1804. Served as Mid. in the *Naiad* at Trafalgar, 1805. Lieut., 1810. Not in Navy List after 1813.

(9) Commander W. G. Agar was born in London. Served as Mid. in the *Naiad* at Trafalgar, 1805. Lieut., 1806. Commander, 1824. Died, when in command of the *Arachne*, sloop, on the North America and West India stations, 1833.

(10) Lieut. J. Higgins served as Mid. in the *Naiad* at Trafalgar, 1805—promoted Lieut. Not in Navy List after 1810.

(11) Commander M. Anthony was the son of Joseph Anthony

of Waterford, and grandson of Peter Anthony, of Carrig Castle, Co. Waterford, Captain in the Irish Brigade in the service of France at Fontenoy. He was born in Waterford in 1784, and entered the service as Mid. in 1801. Served in the boats of the *Hunter* in the unsuccessful attempt to bring out several merchantmen off the island of Cuba, 1803. Mid. in the *Naiad* at Trafalgar, 1805, and rescued several officers and men of the French *Achille* before she blew up. Lieut., 1808. First Lieut. of *Sarpen* in the Walcheren expedition, 1809. Served in the *Stanley* at the defence of Cadiz and Tarifa, 1811. Harbourmaster of Dunmore East, 1818–32. Retired Commander, 1848. Greenwich Hospital pension, 1848. Medal and clasp. Died in 1869.

(12) Lieut. S. Cousins was born in Maidstone, Kent. Served as Mid. in the *Naiad* at Trafalgar, 1805. Lieut., 1806. Not in Navy List after 1819.

(13) Lieut. T. Mockler was promoted to Mid., 1805. Served in that capacity in the *Naiad* at Trafalgar, 1805. Lieut., 1810. Died in 1840.

(14) Lieut. T. V. Cooke was born in London in 1786, and entered the service as Volunteer 1st Class in 1803. Served in the *Naiad* in 1803–6, including the battle of Trafalgar, 1805. Mid., 1806. Master's Mate, 1810. Lieut., 1815. Lieut. in the *Erne*, 1815, escorting the *Bellerophon*, with Napoleon I on board. Died in 1840 on passage home from the West Indies.

(15) Commander J. W. Harvey served as a Volunteer in the *Naiad* at Trafalgar, 1805. Lieut., 1812. Commander, 1815. Drowned at Battle, in Sussex, 1816, aged 24.

(16) Mr. W. Allen served as a Volunteer in the *Naiad* at Trafalgar, 1805. Received the medal and clasp in 1848.

(17) Mr. J. Macansh was appointed Surgeon, R.N., in 1796. Served as Surgeon in the *Naiad* at Trafalgar, 1805. Retired, 1816. Died in 1830.

(18) Mr. T. Menzies became Paymaster and Purser, R.N., in 1801. Served in the *Naiad* at Trafalgar, 1805. Died in 1835.

(19) Mr. J. Corbyn served as Clerk in the *Naiad* at Trafalgar, 1805. Purser, 1806. Died, 1815–16.

(20) Major E. Jones was appointed 2nd Lieut., R.M., in 1795. First Lieut., 1796. Captain, 1805. Served in the *Naiad* at Trafalgar, 1805. Brevet-Major, 1819. Retired, 1826.

(21) Lieut. T. S. Perkins was appointed 2nd Lieut., R.M., in 1798. First Lieut., 1804. Served in the *Naiad* at Trafalgar, 1805. Retired, half-pay, 1816.

XXXI

H.M.S. *SIRIUS*, 36-GUN FRIGATE

Captain . . .	William Prowse (1).
Lieutenants .	William Hepenstal (2).
	David Anderson (3).
	Richard Burton (4).
Master . . .	William Wilkinson (5).
Master's Mates {	William Adair (6).
	John Robinson (7).
Midshipmen .	Thomas Morgan (8).
	James McKenzie.
	Meyrick Lloyd (9).
	George Young.
	John Filmore (10).
	Richard Hambly (11).
Volunteers 1st	Stephen Yonge May (12).
Class	* *Edward Walker* (13).
	† *Morgan George Crofton* (14).
Surgeon . . .	Thomas Robertson (15).
Purser . . .	Rice Williams (16).
Clerk. . . .	Richard Hobbs Goldin (17).
Gunner . . .	Hugh Perry.
Boatswain . .	Matthew Pope.
Carpenter . .	William Mitchell.
1st Lieuts., {	Thomas Moore (18).
Royal Marines	William Murray (19).

The *Sirius*, a frigate of 1049 tons, was built at Dudman's Yard, Deptford, in 1797; and was commissioned the same year under Captain Richard King for service in the North Sea. In the following year she

---

* Rated and served as A.B.   † Rated as Coxswain.

made her first capture. She was cruising off the Texel
on the 24th October 1798, when she fell in with the
Dutch vessels *Furie*, 36, and *Waakzaamheid*, 24, which,
being about two miles apart, were not in a situation for
mutual support. Passing within gunshot of the former,
the *Sirius* stood on until she could nearly fetch the
Waakzaamheid, and Captain King, having prevented the
junction of the two ships, fired at and brought to the
Waakzaamheid, which, after discharging a lee gun,
hauled down her colours. A prize crew was placed on
board her, and the *Sirius* made sail after the *Furie*, which
had taken to her heels, and was soon overtaken. A
running action ensued, at times within musket-shot, the
Furie returning the heavy fire of the *Sirius* with a smart
but ill-directed discharge of cannon and musketry.
This continued for about half an hour, when the *Furie*,
having her hull, masts, rigging, and sails much cut up,
surrendered. The damage done to the *Sirius* was
trifling—a shot through her bowsprit, her rigging and
sails a little injured, and one man wounded by a musket
ball. On the 26th January 1801, the British frigate
Oiseau fell in with and chased the French 36-gun
frigate *Dédaigneuse*, bound from Cayenne to Rochefort
with despatches. The *Oiseau* continued the pursuit
until the following day, when the *Sirius* and *Amethyst*,
frigates, came in sight, and the *Dédaigneuse* turned and
headed for Ferrol. A long chase followed, but late in
the night of the 27th–28th the *Sirius* and *Oiseau* began
a running fight which, after some forty-five minutes'
duration, and the loss of several killed and wounded,
including her captain, ended in the French frigate
hauling down her colours. The British suffered no loss
and very little damage.

In 1802-5, under command of Captain William
Prowse, she was with the fleet off Brest, and in the Bay.

She was with Vice-Admiral Sir Robert Calder in his action with the Franco-Spanish fleet off Finisterre on the 22nd July 1805, and did good service in signalling the result of her very close inspection of Villeneuve's line prior to the battle. When the enemy tacked, the British did likewise, to prevent their opponents escaping them on the opposite tack; but the Franco-Spanish, who had hauled close to the wind, on getting within about three miles of the British fleet, wore in consequence of the *Sirène*, which had the galleon in tow, making signals by guns fired in quick succession that the rear was in danger of being cut off. This was occasioned by the bold approach of the *Sirius*, which, as soon as she had got sufficiently to windward to fetch into the water of the combined line, had tacked, with the intention of carrying by boarding the *Sirène*. While making the necessary preparation to effect his object, Captain Prowse discovered, through the haze on his lee bow, the enemy's van ship, the Spanish 90 *Argonauta*, approaching with the wind nearly abeam. The *Sirius* herself being now in jeopardy, Captain Prowse abandoned his design upon the galleon, and bore up to pass to leeward of the Franco-Spanish line. With a forbearance highly honourable to the Spanish Admiral, Gravina, the *Argonauta* passed the British frigate without firing; and so did the Spanish *Terrible* and *America*. By the time, however, that the *Sirius* had got abreast of the 64 *España*, the *Hero*, the British van ship, then with royals set, hove in stays. Instantly the Spanish ships, all of which had royals and courses set, hoisted their colours and commenced the action, the *España* firing her larboard guns at the *Sirius*, which had two men killed and three wounded. The result of the action is well known. After the Spanish 74 *Firme* struck she was taken in tow by the *Sirius*, and brought to Plymouth.

The *Sirius*, with the *Euryalus*, *Naiad*, and *Phœbe*, as the "eyes of the fleet," did good service in reconnoitring the hostile fleets prior to Trafalgar, during which she was chased and fired upon by one of the enemy's advanced ships; but the frigate, crowding sail, effected her escape. She was present, to windward of the weather column, in the great battle of the 21st October 1805, but was not actually engaged. Her surviving officers and crew, however, received the naval medal and clasp on its issue in 1848.

In December 1805, the *Sirius* was, with the *Polyphemus*, 64, in charge of a convoy from Gibraltar, when they were chased by the French under Willaumez, who captured one or two of the transports. She served in the Mediterranean in 1806-8; and, on the 17th April of the former year, performed a smart action in the capture of the French ship-corvette *Bergère*, of 18 guns. Under Captain Prowse she was cruising to the eastward of Civita Vecchia, when she gained intelligence that a flotilla of French armed vessels was to have sailed that morning for Naples. The *Sirius* immediately crowded sail in that direction and shortly discovered her enemy near the shore; soon after sunset she closed with the flotilla, which was lying near a dangerous shoal awaiting the attack, and drawing within pistol shot opened fire, apparently sailing right in amongst the small craft, for we are told that she used both broadsides. She was most hotly engaged by the *Bergère* and the *Abeille*, another 18. After two hours' hard cannonading most of the French small craft retired to the shoals, where the *Sirius* could not follow them. The *Bergère*, however, offered a determined resistance, and did not strike till she was disabled and had suffered heavy loss. In the *Sirius* nine men were killed and twenty wounded. The action was commemorated by the award of a clasp to the naval medal.

Under Captain Samuel Pym the *Sirius* was, in 1809, serving with the British force under Commodore Josias Rowley, cruising off the isles of France and Bourbon. In September she took part in the combined naval and military expedition which, on the 21st September, captured St. Paul, the harbour which had long been the rendezvous of French cruisers on the Indian station. On this occasion the *Sirius* was closely engaged, her fire most effective, and she took a prominent part in the capture of the French 40-gun frigate *Caroline*. In the summer of the following year she played an important part in the combined operations resulting in the capture of the Ile Bourbon, or Réunion, under Captain Pym, when a party from the ship performed excellent service on shore. Her boats also succeeded in capturing a French brig off St. Paul, with the loss of only two men killed, and in destroying a French schooner laden with supplies for the French army. The *Sirius* bore a distinguished part in Captain Pym's gallant and successful attack and capture of the Isle de la Passe in August 1810, when the boat attack led by Lieut. J. W. Watling was specially commended. In the same month eleven of the seamen under Lieut. Watling, in the gig of the *Sirius*, chased and captured the *Windham*, an Indiaman mounting twenty-six guns, under the batteries on the south-west side of Mauritius. Her last service was in the unsuccessful attack at Grand Port, Isle of France, when she ran upon a coral rock, and to avoid capture, was ordered by Captain Pym to be destroyed. At 9 A.M., on the 25th August 1810, she was set on fire, and at 11 o'clock she blew up, her crew and most of the stores having previously been removed. Captain Pym was acquitted by the court martial of all blame.

(1) Rear-Admiral W. Prowse, C.B., was born in Devonshire in 1753, and entered the navy at an early age in an inferior

rating. He served as A.B. from 1771 to 1778, when he was promoted to Midshipman. During the War of American Independence he served continuously afloat; and, as Master's Mate in the *Albion*, participated in the action off Grenada in 1779, and in that near Martinique in 1781. He was promoted to the rank of Lieutenant in 1782. On the commencement of the war of the French Revolution in 1793 he was appointed to the flagship, *Barfleur*, and as 6th Lieut. in her was present and did good service in Lord Howe's victory of the 1st June 1794—severely wounded, lost a leg. He was promoted to Commander in 1796. He commanded the *Raven*, brig, in the battle of St. Vincent, 1797—promoted Captain; and took part in the subsequent unsuccessful pursuit of the Spanish *Santisima Trinidad* by Captain V. C. Berkeley. As Captain of the frigate *Sirius* he was present in Calder's action off Finisterre in July 1805; was with the reconnoitring frigate squadron prior to Trafalgar; and commanded her in the great battle of the 21st October.* In command of the *Sirius* he performed a very gallant service, when, on the 17th April 1806, he attacked the French flotilla at Civita Vecchia, consisting of the 18-gun corvette *Bergère*, three brig-corvettes, one bombard, one cutter, and three gunboats. He captured the *Bergère* after a gallant fight, and drove the rest to seek shelter at Civita Vecchia. For this service he was honourably mentioned in despatches, and received a valuable sword of honour from the Patriotic Fund. He was created a C.B. in 1815; appointed Colonel, Royal Marines, 1819; and promoted to Rear-Admiral in 1821. He died in 1826.

(2) Commander W. Hepenstal was promoted to Lieut. in 1794. As Lieut. in the *Flora*, frigate, he served in her boats at the capture of the corvette *Mondovi*, 18 guns, in the Archipelago, 1798. Served as 1st Lieut. of the *Sirius* in Sir Robert Calder's action; in the battle of Trafalgar, 1805; and in the action with the French

---

* It is understood that Captain Prowse was not actually in the *Sirius* during the battle, being detained in the *Victory* and unable to get back to his own ship. In Thomas Davidson's picture, published by Arthur Lucas in 1894, he is shown on the deck of the *Victory*, watching his own frigate through a telescope.

flotilla at Civita Vecchia, 1806—mentioned in despatches, promoted Commander. Died in 1809.

(3) Commander D. Anderson was promoted to Lieut. in 1797. Served as Lieut. in the *Sirius* at Trafalgar, 1805. Retired Commander, 1830. Died, 1831.

(4) Commander R. Burton was promoted to Lieut. in 1797. He served as Lieut. in the *Sirius* at Trafalgar, 1805. Commander, 1812. Died in Bayswater, London, W., in 1836.

(5) Commander W. Wilkinson served as a Midshipman at the blockade of the Texel in 1801. Appointed Master, R.N., 1801. Served as Master of the *Rambler* on the coast of France in 1801-2. Master of the *Sirius* at the blockade of Brest and Ferrol; in Sir Robert Calder's action, and at Trafalgar, 1805. Commanded the boats of the *Sirius* at the capture of two feluccas under a heavy fire from the batteries of Tarifa. Master of the *Minotaur* in the expedition to Copenhagen, 1807. Master of the *Christian VII* at the attack on French gunboats and the capture of one in the Basque Roads, 1810. Retired Commander, 1846. Medal and clasps. Died in 1857.

(6) Mr. W. Adair, Master's Mate, was born at Stonehouse, Devonport, in 1790. Appointed Master's Mate, 1805. Served as Master's Mate in the *Sirius* in Sir Robert Calder's action and at Trafalgar, 1805. When in the *Sirius* was killed in the action with the French flotilla off Civita Vecchia, when the *Bergère* was captured, the 17th April 1806.

(7) Mr. J. Robinson served as Master's Mate in the *Sirius* at Trafalgar, 1805; and in the action with the French flotilla and the capture of the *Bergère* off Civita Vecchia, 1806—wounded.

(8) Mr. T. Morgan served as Midshipman in the *Sirius* at Trafalgar, 1805; and in the action with the French flotilla and the capture of the *Bergère* at Civita Vecchia, 1806—promoted to Master's Mate.

(9) Mr. M. Lloyd served as Midshipman in the *Sirius* at Trafalgar, 1805; and in the action with the French flotilla and the capture of the *Bergère* at Civita Vecchia, 1806—wounded.

(10) Captain J. Filmore was born at Portsmouth in 1788.

U

He served as Mid. in the *Sirius* at Trafalgar, 1805. Lieut., 1808. Lieut. in the *Columbine* at the capture of Senegal, 1809. Commander, 1811. Captain, 1824. Died at Plymouth, 1839.

(11) Lieut. R. Hambly was born at Cawsand, Cornwall. Volunteer 1st Class, 1804. Mid., 1805. Served as Mid. in the *Sirius* at Trafalgar, 1805; and in the action with a French flotilla and the capture of the *Bergère* at Civita Vecchia, 1806. Served as Master's Mate in the *Blossom*, and commanded her cutter at the capture of the privateer *Cæsar*, 1810—wounded. Lieut., 1811. Served in the boats of the *Leviathan* at the cutting out of a French convoy at Langueglia, 1812. Served in the Coastguard, 1829–32. Died in 1832.

(12) Lieut. S. Y. May was born at Stoneham. Volunteer 1st Class, 1804. Served in the *Sirius* at Trafalgar, 1805; and in the action with a French flotilla and the capture of the *Bergère* at Civita Vecchia, 1806. Mid., 1806. Lieut., 1815. Died in 1828.

(13) Mr. E. Walker served as A.B. in the *Sirius* at Trafalgar, 1805; and in the action with the French fleet and the capture of the *Bergère* off Civita Vecchia, 1806—promoted Mid.

(14) Sir Morgan G. Crofton, Bart., of Mohill Castle, Co. Antrim, was the son of the second baronet, and was born in 1788. Rated as Coxswain, but served as Mid. in the *Sirius* at Trafalgar, 1805; and at capture of French corvette *Bergère*, 1806. Lieut., 1807. Lieut. in *St. Albans*, and in her boats at attack on Cadiz, 1810. Retired, 1815. Succeeded to the baronetcy, 1834. Medal and three clasps. Died in 1867.

(15) Surgeon T. Robertson became Surgeon, R.N., 1794. Served as Assistant-Surgeon in the *Europa* and *Flying Fish* at the capture of Port au Prince, 1794; of the *Leda* during the operations in Egypt, 1801; of *Dædalus* at the capture of Gorée, 1804; of the *Sirius* in Calder's action, and at Trafalgar, 1805; and at capture of the *Bergère*, 1806. Surgeon of *Norge* at the defence of Cadiz. Was one of the founders of the Seamen's Hospital, Greenwich. War medal and three clasps. Died in Islington, 1851.

(16) Mr. R. Williams was appointed Paymaster and Purser,

R.N., 1793. Served as Purser of the *Sirius* at Trafalgar, 1805. Died in 1826.

(17) Mr. R. H. Goldin served as Clerk in the *Sirius* at Trafalgar, 1805. Appointed Purser, R.N., 1809. Died in 1826.

(18) Lieut. T. Moore was appointed 2nd Lieut., R.M., in 1800. First Lieut., 1804. Served in the *Sirius* in Sir Robert Calder's action, and at Trafalgar, 1805. Resigned, 1805.

(19) Captain W. Murray was appointed 2nd Lieut., R.M., in 1799. First Lieut., 1804. Served in the *Sirius* at Trafalgar, 1805. Captain, 1823. Died in 1833.

XXXII

H.M.S. *PICKLE*, SCHOONER

Lieutenant . . John Richards Lapenotière (1).
Sub-Lieutenant John Kingdon (2).
Midshipman . Charles Hawkins (3).
Second Master George Almy (acting).
Assist.-Surgeon Simon Gage Britton (4).

Formerly the *Sting*, the *Pickle*, a schooner of ten guns, is believed to have been purchased by the British Government at the commencement of the nineteenth century, when she was renamed the *Pickle*. She served in the Mediterranean in 1804, and did good service in saving the crew of the *Magnificent*, a 74, which was wrecked off Brest. The smallest vessel in the battle, she was present, to windward of the weather column, under Lieut. Lapenotière, at Trafalgar, on the 21st October 1805, but was not actually engaged. She, however, had the distinction of being sent home with Lord Collingwood's despatches announcing the victory. On the 3rd January 1807, under Lieut. D. Callaway, she performed a gallant service in boarding and capturing *La Favorite*, a French privateer of fourteen guns. This was her last important service, for, while commanded by Lieut. M. Cannadey, she was unfortunately wrecked and lost when entering Cadiz with despatches, on the 27th July 1808.

(1) Captain J. R. Lapenotière, a son of Lieut. Frederick Lapenotière, R.N., was born in Ilfracombe, in Devonshire, in 1770, and entered the service in 1780. From 1785 to 1788 we find him serving in the South Seas with King George's Sound Company, and he was employed with another expedition in 1791–3. On the commencement of the war with France in 1793 he re-entered the Royal Navy; and in the following year served in Sir John Jervis's flag-ship, the *Boyne*, at the reduction of the French West India islands. He was present at the boarding and capture of the French frigate *Bienvenue* and other vessels in Fort Royal Bay in 1794. He was promoted to the rank of Lieut. in the same year. In command of the hired cutter *Joseph*, he served in the Mediterranean trade in 1800–3, and was frequently engaged. In command of the *Pickle*, schooner, he performed good service in saving the crew of the *Magnificent*, 74, which was wrecked off Brest in 1804. He also commanded her at Trafalgar, 1805, and had the good fortune to be sent home by Lord Collingwood with the despatches announcing the victory. For this service he was promoted to Commander, and received a sword of honour, value 100 guineas, from the Patriotic Fund. We next find him commanding the *Orontes* in the expedition to Copenhagen in 1807, in which ship he effected several captures during the three following years. He was advanced to the rank of Captain in 1811; and died at Fanny Vale, near Liskeard, Cornwall, 1834.

(2) Commander J. Kingdon entered the service in 1796. Became Sub-Lieut., 1805. Served as Sub-Lieut. in the *Pickle* at Trafalgar, 1805. When serving as Sub-Lieut. in the *Inveterate* was wrecked near St. Valery en Caux in 1807, and was taken prisoner. Lieut., 1812. Retired Commander, 1855. Medal and clasp. Died in 1862.

(3) Commander C. Hawkins was born in Exeter, and entered the service in 1797. Served as Mid. in the *Spitfire*, sloop, off Ireland during the rebellion of 1798. Mid. in the *Pickle* at Trafalgar, 1805. Sub-Lieut., 1806. Sub-Lieut. in the *Pickle*, and was one of the boarders on the occasion of the capture of the French privateer *La Favorite*, 1807—wounded.

promoted Lieut. Commanded a semaphore station, 1841–51.
Awarded a Greenwich Hospital pension, 1851. Medal and two
clasps. Died at St. John's Wood, London, in 1854.

(4) Surgeon S. G. Britton graduated as M.D. at St. Andrew's
University. He served as Assistant-Surgeon of the *Pickle* at
Trafalgar, 1805. Became Surgeon, 1806. Was afterwards con-
sulting physician to the North Devon Infirmary. Medal and
clasp. Died in Barnstaple, 1856.

XXXIII

H.M.S. *ENTREPRENANTE*, CUTTER

Lieutenant .	.	Robert Benjamin Young (1).
Midshipmen	.	Thomas Mitchell.
		Abraham Wade.
Surgeon .	. .	Matthew Martin (2).
Second Master and Pilot	}	William Adeane (3).

The *Entreprenante* was captured from the Fench in 1801, and replaced a vessel of the same name which had been captured in 1793. She was commissioned in 1803. In 1805 we find her carrying despatches and sealed orders. Under command of Lieut. R. B. Young she was present to windward of the weather column at Trafalgar, the 21st October 1805, though not actually engaged ; she performed good service in picking up over a hundred and fifty of the crew of the French *Achille* when that ship blew up. She was afterwards employed during the blockade of Brest in 1806–7.

Under command of Lieut. Peter Williams she was engaged in a very gallant action with four French privateers, on the 12th December 1810. The engagement, which took place off the coast of Spain while she was lying becalmed between Malaga and Almeria Bay, commenced at 11 A.M., when the *Entreprenante* commenced firing at the privateers, one of the largest of which lay on her starboard bow, another on her starboard quarter, and the two smaller ones right astern.

The action was maintained with great spirit on both sides at pistol-shot distance, each party firing with round and grape shot, and the cutter with musketry also. At noon the *Entreprenante* had her topmast shot away and was otherwise severely injured, while two of her starboard guns were disabled by the stock of one and the carriage of the other being broken. In this disabled state three attempts were made to board her, each of which was defeated; until finally the French vessels, much disabled, drew off after four hours' hard fighting. Notwithstanding the length and severity of the action, and the more than double force opposed to the *Entreprenante*, the latter escaped with no greater loss than one man killed and ten wounded; the loss of her opponents was estimated at eighty-one killed and wounded. On the return of the *Entreprenante* to Gibraltar her officers and crew received the public acknowledgments of the Commodore of the station.

She was afterwards mostly employed up the Straits until the close of the year 1811, and by 1813 had disappeared from the list of the Royal Navy. Not one of her officers or crew lived to claim the medal and clasp for Trafalgar on its issue in 1847.

(1) Commander R. B. Young was the son of Lieut. Robert Parry Young, R.N., who died in 1798; his grandfather was also a Lieutenant in the Royal Navy. Born in Douglas, in the Isle of Man, in 1773, he entered the service in 1781. When Acting Lieut. in the *Thorn*, he was present at the capture of the French corvette *Le Courier National*, in 1795—mentioned in despatches. He served on shore in the operations against the Caribs at St. Vincent, in the West Indies, in the same year—mentioned in despatches, promoted Lieut. Served as Lieut. in the *Bonne Citoyenne* in the battle of St. Vincent, 1797. Was wrecked in the *Colossus* off Sicily in 1798. Lieut. in the *Savage* in the expedition to Holland in 1799. First Lieut. of the *Goliath* at the capture of *La*

Mignonne, near San Domingo, 1803. Commanded the *Entreprenante*, cutter, at Trafalgar, 1805—sword, value 100 guineas, from the Patriotic Fund. Commanded the *Entreprenante* at the blockade of Brest in 1806–7. First Lieut. of the *Ulysses* in the expedition to Walcheren in 1809. Commander, 1810. Awarded Greenwich Hospital pension, 1839. Died in Exeter in 1846.

(2) Surgeon M. Martin was appointed Surgeon, R.N., in 1804. Served as Surgeon of the *Entreprenante* at Trafalgar, 1805. Died in 1828.

(3) Mr. W. Adeane served as Second Master and Pilot of the *Entreprenante*, at Trafalgar, 1805. Appointed Master, R.N., 1808. Died in 1822.

H.M.S. *IMPLACABLE*

No account of the ships which fought at Trafalgar would be complete without some reference to the old *Implacable*, which, as the *Duguay Trouin*, was one of our worthy foes on that memorable occasion, and is the only survivor, other than the *Victory*, of the great battle of 21st October 1805. Many strange chances and changes mark her passage through the pages of history. Named by the French *Duguay Trouin*, in honour of one of the most distinguished of her naval heroes, René Duguay Trouin, one of the greatest of the Breton sea-rovers—who, after a gallant fight in command of a 40-gun ship against six British vessels, was captured in 1693—she was launched one hundred years later. In August of that year, 1793, she was in Toulon Harbour when Hood and the British Mediterranean Fleet took possession of the arsenal in the name of Louis XVII of France, and held it and the shipping there until December. Then Bonaparte came on the scene, the heights overlooking the harbour were taken, and the guns of the forts were turned on the British ships there. Hood was forced to weigh and make for the open roadstead, but before leaving he set fire to the French ships that he left behind. There were twelve all told, and of these ten were burned to the water's edge. Only the *Duguay Trouin* and the *Héros* were saved, and they were so badly damaged that it was seven years before they were at sea and in action again.

Early in 1802 the *Duguay Trouin* was again fit for service, and, after cruising with the Northern

Squadron for a while, was sent to San Domingo to assist in suppressing the rebellion of Toussaint l' Ouverture and his blacks. Her captain in those days was P. L'Hermite, and by daring seamanship he escaped from Cape François, where, with the *Duquesne* and the *Guerrière*, he was blockaded by a British squadron under Commodore John Loring. On the 24th July the *Duguay Trouin* put to sea, and was chased by the *Elephant* under Captain Dundas, with whom on the following day she had a smart encounter, but got away. The French ship opened with her stern chasers, and the Britisher drew up on the starboard quarter and maintained a long-range fire until the *Guerrière* came in view, when the *Elephant* retired; Dundas, her captain, was somewhat severely criticised for not pushing his attack home. The *Duguay Trouin* and the *Guerrière* then steered for Europe, and sighted no other ship until the 29th August, when, 140 leagues WNW. of Cape Ortegal, they fell in with the British 38-gun frigate *Boadicea*, Captain J. W. D. Dundas. The *Boadicea* immediatel gave chase till the French vessels altered course and in turn went for their daring enemy, with whom they exchanged fire. The *Duguay Trouin* managed to beat off her opponent, but before doing so had her foretopsail brought down, and was hulled so severely that the crew had to keep at the pumps for three days. Even then her adventures were not ended, and before she broke through the cordon and reached port safely, she fought another duel, this time at long range with the 74-gun ship *Culloden*, Captain Barington Dacres. With the *Guerrière* she had been sighted off Ferrol on the 2nd September by Calder in the *Prince of Wales;* and, making for Corunna, was nearly cut off by Sir Edward Pellew's squadron. As it was, she was engaged by the *Culloden*, but reached Corunna in safety without loss or injury.

Three years later, in 1805, she was with Admiral Villeneuve's squadron at Cadiz, and afterwards at Trafalgar, on the celebrated 21st October. In the great battle she was commanded by Captain Claude Touffet, and was one of the French van ships under Admiral Dumanoir Le Pelley, and thus did not take part in the fighting until towards the end. Then she made up for lost time, and was engaged successively with the *Minotaur*, the *Victory*, and the *Téméraire* before Dumanoir, seeing the hopeless nature of the struggle, withdrew, to fight again another day. This chance was not long in coming. On the 2nd November the British frigate *Phœnix*, cruising off Finisterre, sighted four strange sails, and went about, drawing the French squadron, comprising the *Duguay Trouin*, *Mont Blanc*, *Formidable*, and *Scipion*, skilfully under the guns of Sir Richard Strachan's squadron. In the fight that ensued the *Duguay Trouin* at the outset had no opponent, for the *Namur*, which she could have engaged, was some distance off. Accordingly she attempted to take the wind of the *Cæsar*, but got jammed in stays, and had to pass to leeward of the British squadron, receiving two tremendous broadsides at close quarters. One by one the French ships were overpowered. The gallant Captain Touffet was killed, but the *Duguay Trouin* was the last to admit defeat, and did not surrender until half an hour after the others were British prizes. Then she hauled down her colours and became a British prisoner, as the gallant officer after whom she was christened had done a hundred and twelve years before. The French ships had been terribly mauled, and lost seven hundred and forty killed and wounded; the British loss amounted to one hundred and thirty-five killed and wounded. The *Duguay Trouin* was taken to Plymouth Sound, and was renamed the *Implacable*, a name under which she was destined to serve her new masters faithfully for many a year.

Her fighting days were by no means over. As the *Implacable*, and under Captain Thomas Byam Martin, an officer who in twelve years had captured some twenty-five prizes of all rates, she went to the Baltic in 1808 with Vice-Admiral Sir James Saumarez's expedition to co-operate with the Swedish navy in the fight with Russia. There Byam Martin added to his exploits by engaging the Russian 74, *Sewolod*, and silencing her guns in twenty minutes. The Russian ship would have fallen a prize to the *Implacable* had not the former's consorts come up suddenly ; but she eventually ran ashore at the entrance of the port of Rogerswick, and was then captured by the *Implacable* and *Centaur*. The losses in the *Sewolod* amounted to over three hundred killed, wounded, and missing, as against nine killed and fifty-three wounded on the British side. The action was considered of sufficient importance to be commemorated by the naval medal and clasp on its issue in 1848. Later, off the coast of Finland, the boats of the *Implacable* performed several brilliant exploits in cutting out the enemy's armed vessels and transports. On the 7th July 1809, a date also commemorated by the award of a clasp to the naval medal, her boats, in conjunction with those of the *Bellerophon, Melpomene,* and *Prometheus*, attacked in Baro Sound eight Russian gunboats and a convoy of merchant ships carrying provisions and ammunition to the Russian army. Under a tremendous fire six of them were captured.

For the next thirty years she led an uneventful life until in 1839 she was commissioned by Captain Edward Harvey for service in the Mediterranean, and in the following year was fortunate enough to come in for the operations on the coast of Syria and the blockade of

Alexandria, for which a further clasp was awarded with the naval medal. During this period, and when it will be remembered our relations with France were of a somewhat delicate nature, the British Admiral and his officers one day entertained those of Lalande's fine squadron. The French officers were particularly noticeable by their profuse decorations, while ours had no medals or orders to boast of. Our French friends cast longing eyes on the old *Implacable*, about which they asked many questions. When the last of their officers was being piped over the side of the flagship, it evoked the remark to his Admiral from Captain Harvey of the *Implacable*, " If any strange visitant, sir, had looked down your skylight and seen these fellows, he would have supposed them to have been victorious in the old war. But I command a ship we took from them, and she shall sink under me rather than they shall have her again.' The *Implacable* had then, no doubt, a fine reputation; and when she returned to Devonport after the Syrian operations she carried a cock at her masthead, to indicate that in drills and evolutions she had proved the smartest ship in the Mediterranean. She was paid off by Captain Harvey on the 31st January 1842.

After lying idle for a period, she was employed at Devonport in 1855 as a training ship, or school, for naval cadets, until 1860, when she became a training ship for boys for the Royal Navy. In 1881 she and the *Lion* were formed into one establishment and considered as one ship under the name of the *Lion*, when her name was taken from her, to be given sixteen years later to the battleship *Implacable* then ordered to be built. Under the name of the *Lion* she continued as a training ship for boys until finally paid off on the 31st December 1904. Her career, it will thus be seen, has been a remarkable one. With the exception of the *Victory*, she is the sole survivor of the great victory of Trafalgar, and the last of the numerous prizes of the Napoleonic war. It is worthy of notice that when the naval war medal was instituted in 1848, clasps were awarded for Trafalgar, and Sir Richard Strachan's victory, in which she fought against us as the *Duguay Trouin;* while as the *Implacable* in the British service she subsequently earned three clasps to the same medal for the actions of the 26th August 1808 and the 7th July 1809, and the operations on the coast of Syria, 1840, and the Turkish medal for Syria, 1840. A figure-head of the ship is preserved in Devonport Dockyard, but it is not known if it was carried in 1805.

The old ship was advertised for sale at Devonport Dockyard on the 6th October 1908, but was withdrawn on a strong appeal for her retention being made to King Edward VII and the First Lord of the Admiralty. She was again, however, put up for sale six months later, but was eventually loaned to Mr G. E. Wheatly Cobb. The agreement was signed in August 1911, and the ship was duly taken over by him in March 1912. To the liberality and public spirit of this gentleman the country is indebted for the preservation of this invaluable relic of the past, as also for the *Foudroyant,* another battleship intimately associated with the glorious career of Nelson.

TRAFALGAR MEDALS

FOLLOWING the precedent of Lord Howe's victory of the 1st June 1794, and those of St. Vincent, Camperdown, and the Nile, gold medals were awarded by the King to the flag-officers and the captains of the line of battleships present at Trafalgar ; but the services of the junior officers and of the men were not officially recognised until more than forty years after the battle. The gold medal was of the larger size for flag-officers, and bore on the obverse a figure of Britannia, standing on the prow of a vessel, being crowned by Victory with a laurel wreath (see p. 66). The reverse contained the name of the recipient and the date of the action within a wreath of oak and laurel. The medal awarded to captains was similar in design, but omitted the wreath on the reverse (see p. 110). The ribband in both cases was broad white, with blue edges. By flag-officers the medal was worn suspended by a ribband round the neck, and in the case of the captains was fastened to the third or fourth buttonhole on the left side of the coat.

Encouraged by the example set by Mr. Alexander Davidson, Nelson's prize-agent, after the battle of the Nile, Mr. Matthew Boulton, of the Soho Mint, Birmingham, obtained official sanction for the design and issue of a medal to the survivors of Trafalgar. It was issued in gold to flag-officers, in silver to captains and lieutenants, and in bronze or white metal to the junior officers and men; and was authorised to be worn, if desired, as a decoration with a blue ribband. On the obverse is a bust of Nelson, and on the reverse a representation of the battle (see pp. 156, 209).

On the 1st June 1847, her Majesty Queen Victoria graciously repaired the neglect of her predecessors, and authorised the award of a silver medal with clasps to commemorate the various successful actions fought between 1793 and 1840, including Trafalgar. To the persistence of the Army, and particularly to the successful effort of the Duke of Richmond in obtaining the award of a medal to the survivors of the Peninsular War, the Royal Navy and Royal Marines may be said to have been indebted for this tardy recognition of their services. The medal was known as the Naval General Service Medal. On the obverse it bears the head of Queen Victoria, who was not born at the time Trafalgar was fought, and on the reverse the figure of Britannia, seated on a seahorse, holding in her right hand a trident, and in her left an olive-branch. It was the same for all ranks, and was worn on the left breast with a white ribband with blue edges (see p. 219).

INDEX

THE END